AF677753

Adaptive and Nonlinear Control of Robotics

Adaptive and Nonlinear Control of Robotics

Guest Editor

Aman Behal

Basel • Beijing • Wuhan • Barcelona • Belgrade • Novi Sad • Cluj • Manchester

Guest Editor
Aman Behal
Department of Electrical and
Computer Engineering and
the NanoScience Technology
Center
University of Central Florida
Orlando
USA

Editorial Office
MDPI AG
Grosspeteranlage 5
4052 Basel, Switzerland

This is a reprint of the Special Issue, published open access by the journal *Robotics* (ISSN 2218-6581), freely accessible at: https://www.mdpi.com/journal/robotics/special_issues/nonlinear_control.

For citation purposes, cite each article independently as indicated on the article page online and as indicated below:

Lastname, A.A.; Lastname, B.B. Article Title. *Journal Name* **Year**, *Volume Number*, Page Range.

ISBN 978-3-7258-7424-8 (Hbk)
ISBN 978-3-7258-7425-5 (PDF)
https://doi.org/10.3390/books978-3-7258-7425-5

© 2026 by the authors. Articles in this reprint are Open Access and distributed under the Creative Commons Attribution (CC BY) license. The reprint as a whole is distributed by MDPI under the terms and conditions of the Creative Commons Attribution-NonCommercial-NoDerivs (CC BY-NC-ND) license (https://creativecommons.org/licenses/by-nc-nd/4.0/).

Contents

Preface

Mathematically speaking, robot dynamics are represented by systems of highly coupled nonlinear differential equations. While these dynamics can be linearized under restrictive assumptions of exact or partial model knowledge, most practical robot control designs end up with nonlinear closed-loop dynamics. Adaptive control, which includes neural network-/learning-based control designs, particularly necessitates the application of nonlinear control systems analysis techniques. In this Reprint, we would like to focus on emerging techniques in the adaptive and nonlinear control of robotics, as they apply to novel control problems and state-of-the-art robot configurations/designs. This work is directed at graduate students and other researchers in nonlinear controls and robotics.

Aman Behal

Guest Editor

robotics MDPI

Editorial

Adaptive and Nonlinear Control of Robotics

Aman Behal

Department of Electrical and Computer Engineering and the NanoScience Technology Center, University of Central Florida, Orlando, FL 32816, USA; abehal@ucf.edu

It is my pleasure to present the Special Issue "Adaptive and Nonlinear Control of Robotics", which brings together nine original research contributions exploring state-of-the-art control strategies for robotic systems operating under nonlinear dynamics, uncertain parameters, reconfiguration, or complex physical constraints. The platforms considered in this issue—including cable-driven parallel robots, underactuated manipulators, soft continuum arms, industrial manipulators, teleoperation systems, and bio-inspired swimmers—reflect the diversity of modern robotics and the need for robust, adaptive, and energy-efficient control beyond classical linear paradigms.

One contribution investigates adaptive PID control for a reconfigurable cable-driven parallel mechanism, where dynamic changes in topology challenge conventional fixed-gain controllers. By embedding a real-time parameter estimation scheme, the adaptive controller maintains precise pose control despite structural reconfigurations, demonstrating the potential of adaptive control in complex reconfigurable robots [1]. Another study addresses underactuated serial planar manipulators by combining optimal control and nonlinear dynamics to derive minimum-energy trajectories that suppress residual vibrations, showing that underactuated robots can achieve efficient and stable motion with proper control design [2].

Soft robotics is represented through a study on a continuum manipulator for minimally invasive surgery, which compares sliding-mode and adaptive controllers under model uncertainty and elasticity-induced nonlinearity. The experiments demonstrate that adaptive control improves tracking accuracy, albeit with slower transient response, highlighting the practical trade-offs in soft robotic control [3]. In the industrial robotics domain, a "quantum-inspired" sliding-mode controller is applied to a six-joint articulated arm, reducing chattering, improving trajectory-tracking precision, and decreasing energy consumption relative to classical sliding-mode control, pointing toward energy-efficient, high-precision industrial applications [4].

Human–robot interaction and assistive robotics are addressed by a study on an upper-limb exoskeleton, where online tuning of sliding-mode controller gains via a particle swarm optimization algorithm significantly reduces tracking error under unpredictable human-driven disturbances [5]. Another contribution focuses on teleoperation systems with time-varying delays and uncertainties, employing robust adaptive sliding-mode control to enhance stability and tracking performance, which is critical for remote manipulation tasks [6]. The work in [7] proposes and simulates a 3-DOF aircraft-manipulator system for longitudinal virtual flight testing in a wind tunnel, using a coupled dynamic model and PID-controlled inverse kinematics to replicate free-flight trajectories and demonstrate its feasibility.

Execution of dynamic tasks is explored in a study on prescribed-time interception for moving objects using robotic manipulators, combining nonlinear control with trajectory planning to ensure interception at predefined times despite uncertainties [8]. Additionally, event-driven closed-loop control is demonstrated on a three-link bio-inspired swimmer, illustrating that adaptive nonlinear control can extend to unconventional locomotion robots [9].

Collectively, these contributions highlight the maturation of nonlinear and adaptive control from theoretical research into practical, application-ready methodologies. They illustrate how modern control design—through parameter estimation, optimization, sliding-mode control, Lyapunov methods, and metaheuristic tuning—can address real-world challenges in reconfigurable robots, underactuated systems, soft manipulators, energy-efficient motion, human–robot interaction, teleoperation under delays, and dynamic task execution. At the same time, they underscore ongoing challenges: achieving rapid adaptation without compromising stability, balancing precision with transient response, ensuring safe human–robot interaction, reducing computational load for real-time control, and integrating control with higher-level planning and perception.

I sincerely thank all the authors for their significant contributions, the reviewers for their constructive feedback, and the editorial team for their support in bringing this Special Issue to fruition. I hope this compilation serves as a valuable reference for researchers and practitioners striving to design the next generation of robust and adaptive robotic systems.

Funding: This research received no external funding.

Conflicts of Interest: The author declares no conflicts of interest.

References

1. Khoshbin, E.; Otis, M.J.D.; Meziane, R. Design an Adaptive PID Control Based on RLS with a Variable Forgetting Factor for a Reconfigurable Cable-Driven Parallel Mechanism. *Robotics* **2025**, *14*, 165. [CrossRef]
2. Dona', D.; Bettega, J.; Tamellin, I.; Boscariol, P.; Caracciolo, R. Minimum-Energy Trajectory Planning for an Underactuated Serial Planar Manipulator. *Robotics* **2025**, *14*, 98. [CrossRef]
3. Wang, L.; Chen, K.; Franco, E. Robust and Adaptive Control of a Soft Continuum Manipulator for Minimally Invasive Surgery. *Robotics* **2024**, *13*, 162. [CrossRef]
4. Fazilat, M.; Zioui, N. Quantum-Inspired Sliding-Mode Control to Enhance the Precision and Energy Efficiency of an Articulated Industrial Robotic Arm. *Robotics* **2025**, *14*, 14. [CrossRef]
5. Méndez, D.S.; Bedolla-Martínez, D.; Saad, M.; Kali, Y.; Cena, C.E.G.; Álvarez, Á.L. Upper-Limb Robotic Rehabilitation: Online Sliding Mode Controller Gain Tuning Using Particle Swarm Optimization. *Robotics* **2025**, *14*, 51. [CrossRef]
6. Chang, Y.H.; Yang, C.Y.; Lin, H.W. Robust Adaptive-Sliding-Mode Control for Teleoperation Systems with Time-Varying Delays and Uncertainties. *Robotics* **2024**, *13*, 89. [CrossRef]
7. Ishola, A.; Whidborne, J.F.; Tang, G. An Aircraft-Manipulator System for Virtual Flight Testing of Longitudinal Dynamics. *Robotics* **2024**, *13*, 179. [CrossRef]
8. Flores-Campos, J.A.; Torres-San-Miguel, C.R.; Paredes-Rojas, J.C.; Perrusquía, A. Prescribed Time Interception of Moving Objects' Trajectories Using Robot Manipulators. *Robotics* **2024**, *13*, 145. [CrossRef]
9. Nuevo-Gallardo, C.; Mérida-Calvo, L.; Tejado, I.; Vinagre, B.M.; Feliu-Batlle, V. Event-Based Closed-Loop Control for Path Following of a Purcell's Three-Link Swimmer. *Robotics* **2025**, *14*, 110. [CrossRef]

Disclaimer/Publisher's Note: The statements, opinions and data contained in all publications are solely those of the individual author(s) and contributor(s) and not of MDPI and/or the editor(s). MDPI and/or the editor(s) disclaim responsibility for any injury to people or property resulting from any ideas, methods, instructions or products referred to in the content.

https://doi.org/10.3390/robotics15030056

robotics

MDPI

Article

Robust Adaptive-Sliding-Mode Control for Teleoperation Systems with Time-Varying Delays and Uncertainties †

Yeong-Hwa Chang [1,2,*], Cheng-Yuan Yang [1] and Hung-Wei Lin [1]

1 Department of Electrical Engineering, Chang Gung University, Taoyuan City 333, Taiwan
2 Department of Electrical Engineering, Ming Chi University of Technology, New Taipei City 243, Taiwan
* Correspondence: yhchang@mail.cgu.edu.tw
† This paper is an extended version of our paper published in Y.-H. Chang, C.-Y. Yang and H.-W. Lin, "Adaptive control for bilateral teleoperation systems with time-varying delays", 2018 IEEE International Conference on Applied System Invention (ICASI), Chiba, Japan, 2018, pp. 1111–1114, doi: 10.1109/ICASI.2018.8394475.

Abstract: Master–slave teleoperation systems with haptic feedback enable human operators to interact with objects or perform tasks in remote environments. This paper presents a sliding-mode control scheme tailored for bilateral teleoperation systems operating in the presence of unknown uncertainties and time-varying delays. To address unknown but bounded uncertainties, adaptive laws are derived alongside controller design. Additionally, a linear matrix inequality is solved to determine the allowable bound of delays. Stability of the closed-loop system is ensured through Lyapunov–Krasovskii functional analysis. Two-degree-of-freedom mechanisms are self-built as haptic devices. Free-motion and force-perception scenarios are examined, with experimental results validating and comparing performances. The proposed adaptive-sliding-control method increases the position performance from 58.48% to 82.55% and the force performance from 83.48% to 99.77%. The proposed control scheme demonstrates enhanced position tracking and force perception in bilateral teleoperation systems.

Keywords: adaptive control; sliding-mode control; teleoperation system; time-varying delays

1. Introduction

The structure of teleoperation systems typically consists of several key components: human operator, master manipulator, slave manipulator, and communication channel. The interactions between these components form the basis of teleoperation systems, enabling human operators to control systems and interact with remote environments effectively [1,2]. In a teleoperation system, the human operator controls the master manipulator, usually through prescribed trajectories or specific tasks. The slave robot then follows the movements of the master manipulator in a free space, replicating the actions performed by the operator in the remote environment. Integrating haptic feedback into teleoperation systems enhances the operator's situational awareness and dexterity, enabling more intuitive and precise control of the master manipulator while interacting with the remote environment. This contributes to improved task performance and overall efficiency in various teleoperation applications. The applications of teleoperation systems are versatile, such as in unmanned aerial vehicles [3–5], virtual reality [6,7], medical training [8–10], and telesurgery [11–16].

In recent years, significant advancements have been made in the development of teleoperation systems, with several methods and techniques being addressed to improve their performance, robustness, and versatility. In [17], an event-triggered mechanism combined with a PD-like controller was presented for bilateral teleoperation systems to address communication channel congestion. In [18], an adaptive proportional damping controller utilizing an RBF neural network and adaptive control strategy was proposed to enhance stability and performance in a telerobotic system. On the other hand, time-domain-passivity control is a widely used approach to preserve the stability of teleoperation systems. In general, it is expected to maintain the passivity of the system to ensure a safe and stable operation [19,20]. Bavili et al. [21] investigated the problem of asymptotic stability and position tracking in nonlinear teleoperation systems when interacting with non-passive operators and environments. In [22], a passivity controller was presented to compensate for the non-passivity induced by longitudinal slipping and lateral sliding of wheeled robots. In [23], a passivity-based delay predictor was proposed to improve the transparency of a four-channel bilateral teleoperation system. Passivity-based control was utilized to ensure energy stability, and shared variable impedance control can facilitate smooth collaboration in teleoperation [24]. Additionally, a passivity-based nonlinear controller was introduced for bilateral teleoperation system under variable time delay and load disturbance [25]. In [26], a neural network-based four-channel-time-domain-passivity approach was proposed for a teleoperation system with time-varying delays.

Obtaining precise dynamic models for both master and slave manipulators in a teleoperation system can be challenging due to various factors such as nonlinearities, uncertainties, and complex mechanical structures. Adaptive tuning methods have been proposed to overcome this problem. Yang et al. [27] addressed the problem of adaptive tracking control for a teleoperation system with uncertainties in both kinematics and dynamics. In [28], an adaptive fuzzy neural network-backstepping-control scheme was developed for bilateral teleoperation systems to handle time delays and uncertainties. In [29], a fixed-time adaptive neural network-synchronization control was presented for teleoperation systems, handling position-error constraints and time-varying delays. In [30], a type-2 fuzzy neural network was proposed to deal with time-varying delays and uncertainties. In [31], a type-2 fuzzy-based observer was introduced to estimate external force/torque information and simultaneously filter out system disturbances. In [32], an adaptive bilateral control strategy was introduced for underwater manipulator teleoperation, with adaptive RBF network compensation for slave-manipulator uncertainties. In [33], a radial basis function-neural network-based-sliding-mode-control design was developed for nonlinear bilateral teleoperation system with transmission delays and uncertainties. In addition, a sliding-mode controller combined with a nonlinear-disturbance observer was proposed, such that the asymptotical stability can be preserved [34]. Due to the superiority of its robustness, the sliding-mode control has become an effective scheme for network control systems that are subject to time delays, packet losses, uncertainties, disturbances, and/or faults [35].

The presence of communication time delays and model uncertainties can significantly impact the transparency and stability of teleoperation systems [36,37]. For constant delays, a terminal sliding-mode controller was discussed for time-delayed nonlinear teleoperation systems [38]. In [39], an observer-based force control scheme was proposed to guarantee the position and force tracking in nonlinear teleoperation systems, subject to a constant communication time delay. Moreover, a bilateral neural network adaptive controller was designed for a class of teleoperation systems with constant time delays, external disturbances, and internal friction [40]. In practice, it is more attractive to investigate the tracking stability of teleoperation systems subject to time-varying delays. In [41], a general framework was presented to analyze and optimize the transparency of multilateral systems under time-varying delays. In [42], an adaptive control framework was developed to simultaneously handle both unknown kinematics/dynamics and time-varying delays. In [43], a finite-time control method was presented for bilateral teleoperators to ensure the coordination of master and slave manipulators in the presence of time-varying delays, external disturbances, and dynamic uncertainties. Zakerimanesh et al. [44] presented a control framework for bilateral teleoperation systems experiencing bounded time-varying delays in their communication channels.

When analyzing time-delay issues, delay-dependent approaches are generally less conservative than delay-independent approaches. However, the derivation of delay-dependent stability conditions can be more complex than that for delay-independent approaches, particularly because delays are explicitly considered in the design of stabilizing controllers. In general, when dealing with time-delay systems, ensuring closed-loop stability is crucial for the overall performance and reliability of the system. To achieve this, various conditions related to controller parameters are often desired, especially those that explicitly consider the time delays. Lyapunov–Krasovskii functions and linear matrix inequalities (LMIs) are commonly employed tools for investigating the stability of time-delay systems [45–51].

The synthesis problem in time-delayed teleoperation systems involves designing stabilizing controllers to ensure closed-loop stability while minimizing conservatism and preserving transparency in teleoperation. This entails finding less conservative stabilizing controllers that can effectively handle time delays, especially those that vary over time. Delay-dependent approaches are preferred due to their ability to explicitly consider time delays, which leads to more accurate estimation of stability conditions and efficient controller designs. By addressing practical considerations such as time-varying delays, teleoperation systems can achieve robust performance and seamless interaction between the operator and the remote environment. In the works of [52], both symmetric and asymmetric time-varying delays in communication were addressed. Symmetry of the communication delays means that the delays of the forward and backward channels are equal. Symmetric delays could exist in a constrained environment such as a local wire-connected network with a strictly defined protocol. On the other hand, asymmetric communication delays would be more practical in internet or wireless networks. In existing works of asymmetric time-varying delays, the bounds of time-varying delays are usually given in advance, then a delay-dependent controller can be obtained to ensure closed-loop stability. In this paper, it is desired to find the allowable boundary of time-varying communication delays. For the purpose of concise computations, a symmetric teleoperation system is addressed. How to relax this assumption of symmetry would be another interesting topic.

Transparency is a critical issue in teleoperations. Ensuring precise force feedback across versatile environments is a primary task. Our proposed control strategies are designed to maintain high transparency by accurately replicating forces encountered in the remote environment, thus enhancing the user's sense of presence and control. In this work, a novel adaptive-sliding mode control scheme is proposed for bilateral teleoperation systems encountering model uncertainties and time-varying delays. The main contributions are as follows:

1. The proposed method allows for the determination of admissible bounds of time-varying delays by solving linear matrix inequalities (LMIs), thus providing valuable insights into temporal constraints.
2. The derived adaptive laws enable the estimation of bounds for unknown uncertainties, thereby enhancing the robustness of the controller against model uncertainties.
3. Utilizing delay-dependent Lyapunov–Krasovskii functional analysis ensures the closed-loop stability of the teleoperation system, offering theoretical assurances even in the presence of delays and uncertainties.
4. The control scheme addresses both free-motion and force-perception aspects of a general non-passive teleoperation system, thereby expanding its applicability across various scenarios.
5. Conducting master–slave experiments validates the feasibility and effectiveness of the proposed control scheme in real-world settings, demonstrating its practical applicability and performance.

2. Materials and Methods

2.1. Preliminaries

The dynamic model for an nth degree master–slave robotic system can be described using the following equations:

$$M_m(q_m)\ddot{q}_m + C_m(q_m, \dot{q}_m)\dot{q}_m + g_m(q_m) + \delta_m = \tau_m + f_h \tag{1}$$

$$M_s(q_s)\ddot{q}_s + C_s(q_s, \dot{q}_s)\dot{q}_s + g_s(q_s) + \delta_s = \tau_s - f_e \tag{2}$$

where the subscripts m and s represent the master and slave, respectively, q_m and $q_s \in \mathcal{R}^n$ are the vectors joint positions, $M_m(q_m)$ and $M_s(q_s) \in \mathcal{R}^{n\times n}$ are the inertia matrices, $C_m(q_m, \dot{q}_m)$ and $C_s(q_s, \dot{q}_s) \in \mathcal{R}^{n\times n}$ are the Coriolis matrices, $g_m(q_m)$ and $g_s(q_s) \in \mathcal{R}^n$ are the gravitational vectors, τ_m and $\tau_s \in \mathcal{R}^n$ are vectors of input torques, f_h and $f_e \in \mathcal{R}^n$ are the human operation force and the environmental force, and δ_m and δ_s are the unknown uncertainties of the master and slave robots, respectively. In this paper, the human operator's force f_h and the environmental force f_e are non-passive [53,54]:

$$f_h = k_h - D_h\dot{q}_m - K_h q_m \tag{3}$$

$$f_e = k_e - D_e\dot{q}_s - K_e q_s \tag{4}$$

where k_h and k_e are constant vectors of $\mathcal{R}^n$, and D_h and $K_h \in \mathcal{R}^{n\times n}$ are the damping and spring-constant matrices for human force, respectively. In addition, D_e and $K_e \in \mathcal{R}^{n\times n}$ represent the damping and spring-constant matrices for the environmental force, respectively.

Property 1. *The inertia matrix $M_i(q_i)$ is symmetric and positive definite. Let $\overline{\lambda}_i$ be the maximum eigenvalue of $M_i(q_i)$. Then, $M_i(q_i) \leq \overline{\lambda}_i I_n$ where $I_n \in \mathcal{R}^{n\times n}$ is the identity matrix, $i \in \{m,s\}$.*

Property 2. *The matrix $\dot{M}_i(q_i) - 2C_i(q_i, \dot{q}_i)$ is skewed symmetric, $i \in \{m,s\}$.*

Property 3. *There exists a positive constant c_i such that $\|C_i(q_i, \dot{q}_i)\|_2 \leq c_i$, where $\|\cdot\|_2$ represents the $\mathcal{L}_2$ norm, $i \in \{m,s\}$.*

Assumption 1. *Let $\delta_i = [\delta_{i1}\ \delta_{i2}\ \ldots\ \delta_{in}]^T$ be bounded by $\overline{\delta}_i = [\overline{\delta}_{i1}\ \ \overline{\delta}_{i2}\ \ \ldots\ \ \overline{\delta}_{in}\ ]^T$, $|\delta_{ij}| < \overline{\delta}_{ij}$, where $\overline{\delta}_{ij}$ is an unknown constant, $i \in \{m,s\}$, $j = 1, 2, \ldots n$.*

Lemma 1. [55] *Given a positive-definite matrix R, the following inequality holds*

$$2X^T Y \leq X^T R X + Y^T R^{-1} Y, \tag{5}$$

where X and Y are two matrices with proper dimensions.

Lemma 2. [56] *Let $O = \begin{bmatrix} O_{11} & O_{12} \\ O_{12}^T & -O_{22} \end{bmatrix}$ be a matrix with proper dimensions, $O_{22} > 0$. Then the following equation holds:*

$$O < 0 \Longleftrightarrow O_{11} + O_{12}O_{22}^{-1}O_{12}^T < 0. \tag{6}$$

2.2. Adaptive-Sliding-Mode-Controller Design

In the context of the time-delayed teleoperation system described by Equations (1) and (2), a sliding-mode controller will be designed to achieve asymptotically stable sliding motion.

Assumption 2. *The forward and backward communication delays are symmetric, and the time-varying delay $d(t)$ satisfies the conditions that*

$$0 < d(t) \leq \overline{d} < \infty,\ \dot{d}(t) \leq \mu < 1, \tag{7}$$

where $\overline{d}$ and μ are positive constants.

Remark 1. *If $\dot{d}(t) \geq 1$, then the delay will grow faster than the increase in time. As the manipulator devices are required to track some delayed trajectories, the control loop becomes open. Under this circumstance, the controller design and related stability analysis opens a new theoretical problem, which cannot be solved at current stage and needs to be investigated separately* [42].

In the following equations, the notations $q_{m,d}$ and $q_{s,d}$ are used to stand for $q_m(t-d(t))$ and $q_s(t-d(t))$, respectively, for simplicity. The sliding surfaces for the master and slave robots are defined, respectively, as

$$s_m = \dot{q}_m + K_m\left(q_m - q_{s,d}\right)$$
$$s_s = \dot{q}_s + K_s\left(q_s - q_{m,d}\right) \tag{8}$$

where $K_m = diag\{k_{m1}, k_{m2}, \ldots, k_{mn}\} \in \mathcal{R}^{n\times n}$ and $K_s = diag\{k_{s1}, k_{s2}, \ldots, k_{sn}\} \in \mathcal{R}^{n\times n}$, $k_{mj} > 0$, and $k_{sj} > 0$, $j = 1, 2, \ldots, n$. Then, the sliding mode of (8), $s_m = s_s = 0$, can be equivalently described as

$$\dot{q}_m = -K_m\left(q_m - q_{s,d}\right)$$
$$\dot{q}_s = -K_s\left(q_s - q_{m,d}\right) \tag{9}$$

Let the error functions of the master and slave sides, respectively, be defined as

$$e_m = q_m - q_s,\ e_s = q_s - q_m \tag{10}$$

From (9) and (10), it can be determined that

$$\dot{e} = -A_1 e - A_1 e_d \tag{11}$$

where $e = \begin{bmatrix} e_m^T & e_s^T \end{bmatrix}^T$, $e_d = e(t-d(t))$, and $A_1 = diag\{K_m, K_s\}$.

Theorem 1. *The error functions of (10) are asymptotically convergent if the following inequality holds:*

$$\begin{bmatrix} \Theta_{11} & A_1 P_s & 0_{2n} & A_1 \\ P_s A_1 & -\bar{d}^{-1} R_s & 0_{2n} & 0_{2n} \\ 0_{2n} & 0_{2n} & -\tilde{\mu} Q_s & A_1 \\ A_1 & 0_{2n} & A_1 & -\left(\bar{d} R_s\right)^{-1} \end{bmatrix} < 0 \tag{12}$$

where P_s, Q_s, and R_s are symmetric positive-definite matrices of $\mathcal{R}^{2n\times 2n}$, $\Theta_{11} = -4P_s A_1 + Q_s$, $\tilde{\mu} = 1 - \mu$, and 0_{2n} is a zero matrix of dimension $2n \times 2n$.

Proof. A Lyapunov–Krasovskii function is chosen as

$$V_s = e^T P_s e + \int_{t-d(t)}^{t} e^T(s) Q_s e(s) ds + \int_{-\bar{d}}^{0}\int_{t+\theta}^{t} \dot{e}^T(s) R_s \dot{e}(s) ds d\theta. \tag{13}$$

The time derivative of V_s from (11) is derived as

$$\begin{aligned} \dot{V}_s \le\ & 2e^T P_s(-A_1 e - A_1 e_d) + e^T Q_s e - \tilde{\mu} e_d^T Q_s e_d \\ & + \bar{d}(-A_1 e - A_1 e_d)^T R_s (-A_1 e - A_1 e_d) - \textstyle\int_{t-\bar{d}}^{t} \dot{e}^T(s) R_s \dot{e}(s) ds \end{aligned} \tag{14}$$

It is noted that $e_d = e - \int_{t-d(t)}^{t} \dot{e}(s) ds$. Then, from Lemma 1 and Assumption 2, it leads to the following inequality

$$\begin{aligned} \dot{V}_s \le\ & -4e^T P_s A_1 e + \bar{d} e^T P_s A_1 R_s^{-1} A_1 P_s e + e^T Q_s e - \tilde{\mu} e_d^T Q_s e_d + \bar{d} e^T A_1 R_s A_1 e \\ & + 2\bar{d} e^T A_1 R_s A_1 e_d + \bar{d} e_d^T A_1 R_s A_1 e_d = \begin{bmatrix} e \\ e_d \end{bmatrix}^T \Theta \begin{bmatrix} e \\ e_d \end{bmatrix} \end{aligned} \tag{15}$$

where

$$\Theta = \begin{bmatrix} \Theta_1 & \bar{d}A_1R_sA_1 \\ \bar{d}A_1R_sA_1 & \bar{d}A_1R_sA_1 - \tilde{\mu}Q_s \end{bmatrix}, \ \Theta_1 = -4P_sA_1 + Q_s + \bar{d}P_sA_1R_s^{-1}A_1P_s + \bar{d}A_1R_sA_1 \tag{16}$$

From Lemma 2, $\dot{V}_s$ is negative if (12) holds. This implies that the error dynamics of (11) is asymptotically stable. This completes the proof. □

The sliding-mode-based controllers for the torques acting on the delayed teleoperation system are designed as

$$\tau_m = \tau_{eq,m} + \tau_{sw,m} \tag{17}$$

$$\tau_s = \tau_{eq,s} + \tau_{sw,s} \tag{18}$$

where $\tau_{eq,m}$ and $\tau_{eq,s}$ are the equivalent control actions and $\tau_{sw,m}$ and $\tau_{sw,s}$ are the switching controllers. From (1) and (2), considering the uncertainty-free case, the equivalent controllers $\tau_{eq,m}$ and $\tau_{eq,s}$ can be determined as

$$\tau_{eq,m} = -M_mK_m\left(\dot{q}_m - \dot{q}_{s,d}\right) + C_m\dot{q}_m + g_m \tag{19}$$

$$\tau_{eq,s} = -M_sK_s\left(\dot{q}_s - \dot{q}_{m,d}\right) + C_s\dot{q}_s + g_s \tag{20}$$

It is noted that the uncertain terms δ_m and δ_s of (1) and (2) are unknown but bounded. To estimate $\bar{\delta}_m = \begin{bmatrix} \bar{\delta}_{m1} & \bar{\delta}_{m2} & \ldots & \bar{\delta}_{mn} \end{bmatrix}^T$ and $\bar{\delta}_s = \begin{bmatrix} \bar{\delta}_{s1} & \bar{\delta}_{s2} & \ldots & \bar{\delta}_{sn} \end{bmatrix}^T$, the adaptive laws are designated as follows:

$$\dot{\hat{\bar{\delta}}}_m = \begin{cases} \Gamma M_m^{-1}|s_m|, & if\, f_h = 0, \\ 0, & if\, f_h \neq 0. \end{cases} \tag{21}$$

$$\dot{\hat{\bar{\delta}}}_s = \begin{cases} \Gamma M_s^{-1}|s_s|, & if\, f_e = 0, \\ 0, & if\, f_e \neq 0. \end{cases} \tag{22}$$

where $\hat{\bar{\delta}}_m$ and $\hat{\bar{\delta}}_s \in \mathcal{R}^n$, $\Gamma = diag\{\gamma_1, \gamma_2, \ldots, \gamma_n\} \in \mathcal{R}^{n\times n}$, $\gamma_j > 0, j = 1,2,\ldots,n$, $|s_m| = \begin{bmatrix} |s_{m1}| & |s_{m2}| & \ldots & |s_{mn}| \end{bmatrix}^T$, and $|s_s| = \begin{bmatrix} |s_{s1}| & |s_{s2}| & \ldots & |s_{sn}| \end{bmatrix}^T$.

In this paper, the switching controllers are formulated as

$$\tau_{sw,m} = -(\Phi_m + \hat{\Delta}_m)sgn(s_m), \tag{23}$$

$$\tau_{sw,s} = -(\Phi_s + \hat{\Delta}_s)sgn(s_s), \tag{24}$$

in which $\Phi_m = diag\{\phi_{m1}, \phi_{m2}, \ldots, \phi_{mn}\} \in \mathcal{R}^{n\times n}$, $\Phi_s = diag\{\phi_{s1}, \phi_{s2}, \ldots, \phi_{sn}\} \in \mathcal{R}^{n\times n}$, $\phi_{mj} > 0$, $\phi_{sj} > 0$, $j = 1,2,\ldots,n$, and $sgn(\cdot)$ is a standard sign function. In addition, $\hat{\Delta}_m = diag\left\{\hat{\bar{\delta}}_{m1}, \hat{\bar{\delta}}_{m2}, \ldots, \hat{\bar{\delta}}_{mn}\right\}$ and $\hat{\Delta}_s = diag\left\{\hat{\bar{\delta}}_{s1}, \hat{\bar{\delta}}_{s2}, \ldots, \hat{\bar{\delta}}_{sn}\right\}$.

Remark 2. *The required input torques on the master and slave sides are shown in (17) and (18). The input torques include both equivalent and switching control actions. For example, the input torque τ_m can be obtained from $\tau_{eq,m}$ and $\tau_{sw,m}$ in Equations (17), (19) and (23). In (23), an adaptive law for the unknown bounded uncertainties is designed as (21). Similarly, the input torque τ_s can be implemented with Equations (18), (20), (22), and (24). The scheme diagram of the proposed teleoperation system is shown in Figure 1.*

Remark 3. *There could be a potential issue of chattering associated with the use of the sign function in the controller (23) and (24). To address this common chattering problem, a smoothing technique can be employed by replacing the sign function with a continuous approximation, such as a saturation function or a boundary-layer approach.*

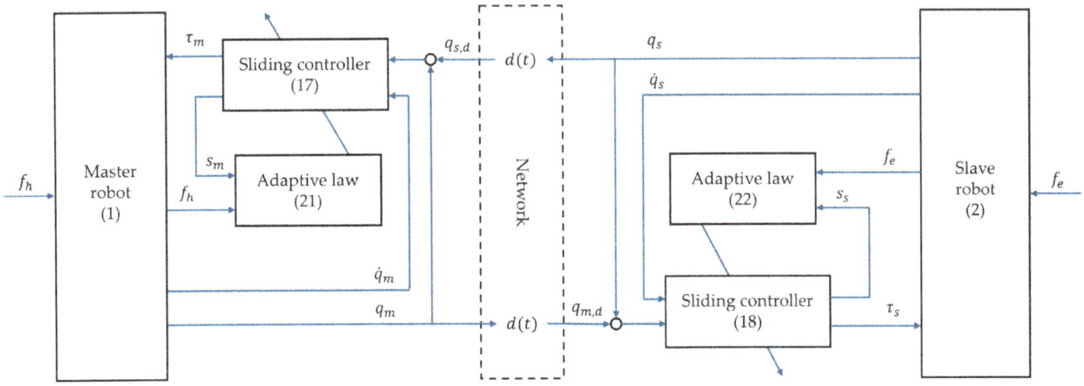

Figure 1. Adaptive-sliding-mode scheme for teleoperation system.

Theorem 2. *Consider the bilateral teleoperation systems (1) and (2). In free motion, $f_h = f_e = \mathbf{0}$, and the state trajectories of teleoperation systems (1) and (2) will be driven onto the sliding surfaces (8) with the controllers (17) and (18) and the adaptive laws (21), (22).*

Proof. Let a Lyapunov function be chosen as

$$V_c = \frac{1}{2}\left(s_m^T s_m + \tilde{\delta}_m^T \Gamma^{-1} \tilde{\delta}_m + s_s^T s_s + \tilde{\delta}_s^T \Gamma^{-1} \tilde{\delta}_s \right) \tag{25}$$

where $\tilde{\delta}_m = \bar{\delta}_m - \hat{\bar{\delta}}_m$, and $\tilde{\delta}_s = \bar{\delta}_s - \hat{\bar{\delta}}_s$ are the estimation errors. The derivative of (8) is obtained as

$$\begin{aligned} \dot{s}_m &= \ddot{q}_m + K_m\left(\dot{q}_m - \dot{q}_{s,d}\right), \\ \dot{s}_s &= \ddot{q}_s + K_s\left(\dot{q}_s - \dot{q}_{m,d}\right). \end{aligned} \tag{26}$$

The derivative of V_c along (26) is

$$\begin{aligned} \dot{V}_c &= s_m^T\left(M_m^{-1}(\tau_m - C_m\dot{q}_m - g_m - \delta_m) + K_m\left(\dot{q}_m - \dot{q}_{s,d}\right)\right) \\ &+ s_s^T\left(M_s^{-1}(\tau_s - C_s\dot{q}_s - g_s - \delta_s) + K_s\left(\dot{q}_s - \dot{q}_{m,d}\right)\right) - \tilde{\delta}_m^T \Gamma^{-1} \dot{\hat{\bar{\delta}}}_m - \tilde{\delta}_s^T \Gamma^{-1} \dot{\hat{\bar{\delta}}}_s. \end{aligned} \tag{27}$$

From Assumption 1, this gives the following:

$$\begin{aligned} \dot{V}_c &< s_m^T\left(M_m^{-1}(\tau_m - C_m\dot{q}_m - g_m) + K_m\left(\dot{q}_m - \dot{q}_{s,d}\right)\right) \\ &+ s_s^T\left(M_s^{-1}(\tau_s - C_s\dot{q}_s - g_s) + K_s\left(\dot{q}_s - \dot{q}_{m,d}\right)\right) \\ &+ |s_m|^T M_m^{-1}\bar{\delta}_m + |s_s|^T M_s^{-1}\bar{\delta}_s - \tilde{\delta}_m^T \Gamma^{-1} \dot{\hat{\bar{\delta}}}_m - \tilde{\delta}_s^T \Gamma^{-1} \dot{\hat{\bar{\delta}}}_s. \end{aligned} \tag{28}$$

Substituting (17), (18), and (21) into (28), it yields

$$\dot{V}_c < -s_m^T \Phi_m M_m^{-1} sgn(s_m) - s_s^T \Phi_s M_s^{-1} sgn(s_s) \tag{29}$$

From (25) to (29), it is evident that the negative definiteness of V_c can be preserved, which means that s_m, s_s, $\tilde{\delta}_m$, and $\tilde{\delta}_m$ are bounded. Therefore, the systems (1) and (2) are stable. Hence, the states of the teleoperation system (1) and (2) will reach the sliding surface (8). The proof is completed. □

2.3. Stability Analysis

Substituting (3), (4), (17), and (18) into (1) and (2), the closed-loop teleoperation systems can be represented as

$$M_m\ddot{q}_m = -M_mK_m\left(\dot{q}_m - \dot{q}_{s,d}\right) + \epsilon_m + k_h - D_h\dot{q}_m - K_hq_m$$

$$M_s\ddot{q}_s = -M_sK_s\left(\dot{q}_s - \dot{q}_{m,d}\right) + \epsilon_s + k_e - D_e\dot{q}_s - K_eq_s. \quad (30)$$

where $\epsilon_m = -\delta_m - \hat{\Delta}_m sgn(s_m) - \Phi_m sgn(s_m)$ and $\epsilon_s = -\delta_s - \hat{\Delta}_s sgn(s_s) - \Phi_s sgn(s_s)$.

Remark 4. *According to Assumption 1 and Theorem 2, the uncertainty terms δ_m and δ_s are bounded and the estimated terms $\hat{\Delta}_m$ and $\hat{\Delta}_s$ are bounded. Thus, both the ϵ_m and ϵ_s are bounded.*

Theorem 3. *With non-passive human and environment forces (3) and (4), the closed-loop teleoperation system (30) is asymptotic stable if the following LMI holds:*

$$\Omega = \begin{bmatrix} \Omega_{11} & 0_n & 0_n & 0_n \\ 0_n & \overline{\lambda}_sK_s - \tilde{\mu}Q & 0_n & 0_n \\ 0_n & 0_n & \Omega_{33} & 0_n \\ 0_n & 0_n & 0_n & \overline{\lambda}_mK_m - \tilde{\mu}Q \end{bmatrix} < 0 \quad (31)$$

where $Q \in \mathcal{R}^{n\times n}$ is a symmetric positive-definite matrix, and

$$\Omega_{11} = -\overline{\lambda}_mK_m + (2c_m + \alpha_m)I_n + Q - 2D_h$$

$$\Omega_{33} = -\overline{\lambda}_sK_s + (2c_s + \alpha_s)I_n + Q - 2D_e \quad (32)$$

in which αm and αs are positive constants and $0n$ is a zero matrix of $\mathcal{R}^{n\times n}$.

Proof. Consider a Lyapunov–Krasovskii function candidate as follows:

$$V = \dot{q}_m^TM_m\dot{q}_m + q_m^TK_hq_m + \int_{t-d(t)}^{t}\dot{q}_m^T(s)Q\dot{q}_m(s)ds + \dot{q}_s^TM_s\dot{q}_s + q_s^TM_sq_s + \int_{t-d(t)}^{t}\dot{q}_s^T(s)Q\dot{q}_s(s)ds \quad (33)$$

From Property 2, the time derivative of V along (30) can be reformulated as

$$V \leq 2\dot{q}_m^T\left(-M_mK_m\left(\dot{q}_m - \dot{q}_{s,d}\right) + C_m\dot{q}_m + \epsilon_m + k_h - D_h\dot{q}_m\right) + 2\dot{q}_s^T\left(-M_sK_s\left(\dot{q}_s - \dot{q}_{m,d}\right) + C_s\dot{q}_s + \epsilon_s + k_e - D_e\dot{q}_s\right) + \dot{q}_m^TQ\dot{q}_m - \tilde{\mu}\dot{q}_{m,d}^TQ\dot{q}_{m,d} + \dot{q}_s^TQ\dot{q}_s - \tilde{\mu}\dot{q}_s^TQ\dot{q}_{s,d}. \quad (34)$$

From Lemma 1, the following inequalities can be obtained:

$$2\dot{q}_m^T(\epsilon_m + k_h) \leq \alpha_m\dot{q}_m^T\dot{q}_m + \frac{1}{\alpha_m}\|\epsilon_m + k_h\|_2^2$$

$$2\dot{q}_s^T(\epsilon_s + k_e) \leq \alpha_s\dot{q}_s^T\dot{q}_s + \frac{1}{\alpha_s}\|\epsilon_s - k_e\|_2^2 \quad (35)$$

and

$$2\dot{q}_m^TK_mM_m\dot{q}_{s,d} \leq \dot{q}_m^TK_mM_m\dot{q}_m + \dot{q}_{s,d}^TK_mM_m\dot{q}_{s,d}$$

$$2\dot{q}_s^TK_sM_s\dot{q}_{m,d} \leq \dot{q}_s^TK_sM_s\dot{q}_s + \dot{q}_{m,d}^TK_sM_s\dot{q}_{m,d} \quad (36)$$

where $\|\cdot\|_2$ represents the $L2$ norm of the signals.

From Properties 1 and 3, substituting (35) and (36) into (34) yields

$$\dot{V} \leq \dot{q}^T \Omega \dot{q} + \frac{1}{\alpha_m} \|\epsilon_m + k_h\|_2^2 + \frac{1}{\alpha_s} \|\epsilon_s - k_e\|_2^2 \tag{37}$$

where $\dot{q} = \begin{bmatrix} \dot{q}_m^T & \dot{q}_{m,d}^T & \dot{q}_s^T & \dot{q}_{s,d}^T \end{bmatrix}^T$. Furthermore, it leads to the following condition,

$$V \leq \overline{\lambda}_\Omega \|\dot{q}\|_2^2 + \rho \tag{38}$$

where $\overline{\lambda}_\Omega < 0$ is the maximum eigenvalue of the matrix $\boldsymbol{\Omega}$, $\rho = \frac{1}{\alpha_m}\|\epsilon_m + k_h\|_2^2 + \frac{1}{\alpha_s}\|\epsilon_s - k_e\|_2^2$. Noting that ρ is bounded, $\rho \leq \overline{\rho}$, $\overline{\rho}$ is a constant. Hence, $\dot{V}$ is negative, if $\|\dot{q}\|_2 > \sqrt{\frac{\overline{\rho}}{-\overline{\lambda}_\Omega}}$. The controller parameters $\boldsymbol{K_m}$ and $\boldsymbol{K_s}$ can be chosen such that $\dot{q}$ will be arbitrarily small. Therefore, the closed-loop system (30) is asymptotically stable. □

3. Experimental Results

In this paper, the master and slave devices are a pair of two-degrees-of-freedom-revolute-prismatic robots. The configuration illustration and 3D framework of the teleoperation devices are shown in Figure 2.

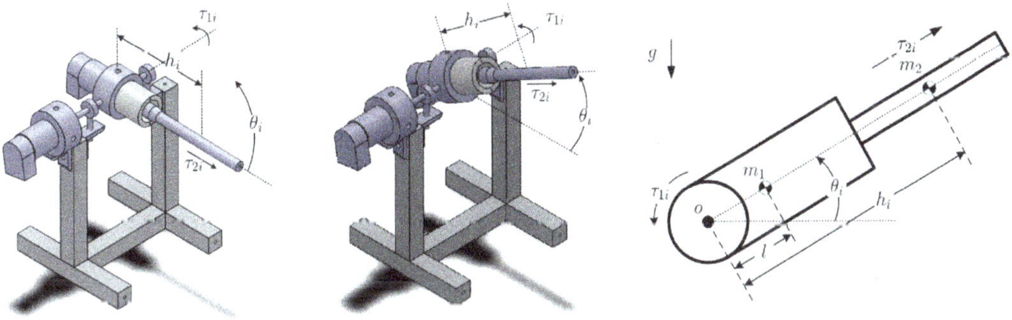

Figure 2. Configuration diagram of the master- and slave-manipulator robots.

The system parameters of the master and slave robots are listed in Table 1.

Table 1. System parameters of teleoperation systems.

m_1	Mass of link 1	0.36 kg
m_2	Mass of link 2	0.027 kg
l	Distance between joint o and center of link 1	0.02 m
g	Gravitational constant	9.8 m/s^2

The dynamic models of (1) and (2) are obtained as

$$\boldsymbol{M}_i(\boldsymbol{q}_i) = \begin{bmatrix} m_1 l^2 + m_2 h_i^2 & 0 \\ 0 & m_2 \end{bmatrix}, \ \boldsymbol{C}_i(\boldsymbol{q}_i, \dot{\boldsymbol{q}}_i) = \begin{bmatrix} 0 & 2m_2 h_i \dot{\theta}_i \\ -m_2 h_i \dot{\theta}_i & 0 \end{bmatrix},$$

$$\boldsymbol{G}_i(\boldsymbol{q}_i) = \begin{bmatrix} (m_1 l + m_2 h_i) g cos(\theta_i) \\ m_2 g sin(\theta_i) \end{bmatrix} \tag{39}$$

$q_i = [\theta_i \quad h_i]^T$, $\ddot{q}_i = [\ddot{\theta}_i \quad \ddot{h}_i]^T$, $\tau_i = [\tau_{1i} \quad \tau_{2i}]^T$, $f_h = [f_{h1} \quad f_{h2}]^T$,$f_e = [f_{e1} \quad f_{e2}]^T$, $i \in \{m,s\}$. In addition, h_i is the length of the joint 2 between the point o and the center of mass of the second link, and θ_i is the angle of the joint 1.

The parameters of the adaptive-sliding-mode controller are set as $\boldsymbol{K}_i = \boldsymbol{diag}\{2,2\}$, $\boldsymbol{\Phi}_i = \boldsymbol{diag}\{2.5,2.5\}$, and $\boldsymbol{\Gamma} = \boldsymbol{diag}\{0.5,0.1\} \times 10^{-3}$, $i \in \{m,s\}$. The disturbance parts are assumed as $\delta_i = \boldsymbol{diag}\{0.5,0.1\} \times \boldsymbol{rand}(\cdot) \times 10^{-3}$ and $\boldsymbol{rand}(\cdot)$ is a uniformly distributed random number. From Theorem 1, the allowable delay bound can be obtained as $\overline{d} = 0.5$ s by solving LMI (12). In experiments, the time delay is chosen as $d(t) = 0.25 + 0.2\sin(t)$ s. The initial states of the master and slave robots are set as $q_m = q_s = [0 \quad 0.145]^T$, and the initial velocities and acceleration are zero. Three types of controllers are adopted for comparison, including the proportional plus damping controller (P + dC) [17,18,45], sliding-mode controller (SC), and the proposed adaptive-sliding-mode controller (ASC). The following indices are considered for performance comparisons: the integral absolute error (IAE), the integral time absolute error (ITAE), the integral square error (ISE), and the integral time square error (ITSE) [57].

In the following, the cases of both free motion and force perception are performed. The experimental setup of a bilateral teleoperation system is shown in Figure 3. The position responses of the master and slave robots are measured by encoders. The control algorithms and signal interfacing are implemented by Raspberry Pi and a PIC18F4331 microprocessor. The sampling time is selected as 20 ms. In these experiments, the time delay is realized by software programming. Furthermore, all of the controller parameters of the teleoperation system are the same as the settings in simulations. The allowable delay bound is determined to be 0.5 s. The behavior of a delay can be accurately captured if the delay is multiple times the length of the sampling time.

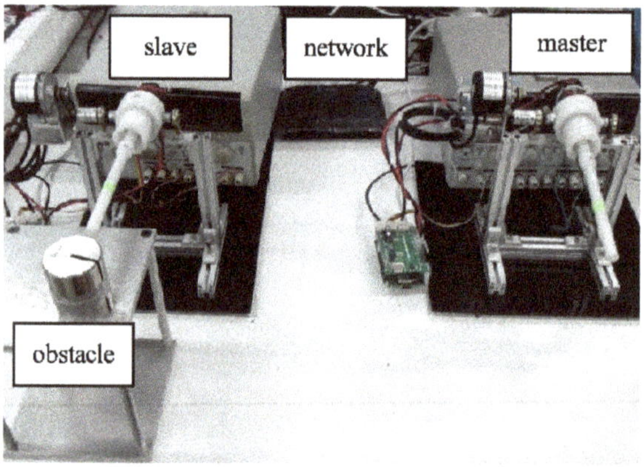

Figure 3. Experimental setup for teleoperation system.

3.1. Case 1: Free Motion (Experiment)

During the free-motion operation, the human operator moves the master robot towards $\theta_m = 1$ rad and $h_m = 0.195$ m, and the operator leaves the device standing still alone for $t > 5$ s. It is desired to see whether the slave robot can track the motion trajectory of the master device stably. As shown in Figures 4 and 5, the steady-state position errors are significantly reduced using the ASC method. Quantitative analyses of different methods are shown in Table 2. The proposed ASC method increases the performance improvement from 70.70% to 90.00%. The video snapshots captured from the ASC are depicted in Figure 6, where the recording time of each snapshot is indicated on the bottom right.

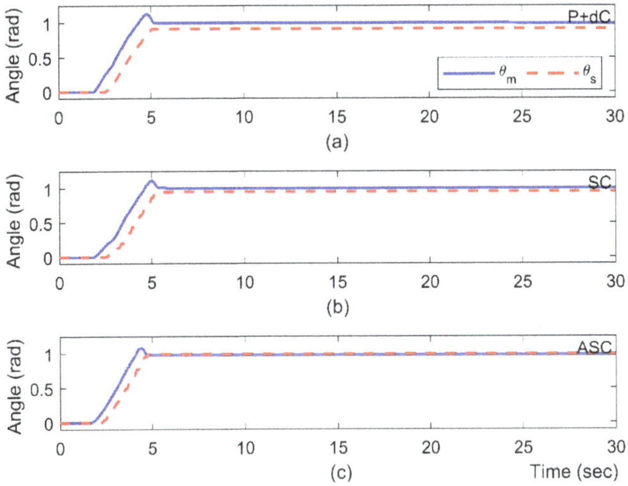

Figure 4. Position responses of joint 1 with different control methods for Case 1: (**a**) P + dC, (**b**) SC, and (**c**) ASC.

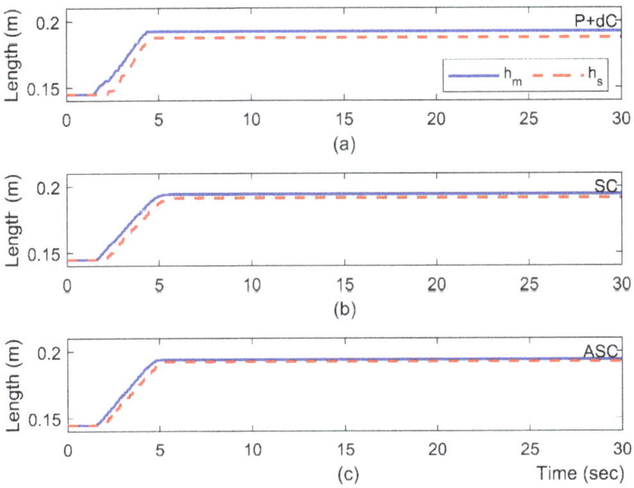

Figure 5. Position responses of joint 2 with different control methods for Case 1: (**a**) P + dC, (**b**) SC, and (**c**) ASC.

Table 2. Experimental comparisons of position errors in Case 1.

		IAE	ITAE	ISE	ITSE
P + dC	Joint 1	21.38	147.72	1983.70	199.68
	Joint 2	0.045	7.79	115.41	0.60
SC	Joint 1	13.38	99.21	1199.80	92.06
	Joint 2	0.019	4.81	68.24	0.21
ASC	Joint 1	6.26	36.91	248.95	22.71
	Joint 2	0.008	2.70	33.85	0.06

unit: joint 1 (rad), joint 2 (m).

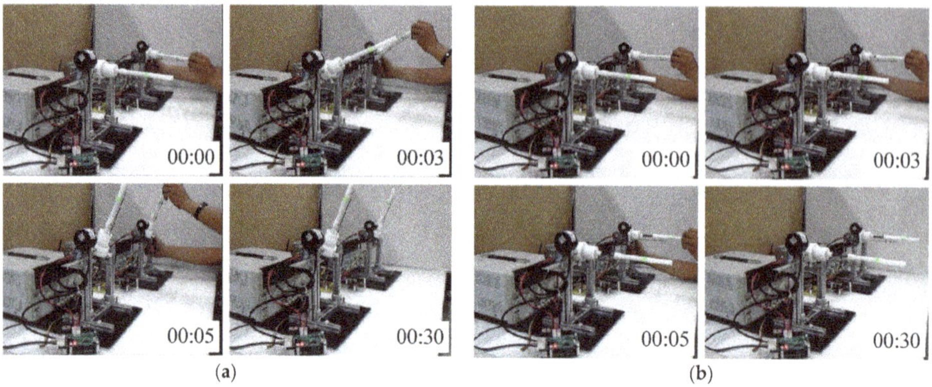

Figure 6. The snapshots of the experimental results for Case 1 (ASC): (**a**) joint 1, and (**b**) joint 2.

3.2. Case 2: Force Perception (Experiment)

In this case, an obstacle is placed on the slave side of the system at a position of roughly $h_s = 0.175$ m and $\theta_s = -0.5$ rad, respectively. As it is following the scheduled movement of the master, the slave robot will contact the pre-placed obstacle. Like in the in the simulation discussions, the force feedback will be conducted in turn for each joint. The experimental results corresponding to different methods are presented in Figures 7–10, where the slave robot contacts the obstacle around $t = 4$ s. From Figures 7 and 8, it can be observed that there exist quite clear biases between the joint positions of master and slave robots with the P + dC method. On the other hand, the proposed ASC controller can provide significant improvements in position tracking and force perception. As the force perception in Figures 9 and 10, the proposed ASC control method has superiority in stably and accurately tracking for $t > 4$ s. Quantitative analyses of the experimental results are summarized in Tables 3 and 4. They indicate that the proposed ASC method increases position performance from 58.48% to 82.55% and improves force performance from 83.48% to 99.77%. The video snapshots of ASC are depicted in Figure 11, where the recording time of each snapshot is indicated on the bottom right.

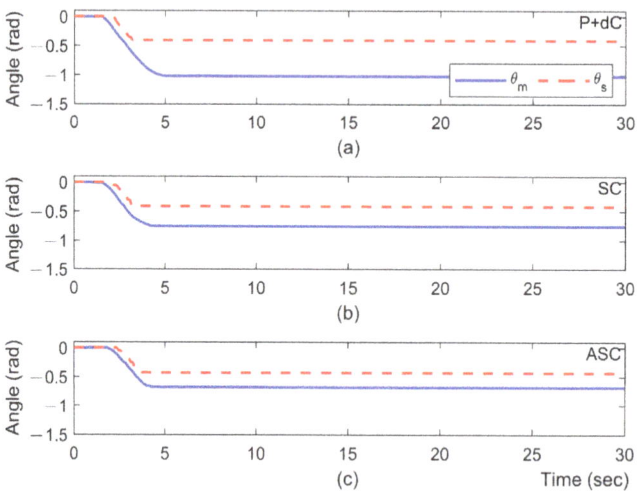

Figure 7. Position responses of joint 1 with different control methods for Case 2: (**a**) P + dC, (**b**) SC, and (**c**) ASC.

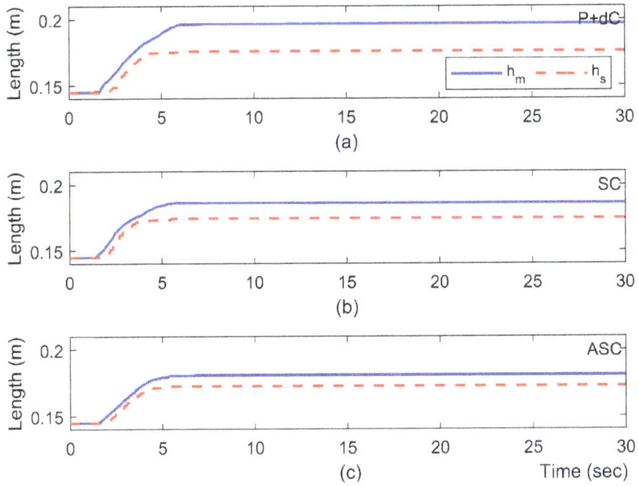

Figure 8. Position responses of joint 2 with different control methods for Case 2: (**a**) P + dC, (**b**) SC, and (**c**) ASC.

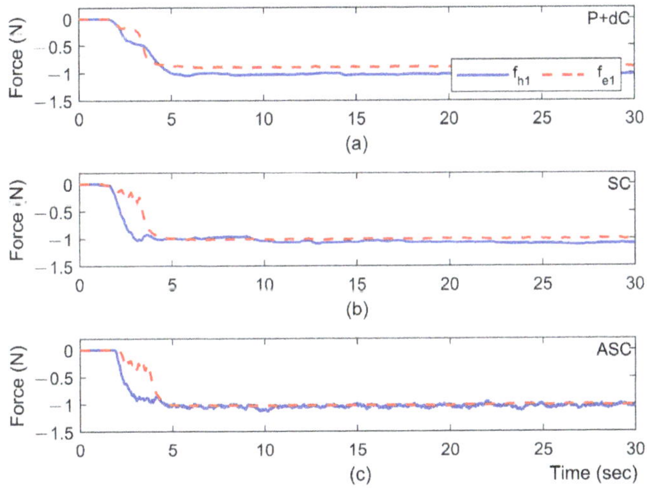

Figure 9. Force responses of joint 1 with different control methods for Case 2: (**a**) P + dC, (**b**) SC, and (**c**) ASC.

Table 3. Experimental comparisons of position responses in Case 2.

		IAE	ITAE	ISE	ITSE
P + dC	Joint 1	493.82	822.78	13,620.00	8319.10
	Joint 2	0.53	27.06	453.25	9.23
SC	Joint 1	155.35	465.18	7588.70	2575.70
	Joint 2	0.18	15.84	262.65	3.09
ASC	Joint 1	85.66	343.22	5655.00	1432.80
	Joint 2	0.17	15.69	241.20	2.60

unit: joint 1 (rad), joint 2 (m).

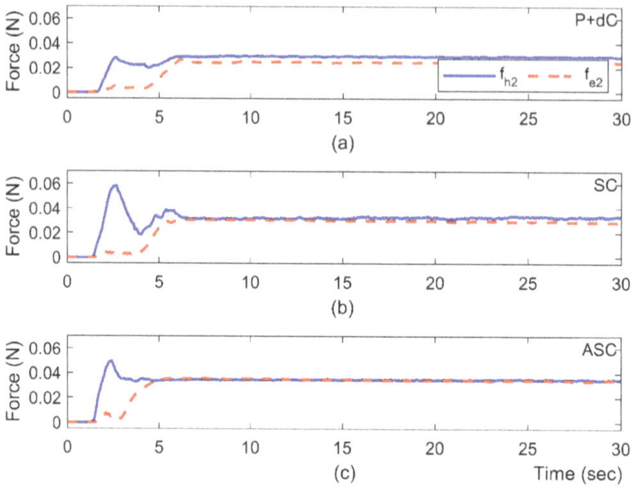

Figure 10. Force responses of joint 2 with different control methods for Case 2: (**a**) P + dC, (**b**) SC, and (**c**) ASC.

Table 4. Experimental comparisons of force errors in Case 2.

		IAE	ITAE	ISE	ITSE
P + dC	Joint 1	24.45	178.45	2497.80	351.22
	Joint 2	0.048	7.23	85.57	0.435
SC	Joint 1	13.28	93.91	1348.60	112.79
	Joint 2	0.036	4.77	54.07	0.195
ASC	Joint 1	2.87	34.35	412.59	15.84
	Joint 2	0.001	0.93	10.41	0.001

unit: joint 1 (N), joint 2 (N).

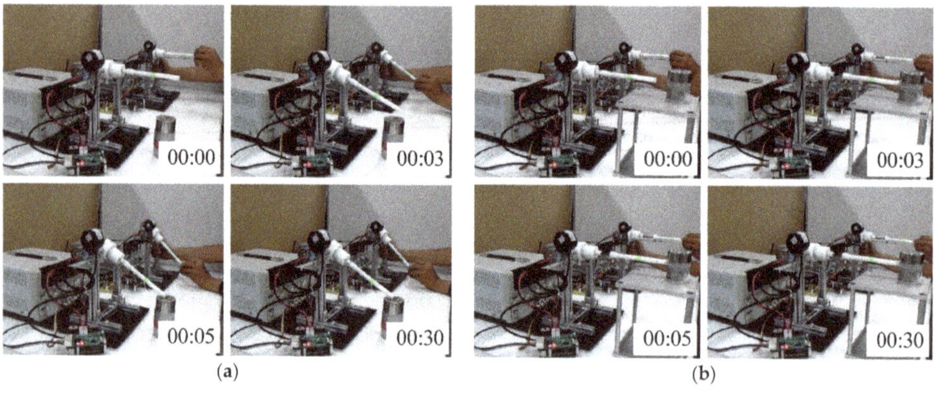

Figure 11. Snapshots of the experimental results for Case 2 (ASC): (**a**) joint 1, and (**b**) joint 2.

Remark 5. *To enhance the reader's understanding of the experimental process and results, experimental videos have been uploaded to YouTube (accessed on 11 June 2024).*

https://www.youtube.com/watch?v=M0uSr1mg5YU
https://www.youtube.com/watch?v=buR8rsf2_ls
https://www.youtube.com/watch?v=0H8ogvjg2TU
https://www.youtube.com/watch?v=jYd8kWvERj0

4. Discussion

A non-passive environment in the context of teleoperation systems refers to an environment where the forces exerted on the slave's side are not purely passive. This means that the slave's side does not simply follow the master's movements passively but may exert forces or exhibit behaviors that are independent or reactive to the master's commands. Building an experimental setup to replicate a non-passive environment presents several challenges due to its inherent complexity and unpredictability. To address these challenges, we conduct a simulation scenario in this study. Key performance indicators in a non-passive teleoperation environment include the closeness of position responses between the master and slave sides and the consistency of force tracking. Smaller errors in position and force tracking generally indicate better system performance.

4.1. Case 3: Free Motion (Simulation)

Additionally, a more general free-motion case is considered, where the joint 1 of the master moves approximately up to 1 rad and then gradually returns to its original position. During the same period, joint 2 smoothly pulls out. The simulation responses are shown in Figures 12–17, and the comparisons of position errors with different control methods are summarized in Table 5. Furthermore, the related control signals regarding to P + dC, SC, and ASC are shown in Figures 13, 15 and 17, respectively. It can be observed that the proposed ASC method can provide better trajectory-tracking capability.

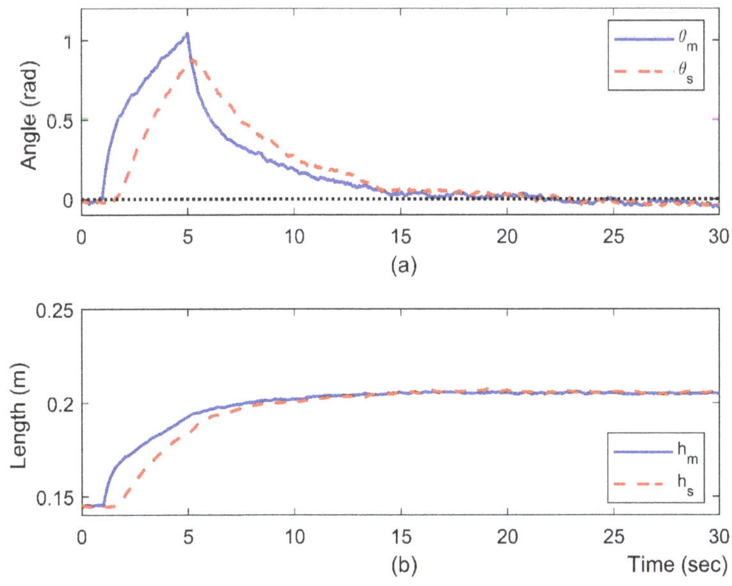

Figure 12. Position responses with P + dC method (Case 3): (**a**) joint 1, and (**b**) joint 2.

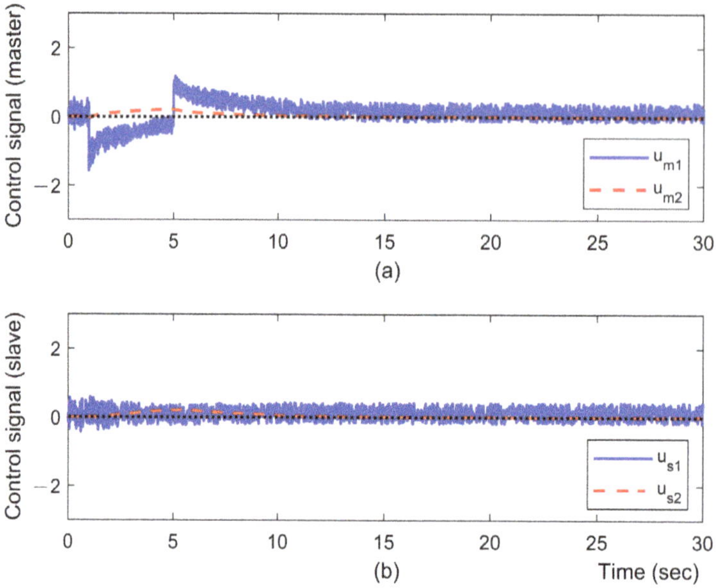

Figure 13. Control signals with P + dC method (Case 3): (**a**) master, and (**b**) slave.

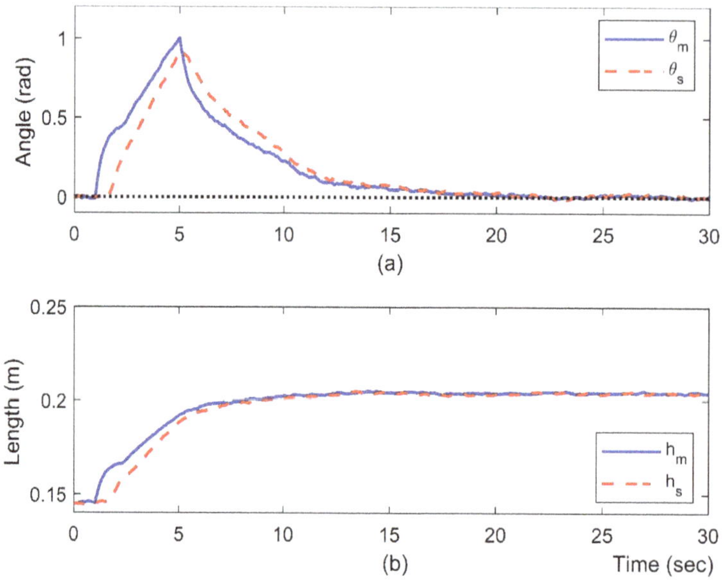

Figure 14. Position responses with SC method (Case 3): (**a**) joint 1, and (**b**) joint 2.

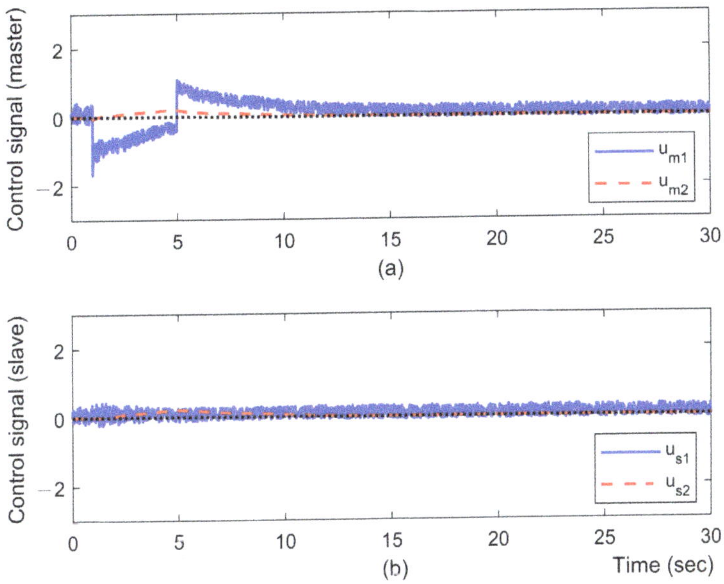

Figure 15. Control signals with SC method (Case 3): (**a**) master, and (**b**) slave.

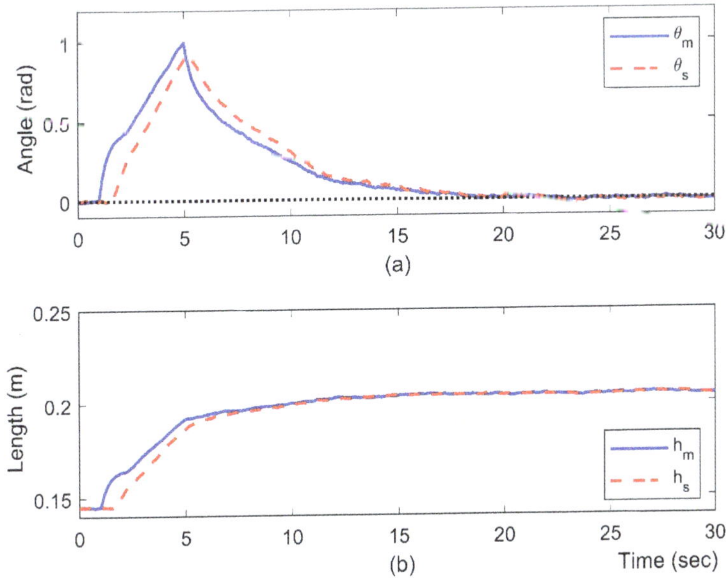

Figure 16. Position responses with ASC method (Case 3): (**a**) joint 1, and (**b**) joint 2.

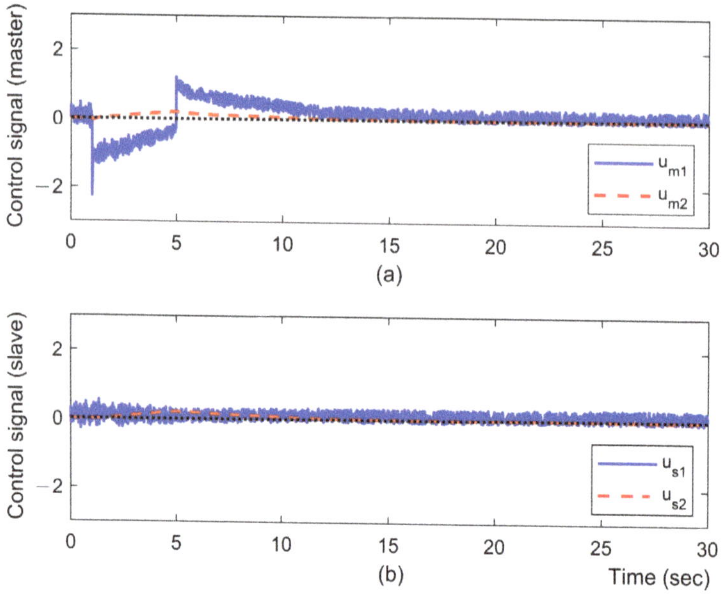

Figure 17. Control signals with ASC method (Case 3): (**a**) master, and (**b**) slave.

Table 5. Simulation comparisons of position errors in Case 3.

		IAE	ITAE	ISE	ITSE
P + dC	Joint 1	1366.5	15,168.1	179.2	1456.9
	Joint 2	26.8	296.3	0.09	0.61
SC	Joint 1	710.1	7420.9	54.4	410.4
	Joint 2	20.5	249.7	0.04	0.32
ASC	Joint 1	643.1	7295.7	44.5	369.0
	Joint 2	18.7	209.6	0.03	0.29

unit: joint 1 (rad), joint 2 (m).

4.2. *Case 4: Non-Passive Human and Environment (Simulation)*

Consider the case that the human operator and environment forces are all non-passive, such as

$$f_h = \begin{cases} k_h - D_h\dot{q}_m - K_h q_m, & 1 \leq t \leq 30 \text{ s} \\ 0 & \text{otherwise} \end{cases} \tag{40}$$

$$f_e = \begin{cases} k_e - D_e\dot{q}_s - K_e q_s, & 5 \leq t \leq 30 \text{ s} \\ 0 & \text{otherwise} \end{cases} \tag{41}$$

where $k_h = \begin{bmatrix} -0.9 & 0.2 \end{bmatrix}^T$, $k_e = \begin{bmatrix} 0.1 & -0.15 \end{bmatrix}^T$, $D_h = D_e = diag\{1,1\}$, and $K_h = K_e = diag\{1,1\}$.

The simulation results of this case are depicted in Figures 18–26, including the position responses, force responses, and control signals of the master and slave robots. The observation revolves around the responses after the addition of the environment force, i.e., from 5 to 30 s. From Figure 24, compared to Figures 18 and 21, the position errors of the master and slave robots are significantly improved using the proposed ASC method. As regards the force responses shown in Figures 19, 22 and 25, all three methods can support a certain degree of inconsistency in the human and environment forces. Similarly, the average position and force errors of 20 repetitions are summarized, from 5 to 30 s, in Tables 6 and 7. It can be observed that the proposed ASC scheme has better performance in both position following and force perception.

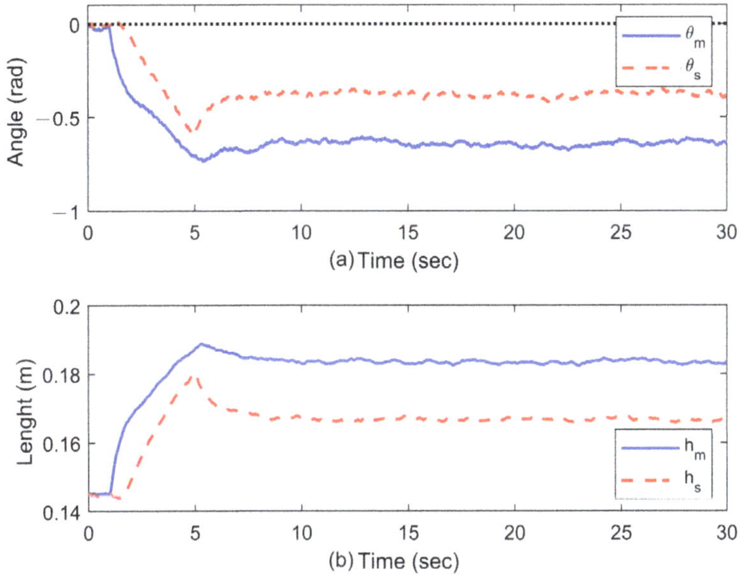

Figure 18. Position responses with P + dC method (Case 4): (**a**) joint 1, and (**b**) joint 2.

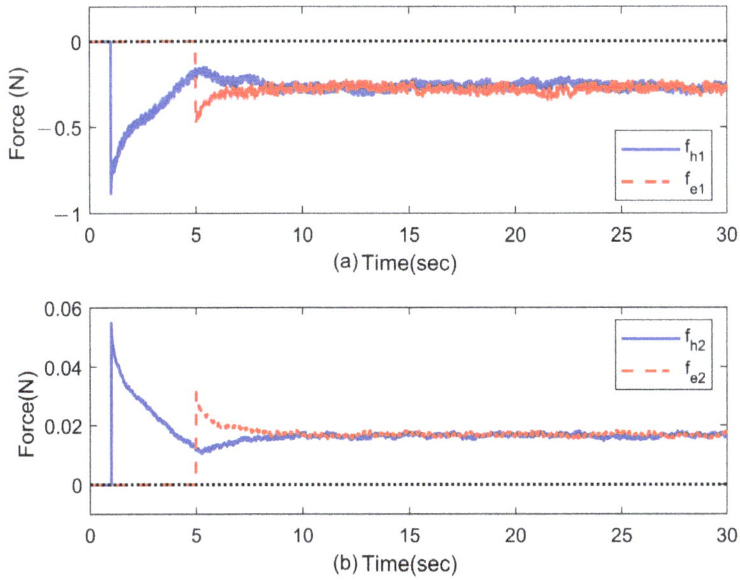

Figure 19. Force responses with P + dC method (Case 4): (**a**) joint 1, and (**b**) joint 2.

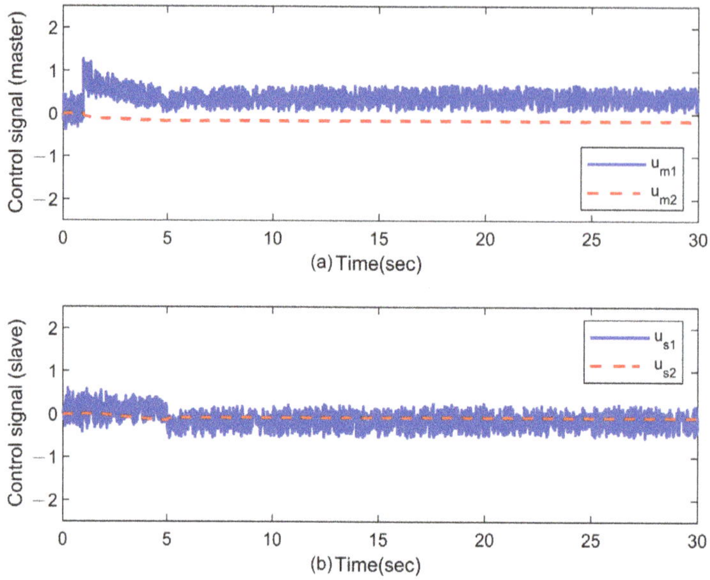

Figure 20. Control signals with P + dC method (Case 4): (**a**) master, and (**b**) slave.

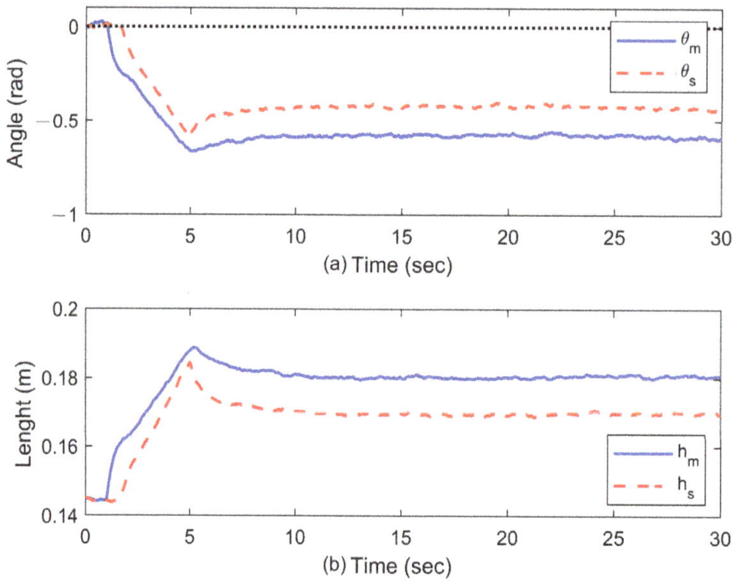

Figure 21. Position responses with SC method (Case 4): (**a**) joint 1, and (**b**) joint 2.

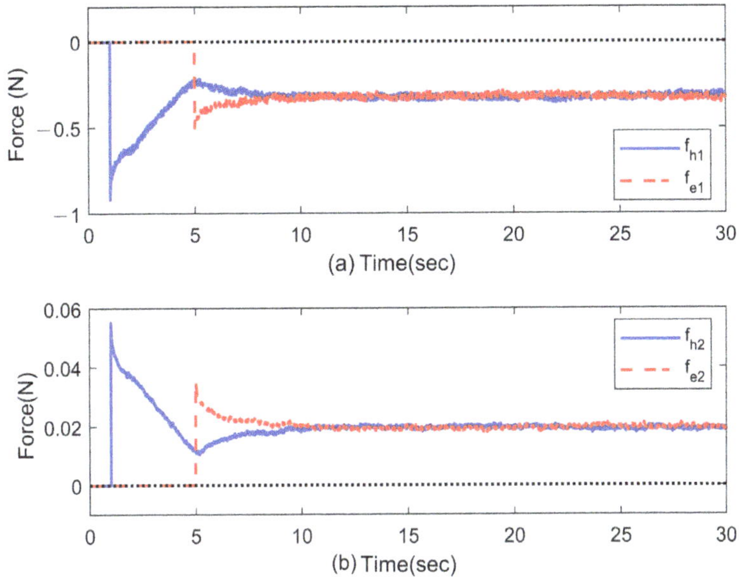

Figure 22. Force responses with SC method (Case 4): (a) joint 1, and (b) joint 2.

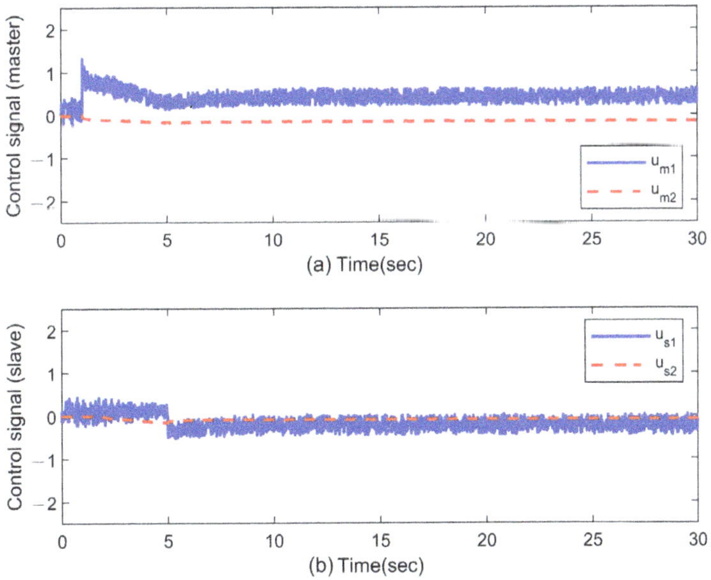

Figure 23. Control signals with SC method (Case 4): (a) master, and (b) slave.

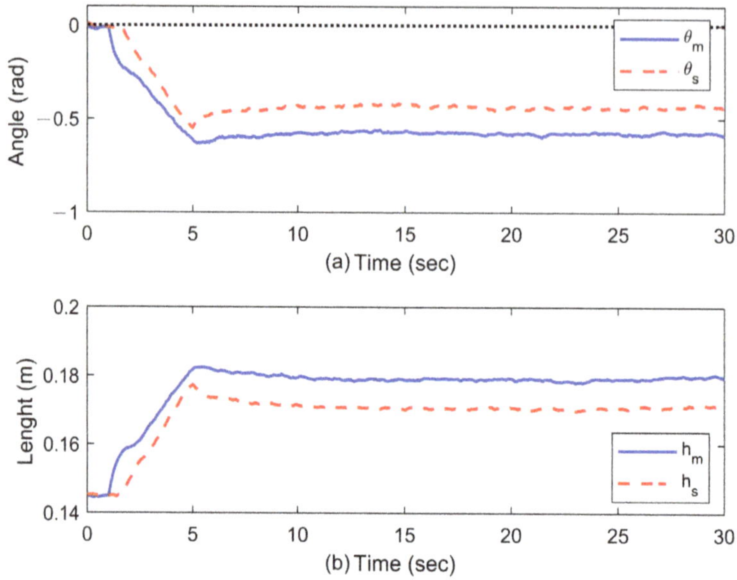

Figure 24. Position responses with ASC method (Case 4): (**a**) joint 1, and (**b**) joint 2.

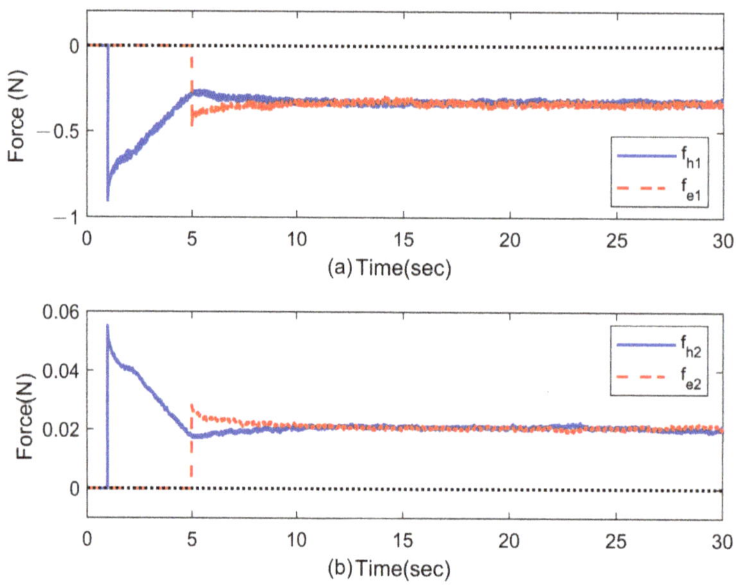

Figure 25. Force responses with ASC method (Case 4): (**a**) joint 1, and (**b**) joint 2.

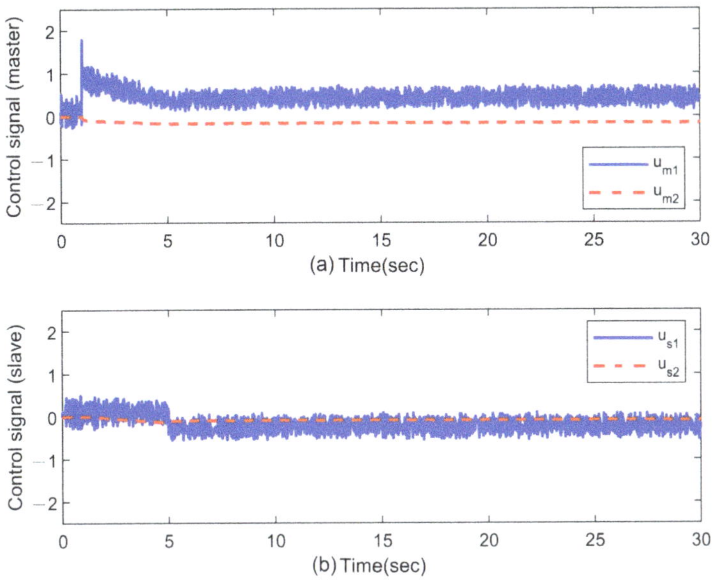

Figure 26. Control signals with ASC method (Case 4): (**a**) master, and (**b**) slave.

Table 6. Simulation comparisons of position errors in Case 4.

		IAE	ITAE	ISE	ITSE
P + dC	Joint 1	66,092.74	116,329.60	1753.97	30,999.84
	Joint 2	413.14	7264.24	6.85	120.94
SC	Joint 1	4312.21	75,538.54	747.91	13,093.91
	Joint 2	271.31	4772.02	2.95	52.16
ASC	Joint 1	3328.01	58,510.62	444.31	7840.92
	Joint 2	207.80	3637.15	1.73	30.30

unit: joint 1 (rad), joint 2 (m).

Table 7. Simulation comparisons of force errors in Case 4.

		IAE	ITAE	ISE	ITSE
P + dC	Joint 1	655.09	8101.66	49.21	355.33
	Joint 2	44.38	508.72	0.24	1.61
SC	Joint 1	643.66	7720.72	44.83	322.15
	Joint 2	35.56	353.51	0.19	1.08
ASC	Joint 1	572.32	5399.46	23.56	153.96
	Joint 2	26.39	168.89	0.08	0.19

unit: joint 1 (N), joint 2 (N).

5. Conclusions

This paper introduces an adaptive-sliding-mode controller that has been designed for a bilateral teleoperation system that is characterized by time-varying communication delays and unknown but bounded uncertainties. The master and slave devices utilized in the system are self-made by the authors, with certain components manufactured using CNC milling and lathe machines. The controller design involves deriving a delay-dependent condition for stability and determining the admissible bound of time delays through linear matrix inequalities. The closed-loop stability of the teleoperation system is ensured via Lyapunov–Krasovskii stability analysis, aligning the stability analysis with the designed controllers and adaptive laws. Both passive and non-passive scenarios involving the human operator and the environment are considered in the design process. A real experimental setup is employed to validate the proposed control scheme, covering free-motion and force-perception tasks. Results indicate that the proposed adaptive-sliding-control method increases position performance from 58.48% to 82.55% and force performance from 83.48% to 99.77%. In conclusion, the proposed control algorithm shows promising potential for application in generalized haptic devices with expanded degrees of freedom. Additionally, our control strategies have successfully addressed a wide range of scenarios and environments, including free motion, force perception, and also both passive and non-passive situations. Furthermore, our experimental results underscore its viability for real-world applications.

Author Contributions: Conceptualization, Y.-H.C. and C.-Y.Y.; methodology, Y.-H.C., C.-Y.Y. and H.-W.L.; software, C.-Y.Y.; validation, Y.-H.C. and C.-Y.Y.; formal analysis, Y.-H.C., C.-Y.Y. and H.-W.L.; investigation, Y.-H.C. and C.-Y.Y.; data curation, C.-Y.Y.; writing—original draft preparation, Y.-H.C. and C.-Y.Y.; writing—review and editing, Y.-H.C. and H.-W.L.; visualization, Y.-H.C. and C.-Y.Y.; supervision, Y.-H.C. and H.-W.L. All authors have read and agreed to the published version of the manuscript.

Funding: This research received no external funding.

Data Availability Statement: The original contributions presented in the study are included in the article, further inquiries can be directed to the corresponding author.

Conflicts of Interest: The authors declare no conflicts of interest.

References

1. Moniruzzaman, M.; Rassau, A.; Chai, D.; Islam, S. Teleoperation methods and enhancement techniques for mobile robots: A comprehensive survey. *Robot. Auton. Syst.* **2022**, *150*, 103973. [CrossRef]
2. Shahbazi, M.; Atashzar, S.F.; Patel, R.V. A systematic review of multilateral teleoperation systems. *IEEE Trans. Haptics* **2018**, *11*, 338–356. [CrossRef] [PubMed]
3. Courtois, H.; Aouf, N.; Ahiska, K.; Cecotti, M. OAST: Obstacle avoidance system for teleoperation of UAVs. *IEEE Trans. Hunan-Mach. Syst.* **2022**, *52*, 157–168. [CrossRef]
4. Zhang, D.; Yang, G.; Khurshid, R.P. Haptic teleoperation of UAVs through control barrier functions. *IEEE Trans. Haptics* **2020**, *13*, 109–115. [CrossRef] [PubMed]
5. Lee, M.; Lee, D. A Distributed two-layer framework for teleoperated platooning of fixed-wing UAVs via decomposition and backstepping. *IEEE Robot. Autom. Lett.* **2021**, *6*, 3655–3662. [CrossRef]
6. Fu, J.; Rota, A.; Shufei Li, A.; Zhao, J.; Liu, Q.; Iovene, E.; Ferrigno, G.; Momi, E. Recent advancements in augmented reality for robotic applications: A survey. *Actuators* **2023**, *12*, 323. [CrossRef]
7. Zhang, Q.; Liu, Q.; Duan, J.; Qin, J. Research on teleoperated virtual reality human–robot five-dimensional collaboration system. *Biomimetics* **2023**, *8*, 605. [CrossRef]
8. Song, C.; Yang, G.; Park, S.; Jang, N.; Jeon, S.; Oh, S.-R.; Hwang, D. On the design of Integrated tele-monitoring operation system for therapeutic devices in isolation intensive care unit. *IEEE Robot. Autom. Lett.* **2022**, *7*, 8705–8712. [CrossRef]
9. Aggravi, M.; Estima, D.A.L.; Krupa, A.; Misra, S.; Pacchierotti, C. Haptic teleoperation of flexible needles combining 3D ultrasound guidance and needle tip force feedback. *IEEE Robot. Autom. Lett.* **2021**, *6*, 4859–4866. [CrossRef]
10. Feng, F.; Zhou, Y.; Hong, W.; Li, K.; Xie, L. Development and experiments of a continuum robotic system for transoral laryngeal surgery. *Int. J. Comput. Assist. Radiol. Surg.* **2022**, *17*, 479–505. [CrossRef]
11. Wakasa, Y.; Hakamada, K.; Morohashi, H.; Kanno, T.; Tadano, K.; Kawashima, K.; Ebihara, Y.; Oki, E.; Hirano, S.; Mori, M. Ensuring communication redundancy and establishing a telementoring system for robotic telesurgery using multiple communication line. *J. Robot. Surg.* **2024**, *18*, 9. [CrossRef]
12. Zhaoa, B.; Nelson, C.A. A sensorless force-feedback system for robot assisted laparoscopic surgery. *Comput. Assist. Surg.* **2019**, *24*, 36–43. [CrossRef] [PubMed]
13. Schleer, P.; Körner, D.; Vossel, M.; Drobinsky, S.; Radermacher, K. Conceptual design of force reflection control for teleoperated bone surgery. *Curr. Dir. Biomed. Eng.* **2020**, *6*, 20200014. [CrossRef]

14. Muñoz, V.F.; Garcia-Morales, I.; Fraile-Marinero, J.C.; Perez-Turiel, J.; Muñoz-Garcia, A.; Bauzano, E.; Rivas-Blanco, I.; Sabater-Navarro, J.M.; de la Fuente, E. Collaborative robotic assistant platform for endonasal surgery: Preliminary in-vitro trials. *Sensors* **2021**, *21*, 2320. [CrossRef]
15. Quek, Z.F.; Provancher, W.R.; Okamura, A.M. Evaluation of skin deformation tactile feedback for teleoperated surgical tasks. *IEEE Trans. Haptics* **2019**, *12*, 102–113. [CrossRef] [PubMed]
16. Patel, R.V.; Atashzar, S.F.; Tavakoli, M. Haptic feedback and force-based teleoperation in surgical robotics. *Proc. IEEE* **2022**, *110*, 1012–1027. [CrossRef]
17. Gong, Y.; Ji, Y. A Novel Passivity Criterion for bilateral teleoperation under event triggered PD-like control with constant time delays. *Int. J. Control Autom. Syst.* **2022**, *20*, 2353–2363. [CrossRef]
18. Bao, J.; Fu, L.; Zhang, H.; Zhang, A.; Guo, W.; Chen, T. An adaptive proportional plus damping control for teleoperation systems with asymmetric time-varying communication delays. *Mathematics* **2022**, *10*, 4675. [CrossRef]
19. Ahmad, U.; Pan, Y.-J. A Time Domain Passivity approach for asymmetric multilateral teleoperation system. *IEEE Access* **2018**, *6*, 519–531. [CrossRef]
20. Ryu, J.-H.; Ha-Van, Q.; Jafari, A. Multilateral teleoperation over communication time delay using the time-domain passivity approach. *IEEE Trans. Control Syst. Technol.* **2020**, *28*, 2705–2712. [CrossRef]
21. Bavili, R.E.; Akbari, A.; Esfanjani, R.M. Passivity-based control of nonlinear teleoperation systems with non-passive interaction forces. *Intell. Serv. Robot.* **2020**, *13*, 419–437. [CrossRef]
22. Li, W.; Liu, Y.; Ding, L.; Wang, J.; Gao, H.; Deng, Z. Teleoperation of wheeled mobile robots subject to longitudinal slipping and lateral sliding by time-domain passivity controller. *Mechatronics* **2022**, *81*, 102705. [CrossRef]
23. Gong, X.; Wang, L.; Mou, Y.; Wang, H.; Wei, X.; Zheng, W.; Yin, L. Improved four-channel PBTDPA control strategy using force feedback bilateral teleoperation system. *Int. J. Control Autom. Syst.* **2022**, *20*, 1002–1017. [CrossRef]
24. Li, R.; Cheng, M.; Ding, R. Passivity-based bilateral shared variable impedance control for teleoperation compliant assembly. *Mechatronics* **2023**, *95*, 10305. [CrossRef]
25. Uyulan, C. Robust passivity-based nonlinear controller design for bilateral teleoperation system under variable time delay and variable load disturbance. *Nonlinear Eng.* **2024**, *13*, 20220358. [CrossRef]
26. Sun, D.; Naghdy, F.; Du, H. Neural Network-based Passivity Control of Teleoperation System under Time-Varying Delays. *IEEE Trans. Cybern.* **2017**, *47*, 1666–1680. [CrossRef] [PubMed]
27. Yang, L.; Chen, Y.; Liu, Z.; Chen, K.; Zhang, Z. Adaptive Fuzzy Control for Teleoperation System with Uncertain Kinematics and Dynamics. *Int. J. Control Autom. Syst.* **2019**, *17*, 1158–1166. [CrossRef]
28. Li, H.; Chou, W. Adaptive FNN backstepping control for nonlinear bilateral teleoperation with asymmetric time delays and uncertainties. *Int. J. Control Autom. Syst.* **2023**, *21*, 3091–3104. [CrossRef]
29. Su, S.; Ji, Y. Fixed-time adaptive neural network synchronization control for teleoperation system with position error constraints and time-varying delay. *Nonlinear Dyn.* **2023**, *111*, 13053–13072. [CrossRef]
30. Kebria, P.M.; Khosravi, A.; Nahavandi, S.; Wu, D.; Bello, F. Adaptive type-2 fuzzy neural-network control for teleoperation systems with delay and uncertainties. *IEEE Trans. Fuzzy Syst.* **2020**, *28*, 2543–2554. [CrossRef]
31. Sun, D.; Liao, Q.; Stoyanov, T.; Kiselev, A.; Loutfi, A. Bilateral telerobotic system using type-2 fuzzy neural network based moving horizon estimation force observer for enhancement of environmental force compliance and human perception. *Automatica* **2019**, *106*, 358–373. [CrossRef]
32. Zhang, J.; Xia, M.; Li, S.; Liu, Z.; Yang, J. The adaptive bilateral control of underwater manipulator teleoperation system with uncertain parameters and external disturbance. *Electronics* **2024**, *13*, 1122. [CrossRef]
33. Huang, F.; Zhang, W.; Chen, Z.; Tang, J.; Song, W.; Zhu, S. RBFNN-based adaptive sliding mode control design for nonlinear bilateral teleoperation system under time-varying delays. *IEEE Access* **2019**, *7*, 11905–11912. [CrossRef]
34. Hao, S.; Hu, L.; Liu, P.X. Sliding mode control for a surgical teleoperation system via a disturbance observer. *IEEE Access* **2019**, *7*, 43383. [CrossRef]
35. Hu, J.; Zhang, H.; Liu, H.; Yu, X. A survey on sliding mode control for networked control systems. *Int. J. Syst. Sci.* **2021**, *52*, 1129–1147. [CrossRef]
36. Guajardo-Benavides, E.; Arteaga, M. On the finite time force estimation for bilateral teleoperation of robot manipulators with time varying delays. *Control Eng. Pract.* **2023**, *138*, 105622. [CrossRef]
37. Zhang, H.; Song, A.; Li, H.; Chen, D.; Fan, L. Adaptive finite-time control scheme for teleoperation with time-varying delay and uncertainties. *IEEE Trans. Syst. Man Cybern. Syst.* **2022**, *52*, 1552–1566. [CrossRef]
38. Guo, S.; Liu, Z.; Li, L.; Ma, Z.; Huang, P. Fixed-time personalized variable gain tracking control for teleoperation systems with time varying delays. *J. Frankl. Inst.* **2023**, *360*, 13015–13032. [CrossRef]
39. Dehghan, S.A.M.; Koofigar, H.R.; Sadeghian, H.; Ekramian, M. Observer-based adaptive force–position control for nonlinear bilateral teleoperation with time delay. *Control Eng. Pract.* **2021**, *107*, 104679. [CrossRef]
40. Wang, Y.; Tian, J.; Liu, Y.; Yang, B.; Liu, S.; Yin, L.; Zheng, W. Adaptive neural network control of time delay teleoperation system based on model approximation. *Sensors* **2021**, *21*, 7443. [CrossRef]
41. Tumerdem, U.; Yilmaz, N. A unifying framework for transparency optimized controller design in multilateral teleoperation with time delays. *Control Eng. Pract.* **2021**, *117*, 104931. [CrossRef]

42. Zhai, D.-H.; Xia, Y. A novel switching-based control framework for improved task performance in teleoperation system with asymmetric timevarying delays. *IEEE Trans. Cybern.* **2018**, *48*, 625–638. [CrossRef] [PubMed]
43. Nguyen, T.-V.; Liu, Y.-C. Advanced finite-time control for bilateral teleoperators with delays and uncertainties. *IEEE Access* **2021**, *9*, 141951. [CrossRef]
44. Zakerimanesh, A.; Hashemzadeh, F.; Torabi, A.; Tavakoli, M. Controlled synchronization of nonlinear teleoperation in task-space with timevarying delays. *Int. J. Control Autom. Syst.* **2019**, *17*, 1875–1883. [CrossRef]
45. Hua, C.-C.; Liu, X.P. Delay-dependent stability criteria of teleoperation systems with asymmetric time-varying delays. *IEEE Trans. Robot.* **2010**, *26*, 925–932. [CrossRef]
46. Deepak, V.; Arun, N.K.; Shihabudheen, K.V. Observer based stabilization of linear time delay systems using new augmented LKF. *IFAC J. Syst. Control* **2023**, *26*, 100231. [CrossRef]
47. Halder, K.; Gillam, L.; Dixit, S.; Mouzakitis, A.; Fallah, S. Stability analysis with LMI based distributed H∞ controller for vehicle platooning under random multiple packet drops. *IEEE Trans. Intell. Transp. Syst.* **2022**, *23*, 23517–23532. [CrossRef]
48. Yang, Y.; Constantinescu, D.; Shi, Y. Input-to-state stable bilateral teleoperation by dynamic interconnection and damping injection: Theory and experiments. *IEEE Trans. Ind. Electron.* **2020**, *67*, 790–799. [CrossRef]
49. Baranitha, R.; Rakkiyappan, R.; Li, X. T–S fuzzy model-based singlemaster multislave teleoperation systems with decentralized communication structure and varying time delays. *IEEE Trans. Fuzzy Syst.* **2020**, *28*, 3406–3417. [CrossRef]
50. Bavili, R.E.; Akbari, A.; Esfanjani, R.M. Controller design for nonlinear bilateral teleoperation systems via total energy shaping. *Mech. Syst. Signal Process.* **2021**, *150*, 107239. [CrossRef]
51. Estrada, E.; Yu, W.; Li, X. Stable bilateral teleoperation with phase transition and haptic feedback. *J. Frankl. Inst.* **2021**, *358*, 1940–1956. [CrossRef]
52. Islam, S.; Liu, X.P.; Saddik, A. Nonlinear adaptive control for teleoperation systems with symmetrical and unsymmetrical time-varying delay. *Int. J. Syst. Sci.* **2015**, *46*, 2928–2938. [CrossRef]
53. Islam, S.; Liu, P.X.; Saddik, A.E. Nonlinear control for teleoperation systems with time varying delay. *Nonlinear Dyn.* **2014**, *76*, 931–954. [CrossRef]
54. Islam, A.; Liu, P.X.; Saddik, A.E.; Yang, Y.B. Bilateral control of teleoperation systems with time delay. *IEEE/ASME Trans. Mechatronics* **2015**, *20*, 1–12. [CrossRef]
55. Hu, J.; Wang, Z.; Gao, H.; Stergioulas, L.K. Robust sliding mode control for discrete stochastic systems with mixed time delays randomly occurring uncertainties, and randomly occurring nonlinearities. *IEEE Trans. Ind. Electron.* **2012**, *59*, 3008–3015. [CrossRef]
56. Sun, Y.G.; Wang, L.; Xie, G. Average consensus in networks of dynamic agents with switching topologies and multiple time-varying delays. *Syst. Control Lett.* **2008**, *57*, 175–183. [CrossRef]
57. Chang, Y.-H.; Chan, W.-S. Adaptive dynamic surface control for uncertain nonlinear systems with interval type-2 fuzzy neural networks. *IEEE Trans. Cybern.* **2014**, *44*, 293–304. [CrossRef]

Disclaimer/Publisher's Note: The statements, opinions and data contained in all publications are solely those of the individual author(s) and contributor(s) and not of MDPI and/or the editor(s). MDPI and/or the editor(s) disclaim responsibility for any injury to people or property resulting from any ideas, methods, instructions or products referred to in the content.

robotics

MDPI

Article

Prescribed Time Interception of Moving Objects' Trajectories Using Robot Manipulators

Juan Alejandro Flores-Campos [1], Christopher René Torres-San-Miguel [2], Juan Carlos Paredes-Rojas [3] and Adolfo Perrusquía [4,*]

[1] Unidad Profesional Interdisciplinaria en Ingeniería y Tecnologías Avanzadas, Instituto Politécnico Nacional, Avenida Instituto Politécnico Nacional 2580, Ciudad de México C.P. 07340, Mexico; jaflores@ipn.mx
[2] Escuela Superior de Ingeniería Mecánica y Eléctrica Zacatenco, Instituto Politécnico Nacional, Avenida Luis Enrique Erro, Adolfo López Mateos, Ciudad de México C.P. 07738, México; ctorress@ipn.mx
[3] Escuela Superior de Ingeniería Mecánica y Eléctrica, Unidad Culhuacán, Instituto Politécnico Nacional, Avenida Santa Ana 1000, Coyoacán, CTM Culhuacán, Ciudad de México C.P. 04440, México; jparedes@ipn.mx
[4] Faculty of Engineering and Applied Sciences, Cranfield University, College Road, Bedford MK43 0AL, UK
* Correspondence: adolfo.perrusquia-guzman@cranfield.ac.uk

Abstract: Trajectory interception is a critical synchronization element in the transportation and manufacturing sectors using robotic platforms. This is usually performed by matching the position and velocity of a target object with the position and velocity of the robot interceptor. However, the synchronization task is exasperated by (i) the proper gain tuning of the controller, (ii) the dynamic response of the robotic platform, (iii) the velocity constraints in the actuators, and (iv) the trajectory profile exhibited by the moving object. This means that the interception time is not controlled, which is critical for energy optimization, resources, and production. This paper proposes a prescribed time trajectory interception algorithm for robot manipulators. The approach uses the finite-time convergence properties of sliding mode control combined with a terminal attractor based on a time base generator. The combined approach guarantees trajectory interception in a prescribed time with robust properties. Simulation studies are conducted using the first three degrees of freedom (DOFs) of a RV-M1 robot under single- and multi-object interception tasks. The results verify the effectiveness of the proposed methodology under different hyperparameter configurations.

Keywords: time interception; robot manipulators; second-order sliding mode control; time base generator; moving objects trajectories.

1. Introduction

Trajectory interception is one of the most common tasks in the transport and manufacturing sectors involving robots. Some potential applications include pick and place [1], maneuvers in combat [2], deceiving targets [3], synchronization [4] and, recently, encryption of communication tasks [5]. In these tasks, time is an important element that needs to be considered in the control design to minimize error threats due to delays in the interception. The most simple control approaches use linear models to predefine the convergence time [6,7]. Also, feedback linearization controllers or dynamic inversion approaches [8] have been considered to first linearize the system dynamics and then apply classic linear control approaches for trajectory interception. This means that knowledge of the dynamics of the robot is required to obtain the control gains that inject a desired behavior and closed-loop performance. However, the model is usually uncertain, and applying feedback linearization controllers is prohibitive due to the inherent modeling error of model-based controllers [9]. On the other hand, model-free controllers such as PD, PID, or sliding mode control (SMC) [10,11] can ensure finite time convergence, but the convergence is usually asymptotic, such that the robot can intercept the object either before or after a desired time.

Therefore, there is a need to ensure that the interception between a robot interceptor and a moving object occurs in a prescribed time to ensure the smooth operation of transport or manufacture operations.

1.1. Related Work

Classical approaches use guidance and navigation controllers (e.g., proportional navigation [12,13]) based on simple geometric relations for the interception of targets. Artificial potential fields [14,15] have been also used to guide autonomous systems toward the trajectory followed by the target. The key idea is to use repellent and attractive forces that suggest the direction where the target is moving. Trajectory optimization techniques, such as covariant Hamiltonian optimization for motion planning (CHOMP) [16] or stochastic trajectory optimization for motion planning (STOMP) [17], have been applied in robot manipulators for motion planning under obstacles. However, these approaches do not consider the interception time [18], which can cause the robot to miss the target or that the interception occur after the desired time.

Other navigation approaches, such as A^* and Dijkstra algorithms [19–22], have been used to calculate an optimal/near-optimal path given some starting and ending points. These approaches assume knowledge of the workspace to find the best path. However, this is computationally intensive if the search space is large. These models are usually improved with some heuristics to reduce the search space and the computational resources [23]. Novel approaches use one-shot learning approaches [24,25] to obtain a path for the interception. These approaches combine deep autoencoders with heuristics [26] to seek a path from any starting point to an ending point under workspaces with obstacles.

Reinforcement Learning (RL) algorithms have been effectively used in interception tasks using diverse architectures ranging from simple tabular methods (e.g., Q-learning) to deep RL models (e.g., deep deterministic policy gradient (DDPG) [27] or soft actor-critic (SAC) [28]), and recently with adversarial learning [2]. The key success of these models is due to a proper reward design that covers all the possible scenarios that the robotic system can meet in the interception task. However, these methods need a large training time, and it is difficult to converge in a prescribed time.

In the last decade, different research has been developed to ensure convergence in prescribed time. The key idea is to use terminal attractors [29] that force the system trajectories to converge into a desired manifold and remain within as time advances. A time base generator (TBG) is usually used to ensure convergence in a prescribed time. Here, an S-shaped function with a parabolic derivative is used to guarantee this behavior. The S-shaped function is designed in terms of polynomials or splines [30]. However, these functions lack robustness across diverse behaviors due to the fixed form of the curves.

1.2. Contributions, Outline and Notations

This paper proposes a model-free robust controller that guarantees interception to moving objects' trajectories in a prescribed time. The approach consists of using a robust second-order sliding mode controller (SMC) enhanced with a time base generator (TBG) for prescribed time convergence to the object trajectory. Lyapunov stability is used to assess the closed-loop stability of the approach. Diverse simulation studies are conducted to show the advantages and challenges of the proposed approach.

The main contributions of this paper are summarized as follows:

- A prescribed time interception algorithm that ensures accurate interception of the trajectories of moving objects.
- A time base generator (TBG) design that permits the control of the path followed by the robot for the interception.
- A second-order sliding mode control that forces the closed-loop trajectories to stay in the sliding surface manifold in the prescribed time given by the TBG.

The outline of this paper is as follows. Section 2 describes the proposed methodology, which includes the preliminaries, TBG design, and sliding mode control design. Section 3 shows the results of the proposed approach under different scenarios and hyperparameter settings. Conclusions are given in Section 4.

Throughout this paper, $\mathbb{N}$, $\mathbb{R}$, $\mathbb{R}^+$, $\mathbb{R}^n$, $\mathbb{R}^{n\times m}$ denote the spaces of natural numbers, real numbers, positive real numbers, real n-vectors, and real $n \times m$-matrices, respectively; I_n is an identity matrix of dimension $n \times n$, $\lambda_{\min}(A)$ and $\lambda_{\max}(A)$ denotes the minimum and maximum eigenvalues of matrix A, respectively; the norms $\|A\| = \sqrt{\lambda_{\max}(A^\top A)}$ and $\|x\|$ stand for the induced matrix and vector Euclidean norms, respectively; where $x \in \mathbb{R}$, $x \in \mathbb{R}^n$, $A \in \mathbb{R}^{n\times n}$ and $n, m \in \mathbb{N}$.

2. Methodology

The proposed methodology is shown in Figure 1 as a simple visualization of the task. We consider a trajectory interception application involving a robot manipulator and objects moving in a known trajectory profile x_r. Cameras are used to measure the position of the objects. Here, the task consists of intercepting the trajectory of each object in a pre-defined time t_f given initial times t_0, t_1, t_2, etc. This is achieved by (1) designing a second-order sliding mode control (SMC) that ensures convergence to the object trajectory in finite time with robust capabilities against exogenous disturbances and model uncertainty, and (2) integrating a time base terminal attractor known as time base generator (TBG) that forces the robot dynamics to intercept the object in a desired time. This means that the finite time convergence of the SMC is modified into a prescribed time control that maintains all its robust properties.

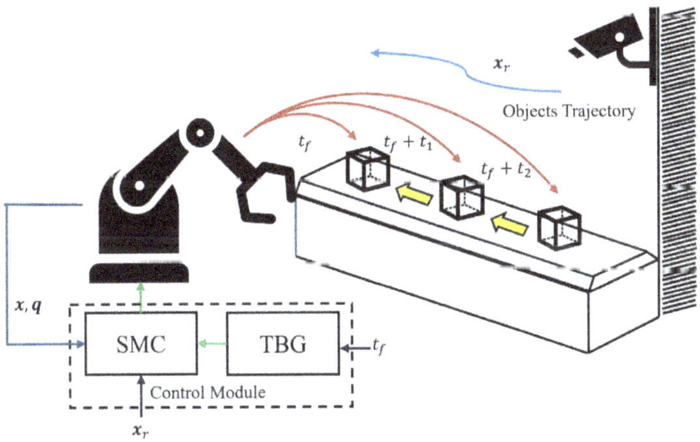

Figure 1. Proposed methodology.

2.1. Robot Dynamic Preliminaries

Consider the dynamic model of a n-rigid robot manipulator [31]

$$M(q)\ddot{q} + C(q,\dot{q})\dot{q} + G(q) = \tau + d, \tag{1}$$

where $q, \dot{q} \in \mathbb{R}^n$ denotes the joint positions and angular velocities, $M(q) \in \mathbb{R}^{n\times n}$ is a positive definite inertia matrix, $C(q,\dot{q}) \in \mathbb{R}^{n\times n}$ stands to the centripetal and Coriolis forces matrix, $G(q) \in \mathbb{R}^n$ is the gravitational torques vector, $d \in \mathbb{R}^n$ is a bounded disturbance vector associated with dissipative terms such as friction, model uncertainties, and exogenous disturbances, and $\tau \in \mathbb{R}^n$ is the vector of applied torques. It is assumed that the Coriolis matrix $C(q,\dot{q})$ satisfies the following Christoffel factorization

$$[C(q,\dot{q})]_{ij} = \sum_k \Gamma_{ijk}(q)\dot{q}_k, \tag{2}$$

where

$$\Gamma_{ijk}(\boldsymbol{q}) = \frac{1}{2}\left[\frac{\partial M_{ij}}{\partial q_k} + \frac{\partial M_{ik}}{\partial q_j} - \frac{\partial M_{jk}}{\partial q_i}\right], \tag{3}$$

are the Christoffel symbols of the first kind, and M_{ij} denotes the (i,j) component of the inertia matrix $\boldsymbol{M}(\boldsymbol{q})$. The Coriolis matrix is skew-symmetric [32], such that it satisfies

$$\boldsymbol{v}^\top\left[\dot{\boldsymbol{M}}(\boldsymbol{q}) - 2\boldsymbol{C}(\boldsymbol{q},\dot{\boldsymbol{q}})\right]\boldsymbol{v} = 0,$$

for any $\boldsymbol{v} \in \mathbb{R}^n$. In addition, the inertia matrix $\boldsymbol{M}(\boldsymbol{q})$, the Coriolis matrix $\boldsymbol{C}(\boldsymbol{q},\dot{\boldsymbol{q}})$, and $\boldsymbol{G}(\boldsymbol{q})$ satisfy

$$\begin{aligned} \beta_0 \leq \lambda_{\min}(\boldsymbol{M}(\boldsymbol{q})) \leq \|\boldsymbol{M}(\boldsymbol{q})\| &\leq \lambda_{\max}(\boldsymbol{M}(\boldsymbol{q})) < \beta_1 \\ \|\boldsymbol{C}(\boldsymbol{q},\dot{\boldsymbol{q}})\| &\leq \beta_2\|\dot{\boldsymbol{q}}\| \\ \|\boldsymbol{G}(\boldsymbol{q})\| &\leq \beta_3, \end{aligned} \tag{4}$$

for some $\beta_i > 0, i = 0,1,2,3$.

The transformation from joint space coordinates to task space coordinates is given by

$$\begin{aligned} \boldsymbol{x} &= f(\boldsymbol{q}), \\ \dot{\boldsymbol{x}} &= \boldsymbol{J}(\boldsymbol{q})\dot{\boldsymbol{q}}, \\ \ddot{\boldsymbol{x}} &= \dot{\boldsymbol{J}}(\boldsymbol{q})\dot{\boldsymbol{q}} + \boldsymbol{J}(\boldsymbol{q})\ddot{\boldsymbol{q}}, \end{aligned} \tag{5}$$

where $f(\boldsymbol{q}) \in \mathbb{R}^m$ is the forward kinematics of the robot, $\boldsymbol{x} \in \mathbb{R}^m$ and $\dot{\boldsymbol{x}} \in \mathbb{R}^m$ are the Cartesian positions and velocities, respectively, and $\boldsymbol{J}(\boldsymbol{q}) \in \mathbb{R}^{m\times n}$ is the Jacobian matrix.

Assumption 1. *In this paper, we consider non-redundant robots, i.e., we assume $m = n$. In addition, we assume that the Jacobian matrix $\boldsymbol{J}(\boldsymbol{q})$ is full rank for any interception task and it is bounded, i.e., $\|\boldsymbol{J}(\boldsymbol{q})\| \leq \varepsilon_J$ where $\varepsilon_J > 0$ is an upper bound.*

Assumption 2. *In this paper, it is assumed that the dynamic parameters (e.g., mass, inertia) of the robot are unknown, whilst the kinematic parameters (e.g., length of links) are known.*

The trajectories followed by the moving objects in the Cartesian space are assumed to be known in advance, and are denoted as $\boldsymbol{x}_r \in \mathbb{R}^m$.

2.2. Time Base Generator (TBG)

The dynamics of the TBG have the following structure:

$$\dot{\xi} = \phi(\xi) = -\gamma(\xi(1-\xi))^\beta, \tag{6}$$

where $\beta \in (0,1)$ is a user-defined constant that shapes the behavior of the TBG, $\gamma > 0$ is a positive constant that ensures convergence in a pre-defined time t_f. We can easily observe that (6) has a stable equilibrium point at $\xi = 0$ and an unstable equilibrium point at $\xi = 1$. Here, we can always ensure convergence to the stable point by choosing an initial condition of $\xi(0) = 1 - \varepsilon$, where $\varepsilon \ll 1$. The convergence time can be computed as follows:

$$t_f = \int_0^{t_f} dt \approx -\int_0^1 \frac{d\xi}{\phi(\xi)} = \frac{1}{\gamma}\frac{\Gamma^2(1-\beta)}{\Gamma(2-2\beta)}, \tag{7}$$

where $\Gamma(\cdot)$ is the Gamma function. Therefore, the constant γ is a function of t_f and β as

$$\gamma = \frac{1}{t_f}\frac{\Gamma^2(1-\beta)}{\Gamma(2-2\beta)}. \tag{8}$$

The acceleration profile of the TBG satisfies the following relation:

$$\ddot{\xi} = \gamma^2\beta(1-2\xi)[\xi(1-\xi)]^{2\beta-1}. \tag{9}$$

Notice that a bounded acceleration is obtained only if $\beta \in [1/2, 1)$, which provides an additional constraint to β. For the jerk effect, we obtain the following relation by differentiating (9)

$$\dddot{\xi} = -\gamma^3\beta(1-2\xi)[\xi(1-\xi)]^{3\beta-2}, \tag{10}$$

which gives another constraint to β, i.e., $\beta \in [2/3, 1)$.

So, we can generate a family of time-varying signals $\xi(t)$ by modifying the parameters t_f and β, which can serve for interception purposes. Figure 2 shows the TBG dynamics under different β values under a fixed $t_f = 1.5$ s.

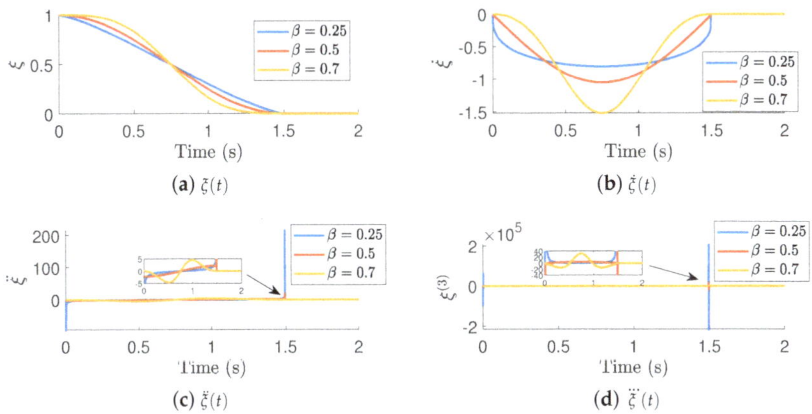

(**a**) $\xi(t)$ (**b**) $\dot{\xi}(t)$ (**c**) $\ddot{\xi}(t)$ (**d**) $\dddot{\xi}(t)$

Figure 2. Time Base Generator under different β values.

The results highlight that small values of β give performances that are proportional to time, which can yield to overshoots if t_f is too small. In addition, small values for β do not comply with the acceleration and jerk constraints, which can be observed as large overshoots in the prescribed time t_f. As β increases, it yields to smoother performances, without overshoots and smooth acceleration and jerk profiles. Figure 3 shows the TBG dynamics under different interception times t_f for a fixed $\beta = 0.7$.

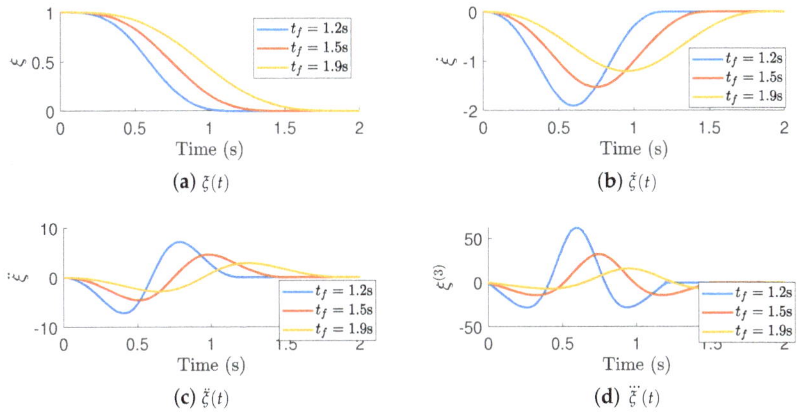

(**a**) $\xi(t)$ (**b**) $\dot{\xi}(t)$ (**c**) $\ddot{\xi}(t)$ (**d**) $\dddot{\xi}(t)$

Figure 3. Time Base Generator under different t_f values.

Here, it is clear that t_f modifies the time of convergence of the TBG, whilst maintaining the smooth performance injected by the β value. Notice that for large interception time, t_f

gives a $\dot{\xi}$ curve with a smaller amplitude magnitude. Conversely, for small interception time, t_f gives large $\dot{\xi}$. This gives an indicator of how we can exploit the TBG dynamics in an adaptive control design. Furthermore, smooth acceleration and jerk profiles are observed in all cases which is highly useful to avoid abrupt movements of the manipulator.

2.3. Sliding Mode Control (SMC) Design

Define the interception errors as

$$\begin{aligned} e &= x - x_r, \\ \dot{e} &= \dot{x} - \dot{x}_r. \end{aligned} \tag{11}$$

For the sliding surface design, consider the following unforced linear time-varying (LTV) system:

$$\dot{m} + \alpha(t)m = 0, \tag{12}$$

where

$$\alpha(t) = -\alpha_0 \frac{\dot{\xi}(t)}{\xi(t) + \delta}, \tag{13}$$

with $\alpha_0 = 1 + \epsilon$, and $\epsilon, \delta \ll 1$ are small positive constants. Figure 4 shows how the gain $\alpha(t)$ changes as ξ and $\dot{\xi}$ evolves in time. Here, we set $\epsilon = \delta = 1 \times 10^{-6}$.

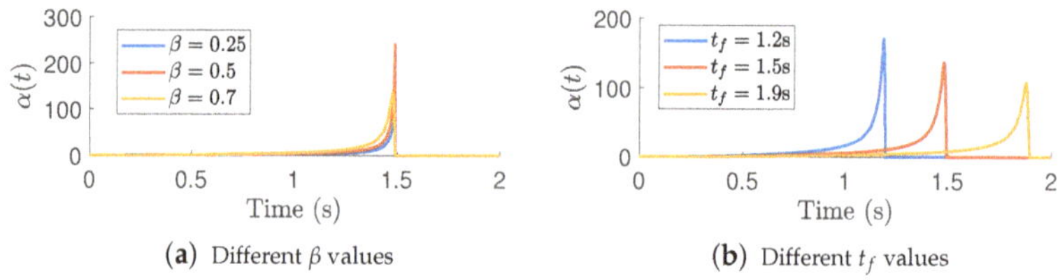

Figure 4. Time-evolution of $\alpha(t)$ under different hyperparameters.

The graphs show that $\alpha(t)$ grows as the TBG approximates to t_f. Here, large enough β values give gains with a smaller amplitude. This is consistent with what we observed in the TBG dynamics, i.e., large β values give smooth performances that attenuate the amplitude of the gain $\alpha(t)$. On the other hand, the effect of t_f is clear, since large interception time yields to smaller gains. Conversely, small interception times give large gains to ensure the interception. This behavior is exploited in the design of the sliding mode controller.

The solution of (12) satisfies the following relation:

$$m(t) = m(t_0)[\xi + \delta]^{1+\epsilon}. \tag{14}$$

Note that when $t = t_f$, we have that $\xi = 0$, and

$$m(t_f) = m(t_0)\delta^{1+\epsilon} > 0. \tag{15}$$

Under this condition, $m(t_f)$ can be set as small as possible by selecting small enough constants δ and ϵ. This is quite useful for the design of the sliding surface, which forces the trajectories to maintain in the manifold and to not escape.

Based on this concept, consider the following sliding surface design:

$$s = \dot{e} + \alpha(t)e. \tag{16}$$

So, based on the previous analysis, we have that when $t = t_f$, it will imply that the interception error $\boldsymbol{e}$ can be arbitrarily small. To avoid the chattering effect and enhance the robust capabilities of the SMC, we consider the following nominal sliding surface, given by

$$\begin{aligned} s_x &= s - s(t_0)\exp^{-k(t-t_0)} + \Lambda\sigma, \\ \dot{\sigma} &= \operatorname{sign}\left(s - s(t_0)\exp^{-k(t-t_0)}\right), \end{aligned} \tag{17}$$

where $k > 0$ and $\Lambda \in \mathbb{R}^{m\times m}$ is a diagonal weight matrix. Notice that the additional term in the sign function ensures that we start in the sliding surface for any initial condition. Then, the following second-order sliding mode control law is used:

$$\tau = -KJ^{+}(q)s_x, \tag{18}$$

where $K \in \mathbb{R}^{n\times n}$ is a diagonal control gain and $J^{+}(q)$ is the Moore–Penrose pseudoinverse of the Jacobian $J(q)$. If we expand the terms in (18), it yields an SMC with a PID structure.

2.4. Stability Analysis

The closed-loop dynamics between (1) and (18) gives

$$M(q)\ddot{q} + C(q,\dot{q})\dot{q} + G(q) = -KJ^{+}(q)s_x + d.$$

The Jacobian mapping (5) is used on the nominal sliding surface as

$$\begin{aligned} s_q &= J^{+}(q)s_x, \\ \dot{s}_q &= J^{+}(q)\left[\dot{s}_x - \dot{J}(q)J^{+}(q)s_x\right], \end{aligned} \tag{19}$$

where s_q denotes the nominal sliding surface in the joint space and $\dot{J}(q)$ is the time-derivative of the Jacobian, which is also bounded, i.e., $\|\dot{J}(q))\| \le \varepsilon_t$ where $\varepsilon_t > 0$. Then, we can rewrite the closed-loop dynamics in terms of this joint space surface as

$$M(q)\dot{s}_q + (C(q,\dot{q}) + K)s_q = -\eta, \tag{20}$$

where $\eta \in \mathbb{R}^n$ is a state-dependent function, given by

$$\eta = M(q)\ddot{q}_s + C(q,\dot{q})\dot{q}_s + G(q) + d,$$

with $\dot{q}_s = J^{+}(q)\left[\dot{x}_r - \alpha(t)e + s(t_0)\exp^{-k(t-t_0)} - \Lambda\sigma\right]$. Notice that

$$\begin{aligned} &\|\dot{q}_s\| \le \varepsilon_J^{-1}(\beta_4 + \alpha(t)\|e\| + \|\Lambda\|\|\sigma\|) \\ &\|\ddot{q}_s\| \le \varepsilon_J^{-1}\left(\beta_5 + \varepsilon_t\varepsilon_J^{-1}\beta_4 + \|\alpha(t)\|\|\dot{e}\| + \varepsilon_J\|\psi(t)\|\|e\| + \varepsilon_t\varepsilon_J^{-1}\|\Lambda\|\|\sigma\|\right), \end{aligned}$$

where $\beta_4, \beta_5 > 0$ and $\psi(t) = \varepsilon_J^{-1}\dot{\alpha}(t) + \frac{\varepsilon_t}{\varepsilon_J^2}\alpha(t)$. Then, by using the bounds (4), we have that

$$\begin{aligned} \|\eta(t)\| \le &\beta_1\left[\varepsilon_J^{-1}\left(\beta_5 + \varepsilon_t\varepsilon_J^{-1}\beta_4 + \|\alpha(t)\|\|\dot{e}\| + \varepsilon_J\|\psi(t)\|\|e\| + \varepsilon_t\varepsilon_J^{-1}\|\Lambda\|\|\sigma\|\right)\right] \\ &+ \beta_2\|\dot{q}\|\left[\varepsilon_J^{-1}(\beta_4 + \alpha(t)\|e\| + \|\Lambda\|\|\sigma\|)\right] + \beta_3 + \|d\|. \end{aligned} \tag{21}$$

Notice that η contains the disturbance vector d, which needs to be compensated by the sliding mode controller. The following theorem is used to verify the practical stability of the proposed approach.

Theorem 1. *Consider the closed-loop system trajectories* (20). *If the control gain* K *satisfies the following relation,*

$$\lambda_{\min}(K) \ge \|\eta(t)\| + \rho, \tag{22}$$

where $\rho > 0$, then the trajectories of the sliding surface s_x remains bounded in a set of radius $\mu = \frac{\|\eta(t)\|}{\lambda_{\min}(K)}$, and the interception error e converges to an arbitrarily small value in a pre-defined time t_f.

Proof of Theorem 1. Consider the Lyapunov function,

$$V = \frac{1}{2} s_q^\top M(q) s_q. \tag{23}$$

The time-derivative of V across the closed-loop trajectories (20) yields

$$\begin{aligned}\dot{V} &= s_q^\top M(q)\dot{s}_q + \frac{1}{2} s_q^\top \dot{M}(q) s_q \\ &= -s_q^\top \left[\eta(t) + (C(q,\dot{q}) + K)s_q\right] + \frac{1}{2} s_q^\top \dot{M}(q) s_q.\end{aligned}$$

Using the skew-symmetric property of the Coriolis matrix gives

$$\begin{aligned}\dot{V} &= -\, s_q^\top K s_q - s_q^\top \eta(t) \\ &\leq -\,\lambda_{\min}(K)\|s_q\|^2 + \|\eta(t)\|\|s_q\| \\ &= -\,\lambda_{\min}(K)\|s_q\|\left(\|s_q\| - \frac{\|\eta(t)\|}{\lambda_{\min}(K)}\right).\end{aligned} \tag{24}$$

$\dot{V}$ is negative definite if

$$\|s_q\| > \frac{\|\eta(t)\|}{\lambda_{\min}(K)} \equiv \mu.$$

Notice that s_q is a function dependent of e, $\dot{e}$, σ, and the initial conditions of the sliding surface; then, for sufficiently small initial errors [33,34] that belong to a small set S_ε of radius $r > 0$ and are centered in s_q, we are allowed to state that there exists a large enough gain K that fulfills (22). Therefore, the nominal joint surface trajectories converge to a bounded set S_μ of radius μ, i.e., $\|s_q\| \leq \mu$ as $t \to \infty$. This means that $\|s_q\|$ is bounded.

Boundedness of s_q and the Jacobian $J(q)$ means that s_x is also bounded, and converges to a bounded set S_ν of radius $\nu \equiv \mu\varepsilon_J$ centered in the equilibrium $s_x = 0$. In other words, this means that S_ν is centered in the sliding surface attractor, such that all the trajectories within S_ν try to converge into the attractor. In the equilibrium point $s_x = 0$, the sliding surface verifies the unforced LTV system,

$$\dot{e} = -\alpha(t)e,$$

whose solution is given by

$$e(t) = e(t_0)[\xi + \delta]^{1+\epsilon}. \tag{25}$$

This allows to conclude that the error trajectories e within S_ν will converge to an error value proportional to (25) with a lower bound of $e(t_0)\delta^{1+\epsilon}$. This completes the proof. □

From the previous proof, we can observe two specific properties of the controller: (1) it converges in a prescribed time to the object trajectory, and (2) it has robust properties against model uncertainty and exogenous disturbances by choosing a large enough gain K and the proper tuning of the gain Λ. The combined contribution gives the proposed approach a unique mechanism to ensure convergence in a prescribed time with robust capabilities.

Remark 1. *The gain Λ is manually tuned, and plays an important role of the performance of the overall controller. Here, the product of $KJ^+(q)\Lambda$ defines the nonlinear gain of the integral term of the proposed SMC controller. This term is in charge of maintaining the closed-loop trajectories within the sliding manifold, whilst attenuating the model uncertainties and disturbances.*

Remark 2. *The computational complexity of the proposed controller is dominated by the product between the inverse of the Jacobian and the control gain* $\mathbf{K}$*, given by* $\mathcal{O}(mn^2) = \mathcal{O}(n^3)$.

3. Results

In this section, we report the results of the proposed approach in the interception of objects in diverse trajectory profiles. Specifically, we consider the following cases: an object following a curve trajectory and a multiple interception task in a robotic assembly task. All computations are executed on an Intel(R) Core(TM) i9-10885H 2.40 GHz, 32 GB RAM, with Matlab/Simulink 2023b and RoboDk 5.7 software. Both Matlab and RoboDK are connected through the RoboDK API. Here, Matlab/Simulink is used for the control design and encoding the robot dynamics, whilst RoboDK is used to obtain a visual representation of the robot and the interception of the target in the Cartesian coordinates.

3.1. RV-M1 Robot

We consider the Mitsubishi RV-M1 robot observed in Figure 5.

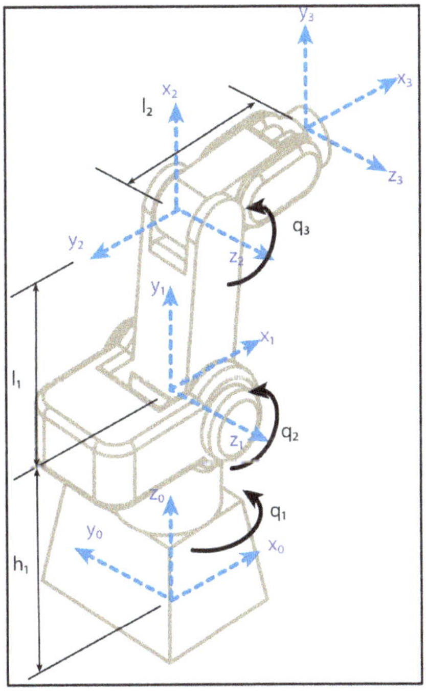

Figure 5. Mitsubishi RV-M1 robot.

The RV-M1 robot is a 5 DOF robot; however, in this paper we only use the first three DOF that control the position of the manipulator, as in [35]. These joint angles are used since the goal of this research is to ensure the interception of the object in a prescribed time regardless its orientation. The control of both the position and orientation for target interception in a prescribed time is topic for future research.

The kinematics of the first three DOF of the RV-M1 robot is given by

$$\begin{bmatrix} X \\ Y \\ Z \end{bmatrix} = \begin{bmatrix} -l_1\cos(q_1)\sin(q_2) + l_2\cos(q_1)\cos(q_2+q_3) \\ -l_1\sin(q_1)\sin(q_2) + l_2\sin(q_1)\cos(q_2+q_3) \\ h_1 + l_1\cos(q_2) + l_2\sin(q_2+q_3) \end{bmatrix}, \tag{26}$$

where $\boldsymbol{q} = [q_1, q_2, q_3]^\top$ denote the joint angles, $\boldsymbol{x} = [X, Y, Z]^\top$ defines the Cartesian position, and h_1 and l_i define the length of each link, with $i = 1, 2$.

The associated Jacobian matrix is given by

$$J(q) = \begin{bmatrix} J_{11} & J_{12} & J_{13} \\ J_{21} & J_{22} & J_{23} \\ 0 & J_{32} & J_{33} \end{bmatrix}, \tag{27}$$

where

$$\begin{aligned}
J_{11} &= \sin(q_1)(l_1 \sin(q_2) - l_2 \cos(q_2 + q_3)) \\
J_{12} &= -\cos(q_1)(l_1 \cos(q_2) + l_2 \sin(q_2 + q_3)) \\
J_{13} &= l_2 \cos(q_1) \sin(q_2 + q_3) \\
J_{21} &= \cos(q_1)(-l_1 \sin(q_2) + l_2 \cos(q_2 + q_3)) \\
J_{22} &= \sin(q_1)(l_1 \cos(q_2) + l_2 \sin(q_2 + q_3)) \\
J_{32} &= -l_1 \sin(q_2) + l_2 \cos(q_3 + q_3) \\
J_{33} &= l_2 \cos(q_2 + q_3).
\end{aligned}$$

The kinematic parameters of the robot are $h_1 = 0.3$ m, $l_1 = 0.25$ m and $l_2 = 0.16$ m. The dynamic parameters have been estimated by the 3D Computer-Aided Design (CAD) drawing of the robot. These parameters are used for simulation purposes. The control gains and parameters of the TBG used in this paper are: $\boldsymbol{K} = 50\boldsymbol{I}_3$, $\boldsymbol{\Lambda} = 5\boldsymbol{I}_3$, $k = 3$ and $\epsilon = \delta = 1 \times 10^{-6}$. The robot model considers friction at the robot joints and complete dynamic model uncertainty.

3.2. *Curve Trajectory*

We test the approach under an object following a curve trajectory, defined by

$$\boldsymbol{x}_r = \begin{bmatrix} 0.24 + 0.1\sin(1.5t) \\ 0.1\cos(1.5t) \\ 0.3 + 0.1\sin(1.5t) \end{bmatrix}, \quad \dot{\boldsymbol{x}}_r = \begin{bmatrix} 0.15\cos(1.5t) \\ -0.15\sin(1.5t) \\ 0.15\cos(1.5t) \end{bmatrix}.$$

In this case, we aim to observe how the hyperparameters of the TBG, i.e., β and t_f affect the performance of the interception algorithm. Consider first the scenario of a fixed interception time of $t = 1.5$ s. We compare the results using $\beta = \{0.25, 0.5, 0.75\}$.

3.2.1. $\beta = 0.25$

Figure 6 shows the trajectory interception for $\beta = 0.25$.

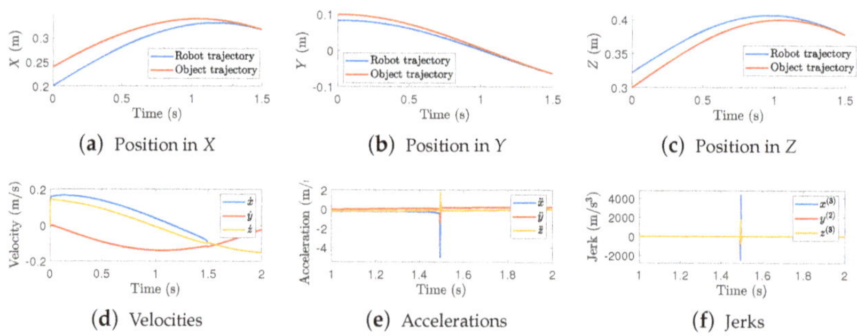

Figure 6. Trajectory interception in each axis. Results for $t_f = 1.5$ s and $\beta = 0.25$.

The results show that, as we previously discussed, a small β makes the robot intercept the object almost linearly. This linear performance produces discontinuous velocities which in consequence shows large accelerations and jerk peaks. Figure 7 shows the 3D interception task between the robot and the object trajectories.

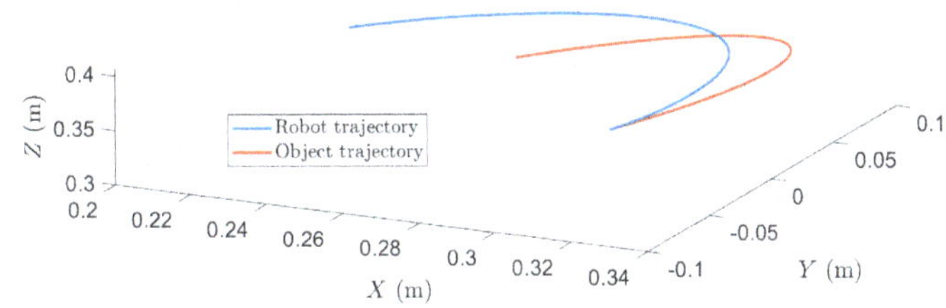

Figure 7. 3D trajectory interception. Results for t_f = 1.5 s and $\beta = 0.25$.

3.2.2. $\beta = 0.5$

Consider the case where $\beta = 0.5$. Figure 8 shows the interception trajectories in the Cartesian space.

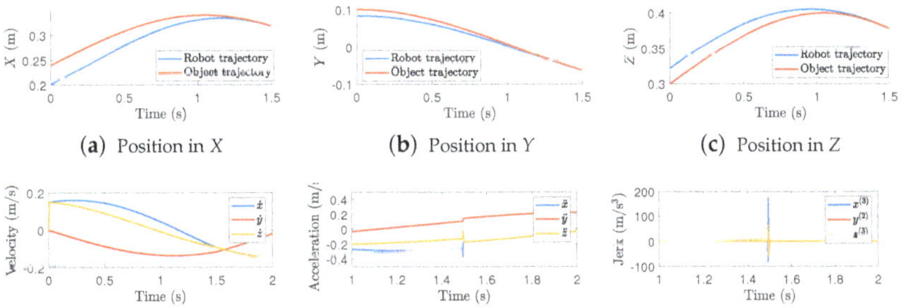

(a) Position in X **(b)** Position in Y **(c)** Position in Z

(d) Velocities **(e)** Accelerations **(f)** Jerks

Figure 8. Trajectory interception in each axis. Results for t_f = 1.5 s and $\beta = 0.5$.

Notice that similar results are obtained in the previous case. In this case, $\beta = 0.5$ offers a smoother evolution of the TBG, i.e., the velocity discontinuities are smaller such that the acceleration and jerk amplitudes are decreased. Figure 9 shows the 3D interception trajectory.

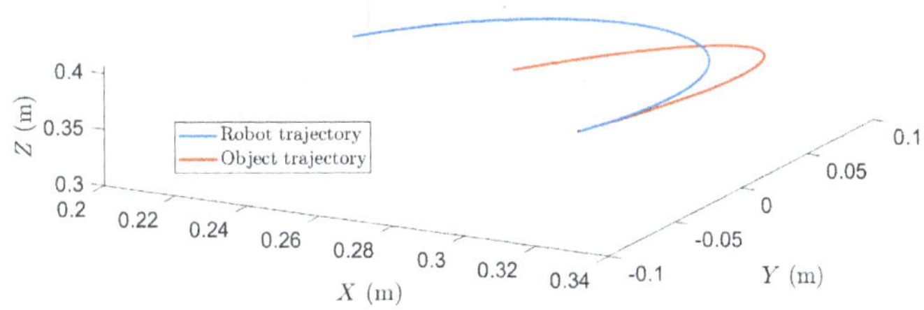

Figure 9. 3D trajectory interception. Results for t_f = 1.5 s and $\beta = 0.5$.

3.2.3. $\beta = 0.75$

Figure 10 shows the interception task for a $\beta = 0.75$.

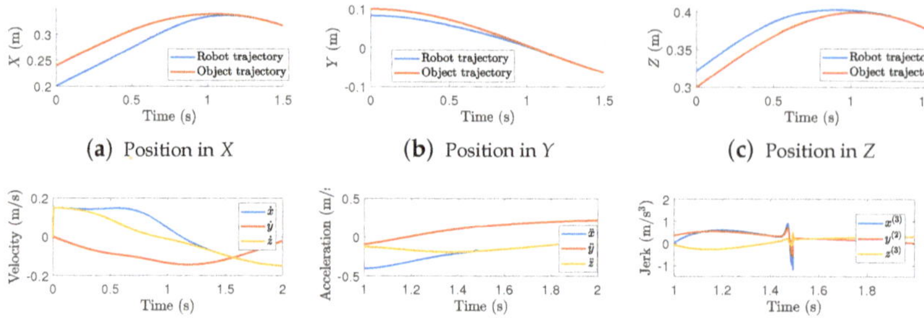

(**a**) Position in X (**b**) Position in Y (**c**) Position in Z

(**d**) Velocities (**e**) Accelerations (**f**) Jerks

Figure 10. Trajectory interception in each axis. Results for t_f = 1.5 s and $\beta = 0.75$.

In contrast to the previous cases, when $\beta = 0.75$ the TBG is smoother, such that it has a large $\dot{\xi}$ that causes the robot to follow a larger trajectory path. However, the robot intercepts the object's trajectory at an early point. This is better observed in the 3D trajectory of Figure 11, where it is shown that the robot adopts a larger path, but converges in the pre-defined time t_f in an early point of the object trajectory. Notice that the acceleration and jerk effects are notably reduced, which gives an indicator that β values close to 1 will give trajectories without peaks in acceleration and jerk.

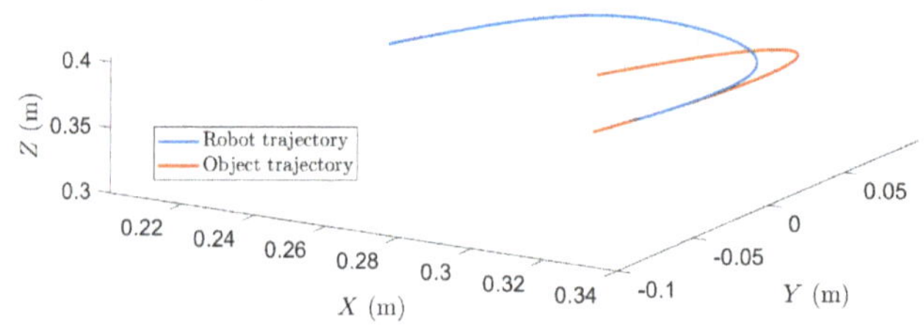

Figure 11. 3D trajectory interception. Results for t_f = 1.5 s and $\beta = 0.75$.

3.2.4. t_f = 1.2 s

In this case, we maintain β fixed to $\beta = 0.75$ and modify the interception time. Figure 12 shows the trajectory interception for an interception time of $t = 1.2$ s.

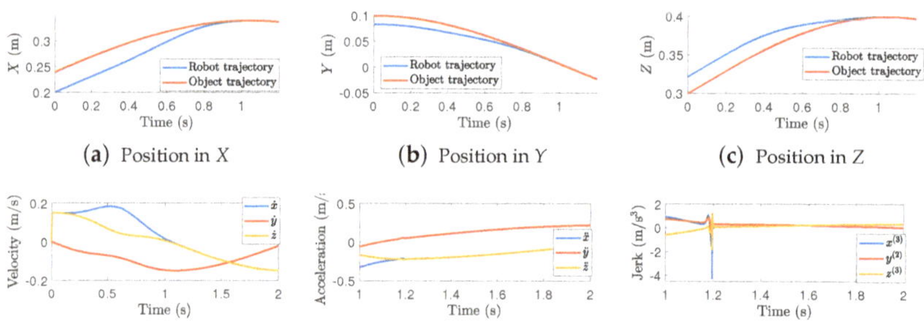

(**a**) Position in X (**b**) Position in Y (**c**) Position in Z

(**d**) Velocities (**e**) Accelerations (**f**) Jerks

Figure 12. Trajectory interception in each axis. Results for t_f = 1.2 s and $\beta = 0.75$.

In this case, we are forcing the robot to intercept the object faster such that it needs to increase $\dot{\xi}$ to obtain a larger $\alpha(t)$. This means that the trajectory will follow a linear trajectory profile that yields to peaks in accelerations and jerks. Figure 13 shows the 3D-interception trajectory. From the graph, it can be observed that the robot takes longer to intercept the object in the pre-defined time t_f. However, as in the previous case, it intercepts the object at an early point, which can lead to issues if the interception is required at a specific point.

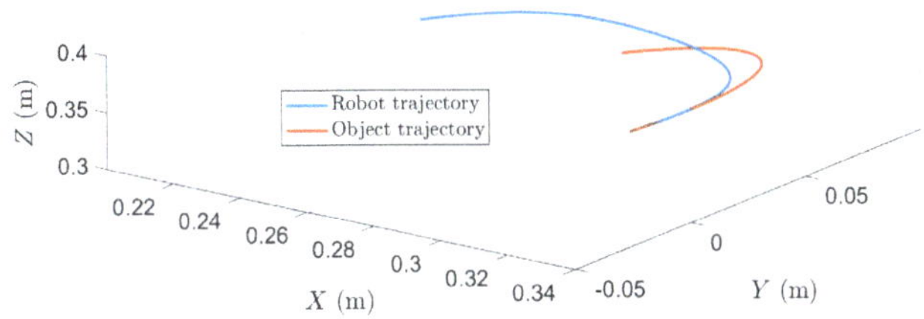

Figure 13. 3D trajectory interception. Results for t_f = 1.2 s and $\beta = 0.75$.

3.2.5. $t_f = 1.9$ s

Figure 14 shows the interception of the trajectory in a pre-defined time $t_f = 1.9$ s. In this scenario, the robot follows a larger path with a slower $\dot{\xi}$ that causes the robot to converge in the pre-defined time but intercepts at an early point. Here, both the acceleration and jerk trajectories exhibit a smooth profile with small overshoots due to the interception.

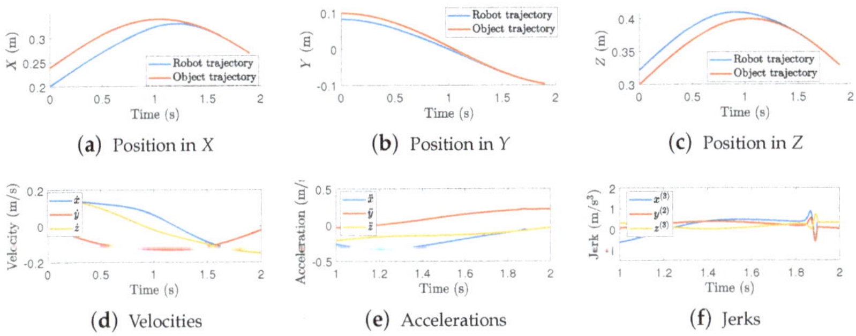

Figure 14. Trajectory interception in each axis. Results for t_f = 1.9 s and $\beta = 0.75$.

Figure 15 shows the 3D-trajectory interception. This case is more evident since the robot follows a large trajectory and converges in the pre-defined time to an early point, whilst the position of the object at time t_f is at a forward position.

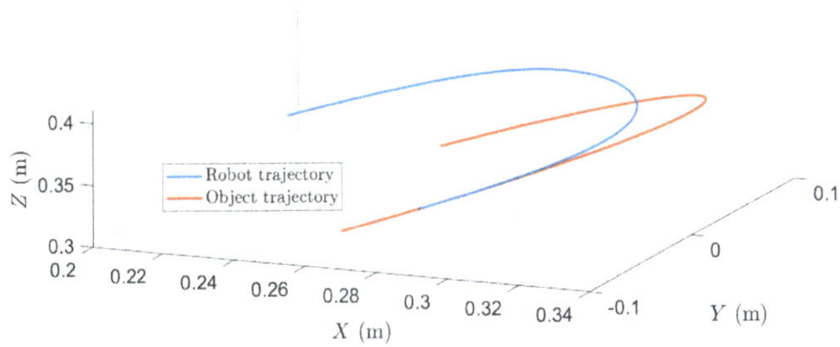

Figure 15. 3D trajectory interception. Results for t_f = 1.9 s and $\beta = 0.75$.

3.3. Multiple Interception in Robotic Assembly Tasks

The proposed approach is challenged in a robotic assembly task. The approach consists of the interception (pick and place) of objects coming from different conveyors. Traditional approaches use different robots to pick objects from their respective conveyor. Here, we aim to reduce the necessity of multiple robots by using a unique robot dedicated to the pick and place of objects in a prescribed time. In this study, we assume the objects have the same orientation such that the robot can pick them without modifying the joint angles of the wrist, i.e., we only use the first three DOF joints of the robot for the pick and place task. Future work will consider objects with different orientations such that the interception task is more challenging.

The proposed experiment consists of the picking and placing of three objects coming from three different conveyors. Each object is assumed to have a constant velocity of $v_y = 0.1$ m/s in the y-axis. The trajectories and positions of each conveyor are summarized in Table 1.

Table 1. Conveyors trajectories in (m).

Conveyor 1	Conveyor 2	Conveyor 3
$x \quad = 0.3$	$x \quad = 0.2$	$x \quad = 0.25$
$y \quad = y_0 + v_y t$	$y \quad = y_0 + v_y t$	$y \quad = y_0 + v_y t$
$z \quad = 0.15$	$z \quad = 0.25$	$z \quad = 0.15$

The initial position of the gripper is $(x_0, y_0, z_0) = (0.2016, 0.0835, 0.3222)$ m. For the object in conveyor 1, we set an interception time of $t_f = 0.5$ s to pick the object and wait 0.30 s to pick the second object in the conveyor 2 in an interception time of $t_f = 1.4$ s. After this, the robot waits 0.10 s to pick the third object in a time of $t_f = 2$ s. Figure 16 shows the velocity error $\dot{e} = (e_x, e_y, e_z)$ for the proposed assembly task.

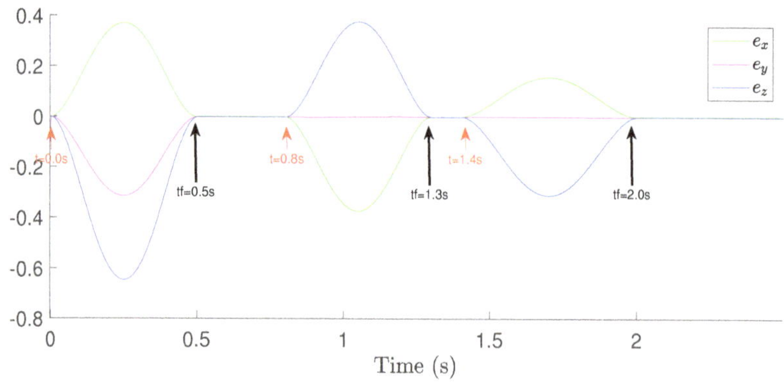

Figure 16. Cartesian velocity error in the assembly task.

Notice that for each interception trajectory, the Cartesian velocity error $\dot{e}$ converges in the prescribed times t_f. For short interception times (object 1), the gain $\alpha(t)$ increases such that the robot follows a faster path given by a large $\dot{\xi}$ to converge in the desired time. On the other hand, for large interception times (object 3), has a low gain $\alpha(t)$ that produces a short path that smoothly converges in the prescribed time t_f.

Figure 17 shows how the torques change each time the TBG is applied. Notice that the torques remain bounded and stable, which shows how the torques slightly increase for short interception times and small values for long interception times. Figure 18 shows the trajectories of the robot throughout the assembly task. Notice that, since the trajectories are not continuous, discontinuous accelerations are obtained, which yield large jerks. However, this is a common pattern in robot manipulators when they start from an initial condition that is relative far from the desired position. This is usually attenuated by adding a low-pass filter in each new target interception goal. This will create a smooth trajectory profile that the robot will be able to handle in a smoother way.

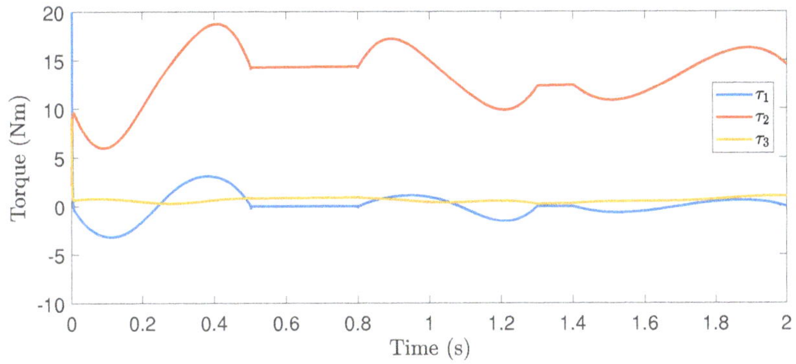

Figure 17. Torques applied to the robot.

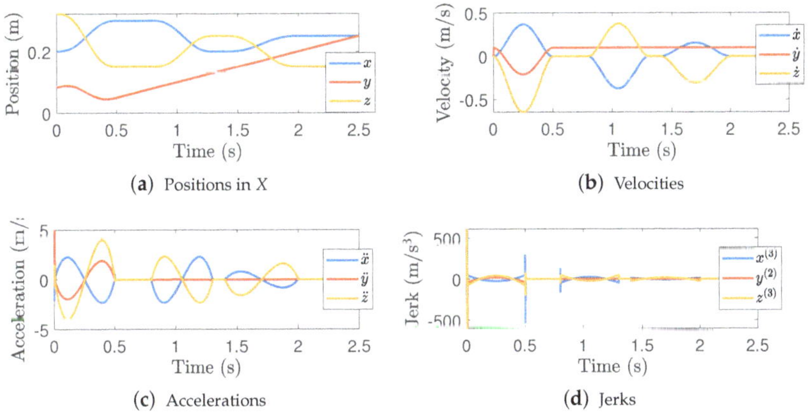

Figure 18. Robot trajectories for the assembly task.

Figure 19 shows the trajectory profile of the robot for the interception of the three objects in the prescribed times. Here, the trajectory followed by the robot is smooth and continuous, this demonstrates the benefits of the proposed technique and the reduction in resources and time.

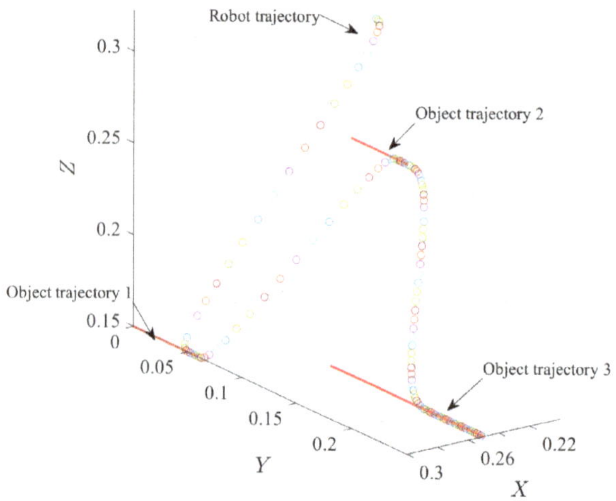

Figure 19. Multiple interception trajectories.

4. Conclusions

This paper proposes a novel interception algorithm for moving objects using robot manipulators. The task is achieved by using a novel time base generator that allows the interception in a prescribed time. Here, we introduce a new parameter that modifies the behavior of the TBG according to the task and prescribed time. A second-order sliding mode controller is designed to ensure tracking of the object and robustness against modeling errors and uncertainties. The proposed sliding-mode controller adopts a TBG-based varying gain to ensure the closed-loop trajectories converge and remain within the sliding manifold. The stability and boundedness of the closed-loop system trajectories are verified using Lyapunov stability theory. Diverse simulation studies using a RV-M1 robot model are conducted to show the advantages of the proposed approach in the interception of objects in prescribed time. Two cases were considered: an object following a curved trajectory and a multi-interception task. The results demonstrate the feasibility and robustness of the approach to intercept objects in different prescribed times and tasks. Future work will consider the extension of the proposed approach when either the trajectories of the objects are unknown or when these trajectories do not follow a repetitive pattern. Furthermore, future research will include the interception of objects with different orientations.

Author Contributions: Conceptualization, J.A.F.-C. and A.P.; methodology, J.A.F.-C.; software, C.R.T.-S.-M.; validation, J.C.P.-R., J.A.F.-C. and A.P.; formal analysis, J.A.F.-C.; investigation, A.P.; resources, J.C.P.-R.; writing—original draft preparation, A.P.; writing—review and editing, A.P.; visualization, C.R.T.-S.-M.; supervision, A.P.; project administration, J.A.F.-C.; funding acquisition, A.P. All authors have read and agreed to the published version of the manuscript.

Funding: This research received funding under projects: SIP 20240710, SIP 20240701, and SIP 20242785.

Institutional Review Board Statement: Not applicable.

Informed Consent Statement: Not applicable.

Data Availability Statement: The original contributions presented in the study are included in the article material, further inquiries can be directed to the corresponding author.

Conflicts of Interest: The authors declare no conflicts of interest.

Abbreviations

The following abbreviations are used in this manuscript:

CAD	Computer-Aided Design
CHOMP	Covariant Hamiltonian optimization for motion planning
DDPG	Deep Deterministic Policy Gradient
DOF	Degree of Freedom
RL	Reinforcement Learning
SAC	Soft Actor Critic
SMC	Sliding Mode Control
STOMP	Stochastic trajectory optimization for motion planning
TBG	Time Base Generator

References

1. Lobbezoo, A.; Qian, Y.; Kwon, H.J. Reinforcement learning for pick and place operations in robotics: A survey. *Robotics* **2021**, *10*, 105. [CrossRef]
2. Wang, L.; Hu, J.; Xu, Z.; Zhao, C. Autonomous maneuver strategy of swarm air combat based on DDPG. *Auton. Intell. Syst.* **2021**, *1*, 15. [CrossRef]
3. Meng, X.; Sun, B.; Zhu, D. Harbour protection: Moving invasion target interception for multi-AUV based on prediction planning interception method. *Ocean. Eng.* **2021**, *219*, 108268. [CrossRef]
4. Flores-Campos, J.A.; Perrusquía, A.; Hernández-Gómez, L.H.; González, N.; Armenta-Molina, A. Constant speed control of slider-crank mechanisms: A joint-task space hybrid control approach. *IEEE Access* **2021**, *9*, 65676–65687. [CrossRef]
5. Guo, W.; Wei, Z.; Gonzalez, O.; Perrusquía, A.; Tsourdos, A. Control layer security: A new security paradigm for cooperative autonomous systems. *IEEE Veh. Technol. Mag.* **2023**, *99*, 2–11. [CrossRef]
6. Ye, H.; Song, Y. Prescribed-time control for linear systems in canonical form via nonlinear feedback. *IEEE Trans. Syst. Man Cybern. Syst.* **2022**, *53*, 1126–1135. [CrossRef]
7. Zhou, B.; Zhang, Z.; Michiels, W. Functional and dual observer based prescribed-time control of linear systems by periodic delayed feedback. *Automatica* **2024**, *159*, 111406. [CrossRef]
8. Friedman, A.; Friedman, A. Dynamic Inversion and Control of Nonlinear Systems. In *Mathematics in Industrial Problems*; Springer: New York, NY, USA, 1988; pp. 114–120.
9. Hou, Z.S.; Wang, Z. From model-based control to data-driven control: Survey, classification and perspective. *Inf. Sci.* **2013**, *235*, 3–35. [CrossRef]
10. Moreira, M.; Papp, E.; Ventura, R. Interception of non-cooperative UAVs. In Proceedings of the 2019 IEEE International Symposium on Safety, Security, and Rescue Robotics (SSRR), Wurzburg, Germany, 2–4 September 2019; IEEE: Piscataway, NJ, USA, 2019; pp. 120–125.
11. Wenjie, Z.; Shengnan, F.; Wei, L.; Qunli, X. An impact angle constraint integral sliding mode guidance law for maneuvering targets interception. *J. Syst. Eng. Electron.* **2020**, *31*, 168–184.
12. Li, Y.; Yan, L.; Zhao, J.g.; Liu, F.; Wang, T. Combined proportional navigation law for interception of high-speed targets. *Def. Technol.* **2014**, *10*, 298–303. [CrossRef]
13. Sinha, A.; Kumar, S.R.; Mukherjee, D. Cooperative integrated guidance and control design for simultaneous interception. *Aerosp. Sci. Technol.* **2022**, *120*, 107262. [CrossRef]
14. Tsuji, T.; Tanaka, Y.; Morasso, P.G.; Sanguineti, V.; Kaneko, M. Bio-mimetic trajectory generation of robots via artificial potential field with time base generator. *IEEE Trans. Syst. Man, Cybern. Part (Appl. Rev.)* **2002**, *32*, 426–439. [CrossRef]
15. Duhé, J.F.; Victor, S.; Melchior, P. Contributions on artificial potential field method for effective obstacle avoidance. *Fract. Calc. Appl. Anal.* **2021**, *24*, 421–446. [CrossRef]
16. Ratliff, N.; Zucker, M.; Bagnell, J.A.; Srinivasa, S. CHOMP: Gradient optimization techniques for efficient motion planning. In Proceedings of the 2009 IEEE International Conference on Robotics and Automation, Kobe, Japan, 12–17 May 2009; IEEE: Piscataway, NJ, USA, 2009; pp. 489–494.
17. Kalakrishnan, M.; Chitta, S.; Theodorou, E.; Pastor, P.; Schaal, S. STOMP: Stochastic trajectory optimization for motion planning. In Proceedings of the 2011 IEEE iNternational Conference on Robotics and Automation, Shanghai, China, 9–13 May 2011; IEEE: Piscataway, NJ, USA, 2011; pp. 4569–4574.
18. Kumar, S.R.; Mukherjee, D. Terminal time-constrained nonlinear interception strategies against maneuvering targets. *J. Guid. Control. Dyn.* **2021**, *44*, 200–209. [CrossRef]
19. Zhaoying, L.; Ruoling, S.; Zhao, Z. A new path planning method based on sparse A* algorithm with map segmentation. *Trans. Inst. Meas. Control.* **2022**, *44*, 916–925. [CrossRef]
20. Li, Z.; Li, H. Study of the interception scheme based on A* path finding algorithm in computer game. *J. Comput. Commun.* **2020**, *8*, 32–49. [CrossRef]

21. Khachiyan, L.; Gurvich, V.; Zhao, J. Extending dijkstra's algorithm to maximize the shortest path by node-wise limited arc interdiction. In Proceedings of the Computer Science–Theory and Applications: First International Computer Science Symposium in Russia, CSR 2006, St. Petersburg, Russia, 8–12 June 2006; Proceedings 1; Springer: Berlin/Heidelberg, Germany, 2006; pp. 221–234.
22. Luo, M.; Hou, X.; Yang, J. Surface optimal path planning using an extended Dijkstra algorithm. *IEEE Access* **2020**, *8*, 147827–147838. [CrossRef]
23. Candra, A.; Budiman, M.A.; Hartanto, K. Dijkstra's and a-star in finding the shortest path: A tutorial. In Proceedings of the 2020 International Conference on Data Science, Artificial Intelligence, and Business Analytics (DATABIA), Medan, Indonesia, 16–17 July 2020; IEEE: Piscataway, NJ, USA, 2020; pp. 28–32.
24. Bian, T.; Xing, Y.; Zolotas, A. End-to-End One-Shot Path-Planning Algorithm for an Autonomous Vehicle Based on a Convolutional Neural Network Considering Traversability Cost. *Sensors* **2022**, *22*, 9682. [CrossRef]
25. Kulvicius, T.; Herzog, S.; Lüddecke, T.; Tamosiunaite, M.; Wörgötter, F. One-shot multi-path planning for robotic applications using fully convolutional networks. In Proceedings of the 2020 IEEE International Conference on Robotics and Automation (ICRA), Paris, France, 31 May–31 August 2020; IEEE: Piscataway, NJ, USA, 2020; pp. 1460–1466.
26. Ha, J.S.; Park, Y.J.; Chae, H.J.; Park, S.S.; Choi, H.L. Adaptive path-integral autoencoders: Representation learning and planning for dynamical systems. *Adv. Neural Inf. Process. Syst.* **2018**, *31*, 124008. [CrossRef]
27. Du, Y.; Zhang, X.; Cao, Z.; Wang, S.; Liang, J.; Zhang, F.; Tang, J. An optimized path planning method for coastal ships based on improved DDPG and DP. *J. Adv. Transp.* **2021**, *2021*, 7765130. [CrossRef]
28. Nasonov, I.; Galyaev, A.; Medvedev, A. Neural Network Algorithm for Intercepting Targets moving along known trajectories by a Dubins' car. *arXiv* **2023**, arXiv:2304.06169v1.
29. Azar, A.T.; Serrano, F.E. Stabilization of port Hamiltonian chaotic systems with hidden attractors by adaptive terminal sliding mode control. *Entropy* **2020**, *22*, 122. [CrossRef] [PubMed]
30. Domínguez Ramírez, O.A.; Parra Vega, V.; Díaz Montiel, M.G.; Pozas Cárdenas, M.J.; Hernández Gómez, R.A. *Cartesian Sliding PD Control of Robot Manipulator for Tracking in Finite Time: Theory and Experiments*; DAAAM International: Viena, Austria, 2008; pp. 257–272.
31. de Wit, C.C.; Siciliano, B.; Bastin, G. *Theory of robot control*; Springer Science & Business Media: Berlin/Heidelberg, Germany, 2012.
32. Perrusquía, A.; Flores-Campos, J.A.; Torres-San-Miguel, C.R. A novel tuning method of PD with gravity compensation controller for robot manipulators. *IEEE Access* **2020**, *8*, 114773–114783. [CrossRef]
33. Spong, M.W.; Thorp, J.S.; Kleinwaks, J.M. Robust microprocessor control of robot manipulators. *Automatica* **1987**, *23*, 373–379. [CrossRef]
34. Abdallah, C.; Dawson, D.M.; Dorato, P.; Jamshidi, M. Survey of robust control for rigid robots. *IEEE Control. Syst. Mag.* **1991**, *11*, 24–30.
35. Kumar, R.; Kalra, P.; Prakash, N.R. A virtual RV-M1 robot system. *Robot.-Comput.-Integr. Manuf.* **2011**, *27*, 994–1000. [CrossRef]

Disclaimer/Publisher's Note: The statements, opinions and data contained in all publications are solely those of the individual author(s) and contributor(s) and not of MDPI and/or the editor(s). MDPI and/or the editor(s) disclaim responsibility for any injury to people or property resulting from any ideas, methods, instructions or products referred to in the content.

robotics

MDPI

Article

Robust and Adaptive Control of a Soft Continuum Manipulator for Minimally Invasive Surgery

Liujia Wang [1], Kaiwen Chen [1,2] and Enrico Franco [2,3,*]

1 Department of Electrical and Electronic Engineering, Imperial College London, London SW7 2AZ, UK; liujia.wang23@imperial.ac.uk (L.W.); kaiwen.chen16@imperial.ac.uk (K.C.)
2 Hamlyn Centre for Robotic Surgery, Imperial College London, London SW7 2AZ, UK
3 Department of Mechanical Engineering, Imperial College London, London SW7 2AZ, UK
* Correspondence: e.franco11@imperial.ac.uk

Abstract: This article investigates the model-based control in configurations space of a soft continuum manipulator for minimally invasive surgery. The main control challenges for these types of systems are the presence of model uncertainties and nonlinearities. To this end, a sliding-mode controller, a Lyapunov redesign controller, and an adaptive controller have been designed and compared by means of simulations and experiments on a prototype. The results indicate that the adaptive controller yields better accuracy but a slower transient. Conversely, the sliding-mode controller and Lyapunov redesign yield a faster response but can result in chattering or steady-state errors.

Keywords: soft robotics; nonlinear systems; adaptive control; robust control

1. Introduction

Thanks to the development of robotics in the medical industry, the flexibility, accuracy, and safety of surgical procedures are constantly increasing. Traditional rigid robots can be unsuitable to operate on complex physiological structures and narrow pathways in the body and may cause unnecessary injuries. To prevent rigid robots from causing injuries during surgery, accurate control needs to be achieved. However, this is very challenging as rigid robots often face problems such as lack of sensor feedback, signal delays, and noise; see [1,2]. Conversely, soft robots are compliant and can operate without harming the human body. Several research works (see [3,4]) indicate that soft robots provide better safety and flexibility compared to rigid robots when interacting with patients. This suggests that soft robots possess great potential in the future medical and healthcare industry. However, the complexity, uncertainty, and nonlinearity in the kinematics and dynamics of soft robots make the underlying control problems challenging. In addition, existing models of soft robots are usually inaccurate, which demands robust control methods. Solving this problem will improve the performance of soft robots, resulting in better versatility and therefore widening the application of soft robots in surgical practice. To date, a variety of control methods have been applied to soft robots, including linear control techniques, nonlinear control techniques, and machine learning [5].

The main modeling approaches for soft robots [6] include beam theory [7] and finite-dimensional approximations [5]. For relatively thin soft robots, such as tentacles and probes, the rod model can describe the continuum's dynamic behavior well with partial differential equations (PDEs). Rod models are usually based on the classical beam theory, such as Euler–Bernoulli and Timoshenko–Ehrenfest beams; however, these are not intended for the large deformations generated by soft robots. Ref. [8] proposed a rod model-based gripping approach for a pneumatic soft manipulator using Euler's theory for the elastica, which accurately calculates the shape change and load capacity of the manipulator. Moreover, several works have used the classical Cosserat rod model considering the bending, torsion, shear, and three-dimensional rotation of the rod, yielding consistent theoretical and experimental results; see [9–11]. This indicates that when model assumptions are valid, the rod model is highly accurate despite its complexity.

The rod models yield much higher accuracy than finite-dimensional approximated models. However, due to their complex nonlinear formulations and corresponding PDEs, it is difficult to realize model-based control for soft robots [12]. The finite element method (FEM) approach discretizes the soft robot into a mesh for detailed modeling and computational processing. The FEM has been shown to accurately simulate the deformation and nonlinear behavior of soft robots in quasi-static conditions. However, due to the complexity of the models, learning-based control techniques (see, e.g., [13–15]) are frequently employed in simulations and experiments. Although the FEM is a finite-dimensional model, the nonlinear modeling of each unit is complicated and computationally inefficient for real-time control. Hence finite-dimensional models often use either the piecewise constant curvature (PCC) approximation or the rigid-link approximation [5] for model-based control. PCC is favorable to situations where there is a trade-off between accuracy and computational complexity [16]. Although PCC is a popular choice for modeling and control of soft robots, it poses a significant control challenge due to the resulting underactuation. In general, underactuated and nonlinear systems require more complex strategies to handle the lack of actuators and the nonlinear dynamics. The constant curvature (CC) approximation, a special case of PCC, while further simplified, avoids the problem of underactuation and achieves an effective balance between modeling accuracy and computational complexity.

With the progress of artificial intelligence and machine learning, learning-based control methods for soft robots have made remarkable progress. Learning-based control methods avoid physical modeling of the robot and allow dealing with complex systems. However, these methods require a large amount of training data, making it difficult to achieve precise and fast control in unknown scenarios [17]. In addition, explainability and stability issues remain challenges. Finally, legal requirements and acceptance by the medical community impose that robot control remains subordinate to clinicians, preventing complete autonomy and full reliance on machine learning in critical tasks [18,19].

Currently, model-based control is still under extensive study. Model-based control of soft robots can be inspired by that of rigid-link robots [5]. Early works applied robust control to soft robots. For instance, [20] designed a linear H-infinity controller by treating the nonlinear dynamics as an uncertainty. Sliding-mode control has been employed to address nonlinearity and underactuation; however, this approach suffers from chattering [21,22]. To reduce chattering and corresponding vibrations in soft robots, a saturation function is employed in [23]; however, this results in a small tracking error. Model predictive control (MPC) has been applied to nonlinear systems and for the control of soft robots [24]. However, solving optimization problems for multi degree-of-freedom (DOF) nonlinear models remains a challenge. Nonlinear adaptive controllers for rigid-body robots can also be applied to soft robots, but the offline computation of the regressors and the slow convergence rate still limit their effectiveness [25,26]. Moreover, energy shaping approaches have been used for regulation tasks and are suitable for dealing with nonlinear and underactuated systems [27]. Energy-shaping control of soft robots has been shown to achieve good performance in the presence of uncertainties [28–30]. However, most energy-shaping approaches are intended for regulation and do not translate easily to tracking tasks.

In summary, the main challenges in soft robot control are model uncertainties and nonlinearity. Accurate models increase the computational complexity of the controller and make it difficult to achieve real-time control. Simple approximate models require strong robustness properties of the controller to deal with the uncertainty caused by model mismatch, which typically applies to inertia, viscous friction, and bending stiffness. Developing and performing computationally efficient control algorithms that meet the requirements of real-world applications remains a challenge. This work investigates the model-based control of a soft continuum manipulator using a simplified model and either a robust control approach or an adaptive controller. The main contributions of this work include the following points:

- A simplified dynamical model of a soft continuum manipulator obtained with the CC assumption.
- A new implementation of a sliding-mode controller and of a Lyapunov redesign approach intended to dominate bounded uncertainties resulting from the model mismatch.
- An adaptive controller designed for the proposed model to compensate uncertainties without prior knowledge of their bound.

The controllers have been compared by means of simulations and experiments on a prototype with uncertain bending stiffness. The rest of this paper is organized as follows. Section 2 describes the system model. Section 3 presents the controller design. Section 4 contains the result of simulations, while Section 5 contains experimental results. Section 6 concludes the paper.

2. System Model

2.1. *Soft Robotic Manipulator*

This work investigates the control of a three-chamber pneumatic silicone soft robotic manipulator manufactured by Treratanakulchai et al. [31]. The pneumatic actuation results in the bending of the manipulator without elongation due to an inextensible central core. The model of a manipulator consisting of two actuated segments connected in series is shown in Figure 1. Two rigid disks, represented by the white sections in the figure, connect the soft segments together.

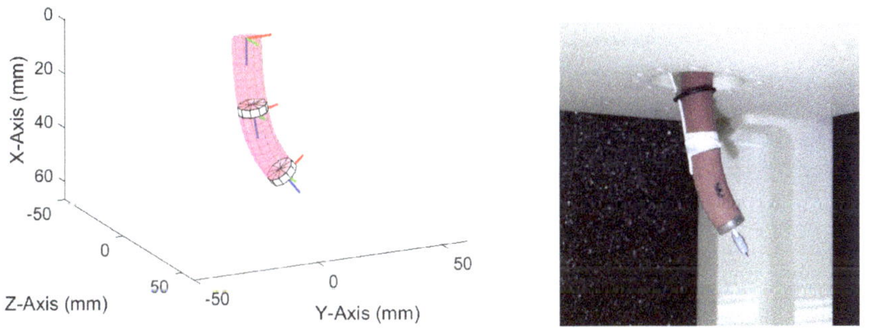

(**a**) Digital twin (**b**) Prototype

Figure 1. Digital twin (**a**) and prototype (**b**) for two-segment soft robotic manipulator.

For simplicity, the system was modeled using the CC approximation, thus each actuated soft segment is represented with exactly one constant-curvature arc, which avoids issues related to underactuation [16].

2.2. *Kinematics Model*

To simplify the kinematics analysis of the three-dimensional model, the robotic arm is analyzed in a bending plane, which is shown in Figure 2a. Each segment has a length of L and a mass of m. The segments are connected with a separation disk, and a position and orientation sensor is mounted on the tip. The cross-section structure is shown in Figure 2b.

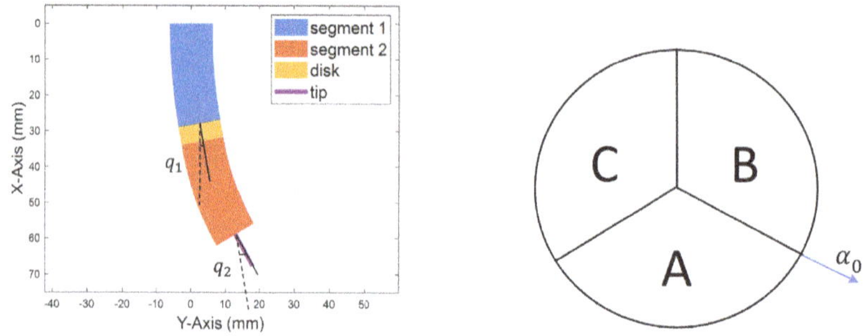

(**a**) Two-segment manipulator (**b**) Cross-section structure

Figure 2. Illustration for the manipulator on the bending plane and cross-section.

An additional coordinate $s \in [0,1]$ is introduced to describe the shape of the soft manipulator in terms of positions and orientations of each infinitesimal element in the soft segment (i.e., $s = 0$ at the base and $s = 1$ at the tip) [5]. Considering a single-segment arm with base orientation aligned with the direction of gravity, its position and orientation can be represented by the shape vector

$$x_0(s,t) = h(s,q(t)) = \left[\underbrace{\left[\frac{L}{q(t)} \sin(sq(t)), \ \ \frac{L}{q(t)} - \frac{L}{q(t)} \cos(sq(t)) \right]^\top}_{X_0(s,t)^\top}, \ \ sq(t) \right]^\top, \tag{1}$$

expressing the displacement in the x-axis, y-axis, and orientation as a function of time t, respectively, where X_0 is the position vector. Since the second segment does not have its base aligned with the direction of gravity, the displacement and rotation matrices resulting from the first segment need to be taken into account. The displacement depends on the end position of the first segment $E(t)$ and the length of the disk d. The angle of rotation of the base about the z-axis in the positive direction is denoted as ϕ, and the rotation matrix is

$$R(\phi) = \begin{bmatrix} \cos(\phi) & -\sin(\phi) \\ \sin(\phi) & \cos(\phi) \end{bmatrix}. \tag{2}$$

The position of the second segment in the base coordinate frame is

$$X(s,t) = R(\phi) \left[\frac{L}{q(t)} \sin(sq(t)) + d \ \ \ \frac{L}{q(t)} - \frac{L}{q(t)} \cos(sq(t)) \right]^\top + E(t). \tag{3}$$

Denoting the bending angles of segment 1 and segment 2 in the model as q_1 and q_2, respectively (see Figure 2), the shape of the soft manipulator is given by the shape vectors

$$x_1(s,t) = \left[\frac{L}{q_1(t)} \sin(sq_1(t)) \ \ \ \frac{L}{q_1(t)} - \frac{L}{q_1(t)} \cos(sq_1(t)) \ \ \ sq_1(t) \right]^\top, \tag{4}$$

$$x_2(s,t) = \begin{bmatrix} R & 0 \\ 0 & 1 \end{bmatrix} \left[\frac{L}{q_2(t)} \sin(sq_2(t)) + d \ \ \ \frac{L}{q_2(t)} - \frac{L}{q_2(t)} \cos(sq_2(t)) \ \ \ sq_2(t) \right]^\top + x_1(1,t). \tag{5}$$

If the model has more segments, the same method can be employed recursively for subsequent shape vectors. If follows from (5) that the kinematics model has removable singularities at zero. (A removable singularity is a singular point where a function is undefined but can be resolved by methods such as Taylor expansion or taking left and right limits to make the function continuous.) In this work, the singularities will be approximated by linear interpolation in a specific interval, as shown in Figure 3.

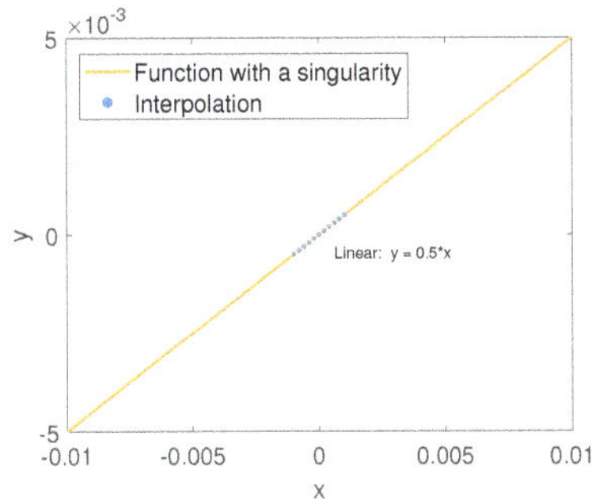

Figure 3. Interpolation of $y = \frac{1-\cos(x)}{x}$ around $x = 0$.

2.3. Dynamic Model

The equation of motion for the soft manipulator is derived from the Euler–Lagrangian formulation

$$\frac{d}{dt}\left(\frac{\partial L(q,\dot{q})}{\partial \dot{q}_i}\right) - \frac{\partial L(q,\dot{q})}{\partial q_i} = \tau_i - D(q,\dot{q})\dot{q}, \; i = 1,...,n \tag{6}$$

where $L(q,\dot{q}) = T(q,\dot{q}) - V(q)$ is the Lagrangian function with $T(q,\dot{q})$ as the kinetic energy and $V(q)$ as the potential energy. The bending angles of each segment are taken as generalized position coordinates.

Denoting the position of the soft robotic segments as X_1 and X_2 and denoting the bending stiffness of each segment as $k_1(s)$ and $k_2(s)$ yields

$$T(q,\dot{q}) = \frac{1}{2}\int_0^1 \dot{X_1}^\top m\dot{X}_1\, ds + \frac{1}{2}\int_0^1 \dot{X_2}^\top m\dot{X}_2\, ds \tag{7}$$

$$V(q) = -mg\left(\int_0^1 [1 \;\; 0]X_1\, ds + \int_0^1 [1 \;\; 0]X_2\, ds\right) + \int_0^1 k_1(s)\, ds\, q_1 + \int_0^1 k_2(s)\, ds\, q_2 \tag{8}$$

The resulting dynamics equation is

$$M(q)\ddot{q} + C(q,\dot{q})\dot{q} + G(q) + D(q,\dot{q})\dot{q} + K(q) = \tau, \tag{9}$$

where $q, G, K, \tau, \in \mathbb{R}^n$ are the angles, vector of gravity forces, vector of elastic forces, and control input, while $M, C, D \in \mathbb{R}^{n\times n}$ are the inertia matrix, the matrix of Coriolis and Centrifugal forces, and the physical damping matrix, which are detailed below. The complete expressions of the matrices M, C, G are given in Appendix A.

Inertia Matrix. The inertia matrix of a mechanical system is positive definite. Considering the model as a thin rod with uniform mass distribution, the inertia matrix can be written as

$$M(q) = \int_0^1 J^\top(q,s)\begin{bmatrix} mI & 0 \\ 0 & 0 \end{bmatrix} J(q,s)\, ds, \tag{10}$$

where J is the Jacobian of the forward kinematics mapping. Alternatively, extracting the factor multiplied by $\ddot{q}$ in the Euler–Lagrangian Equation (6) with $\tau = 0$ yields the inertia matrix (10).

Coriolis and Centrifugal Matrix. The Coriolis matrix is not unique for the same inertia matrix, and the proposed model uses Christoffel symbols of the first kind [32], that is

$$c_{kj} = \sum_{i=1}^{n} \Gamma_{ijk}(q)\dot{q}_i, \tag{11}$$

where

$$\Gamma_{ijk} = \frac{1}{2}\left\{\frac{\partial m_{kj}}{\partial q_i} + \frac{\partial m_{ki}}{\partial q_j} - \frac{\partial m_{ij}}{\partial q_k}\right\}. \tag{12}$$

Gravitational Torque. The gravitational torque can be calculated directly as in [5], that is

$$G(q,\phi) = -mg\left(\int_0^1 J(s,q)\,ds\right)^\top \begin{bmatrix}\cos(\phi)\\ \sin(\phi)\\ 0\end{bmatrix}. \tag{13}$$

In addition, the gravitational torque can be obtained by the known inertia matrices and Coriolis matrix via the Euler–Lagrangian Equation (6), which yields (13).

Stiffness and Damping. The elasticity and damping of soft robots mainly depend on the Young's modulus and the energy dissipation of the material. Thus the model considers the elasticity and damping of the system to be decoupled, without each segment affecting the other. This yields stiffness and damping matrices that are diagonal and positive definite. Assuming that the manipulator is characterized by uniform elasticity and damping, the stiffness matrix is diagonal and the elastic force is

$$K(q) = \mathrm{diag}(k(q_i))q, \tag{14}$$

where $k(q)$ is the stiffness coefficient. The damping matrix $D(q,\dot{q})$ is diagonal and contains the damping coefficient for each segment, that is $D(q,\dot{q}) = \mathrm{diag}(d(q_i,\dot{q}_i))$.

3. Controller Design in Configuration Space

This section contains the main contribution of this work, which is the implementation of robust and adaptive control techniques for the CC model proposed. The derivation of the control methods is inspired by [32,33].

3.1. Feedback Linearization

Employing an *inverse dynamics control* [33], that is

$$\tau = M(q)a + C(q,\dot{q})\dot{q} + G(q) + D(q,\dot{q})\dot{q} + K(q), \tag{15}$$

where $q = [q_1\ q_2 \ldots q_i]^\top$, yields a linear decoupled closed-loop system

$$\ddot{q} = a, \tag{16}$$

where a is the desired acceleration used as a control input (i.e., commonly referred to as "outer loop control"; see [33]). The linearly decoupled system (16) allows each q_i to be independently controlled.

Denoting the reference position as q^d and the position error as $\tilde{q} = q - q^d$, respectively, and aiming for a closed-loop system representative of the second-order system, that is

$$\ddot{\tilde{q}} + k_d\,\dot{\tilde{q}} + k_p\,\tilde{q} = 0, \tag{17}$$

where $k_d \succ 0, k_p \succ 0 \in \mathbb{R}^{n\times n}$ are positive definite matrices, the outer-loop control is designed as

$$a = \ddot{q}^d - k_d(\dot{q} - \dot{q}^d) - k_p(q - q^d). \tag{18}$$

3.2. Robust Feedback Linearization

The control law (18) is applicable if the model does not have uncertainty. However, a robust controller is required because of the approximations intrinsic to the soft manipulator model. Denote the estimates (i.e., reasonable "guesses" from prior information) of M, C, G, D, and K as $\hat{M}$, $\hat{C}$, $\hat{G}$, $\hat{D}$, and $\hat{K}$. The difference between nominal and real values is denoted as $\tilde{(\cdot)} = \hat{(\cdot)} - (\cdot)$. The new control law can be designed as

$$\tau = \hat{M}(q)a + \hat{C}(q,\dot{q})\dot{q} + \hat{G}(q) + \hat{D}(q,\dot{q})\dot{q} + \hat{K}(q). \tag{19}$$

The linear closed-loop system (16) cannot be obtained in this case, and the model uncertainty η has to be taken into account. Substituting (19) into (9) yields the linearized system

$$\ddot{q} = a + \eta(q, \dot{q}, \ddot{q}), \tag{20}$$

where

$$\eta(q, \dot{q}, \ddot{q}) = (M^{-1}\hat{M} - I)a + M^{-1}(\tilde{C}\dot{q} + \tilde{G} + \tilde{D}\dot{q} + \tilde{K}). \tag{21}$$

The following assumptions are introduced for controller design purposes.

Assumption 1. *The model uncertainty has a known bound $\rho(q, \dot{q}, \ddot{q}) > 0$, that is*

$$\|\eta(q, \dot{q}, \ddot{q})\| < \rho. \tag{22}$$

Assumption 2. *The estimate of the inertia matrix satisfies the assumption*

$$\|M^{-1}(q)\hat{M}(q) - I\| \leq 1. \tag{23}$$

Remark 1. *If Assumption 1 is violated, the controller proposed in Section 3.3 is unable to provide a compensation large enough to cancel the uncertainty, resulting in a steady-state error. If Assumption 2 is violated, the measurement uncertainty fails to meet the bounded condition, with adverse effects on stability and performance [34].*

To compensate for the uncertainty η, an additional control signal δa is introduced alongside a, that is

$$a = \ddot{q}^d - k_d(\dot{q} - \dot{q}^d) - k_p(q - q^d) + \delta a, \tag{24}$$

yielding the closed-loop system

$$\ddot{\tilde{q}} + k_d\dot{\tilde{q}} + k_p\tilde{q} + \delta u + \eta = 0. \tag{25}$$

Defining the error vector $e = \begin{bmatrix} e_1 \\ e_2 \end{bmatrix} = \begin{bmatrix} \tilde{q} \\ \dot{\tilde{q}} \end{bmatrix}$, the closed-loop system (25) in state space yields

$$\dot{e} = \begin{bmatrix} 0 & I \\ -k_p & -k_d \end{bmatrix} e + \begin{bmatrix} 0 \\ I \end{bmatrix} (\delta a + \eta), \tag{26}$$

with $A = \begin{bmatrix} 0 & I \\ -k_p & -k_d \end{bmatrix}$ and $B = \begin{bmatrix} 0 \\ I \end{bmatrix}$.

3.3. Sliding-Mode Control and Lyapunov Redesign

According to the state-space Equation (26), a sliding surface is designed as

$$s = \{(\tilde{q}, \dot{\tilde{q}}) : \dot{\tilde{q}} + \lambda\tilde{q} = 0\}, \tag{27}$$

with a positive definite parameter λ. On the sliding surface, the evolution of the trajectories is governed by the first-order dynamics $\dot{\tilde{q}} = -\lambda\tilde{q}$, which exponentially converges to $\tilde{q} = 0$. The time derivative of the sliding variable is

$$\dot{s} = \dot{e}_2 + \lambda\dot{e}_1 = -k_p e_1 - k_d e_2 + \lambda e_2 + (\delta a + \eta). \tag{28}$$

Setting $k_p = \lambda^2$ and $k_d = 2\lambda$, yields

$$\dot{s} = -\lambda^2 e_1 - \lambda e_2 + (\delta a + \eta) = -\lambda s + (\delta a + \eta). \tag{29}$$

Defining the Lyapunov function candidate $V = \frac{1}{2}s^\top s$ and computing its time derivative along the trajectories of the closed-loop system (29) yields

$$\dot{V} = s^\top \dot{s} = s^\top(-\lambda s + (\delta a + \eta)) = -\lambda||s||^2 + s^\top(\delta a + \eta). \tag{30}$$

Setting the auxiliary control input as

$$\delta a = -\rho \frac{s}{||s||} \tag{31}$$

and substituting it into $\dot{V}$ yields

$$\begin{aligned} \dot{V} =& -\lambda||s||^2 - \rho||s|| + s^\top \eta \\ \leq& -\lambda||s||^2 - \rho||s|| + ||s||\,||\eta|| \\ =& -\lambda||s||^2 - (\rho - ||\eta||)||s|| \leq 0. \end{aligned} \tag{32}$$

Consequently, the trajectory of the closed-loop system converges to the sliding surface in finite time (detailed proof can be found in Section 14.1 of [35]) and then converges to $\tilde{q} = 0$ exponentially.

Since the SMC control law is discontinuous, it can lead to a chattering phenomenon in the presence of delays [36]. A continuous control law can mitigate this issue. To this end, the SMC controller can be derived from a slightly different perspective, which is known as the Lyapunov redesign. Introducing the matrix A Hurwitz, define the Lyapunov function

$$V = e^\top Pe, \tag{33}$$

where $P = P^\top > 0$ solves the Riccati equation

$$A^\top P + PA + Q = 0, \tag{34}$$

with any given positive definite $Q = Q^\top \succ 0$. Computing the time derivative of (33) yields

$$\dot{V} = -e^\top Qe + 2e^\top PB(\delta a + \eta). \tag{35}$$

The control law δa for the Lyapunov redesign technique is selected as

$$\delta a = \begin{cases} -\rho \dfrac{B^\top Pe}{||B^\top Pe||} & \text{if } ||B^\top Pe|| > \epsilon, \\ -\dfrac{\rho}{\epsilon} B^\top Pe & \text{if } ||B^\top Pe|| \leq \epsilon. \end{cases} \tag{36}$$

The control laws for the Lyapunov redesign and SMC have a similar form since $B^\top Pe$ corresponds to the sliding-mode surface s. The key difference is the continuity of the control law (36), which reduces the occurrence of chattering. When the error tolerance ϵ is set to 0, the controller (33) reduces to the SMC control law (31). A visual comparison between the two control laws is shown in Figure 4.

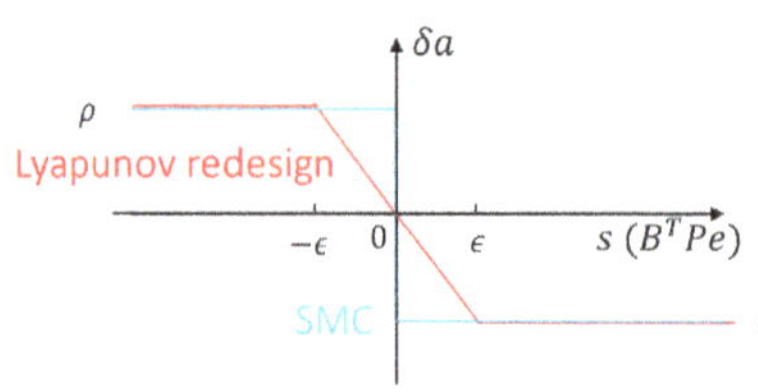

Figure 4. Graphical comparison of the SMC control law (31) and the Lyapunov redesign (36).

3.4. Adaptive Control

Adaptive control of robots is based on the linearity property with respect to the parameters of multi-link robots (also known as "linear parametrization property"), according to which the dynamics model (9) can be written as

$$M(q)\ddot{q} + C(q,\dot{q})\dot{q} + G(q) + D(q,\dot{q})\dot{q} + K(q) = Y(q,\dot{q},\ddot{q})\Theta, \tag{37}$$

where $Y(q,\dot{q},\ddot{q})$ is the $(n \times l)$-dimensional regressor and $\Theta \in \mathbb{R}^l$ is the vector of unknown parameters. The following assumption is introduced for controller design purposes.

Assumption 3. *The vector of unknown parameters* Θ *is constant.*

The control law (19) can be written in the form

$$\tau = \hat{M}(q)a + \hat{C}(q,\dot{q})\dot{q} + \hat{G}(q) + \hat{D}(q,\dot{q})\dot{q} + \hat{K}(q) = Y(q,\dot{q},\ddot{q})\hat{\Theta}, \tag{38}$$

where $\hat{\Theta}$ is the vector of nominal parameters. However, this approach has drawbacks in practice as the acceleration is often difficult to measure accurately. Therefore, a passivity-based adaptive control approach that avoids the measurement of acceleration is employed in this section. Passivity-based control takes advantage of the passivity property of mechanical systems, according to which the control torque τ and the velocity $\dot{q}$ constitute a passive pair; see [37]. The control law is chosen as

$$\tau = \hat{M}(q)a + \hat{C}(q,\dot{q})v + \hat{G}(q) + \hat{D}(q,\dot{q})v + \hat{K}(q) - Fr, \tag{39}$$

where

$$\begin{aligned} v &\triangleq \dot{q}^d - \Lambda\tilde{q}, \\ a &\triangleq \dot{v} = \ddot{q}^d - \Lambda\dot{\tilde{q}}, \\ r &\triangleq \dot{q} - v = \dot{\tilde{q}} + \Lambda\tilde{q}, \end{aligned} \tag{40}$$

with diagonal and positive definite matrices Λ and F representing the tuning parameters; see [38]. Substituting the control law (39) into (9) yields

$$M\dot{r} + Cr + Dr + Fr = Y(q,\dot{q},a,v)\tilde{\Theta}. \tag{41}$$

To ensure convergence of the error e to zero and boundedness of the parameter estimates, the update law for the vector $\hat{\Theta}$ is designed by choosing the Lyapunov function

$$V = \frac{1}{2}r^\top M(q)r + \tilde{q}^\top \Lambda K \tilde{q} + \frac{1}{2}\tilde{\Theta}^\top \Gamma \tilde{\Theta}. \tag{42}$$

Computing the time derivative of (42) along the trajectories of the closed-loop system (41), while recalling the skew-symmetry property of mechanical systems, that is $r^\top(\dot{M} - 2C)r = 0$, yields

$$\dot{V} = \tilde{\Theta}^\top (Y^\top r + \Gamma\dot{\hat{\Theta}}) - \begin{bmatrix}\tilde{q} & \dot{\tilde{q}}\end{bmatrix}^\top \begin{bmatrix}\Lambda^\top F \Lambda & \Lambda D \\ D\Lambda & F\end{bmatrix} \begin{bmatrix}\tilde{q} \\ \dot{\tilde{q}}\end{bmatrix}. \tag{43}$$

The update law for the vector $\hat{\Theta}$ is selected as

$$\dot{\hat{\Theta}} = -\Gamma^{-1} Y^\top r, \tag{44}$$

which substituted into (43) yields $\dot{V} \leq 0$, provided that the matrix $\begin{bmatrix}\Lambda^\top F \Lambda & \Lambda D \\ D\Lambda & F\end{bmatrix}$ is positive definite. Employing a standard convergence argument in adaptive control based on Barbalat's Lemma, it follows that the error vector converges to zero asymptotically.

4. Simulation Results

4.1. Single-Segment Soft Manipulator

Numerical simulations have been performed in MATLAB using the following parameters that are based on the estimated experimental data: length $L = 56 \times 10^{-3}$ m, mass $m = 6 \times 10^{-3}$ kg, gravitational acceleration $g = 9.81$ m/s^2, singularity tolerance tol $= 0.01$, elastic modulus $k = 0.015$ Nm/rad, and damping coefficient $D = 0.001$ Nms/rad.

Note that the single-segment soft robot has only one degree of freedom on the bending plane. To better visualize the performance of the controller, two reference trajectories, $q^d = \frac{\pi}{6}$ and $q^d = \frac{\pi}{6}\sin(0.5t) + \frac{\pi}{3}$, have been used. The simulation results are shown in Figures 5 and 6. All controllers perform well if there are no model uncertainties. However, the control input of the SMC law (31) is persistently switching with $\rho = 30$.

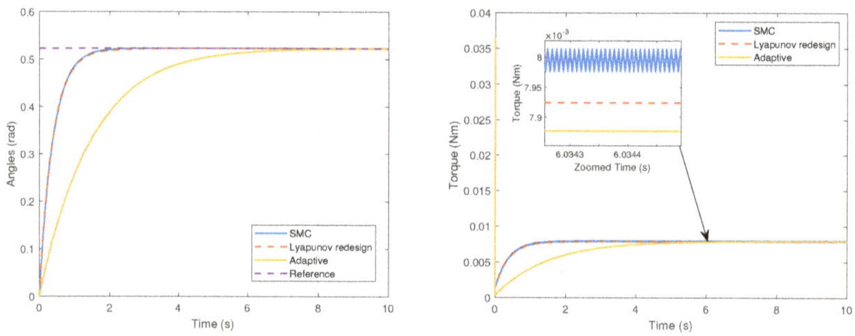

(**a**) Time history of q (**b**) Time history of τ

Figure 5. Step response for ideal single-segment soft manipulator.

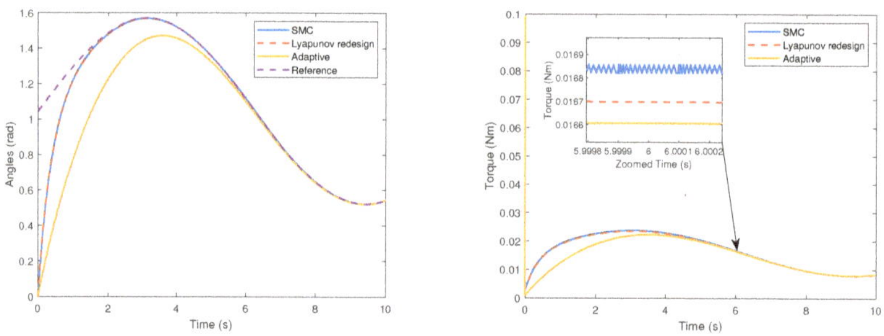

(**a**) Time history of q (**b**) Time history of τ

Figure 6. Sine response for ideal single-segment soft manipulator.

After introducing a model uncertainty of 2% on K, the adaptive control still tracks the signal perfectly, but the SMC and Lyapunov redesign both lead to non-zero steady-state errors; see Figures 7 and 8. From the results, it can be seen that the control laws of SMC and Lyapunov redesign do not switch. This is due to the fact that the switching gain ρ does not accurately estimate the upper bound of the uncertainty, violating Assumption 1.

After increasing the switching gain ρ to 300 such that Assumption 1 is verified (see results in Figures 9 and 10), the SMC control (31) and the Lyapunov redesign (36) yield improved performance. When the output q approaches the reference signal q^d, the control input of the SMC (31) begins chattering, which the Lyapunov redesign (36) effectively avoids at the cost of a tiny steady-state error. Additionally, since the model uncertainty η is a function of t, q, and $\dot{q}$, it is difficult in practice to select a sufficiently large ρ a priori such that $||\eta|| < \rho$ at all times.

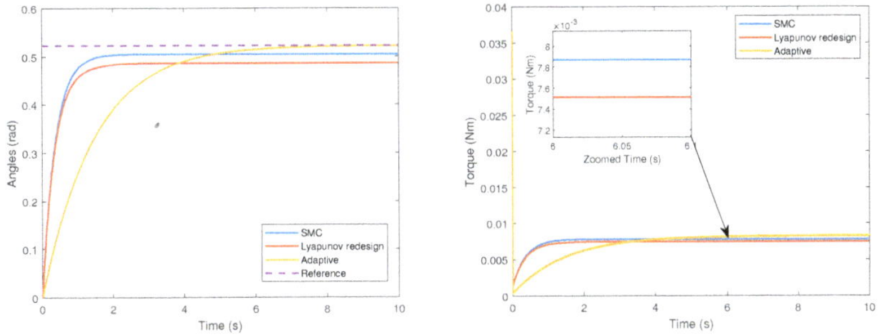

(**a**) Time history of q (**b**) Time history of τ

Figure 7. Step response for single-segment manipulator with model uncertainties and $\rho = 30$.

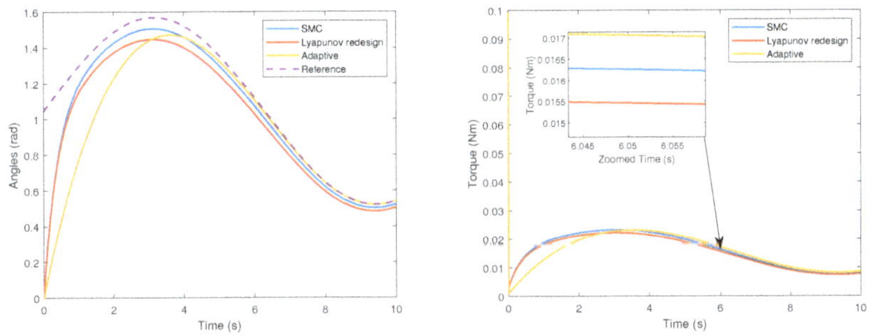

(**a**) Time history of q (**b**) Time history of τ

Figure 8. Sine response for single-segment manipulator with model uncertainties and $\rho = 30$.

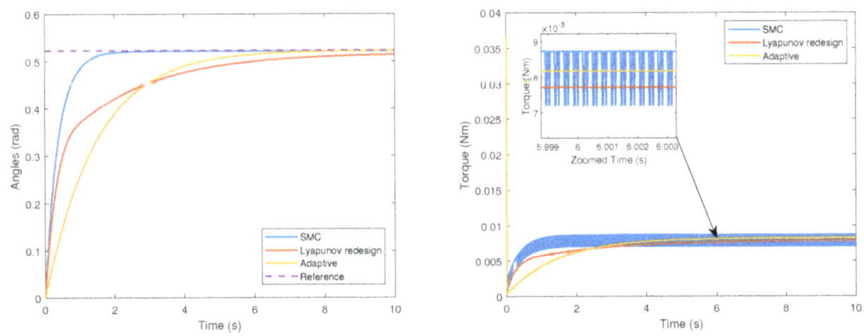

(**a**) Time history of q (**b**) Time history of τ

Figure 9. Step response for single-segment manipulator with model uncertainties and $\rho = 300$.

The time history of $\hat{\Theta}$ for the adaptive controller is illustrated in Figure 10c for completeness. The Integral Absolute Error (IAE) for each controller is shown in Table 1. The SMC performs best in terms of tracking error but it causes chattering, while the Lyapunov redesign avoids chattering at the cost of a steady-state error. With the tuning parameters used, the slow convergence of the adaptive controller leads to a larger IAE.

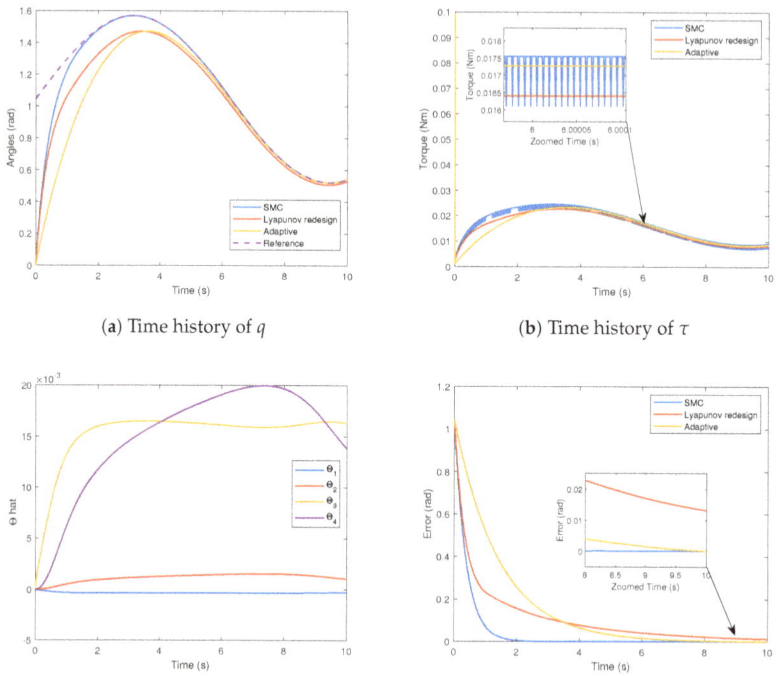

(a) Time history of q

(b) Time history of τ

(c) Time history of $\hat{\Theta}$ for adaptive control.

(d) Time history of errors

Figure 10. Sine response for single-segment manipulator with model uncertainties and $\rho = 300$.

Table 1. Integral of Absolute Error (IAE) with a discounting factor $\gamma = 0.5$ for a single-segment model.

Control Method	IAE
SMC	0.3120
Lyapunov Redesign	0.4732
Adaptive Control	0.7533

4.2. Two-Segment Soft Manipulator

The parameters of the two-segment manipulator have been set as follows: length $L = 28 \times 10^{-3}$ m, mass $m = 3 \times 10^{-3}$ kg, gravitational acceleration $g = 9.81$ m/s^2, singularity tolerance tol $= 0.01$, elastic modulus $k = 0.02$ Nm/rad, and damping coefficient $D = 0.001$ Nms/rad. The reference positions are $q^d = [\frac{\pi}{18}, \frac{\pi}{9}]^\top$ and $q^d = [\frac{\pi}{36}\sin(0.5t) + \frac{\pi}{18}, \frac{\pi}{18}\sin(0.5t) + \frac{\pi}{9}]^\top$

The simulation for the two-segment model yields similar results to the one-segment model(see Figures 11–16 and Table 2), where q_1 refers to the proximal segment and q_2 refers the distal one. The model uncertainty corresponds to 0.2% of K, while ρ is set to initially 30 and then increased to 500 so that Assumption 1 is verified.

Table 2. IAE with a discounting factor $\gamma = 0.5$ for two-segment model.

Control Method	IAE
SMC	0.2503
Lyapunov Redesign	0.2603
Adaptive Control	0.3845

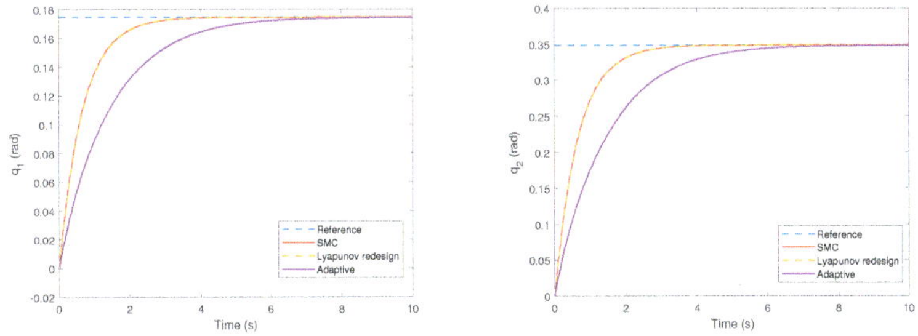

(a) Time history of q_1 (b) Time history of q_2

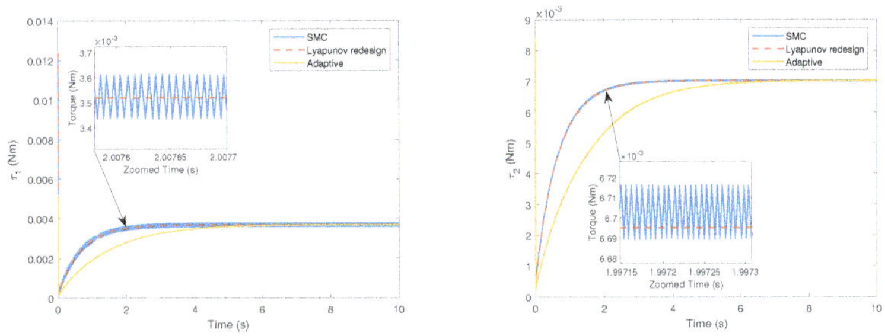

(c) Time history of τ_1 (d) Time history of τ_2

Figure 11. Step response for ideal two-segment manipulator.

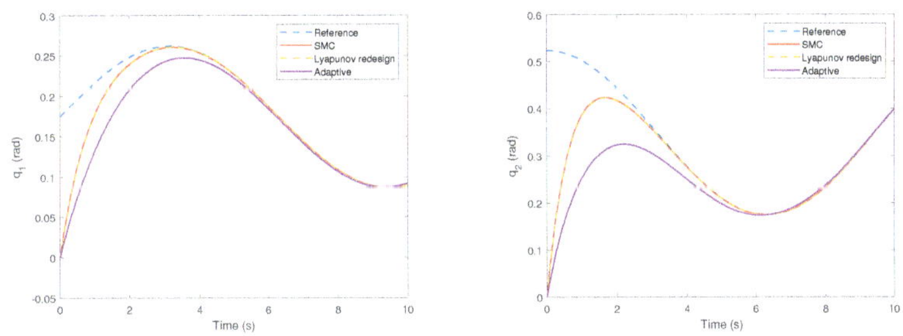

(a) Time history of q_1 (b) Time history of q_2

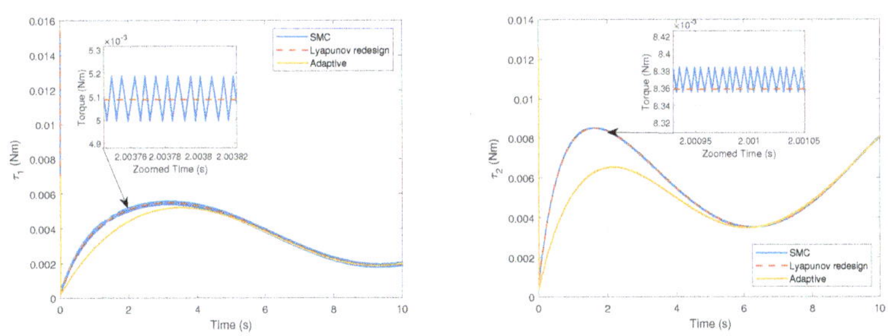

(c) Time history of τ_1 (d) Time history of τ_2

Figure 12. Sine response for ideal two-segment manipulator.

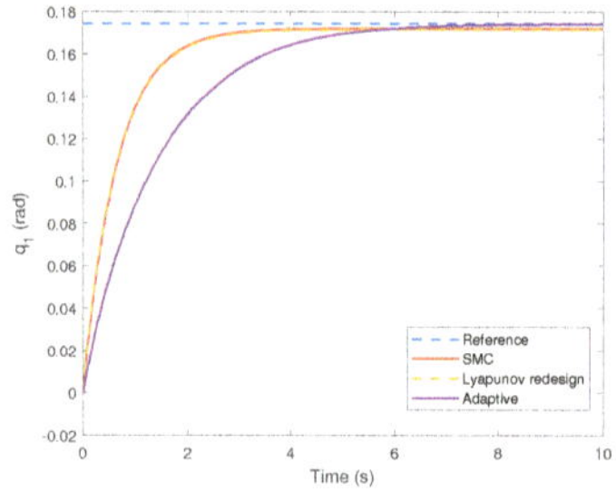

(**a**) Time history of q_1

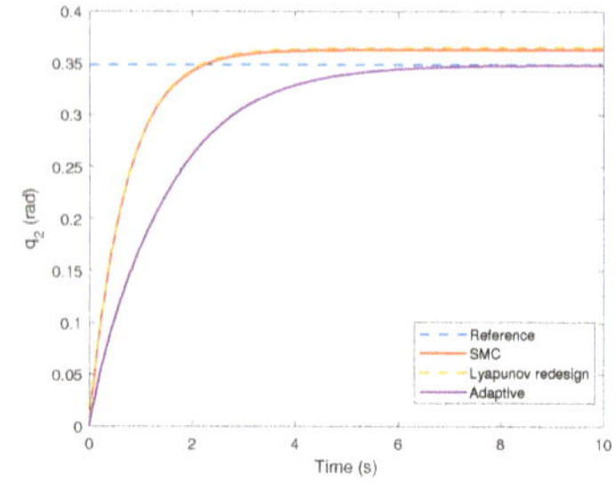

(**b**) Time history of q_2

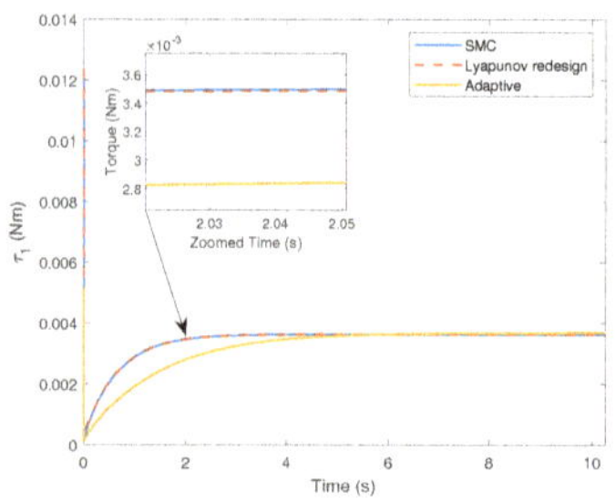

(**c**) Time history of τ_1

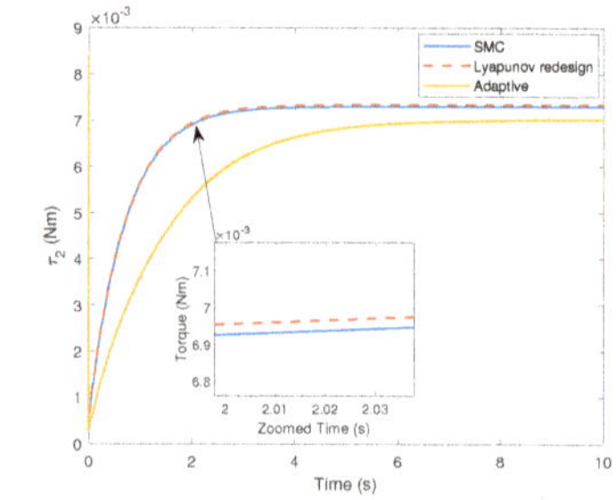

(**d**) Time history of τ_2

Figure 13. Step response for two-segment manipulator with model uncertainties and $\rho = 30$.

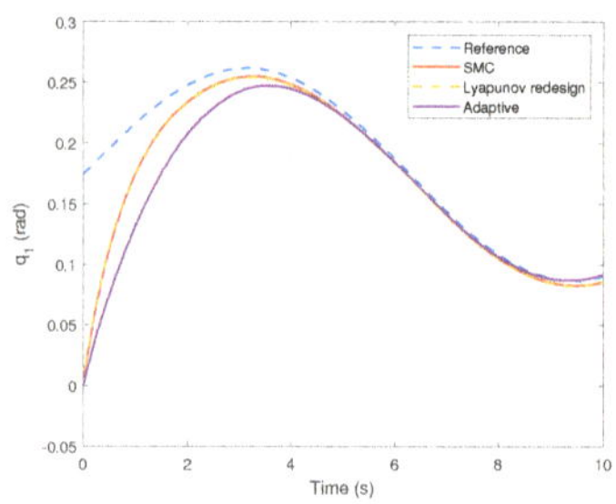

(**a**) Time history of q_1

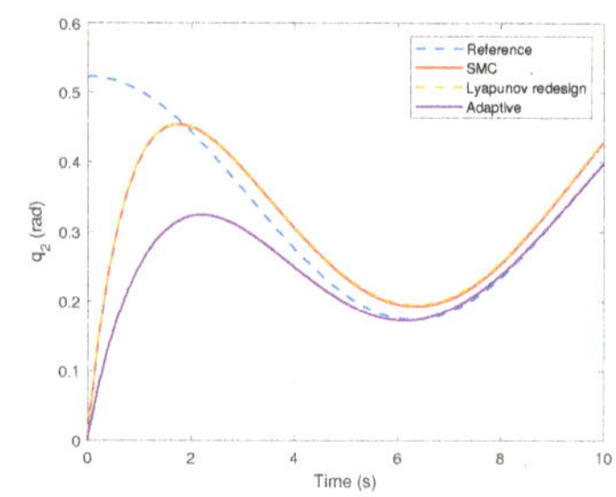

(**b**) Time history of q_2

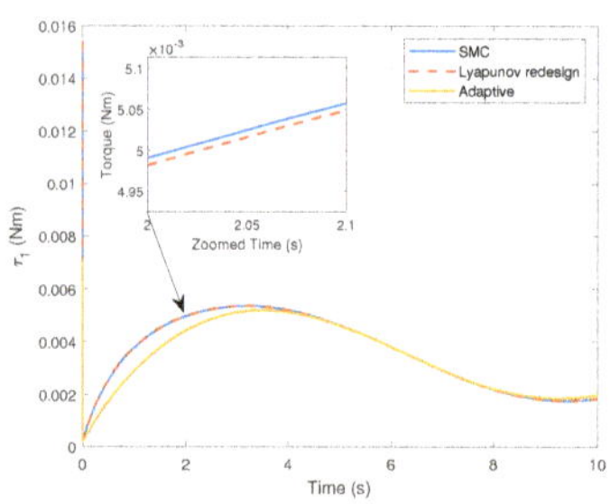

(**c**) Time history of τ_1

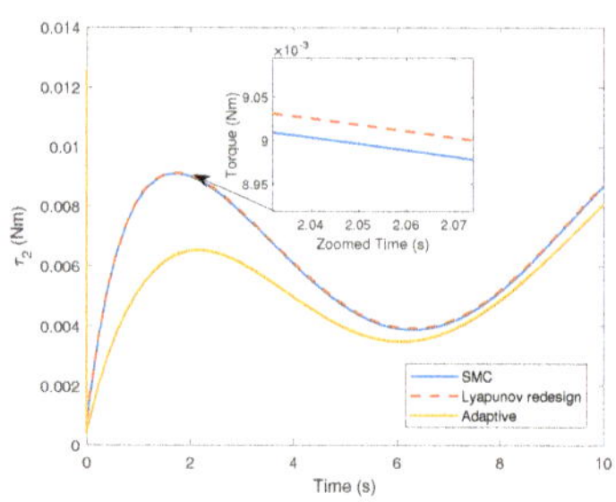

(**d**) Time history of τ_2

Figure 14. Sine response for two-segment manipulator with model uncertainties and $\rho = 30$.

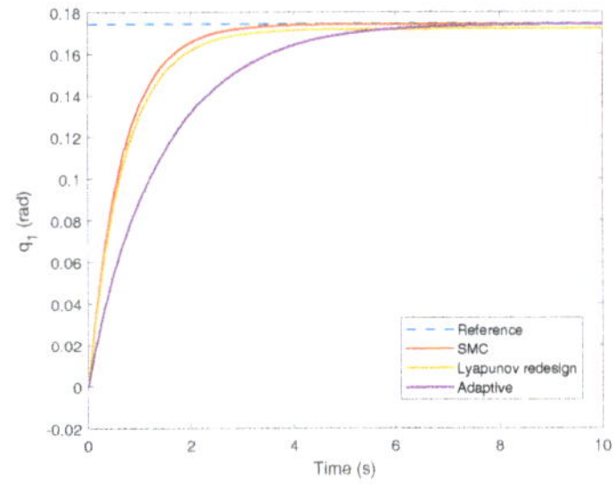

(**a**) Time history of q_1

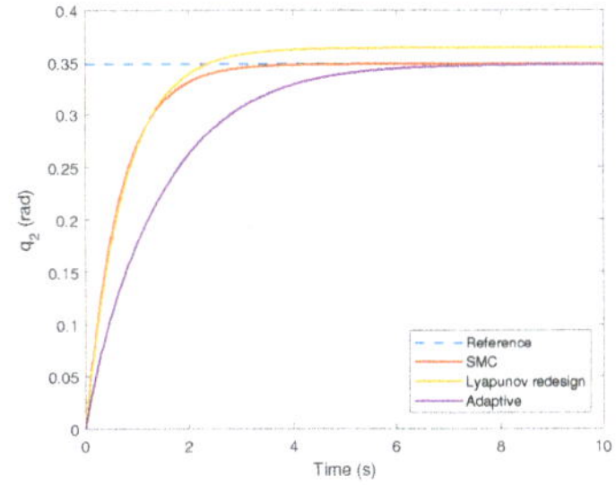

(**b**) Time history of q_2

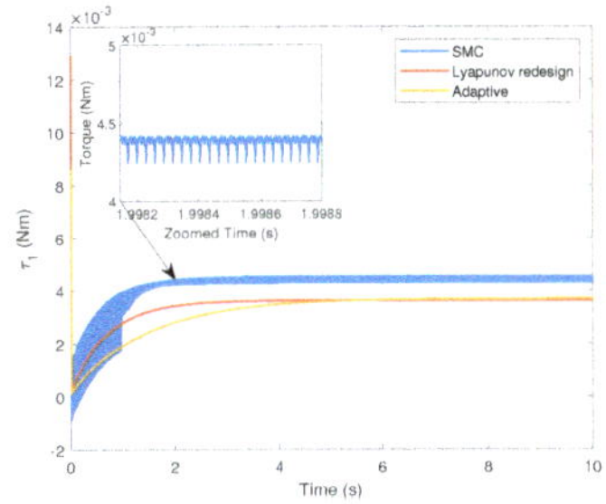

(**c**) Time history of τ_1

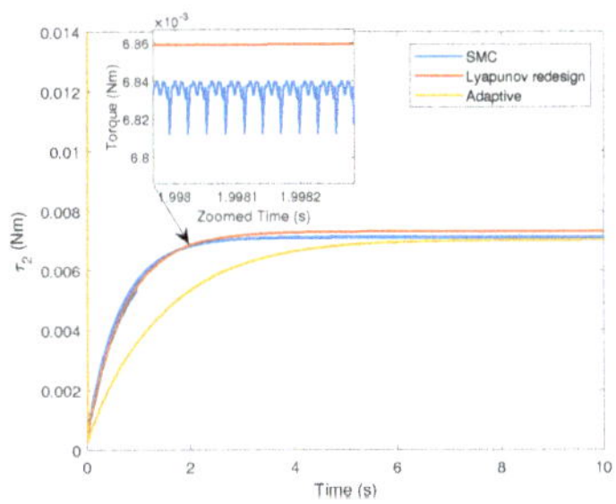

(**d**) Time history of τ_2

Figure 15. Step response for two-segment manipulator with model uncertainties and $\rho = 500$.

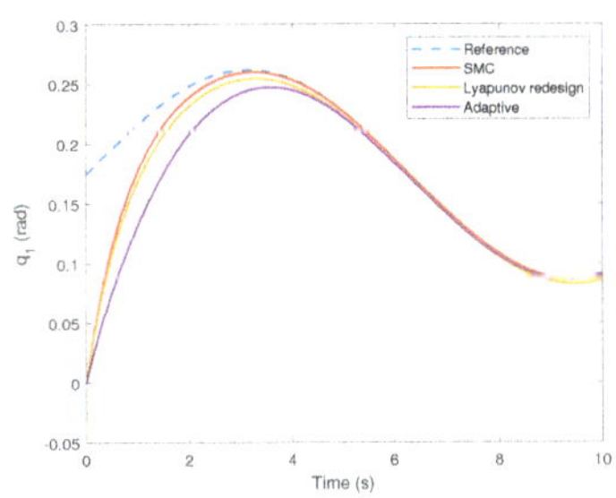

(**a**) Time history of q_1

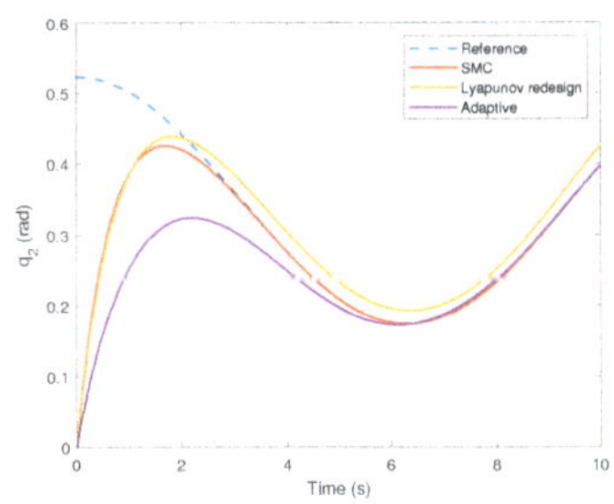

(**b**) Time history of q_2

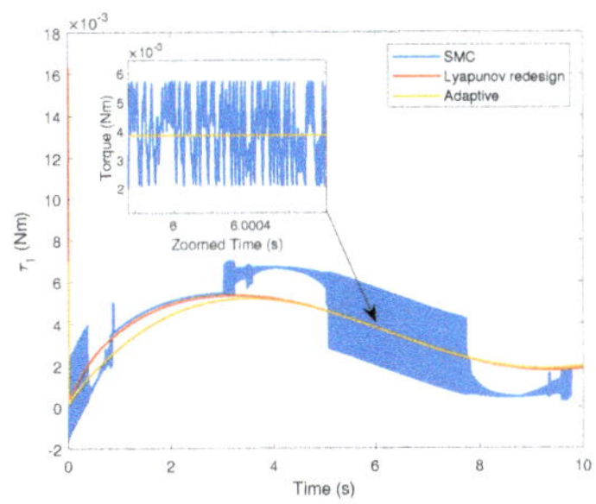

(**c**) Time history of τ_1

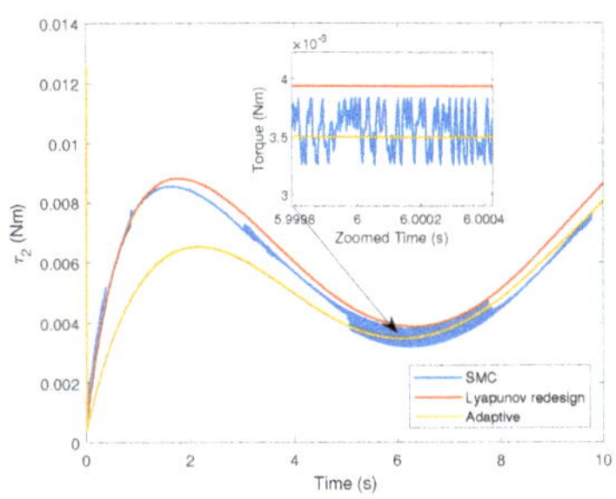

(**d**) Time history of τ_2

Figure 16. Sine response for two-segment manipulator with model uncertainties and $\rho = 500$.

Based on the simulation results, the SMC controller (31) gives the fastest response, provided that Assumptions 1 and 2 are satisfied. However, the discontinuous control law can result in chattering, which becomes a challenge when the sampling step is not sufficiently small or when there is a delay in the system. Instead, the Lyapunov redesign (36) avoids chattering, but at the cost of steady-state error. This is because smaller errors in the range $[-\epsilon, \epsilon]$ do not result in a sufficient control action to compensate for uncertainties. The adaptive controller (39) converges slowly to the reference signal due to its asymptotic stability properties, without requiring prior knowledge of the disturbance bound. In addition, the adaptive control law is smooth, which is beneficial in practical applications. The IAE for each controller is shown in Table 2.

5. Experimental Results

5.1. Hardware Setup

Six pressure regulators (Tecno Basic, Hoerbiger, Schongau, Germany) are used to actuate two three-chamber soft manipulators. Two electromagnetic (EM) sensors (Aurora NDI, Waterloo, ON, Canada) are used to measure the bending angle of each segment, q_1 and q_2. The hardware setup is illustrated in Figure 17. All devices are connected to a workstation using serial links, and the controllers are implemented in MATLAB. Due to the small movement of the individual segments that is susceptible to measurement errors, experiments for the single-segment case are realized by supplying the same air pressure to both segments (i.e., the two segments behave effectively as one). Only the sensor at the end-effector is used in such a case. The sensor arrangement is shown in Figure 18.

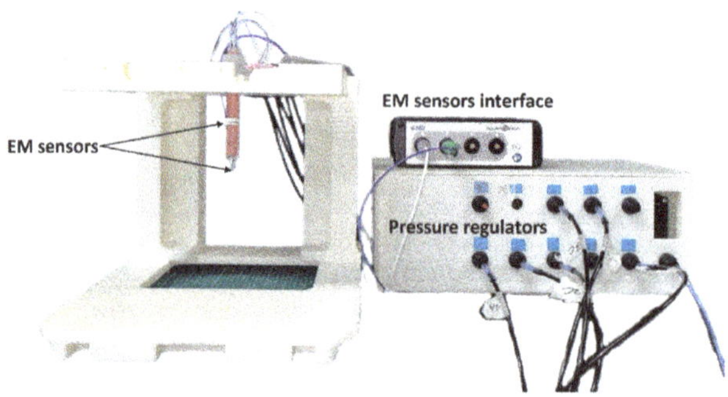

Figure 17. Image of the experimental setup.

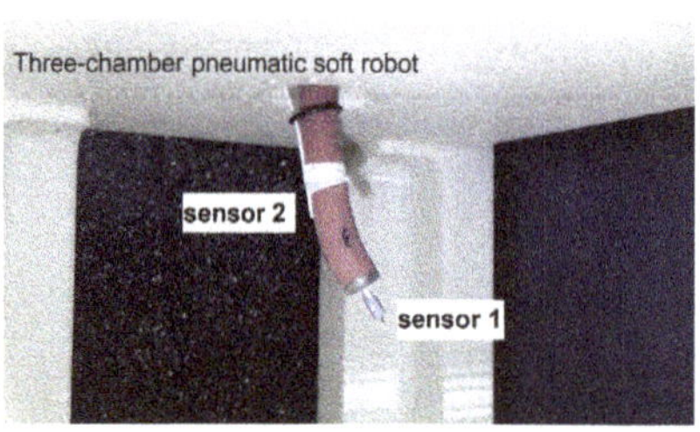

Figure 18. Detailed view of soft robotic manipulator.

The connection between different components is shown in Figure 19, where the controllers are the same as in the simulations.

Additional conversion factors, described below, are needed so that the physical quantities correspond to the model parameters in Section 2.2.

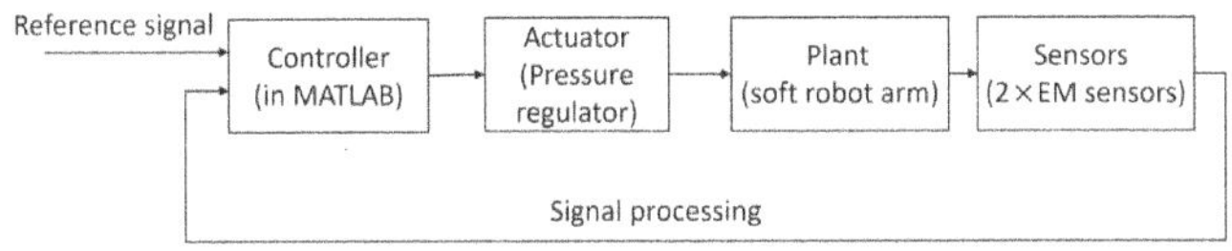

Figure 19. System integration diagram.

Reference frame calibration. This procedure is required since the soft manipulator may be installed with a slightly different orientation after each test. At the start of each experiment, one of the internal chambers of each segment is inflated such that the end-effector moves away from the rest position identifying the positive direction of the x-axis. The position of the end-effector at rest serves as a reference point, and the origin of the coordinate system is set above it at a distance L.

Velocity estimation. Since the EM sensor can only measure position and orientation, a high-pass filter $G(s) = \frac{s}{Ts+1}$ is used in the experiments to estimate angular velocity. This transfer function implies that the time derivative of the position is low-pass filtered to remove the high-frequency noise from the sensor. The sampling frequency of the sensor is around 20 Hz; therefore, frequencies above 10 Hz should be filtered out according to the Nyquist Sampling Theorem, that is $f = \frac{1}{2\pi T} < 10$.

Pneumatic actuation. The air pressure P_α required to produce the required torque has to be distributed among the three chambers to accomplish the control task. A cross-section of the chambers is shown in Figure 2b. If the original direction of the bending plane is set to the direction of the chamber C and the angle of the bending plane is set to α_0, then the relationship between the pressures in each chamber is

$$\begin{bmatrix} \cos\left(-\frac{2\pi}{3} - \alpha_d\right) & \cos\left(\frac{2\pi}{3} - \alpha_d\right) & \cos(-\alpha_d) \\ \sin\left(-\frac{2\pi}{3} - \alpha_d\right) & \sin\left(\frac{2\pi}{3} - \alpha_d\right) & \sin(-\alpha_d) \end{bmatrix} \begin{bmatrix} P_A \\ P_B \\ P_C \end{bmatrix} = \begin{bmatrix} P_\alpha \\ 0 \end{bmatrix}, \tag{45}$$

where the α_d is the angle between the desired bending plane and the original direction. The air pressures corresponding to each chamber P_A, P_B, and P_C are computed from the least squares solution of the Equation (45) and subsequently adding a translation in the Kernel $\begin{bmatrix} 1 & 1 & 1 \end{bmatrix}^\top$ direction to ensure that the pressures are positive and the minimum pressure is zero.

Safety considerations. To ensure that the experimental equipment is not damaged, the upper and lower pressure bounds for each chamber are set to 1.5 bar and 0. A pressure of 1.5 bar bends a segment by approximately 30 degrees without payload, and the reference signal has been set within this range. Considering that the proximal soft robotic segment is also affected by the gravity of the distal segment, smaller reference values q_d should be used for q_1.

Measured Parameters. The parameters for each segment are given in Table 3.

Table 3. Parameters in experiment.

Parameters	Length L (m)	Mass m (kg)	Diameter (m)
Values	28×10^{-3}	3×10^{-3}	10×10^{-3}

Elasticity and gravity. By slowly inflating a chamber, a relationship between pressure and bending angle can be obtained. This relationship reflects the effects of elasticity and gravity on the system for the specific setup; see Figure 20.

Relationship between bending moment and air pressure. A linear relationship exists between air pressure and bending moment. Pressure is assumed to act at the center of each chamber. The corresponding torque generated with an input air pressure of 1 bar is

$$\tau_0 = \text{pressure} \times \text{area} \times \text{distance}, \tag{46}$$

where the distance is measured between the center of pressure and the shaft center. The dynamics of the pressure regulator are neglected in this work since it is considerably faster than that of the soft manipulator. Substituting the experimental parameters gives $\tau_0 \approx 0.0065\ \mathrm{N \cdot m}$. In addition, since each chamber can only be inflated to produce a positive moment (i.e., the pressure regulators do not draw a vacuum), a negative moment needs to be realized by inflating two opposite chambers.

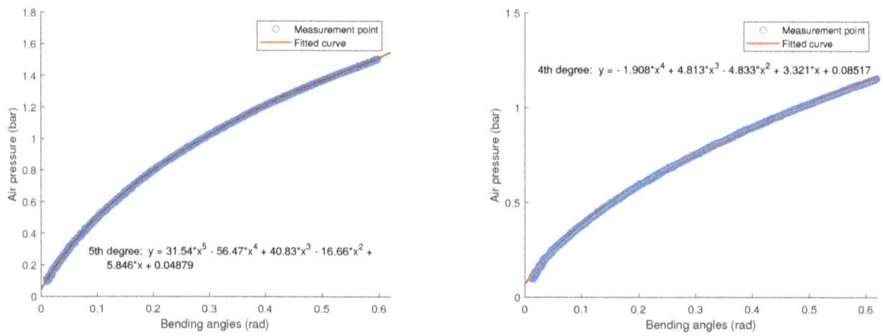

(**a**) Single segment (**b**) Two segments

Figure 20. Relationship between pressure and bending angles for (**a**) one segment, and (**b**) two segments.

5.2. Results for Single-Segment Manipulator

The parameters used for the single-segment experiment are shown in Table 4 and the results are shown in Figures 21–23. The reference position is $q_d = \frac{\pi}{6}$, which represents a step input for the bending angle.

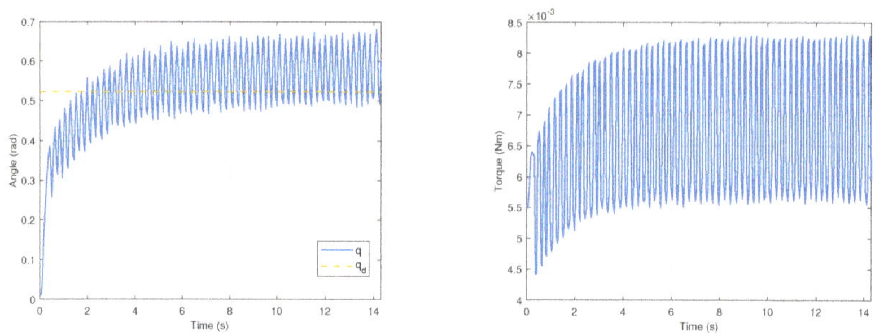

(**a**) Time history for the angle q. (**b**) Time history for control input τ.

Figure 21. Set-point regulation for single-segment manipulator with SMC (31).

Table 4. Controller parameters for single-segment experiment.

Parameters	Values
k_p	8000
k_d	5000
ρ	3000
k_p	8000
k_d	3000
ρ	1000
ϵ	0.01
Γ	0.15
Λ	0.7
F	0.1

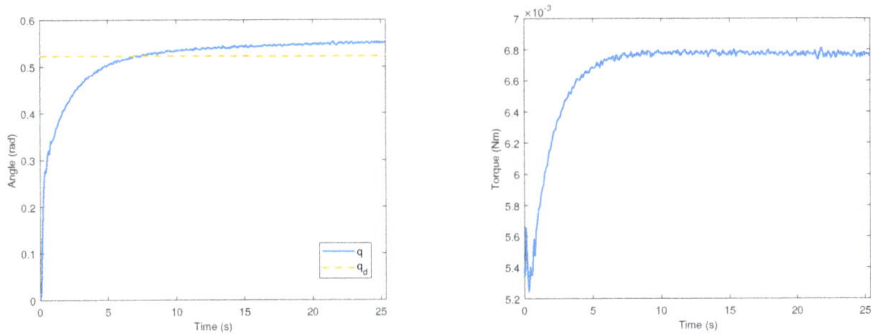

(**a**) Time history for the angle q. (**b**) Time history for control input τ.

Figure 22. Set-point regulation for single-segment manipulator with Lyapunov redesign controller (36).

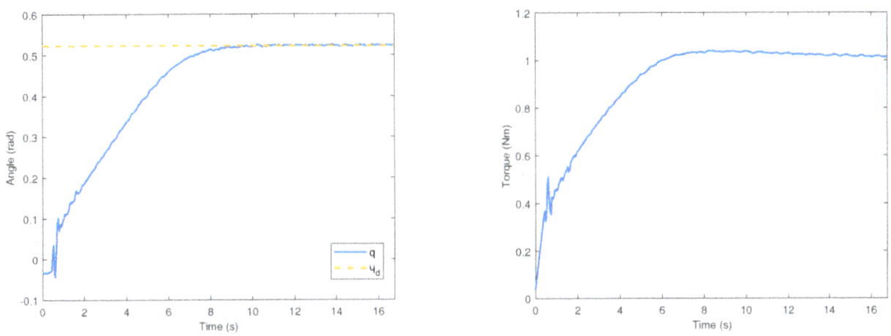

(**a**) Time history for the angle q. (**b**) Time history for control input τ.

Figure 23. Set-point regulation for single-segment manipulator with adaptive controller (44).

5.3. Results for Two-Segment Manipulator

The parameters used for the two-segment experiment are shown in Table 5 and the results are shown in Figures 24–26.

Table 5. Controller parameters for two-segment experiment.

Parameters	Values
k_p	$\begin{bmatrix} 15{,}000 & 0 \\ 0 & 20{,}000 \end{bmatrix}$
k_d	$\begin{bmatrix} 1 & 0 \\ 0 & 100 \end{bmatrix}$
ρ	3000
k_p	$\begin{bmatrix} 10{,}000 & 0 \\ 0 & 200{,}000 \end{bmatrix}$
k_d	$\begin{bmatrix} 1 & 0 \\ 0 & 100 \end{bmatrix}$
ρ	1100
ϵ	0.01
Γ	0.03
Λ	$\begin{bmatrix} 1.44 & 0 \\ 0 & 0.8 \end{bmatrix}$
F	0.01

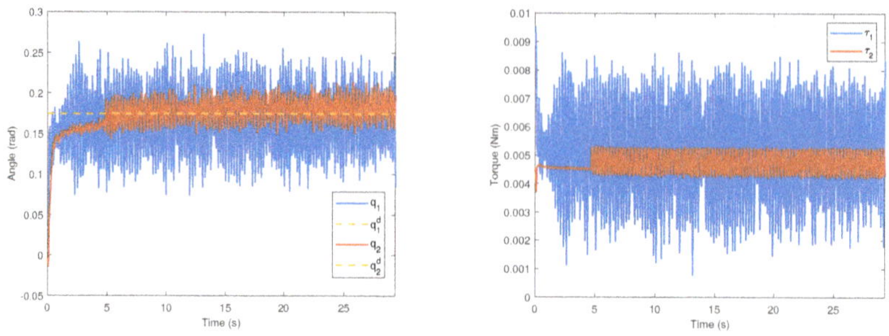

(**a**) Time history for the angles q_1 and q_2. (**b**) Time history for the control input τ_1 and τ_2.

Figure 24. Set-point regulation for two-segment manipulator with SMC (31).

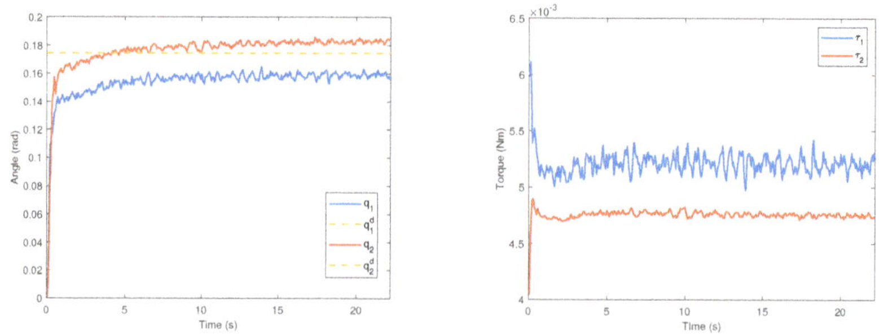

(**a**) Time history for the angles q_1 and q_2. (**b**) Time history for input τ_1 and τ_2.

Figure 25. Set-point regulation test for two-segment manipulator with Lyapunov redesign (36).

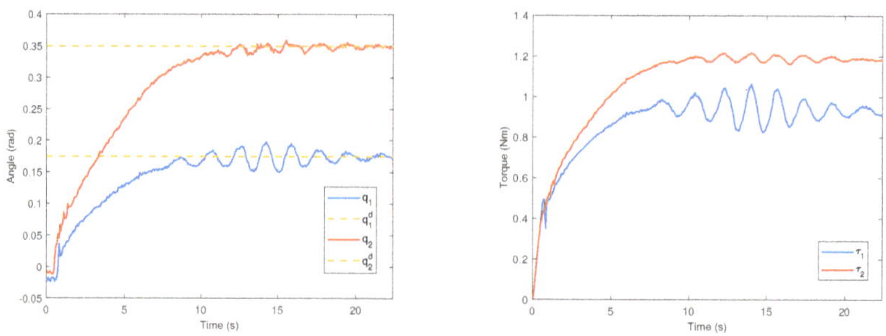

(**a**) Time history for the angles q_1 and q_2. (**b**) Time history for the control input τ_1 and τ_2.

Figure 26. Set-point regulation for two-segment manipulator with adaptive controller (44).

5.4. Discussion

The experimental results show that SMC (31) produces significant oscillations due to its discontinuous control law. This is a notable difference compared to the simulation results, and it is due to the delay in signal transmission resulting from the sensors and the frequency of pressure regulators. This issue degrades the performance of the SMC controller and poses a risk of damaging the experimental equipment. In contrast, the performances of the Lyapunov redesign (36) and the adaptive controller (44) are more consistent with the simulation results. However, the Lyapunov redesign suffers from a steady-state error that is difficult to eliminate, thus failing to achieve the regulation goal in the experiments. The adaptive control is able to track the reference position accurately, although it requires a longer time to reach steady-state with the chosen tuning parameters.

In spite of the positive results, the experimental study has highlighted a number of limitations related to the hardware, which are listed below.

Sensor inaccuracy. The measurements of the EM sensors contain noise, which has a large effect on the velocity estimation. In the experiments, the effect of velocity feedback can be minimized; however, this limits the performance of the system and may introduce oscillations.

Pressure regulator dead zone. The pressure regulators do not respond to very small pressure commands, so a perturbation tends to occur near an angle of zero in the experiments, and the relationship between air pressure and bending angle near zero cannot be measured accurately.

Material Fatigue. The material of the soft manipulator gradually loses its elasticity after repeated deformations. Although the relationship between pressure and bending angle was measured initially, follow-up experiments are required to continuously update this relationship. However, online measurements are unrealistic in real-world applications. Thus, adaptive control has a greater advantage in responding to changes in material properties because it does not require exact parameter values.

Material heterogeneity. The relationship between air pressure and the bending angle is asymmetric in different directions, which affects the control accuracy.

6. Conclusions

In this work, a CC model has been developed for an existing soft robotic manipulator, and model-based control methods for soft robots have been investigated. In particular, an SMC, a Lyapunov redesign controller, and a passivity-based adaptive controller have been designed. The simulations and the experiments show that the adaptive controller yields superior performance in the presence of uncertainties.

Nevertheless, the CC assumption is restrictive in practice, since it is not verified in the presence of payloads or contacts with the environment. Future work will investigate more accurate modeling methods such as PCC or Cosserat rod theory. Finally, predictive control will be investigated to further enhance the performance of soft robots in dynamic environments.

Author Contributions: Conceptualization, L.W., K.C. and E.F.; Methodology, L.W., K.C. and E.F.; Software, L.W. and K.C.; Validation, L.W., K.C. and E.F.; Formal Analysis, L.W. and K.C.; Investigation, L.W., K.C. and E.F.; Resources, L.W., K.C. and E.F.; Data Curation, L.W. and K.C.; Writing—Original Draft Preparation, L.W.; Writing—Review and Editing, L.W., K.C. and E.F.; Visualization, L.W.; Supervision, K.C. and E.F.; Project Administration, K.C. and E.F.; Funding Acquisition, E.F. All authors have read and agreed to the published version of the manuscript.

Funding: This work has been funded by the Engineering and Physical Sciences Research Council (grant EP/X033546/1).

Data Availability Statement: Data are available from the authors upon reasonable request.

Conflicts of Interest: The authors declare no conflicts of interest.

Abbreviations

The following abbreviations are used in this manuscript:

CC	Constant Curvature
FEM	Finite Element Model
MPC	Model Predictive Control
PCC	Piecewise Constant Curvature
PD	Proportional-derivative
PDE	Partial Differential Equation
SMC	Sliding-Mode Control

Appendix A. Expressions of M, C, G in (9)

Matrices M, C, G for single-segment soft manipulator

$$M = \frac{L^2\, m\, (6\, q - 12\, \sin(q) + q^3 + 6\, \cos(q)\, q)}{3\, q^5} \tag{A1}$$

$$C = -\frac{L^2\, m\, \dot{q}\, (12\, q - 30\, \sin(q) + q^3 + 18\, \cos(q)\, q + 3\, \sin(q)\, q^2)}{3\, q^6} \tag{A2}$$

$$G = -\frac{g\, m\, (2\, L\, \cos(q) - 2\, L + L\, \sin(q)\, q)}{q^3} \tag{A3}$$

Matrices M, C, G for two-segment soft manipulator

$$M = \begin{bmatrix} m_{11} & m_{12} \\ m_{21} & m_{22} \end{bmatrix}, \tag{A4}$$

where

$$\begin{aligned}
m_{11} = {} & \frac{12\, L^2\, m_1\, {q_1}^2\, {q_2}^5 + 12\, L^2\, m_2\, {q_1}^2\, {q_2}^5 + 12\, L^2\, m_2\, {q_1}^4\, {q_2}^3 + 2\, L^2\, m_1\, {q_1}^4\, {q_2}^5 + 6\, L^2\, m_2\, {q_1}^4\, {q_2}^5 - 12\, L^2\, m_2\, {q_1}^5 {q_2}^4}{6\, {q_1}^6\, {q_2}^5} \\
& + \frac{12\, L^2\, m_2\, {q_1}^6\, {q_2}^3 + 6\, {d_2}^2\, m_2\, {q_1}^6\, {q_2}^5 + 12\, L\, d_2\, m_2\, {q_1}^4\, {q_2}^5 + 12\, L\, d_2\, m_2\, {q_1}^6\, {q_2}^3 - 24\, L^2\, m_1\, q_1\, {q_2}^5\, \sin(q_1)}{6\, {q_1}^6\, {q_2}^5} \\
& + \frac{12\, L^2\, m_2\, {q_1}^4\, {q_2}^3\, \cos(q_1 + q_2) + 12\, L^2\, m_1\, {q_1}^2\, {q_2}^5\, \cos(q_1) - 12\, L^2\, m_2\, {q_1}^2\, {q_2}^5\, \cos(q_1) - 12\, L^2\, m_2\, {q_1}^4\, {q_2}^3\, \cos(q_1)}{6\, {q_1}^6\, {q_2}^5} \\
& + \frac{-12\, L^2\, m_2\, {q_1}^4\, {q_2}^3\, \cos(q_2) - 12\, L^2\, m_2\, {q_1}^3\, {q_2}^5\, \sin(q_1) + 12\, L^2\, m_2\, {q_1}^4\, {q_2}^4\, \sin(q_1) + 12\, L^2\, m_2\, {q_1}^5\, {q_2}^3\, \sin(q_2)}{6\, {q_1}^6\, {q_2}^5} \\
& + \frac{-12\, L^2\, m_2\, {q_1}^6\, {q_2}^2\, \sin(q_2) - 12\, L\, d_2\, m_2\, {q_1}^4\, {q_2}^5\, \cos(q_1) - 12\, L\, d_2\, m_2\, {q_1}^6\, {q_2}^3\, \cos(q_2)}{6\, {q_1}^6\, {q_2}^5}, \\
m_{12} = {} & \frac{3\, L^2\, m_2\, {q_1}^6\, {q_2}^3 - 12\, L^2\, m_2\, {q_1}^5\, {q_2}^2 - 6\, L^2\, m_2\, {q_1}^4\, {q_2}^3 + 6\, L^2\, m_2\, {q_1}^6\, q_2 - 6\, L\, d_2\, m_2\, {q_1}^6\, {q_2}^3 - 6\, L^2\, m_2\, {q_1}^6\, q_2\, \cos(q_2)}{6\, {q_1}^6\, {q_2}^5} \\
& + \frac{6\, L^2\, m_2\, {q_1}^4\, {q_2}^3\, \cos(q_1 + q_2) - 12\, L^2\, m_2\, {q_1}^4\, {q_2}^2\, \sin(q_1 + q_2) + 6\, L^2\, m_2\, {q_1}^4\, {q_2}^3\, \cos(q_1) - 6\, L^2\, m_2\, {q_1}^4\, {q_2}^3\, \cos(q_2)}{6\, {q_1}^6\, {q_2}^5} \\
& + \frac{12\, L^2\, m_2\, {q_1}^5\, {q_2}^2\, \cos(q_2) + 12\, L^2\, m_2\, {q_1}^4\, {q_2}^2\, \sin(q_1) + 12\, L^2\, m_2\, {q_1}^4\, {q_2}^2\, \sin(q_2) + 6\, L^2\, m_2\, {q_1}^5\, {q_2}^3\, \sin(q_2)}{6\, {q_1}^6\, {q_2}^5} \\
& + \frac{-6\, L^2\, m_2\, {q_1}^6\, {q_2}^2\, \sin(q_2) + 12\, L\, d_2\, m_2\, {q_1}^6\, {q_2}^2\, \sin(q_2) - 6\, L\, d_2\, m_2\, {q_1}^6\, {q_2}^3\, \cos(q_2)}{6\, {q_1}^6\, {q_2}^5}, \\
m_{21} = {} & m_{12}, \\
m_{22} = {} & \frac{2\, L^2\, m_2\, {q_1}^5\, {q_2}^3 - 24\, L^2\, m_2\, {q_1}^5\, \sin(q_2) + 12\, L^2\, m_2\, {q_1}^5\, q_2 + 12\, L^2\, m_2\, {q_1}^5\, q_2\, \cos(q_2)}{6\, {q_1}^5\, {q_2}^5};
\end{aligned}$$

$$C = \begin{bmatrix} c_{11} & c_{12} \\ c_{21} & c_{22} \end{bmatrix}, \tag{A5}$$

where

$$\begin{aligned}
c_{11} = {} & -\frac{L\, m}{3\, {q_1}^6\, {q_2}^4} (24\, L\, \dot{q}_1\, q_1\, {q_2}^4 + 6\, L\, \dot{q}_2\, {q_1}^4\, q_2 + 6\, L\, \dot{q}_2\, {q_1}^6\, q_2 + 6\, d_2\, \dot{q}_2\, {q_1}^6\, q_2 + 6\, L\, \dot{q}_1\, {q_1}^3\, {q_2}^2 + 4\, L\, \dot{q}_1\, {q_1}^3\, {q_2}^4 \\
& - 3\, L\, \dot{q}_1\, {q_1}^4\, {q_2}^3 - 3\, L\, \dot{q}_2\, {q_1}^5\, {q_2}^2 - 30\, L\, \dot{q}_1\, {q_2}^4\, \sin(q_1) - 9\, L\, \dot{q}_2\, {q_1}^6\, \sin(q_2) + 6\, d_2\, \dot{q}_1\, {q_1}^3\, {q_2}^4 + 6\, L\, \dot{q}_1\, q_1\, {q_2}^4\, \cos(q_1) \\
& - 6\, L\, \dot{q}_2\, {q_1}^4\, q_2\, \cos(q_1) - 6\, L\, \dot{q}_2\, {q_1}^4\, q_2\, \cos(q_2) + 3\, L\, \dot{q}_2\, {q_1}^6\, q_2\, \cos(q_2) + 6\, L\, \dot{q}_2\, {q_1}^5\, q_2\, \sin(q_2) - 6\, d_2\, \dot{q}_2\, {q_1}^6\, q_2\, \cos(q_2) \\
& + 6\, L\, \dot{q}_1\, {q_1}^3\, {q_2}^2\, \cos(q_1 + q_2) + 3\, L\, \dot{q}_1\, {q_1}^4\, {q_2}^2\, \sin(q_1 + q_2) + 3\, L\, \dot{q}_2\, {q_1}^4\, {q_2}^2\, \sin(q_1 + q_2) - 6\, L\, \dot{q}_1\, {q_1}^3\, {q_2}^2\, \cos(q_1) \\
& - 6\, L\, \dot{q}_1\, {q_1}^3\, {q_2}^2\, \cos(q_2) + 3\, L\, \dot{q}_1\, {q_1}^3\, {q_2}^4\, \cos(q_1) - 3\, L\, \dot{q}_1\, {q_1}^4\, {q_2}^3\, \cos(q_1) - 3\, L\, \dot{q}_2\, {q_1}^5\, {q_2}^2\, \cos(q_2) \\
& - 9\, L\, \dot{q}_1\, {q_1}^2\, {q_2}^4\, \sin(q_1) + 6\, L\, \dot{q}_1\, {q_1}^3\, {q_2}^3\, \sin(q_1) - 3\, L\, \dot{q}_1\, {q_1}^4\, {q_2}^2\, \sin(q_1) + 3\, L\, \dot{q}_1\, {q_1}^4\, {q_2}^2\, \sin(q_2) + 3\, L\, \dot{q}_2\, {q_1}^4\, {q_2}^2\, \sin(q_1) \\
& - 3\, L\, \dot{q}_2\, {q_1}^4\, {q_2}^2\, \sin(q_2) - 6\, d_2\, \dot{q}_1\, {q_1}^3\, {q_2}^4\, \cos(q_1) - 3\, d_2\, \dot{q}_1\, {q_1}^4\, {q_2}^4\, \sin(q_1) - 3\, d_2\, \dot{q}_2\, {q_1}^6\, {q_2}^2\, \sin(q_2) \\
& + 6\, L\, \dot{q}_2\, {q_1}^4\, q_2\, \cos(q_1 + q_2)),
\end{aligned}$$

$$
\begin{aligned}
c_{12} = {} & \frac{L\,m}{{q_1}^2\,{q_2}^5}(2\,L\,\dot{q}_1\,{q_2}^2 + 4\,L\,\dot{q}_2\,{q_1}^2 - 2\,L\,\dot{q}_2\,{q_2}^2 - 6\,L\,\dot{q}_2\,q_2\,\sin(q_1+q_2) - L\,\dot{q}_1\,q_1\,{q_2}^3 + 6\,L\,\dot{q}_2\,q_2\,\sin(q_1) \\
& + 6\,L\,\dot{q}_2\,q_2\,\sin(q_2) + 2\,L\,\dot{q}_1\,{q_2}^2\,\cos(q_1+q_2) + 4\,L\,\dot{q}_2\,{q_2}^2\,\cos(q_1+q_2) + L\,\dot{q}_1\,{q_2}^3\,\sin(q_1+q_2) + L\,\dot{q}_2\,{q_2}^3\,\sin(q_1+q_2) \\
& + 2\,L\,\dot{q}_1\,{q_1}^2\,{q_2}^2 + L\,\dot{q}_2\,{q_1}^2\,{q_2}^2 - 2\,L\,\dot{q}_1\,{q_2}^2\,\cos(q_1) - 2\,L\,\dot{q}_1\,{q_2}^2\,\cos(q_2) - 4\,L\,\dot{q}_2\,{q_1}^2\,\cos(q_2) + 2\,L\,\dot{q}_2\,{q_2}^2\,\cos(q_1) \\
& - 4\,L\,\dot{q}_2\,{q_2}^2\,\cos(q_2) + L\,\dot{q}_1\,{q_2}^3\,\sin(q_1) - L\,\dot{q}_1\,{q_2}^3\,\sin(q_2) - L\,\dot{q}_2\,{q_2}^3\,\sin(q_2) + 2\,d_2\,\dot{q}_1\,{q_1}^2\,{q_2}^2 - 2\,d_2\,\dot{q}_2\,{q_1}^2\,{q_2}^2 \\
& - 6\,L\,\dot{q}_2\,q_1\,q_2 - L\,\dot{q}_1\,q_1\,{q_2}^3\,\cos(q_2) - L\,\dot{q}_2\,q_1\,{q_2}^3\,\cos(q_2) + 2\,L\,\dot{q}_1\,q_1\,{q_2}^2\,\sin(q_2) - 3\,L\,\dot{q}_1\,{q_1}^2\,q_2\,\sin(q_2) \\
& + 4\,L\,\dot{q}_2\,q_1\,{q_2}^2\,\sin(q_2) - 4\,L\,\dot{q}_2\,{q_1}^2\,q_2\,\sin(q_2) + 6\,d_2\,\dot{q}_2\,{q_1}^2\,q_2\,\sin(q_2) + L\,\dot{q}_1\,{q_1}^2\,{q_2}^2\,\cos(q_2) + L\,\dot{q}_2\,{q_1}^2\,{q_2}^2\,\cos(q_2) \\
& - 2\,d_2\,\dot{q}_1\,{q_1}^2\,{q_2}^2\,\cos(q_2) - 4\,d_2\,\dot{q}_2\,{q_1}^2\,{q_2}^2\,\cos(q_2) - d_2\,\dot{q}_1\,{q_1}^2\,{q_2}^3\,\sin(q_2) - d_2\,\dot{q}_2\,{q_1}^2\,{q_2}^3\,\sin(q_2) + 6\,L\,\dot{q}_2\,q_1\,q_2\,\cos(q_2)), \\
c_{21} = {} & -\frac{L\,\dot{q}_1\,m}{{q_1}^3\,{q_2}^4}(4\,L\,q_2\,\sin(q_1) - 2\,L\,{q_2}^2 + 4\,L\,q_2\,\sin(q_2) - 2\,d_2\,{q_1}^3\,q_2 + 2\,L\,{q_2}^2\,\cos(q_1+q_2) + L\,{q_1}^2\,{q_2}^2 + 2\,L\,{q_2}^2\,\cos(q_1) \\
& - 2\,L\,{q_2}^2\,\cos(q_2) + 3\,L\,{q_1}^3\,\sin(q_2) - 4\,L\,q_1\,q_2 - 4\,L\,q_2\,\sin(q_1+q_2) - 2\,L\,{q_1}^3\,q_2 + L\,{q_1}^2\,{q_2}^2\,\cos(q_2) + d_2\,{q_1}^3\,{q_2}^2\,\sin(q_2) \\
& + 4\,L\,q_1\,q_2\,\cos(q_2) - L\,{q_1}^3\,q_2\,\cos(q_2) + 2\,L\,q_1\,{q_2}^2\,\sin(q_2) - 2\,L\,{q_1}^2\,q_2\,\sin(q_2) + 2\,d_2\,{q_1}^3\,q_2\,\cos(q_2)), \\
c_{22} = {} & -\frac{L^2\,\dot{q}_2\,m\,(12\,q_2 - 30\,\sin(q_2) + 3\,{q_2}^2\,\sin(q_2) + 18\,q_2\,\cos(q_2) + {q_2}^3)}{3\,{q_2}^6};
\end{aligned}
$$

and

$$
G = \begin{bmatrix} -\frac{g\,m\,(2\,L\,{q_2}^2 - L\,{q_1}^3\,\sin(q_1+q_2) - 2\,L\,{q_2}^2\,\cos(q_1) + L\,{q_1}^3\,\sin(q_1) - L\,{q_1}^2\,{q_2}^2\,\cos(q_1) + d_2\,{q_1}^3\,{q_2}^2\,\sin(q_1) + L\,{q_1}^3\,q_2\,\cos(q_1))}{{q_1}^3\,{q_2}^2} \\ \frac{L\,g\,m\,(2\,\cos(q_1+q_2) - 2\,\cos(q_1) + q_2\,\sin(q_1+q_2) + q_2\,\sin(q_1))}{{q_2}^3} \end{bmatrix}. \tag{A6}
$$

References

1. Mohareri, O.; Salcudean, S.E.; Nguan, C. Asymmetric force feedback control framework for teleoperated robot-assisted surgery. In Proceedings of the 2013 IEEE International Conference on Robotics and Automation, Karlsruhe, Germany, 6–10 May 2013; pp. 5800–5806.
2. Abadi, A.S.S.; Ordys, A.; Pierscionek, B. Controlling a teleoperated robotic eye surgical system under a communication channel's unknown time delay. In Proceedings of the 2023 27th International Conference on Methods and Models in Automation and Robotics (MMAR), Miedzyzdroje, Poland, 21–24 August 2023; pp. 211–215.
3. Trivedi, D.; Rahn, C.D.; Kier, W.M.; Walker, I.D. Soft Robotics: Biological Inspiration, State of the Art, and Future Research. *Appl. Bionics Biomech.* **2008**, *5*, 17–99. [CrossRef]
4. Alici, G. Softer is harder: What differentiates soft robotics from hard robotics? *MRS Adv.* **2018**, *3*, 1557–1568. [CrossRef]
5. Della Santina, C.; Duriez, C.; Rus, D. Model-based Control of Soft Robots: A Survey of the State of the Art and Open Challenges. *IEEE Control Syst. Mag.* **2023**, *43*, 30–65. [CrossRef]
6. Baker, J.; Christofides, P.D. Finite-dimensional approximation and control of non-linear parabolic PDE systems. *Int. J. Control* **2000**, *73*, 439–456. [CrossRef]
7. Mochiyama, H.; Kobayashi, H. The shape Jacobian of a manipulator with hyper degrees of freedom. In Proceedings of the 1999 IEEE International Conference on Robotics and Automation (ICRA), Detroit, MI, USA, 10–15 May 1999; Volume 4, pp. 2837–2842.
8. Zhou, X.; Majidi, C.; O'Reilly, O.M. Soft Hands: An Analysis of Some Gripping Mechanisms in Soft Robot Design. *Int. J. Solids Struct.* **2015**, *64–65*, 155–165. [CrossRef]
9. Gilbert, H.B.; Godage, I.S. Validation of an Extensible Rod Model for Soft Continuum Manipulators. In Proceedings of the 2019 2nd IEEE International Conference on Soft Robotics (RoboSoft), Seoul, Korea, 14–18 April 2019; pp. 711–716.
10. Roshanfar, M.; Taki, S.; Sayadi, A.; Cecere, R.; Dargahi, J.; Hooshiar, A. Hyperelastic Modeling and Validation of Hybrid-Actuated Soft Robot with Pressure-Stiffening. *Micromachines* **2023**, *14*, 900. [CrossRef]
11. Till, J.; Aloi, V.; Rucker, C. Real-Time Dynamics of Soft and Continuum Robots Based on Cosserat Rod Models. *Int. J. Robot. Res.* **2019**, *38*, 723–746. [CrossRef]
12. Berthold, R.; Bartholdt, M.N.; Wiese, M.; Kahms, S.; Spindeldreier, S.; Raatz, A. A Preliminary Study of Soft Material Robotic Modelling: Finite Element Method and Cosserat Rod Model. In Proceedings of the 2021 9th International Conference on Control, Mechatronics and Automation (ICCMA), Belval, Luxembourg, 11–14 November 2021; pp. 7–13.
13. Duriez, C. Control of Elastic Soft Robots Based on Real-Time Finite Element Method. In Proceedings of the 2013 IEEE International Conference on Robotics and Automation, Karlsruhe, Germany, 6–10 May 2013; pp. 3982–3987
14. Ding, L.; Niu, L.; Su, Y.; Yang, H.; Liu, G.; Gao, H.; Deng, Z. Dynamic Finite Element Modeling and Simulation of Soft Robots. *Chin. J. Mech. Eng.* **2022**, *35*, 24. [CrossRef]
15. Martin-Barrio, A.; Terrile, S.; Diaz-Carrasco, M.; del Cerro, J.; Barrientos, A. Modelling the Soft Robot Kyma Based on Real-Time Finite Element Method. *Comput. Graph. Forum* **2020**,*39*, 289–302. [CrossRef]

16. Webster, R.J., III; Jones, B.A. Design and Kinematic Modeling of Constant Curvature Continuum Robots: A Review. *Int. J. Robot. Res.* **2010**, *29*, 1661–1683. [CrossRef]
17. Wang, X.; Li, Y.; Kwok, K.-W. A Survey for Machine Learning-Based Control of Continuum Robots. *Front. Robot. AI* **2021**, *8*, 730330. [CrossRef] [PubMed]
18. Lee, A.; Baker, T.S.; Bederson, J.B.; Rapoport, B.I. Levels of autonomy in FDA-cleared surgical robots: A systematic review. *npj Digit. Med.* **2024**, *7*, 1. [CrossRef] [PubMed]
19. Fiorini, P.; Goldberg, K.Y.; Liu, Y.; Taylor, R.H. Concepts and Trends in Autonomy for Robot-Assisted Surgery. *Proc. IEEE* **2022**, *110*, 7, 993–1011. [CrossRef] [PubMed]
20. Shu, A.; Deutschmann, B.; Dietrich, A.; Ott, C.; Albu-Schäffer, A. Robust $H\infty$ Control of a Tendon–Driven Elastic Continuum Mechanism via a Systematic Description of Nonlinearities. *IFAC-PapersOnLine* **2018**, *51*, 386–392. [CrossRef]
21. Abu Alqumsan, A.; Khoo, S.; Norton, M. Multi-Surface Sliding Mode Control of Continuum Robots with Mismatched Uncertainties. *Meccanica* **2019**, *54*, 2307–2316. [CrossRef]
22. Luo, M.; Skorina, E.H.; Tao, W.; Chen, F.; Ozel, S.; Sun, Y.; Onal, C.D. Toward modular soft robotics: Proprioceptive curvature sensing and sliding-mode control of soft bidirectional bending modules. *Soft Robot.* **2017**, *4*, 117–125. [CrossRef]
23. Khan, A.H.; Li, S. Sliding mode control with PID sliding surface for active vibration damping of pneumatically actuated soft robots. *IEEE Access* **2020**, *8*, 88793–88800. [CrossRef]
24. Best, C.M.; Gillespie, M.T.; Hyatt, P.; Rupert, L.; Sherrod, V.; Killpack, M.D. A New Soft Robot Control Method: Using Model Predictive Control for a Pneumatically Actuated Humanoid. *IEEE Robot. Autom. Mag.* **2016**, *23*, 75–84. [CrossRef]
25. Weerakoon, L.; Chopra, N. Bilateral Teleoperation of Soft Robots under Piecewise Constant Curvature Hypothesis: An Experimental Investigation. In Proceedings of the 2020 American Control Conference (ACC), Denver, CO, USA, 1–3 July 2020; pp. 2124–2129.
26. Trumić, M.; Della Santina, C.; Jovanović, K.; Fagiolini, A. Adaptive Control of Soft Robots Based on an Enhanced 3D Augmented Rigid Robot Matching. In Proceedings of the 2021 American Control Conference (ACC), New Orleans, LA, USA, 25–28 May 2021; pp. 4991–4996.
27. Chopra, N.; Fujita, M.; Ortega, R.; Spong, M.W. Passivity-Based Control of Robots: Theory and Examples from the Literature. *IEEE Control Syst. Mag.* **2022**, *42*, 63–73. [CrossRef]
28. Franco, E.; Garriga-Casanovas, A.; Donaire, A. Energy Shaping Control with Integral Action for Soft Continuum Manipulators. *Mech. Mach. Theory* **2021**, *158*, 104250. [CrossRef]
29. Arpenti, P.; Franco, E.; Donaire, A. Integral passivity-based control of an underactuated hydraulic soft manipulator with uncertain nonlinear stiffness. *IFAC-PapersOnLine* **2024**, *58*, 13–18. [CrossRef]
30. Franco, E.; Ayatullah, T.; Sugiharto, A.; Garriga-Casanovas, A.; Virdyawan, V. Nonlinear energy-based control of soft continuum pneumatic manipulators. *Nonlinear Dyn.* **2021**, *106*, 229–253. [CrossRef]
31. Garriga-Casanovas, A.; Treratanakulchai, S.; Franco, E.; Zari, E.; Ferrandy, V.; Virdyawan, V.; Rodriguez y Baena, F. Optimised Design and Performance Comparison of Soft Robotic Manipulators. In Proceedings of the 2022 7th International Conference on Mechanical Engineering and Robotics Research (ICMERR), Krakow, Poland, 9–10 December 2022; pp. 129–136.
32. Spong, M.W. An Historical Perspective on the Control of Robotic Manipulators. *Annu. Rev. Control. Robot. Auton. Syst.* **2022**, *5*, 1–31. [CrossRef]
33. Spong, M.W.; Hutchinson, S.; Vidyasagar, M. *Robot Modeling and Control*; John Wiley & Sons: Hoboken, NJ, USA, 2020.
34. Spong, M.W.; Vidyasagar, M. Robust Linear Compensator Design for Nonlinear Robotic Control. *IEEE J. Robot. Autom.* **1987**, *3*, 345–351. [CrossRef]
35. Khalil, H.K. *Nonlinear Systems*, 3rd ed.; Pearson New International Edition; Pearson: Harlow, UK, 2014.
36. Young, K.D.; Utkin, V.I.; Ozguner, U. A Control Engineer's Guide to Sliding Mode Control. *IEEE Trans. Control Syst. Technol.* **1999**, *7*, 328–342. [CrossRef]
37. Ortega, R.; Spong, M.W. Adaptive Motion Control of Rigid Robots: A Tutorial. *Automatica* **1989**, *25*, 877–888. [CrossRef]
38. Slotine, J.-J.E.; Li, W. *Applied Nonlinear Control*; Prentice Hall: Englewood Cliffs, NJ, USA, 1991.

Disclaimer/Publisher's Note: The statements, opinions and data contained in all publications are solely those of the individual author(s) and contributor(s) and not of MDPI and/or the editor(s). MDPI and/or the editor(s) disclaim responsibility for any injury to people or property resulting from any ideas, methods, instructions or products referred to in the content.

robotics

MDPI

Article

An Aircraft-Manipulator System for Virtual Flight Testing of Longitudinal Flight Dynamics

Ademayowa A. Ishola [1,*], James F. Whidborne [1] and Gilbert Tang [2]

[1] Centre for Aeronautics, Cranfield University, Cranfield MK43 0AL, UK; j.f.whidborne@cranfield.ac.uk
[2] Centre for Robotics and Assembly, Cranfield University, Bedfordshire MK43 0AL, UK; g.tang@cranfield.ac.uk
* Correspondence: ademayowa.ishola@cranfield.ac.uk

Abstract: A virtual flight test is the process of flying an aircraft model inside a wind tunnel in a manner that replicates free-flight. In this paper, a 3-DOF aircraft-manipulator system is proposed that can be used for longitudinal dynamics virtual flight tests. The system consists of a two rotational degrees-of-freedom manipulator arm with an aircraft wind tunnel model attached to the third joint. This aircraft-manipulator system is constrained to operate for only the longitudinal motion of the aircraft. Thus, the manipulator controls the surge and heave of the aircraft whilst the pitch is free to rotate and can be actively controlled by means of an all-moving tailplane of the aircraft if required. In this initial study, a flight dynamics model of the aircraft is used to obtain dynamic response trajectories of the aircraft in free-flight. A model of the coupled aircraft-manipulator system developed using the Euler method is presented, and PID controllers are used to control the manipulator so that the aircraft follows the free-flight trajectory (with respect to the air). The inverse kinematics are used to produce the reference joint angles for the manipulator. The system is simulated in MATLAB/Simulink and a virtual flight test trajectory is compared with a free-flight test trajectory, demonstrating the potential of the proposed system for virtual flight tests.

Keywords: flight dynamics; aircraft manipulator; wind tunnel test; simulation; robot manipulator; virtual flight test

1. Introduction

Wind tunnel testing is a well-established experimental method used in aircraft analysis, and the study of fundamental flight physics and aerodynamics. While most wind tunnel experiments use static models, dynamic wind tunnel testing is useful for examining non-steady aerodynamics [1] as well as for investigating flight dynamics, especially in nonlinear flight regimes, such as those involving high angles of attack, unsteady aerodynamics, spin, and upset recovery. It is also useful for identifying aerodynamic and flight dynamic parameters [2]. For a review, see Huang and Wang [3]. However, there is also a longstanding ambition of wind tunnel testing to be able to 'fly' an aircraft inside a wind tunnel [3]. This is a challenging ambition that has limited the experience to a few very large facilities and to a few specific flight regimes. In particular, spin testing in vertical tunnels has been performed for many decades [4] and is a continuous area of interest [5].

A capability to fly the aircraft inside a wind tunnel can be seen as part of a "virtual flight testing" process [6]. Huang and Wang [3] give a definition of virtual flight testing as "flight" in a tunnel with constraints on the three translational Degrees Of Freedom (DOF). Three-rotational DOF dynamic wind tunnel testing and virtual flight testing has become fairly common over the last decade [7–13]. Recently, Tai proposed extending virtual flight testing to 4-DOF [14], but both 4- and 5-DOF dynamic wind tunnel testing have been successfully performed for some time [15–19].

Manipulators have often been proposed to improve wind tunnel experiments for various reasons, such as to provide dynamic response so that unsteady aerodynamic effects can be investigated. For example, Asai et al. [20] developed a 2-DOF passive robot model to allow for the lateral motion of a delta wing , and Wei et al. [21] developed a 3-DOF manipulator actuated based on commands sent to the corresponding motor for variable angles of pitch, roll, and yaw. Other passive devices include an unforced pitch-axis, a 1-DOF dynamic wind tunnel test rig [22], and a 3-DOF dynamic wind tunnel test apparatus consisting of a momentum arm attached to a rigid frame [23], which allowed rotation about a gimbal for pitch and yaw with a wrist designed for roll.

Pattinson et al. suggested the use of a robotics framework with advanced capabilities in wind tunnels [24] but did not develop the idea in their paper. Some active controlled manipulator systems have been used for wind tunnel testing. For example, cable-based manipulators (to reduce interference effects) have been proposed and investigated, for example, in [25,26]. Another example is the use of a 6-DOF manipulator as part of a captive trajectory simulation system operating inside the trisonic blowdown wind tunnel facilities at the National Research Council in Canada [27]. But it appears that using a manipulator to reproduce natural flight response in a wind tunnel ha0s never been attempted. Hence, this paper proposes an aircraft-manipulator system (AMS) that performs just that. The system has a 2-DOF manipulator connected to an aircraft model that is free to pitch, which, as we show in simulation, can replicate longitudinal free-flight in a wind tunnel and, hence, can be used for virtual flight testing. A schematic of the manipulator sited in a wind tunnel is shown in Figure 1. The manipulator provides the translational variation in the wind tunnel, while the aircraft is free to pitch according to the aerodynamic forces it experiences.

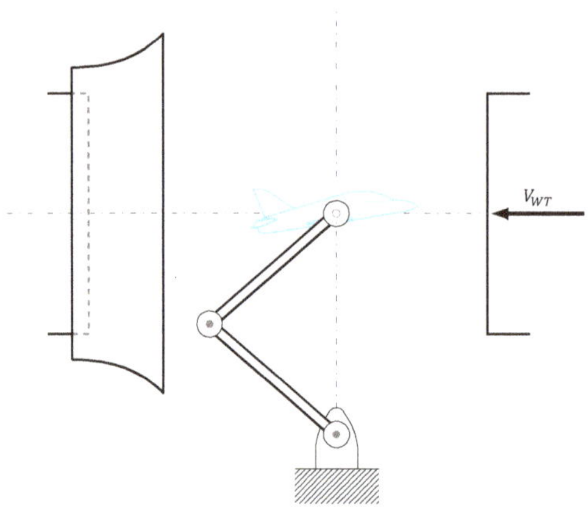

Figure 1. Schematic of the aircraft-manipulator system sited in the working section of an open-section wind tunnel (not to scale). The wind tunnel airspeed is shown as V_{WT}.

The motion of an aircraft is determined by its flight dynamics, the analysis of which is important for determining not only the stability of the aircraft, but also for the handling qualities, that is, how easy it is for the pilot to control the aircraft. Classical configuration, rigid-body, fixed-wing aircraft are usually modelled with 6-DOF (roll, pitch, yaw, surge, sway, heave) using the Newton–Euler equations, and following steady-state analysis (or 'trim'), the equations are often linearised so that modal analysis can be performed. The longitudinal dynamics (pitch, surge, heave) are fairly well decoupled from the lateral dynamics (roll, yaw, sway), and these are controlled, and analysed, separately. The longitudinal dynamics are typically controlled with an elevator and with the engine thrust, while the lateral dynamics by the ailerons and rudder. The longitudinal dynamics are typically characterised by two modes, namely the the high-frequency *short period mode* and the low-frequency *phugoid mode* e.g., [28]. There are several useful texts on flight dynamics, for example, [28–30].

The aircraft used for the modelling of the proposed AMS is based on a 1/12th scaled BAe Hawk aircraft that has been used in a 4-DOF dynamic rig at Cranfield University for parameter identification [2,15,16,19]. In that rig, the aircraft is free to pitch, roll, yaw, and heave; and the control of the aircraft is enacted by the classical elevator, rudder, and aileron moving surfaces [19]. However, the surge motion is constrained, thus limiting the virtual flight, because the velocity in the incident wind direction cannot be increased (unless the wind tunnel speed were increased), and so the aircraft lacks a controlled propulsion system and kinetic energy cannot be injected into the system. Thus, the phugoid mode cannot be accurately reproduced with the Cranfield University's 4-DOF dynamic rig. Note also that the phugoid mode in this rig can be very unstable because the airspeed decreases as the model approaches the tunnel walls, and so the lift reduces as the aircraft descends and the aircraft accelerates towards the lower tunnel wall.

In this paper, we demonstrate the feasibility of the proposed AMS system by means of simulation. A flight dynamics model of the 1/12th scaled BAe Hawk is used to generate a free-flight trajectory that excites both the short period mode and the phugoid. By an inversion of the AMS kinematics, the references for the manipulator joint angles for a wind tunnel flight are obtained. From a model of the dynamics and aerodynamics of the AMS system, the wind tunnel flight is simulated and the responses are analysed. As well as for determining aerodynamic relationships, it is envisaged that the system can be used for testing flight control laws and handling qualities. It could also be used as an educational demonstrator to show the longitudinal dynamics. Note that the aircraft-manipulator concept was originally proposed in a presentation [31], but simulations were not performed. Note also that a summary of some other simulation results from the AMS model were presented recently [32] in an extended abstract.

The nonlinear longitudinal flight dynamics of the BAe Hawk aircraft model in free-flight are presented in Section 2. Section 3 presents a nonlinear model of the proposed AMS, including the inverse kinematics, the AMS dynamics, and a PID controller for the control of the manipulator joints. Simulation results of a test trajectory are presented in Section 4, both the short period mode of the longitudinal response and low-frequency phugoid response mode. Simulation plots for free-flight trajectories and the controlled aircraft-manipulator trajectories are evaluated, and the results demonstrate the potential of the system. The potential of the system for virtual flight tests in a wind tunnel is discussed in Section 5 and some limitations of the work are highlighted. Suggestions for future research are also given. Finally, the conclusions are presented in Section 6.

2. Scaled Aircraft Flight Dynamics

The aircraft considered in this study is a 1/12th scaled BAe Hawk aircraft model shown in Figure 2 originally developed at Cranfield University [15,33] for dynamic wind tunnel testing. It has a fixed low-mounted main wing with wingspan of 780 mm fitted with ailerons, a single vertical tail fin and an all-moving, symmetric, horizontal tail stabilizer that is used for pitch control. It is attached to the end of the second manipulator arm via a gimbal (located in the cavity visible at the top of the fuselage), which can rotate in three directions, but here, it is constrained to pitch rotation only.

The flight dynamics model for the aircraft is described in this section, and is a fairly standard simplified model for a fixed-wing rigid-body aircraft; see, for example, [28,34]. Consider the aircraft flying wing-level in still air with negligible lateral perturbations. The motion is thus restricted to the 3-DOF longitudinal frame shown in Figure 3, where (u, w) is the pair of velocity components in the aircraft body frame with origin at the centre of gravity, θ is the pitch angle from the horizontal, V_T is the total air speed, α is the angle of attack, γ is the flight path angle, L is the lift force, D is the drag force, M is the pitch moment, $W = m_a g$ is the aircraft weight where m_a is the mass of the aircraft, g is the acceleration due to gravity, and T is the thrust.

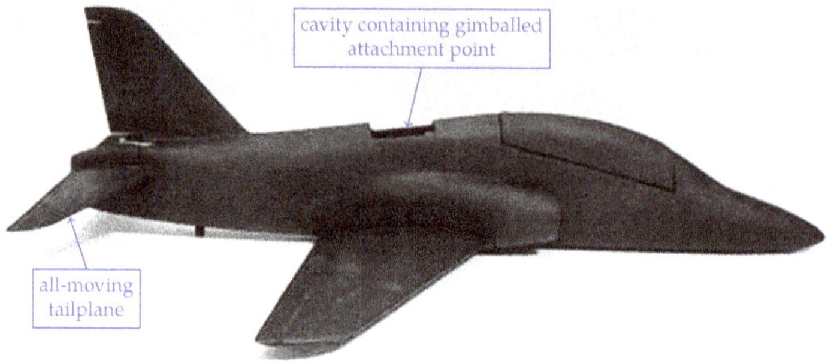

Figure 2. A 1/12th scaled BAe Hawk aircraft.

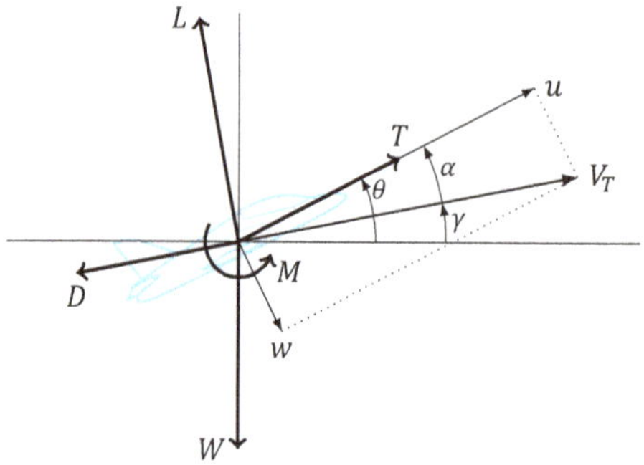

Figure 3. Configuration for 3-DOF aircraft longitudinal dynamics.

2.1. Aerodynamics

The lift, drag, and moment for the aircraft are, respectively,

$$L = \bar{q} S_w C_L, \qquad D = \bar{q} S_w C_D, \qquad M = \bar{q} S_w \bar{c} C_m, \tag{1}$$

where S_w is the wing area, $\bar{c}$ is the mean aerodynamic chord, C_L is the total lift coefficient, C_D is the drag coefficient, C_m is the pitch moment coefficient, and $\bar{q}$ is the dynamic pressure given by $\bar{q} = \frac{1}{2}\rho V_T^2$, where ρ is the density of air.

The total lift coefficient is given by [15,28]

$$C_L = C_{Lw} + \frac{S_t}{S_w} C_{Lt} \tag{2}$$

where C_{Lw} is the wing/body lift coefficient, C_{Lt} is the tail lift coefficient and S_t is the tailplane area. The body/wing lift coefficient is given by $C_{Lw} = C_{Lw\alpha}\alpha + C_{L0}$ where $C_{Lw\alpha}$ is the lift curve slope, α is the angle of attack, and C_{L0} is the lift coefficient at zero angle of attack. The tail lift coefficient is given by $C_{Lt} = C_{Lt\alpha}\,\alpha_t$, where $C_{Lt\alpha}$ is the tail lift curve slope, and α_t is the tailplane incidence given by $\alpha_t = \alpha - \varepsilon + \delta_t$ where δ_t is tailplane control angle and ε is the downwash angle at the tail. From [28],

$$\alpha - \varepsilon = \alpha\left(1 - \frac{\mathrm{d}\varepsilon}{\mathrm{d}\alpha}\right). \tag{3}$$

The drag coefficient C_D is given by

$$C_D = C_{D0} + \sigma C_L^2 \tag{4}$$

where C_{D0} is the drag coefficient at zero lift, and σ is the induced drag factor that can be calculated from $\sigma = 1/(\pi e AR)$ where e is the Oswald efficiency factor, and $AR = S_w/\bar{c}^2$ is the aspect ratio.

The pitch moment coefficient C_m is [28,34,35]

$$C_m = C_{m0} + C_{Lw}(h_{cg} - h_0) - \bar{V}_H\left(\frac{C_{Lt\alpha}}{C_{Lw\alpha}}C_{Lw}\left(1 - \frac{d\varepsilon}{d\alpha}\right) + C_{Lt\alpha}\delta_t\right) + \frac{\bar{c}}{2V_T}C_{mq}q \quad (5)$$

where C_{m0} is the initial pitch moment coefficient, C_{mq} is the pitch damping derivative, q is the pitch rate, h_{cg} is position of the centre of gravity, h_0 is the aerodynamic centre position, $\bar{c}$ is the mean aerodynamic chord, and $\bar{V}_H$ is tailplane volume coefficient, given by

$$\bar{V}_H = \frac{S_t l_t}{S_w \bar{c}} \quad (6)$$

where l_t is the tail moment arm.

2.2. Flight Dynamics

From Figure 3, the nonlinear flight dynamic equations of motion in the longitudinal plane are given (also see [28]) as

$$\begin{bmatrix} m_a\dot{u} + m_a q w \\ -m_a q u + m_a\dot{w} \\ \dot{q} I_y \end{bmatrix} = \begin{bmatrix} L\sin\alpha - D\cos\alpha + T - m_a g\sin\theta \\ -L\cos\alpha - D\sin\alpha + m_a g\cos\theta \\ M \end{bmatrix} \quad (7)$$

where $q = \dot{\theta}$ is the pitch rate and I_y is the moment of inertia about the body's y-axis.

From the still air assumption, the wind speed V_T and angle of attack α are related to the body velocities by

$$V_T = \sqrt{u^2 + w^2}, \quad (8)$$

$$\alpha = \mathtt{atan2}(w, u). \quad (9)$$

The velocity of the aircraft in the earth axes is given by

$$\begin{bmatrix} \dot{x}_e \\ \dot{h}_e \end{bmatrix} = \begin{bmatrix} \cos\theta & \sin\theta \\ \sin\theta & -\cos\theta \end{bmatrix}\begin{bmatrix} u \\ w \end{bmatrix}, \quad (10)$$

where (x_e, h_e) is the position in the earth axes.

From (5), the aircraft longitudinal trim (steady-state) condition can be derived as

$$\delta_{t_{trim}} = \frac{1}{\bar{V}_H C_{Lt\alpha}}\left(C_{m0} + C_{Lw}(h_{cg} - h_0)\right) - \frac{C_{Lw}}{C_{Lw\alpha}}\left(1 - \frac{d\varepsilon}{d\alpha}\right). \quad (11)$$

The trim angle of attack α and subsequent pitch, θ, and the thrust at trim can be calculated iteratively from (1)–(7).

3. Aircraft-Manipulator System Dynamics

A dynamic model of the aircraft-manipulator system (AMS) is required to simulate the system. The configuration is shown in Figure 4, whereby a 1/12th scaled BAe Hawk aircraft model is mounted onto the tip of a two-link revolute jointed manipulator via a joint that allows free pitch movement. The kinematics and dynamics of a two-link manipulator are well known, e.g., [36], and the extension to include the aircraft model is straightforward.

The horizontal axis is taken as x and the vertical (the height) is denoted as h. The first link has a length l_1 and mass m_1 with a centre of mass at the mid-point of the link and moment of inertia I_1. Similarly, the second link has a length l_2 and mass m_2 with a centre of mass at the mid-point of the link and moment of inertia I_2. The links are assumed to be stiff and to have insignificant aerodynamic forces. There are servo motors attached to the first two joints that provide torques of τ_1 and τ_2 to control the joint angles θ_1 and θ_2. The joints are all assumed to be friction-free.

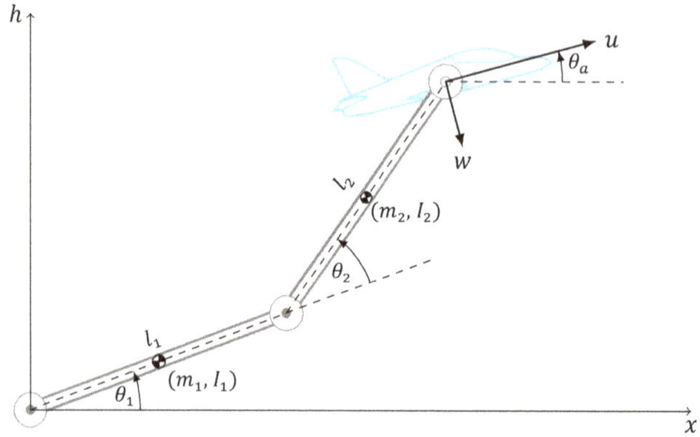

Figure 4. Manipulator aircraft system configuration.

A joint at the centre of mass of the aircraft model is attached to the tip of the second link. The aircraft joint is free to allow pitch rotation, and pitch angle with the horizontal is denoted by θ_a. The aircraft body velocity components u and w are shown, and the position of the aircraft (third joint) is denoted by (x_a, h_a).

3.1. Kinematics

The aircraft model position is related to the joint angles by

$$\begin{bmatrix} x_a \\ h_a \end{bmatrix} = \begin{bmatrix} l_1 \cos\theta_1 + l_2 \cos(\theta_1 + \theta_2) \\ l_1 \sin\theta_1 + l_2 \sin(\theta_1 + \theta_2) \end{bmatrix}, \tag{12}$$

with rates given by

$$\begin{bmatrix} \dot{x}_a \\ \dot{h}_a \end{bmatrix} = \begin{bmatrix} -l_1 \sin\theta_1 - l_2 \sin(\theta_1 + \theta_2) & -l_2 \sin(\theta_1 + \theta_2) \\ l_1 \cos\theta_1 + l_2 \cos(\theta_1 + \theta_2) & l_2 \cos(\theta_1 + \theta_2) \end{bmatrix} \begin{bmatrix} \dot{\theta}_1 \\ \dot{\theta}_2 \end{bmatrix}. \tag{13}$$

The inverse kinematics are well known, e.g., [36] (p. 30), and are given by

$$\theta_2 = \pm\,\text{atan2}\Big(\chi, x_a^2 + h_a^2 - l_1^2 - l_2^2\Big), \tag{14}$$

where $\chi = \sqrt{(x_a^2 + h_a^2 + l_1^2 + l_2^2)^2 - 2\left[(x_a^2 + h_a^2)^2 + l_1^4 + l_2^4\right]}$ and

$$\theta_1 = \text{atan2}(h_a, x_a) \mp \text{atan2}\Big(\chi, x_a^2 + h_a^2 + l_1^2 - l_2^2\Big). \tag{15}$$

Note that for the wind tunnel configuration shown in Figure 4, generally the negative value of θ_2 is chosen (i.e., the elbow-up configuration) because this decreases the downwash aerodynamic effects of the links.

The angular rates are obtained from (13) as

$$\begin{bmatrix} \dot{\theta}_1 \\ \dot{\theta}_2 \end{bmatrix} = \frac{1}{d} \begin{bmatrix} l_2 \cos(\theta_1 + \theta_2) & l_2 \sin(\theta_1 + \theta_2) \\ -l_1 \cos\theta_1 - l_2 \cos(\theta_1 + \theta_2) & -l_1 \sin\theta_1 - l_2 \sin(\theta_1 + \theta_2) \end{bmatrix} \begin{bmatrix} \dot{x}_a \\ \dot{h}_a \end{bmatrix} \tag{16}$$

where the determinant $d = l_1 l_2 (\cos\theta_1 \sin(\theta_1 + \theta_2) - \sin\theta_1 \cos(\theta_1 + \theta_2))$.

3.2. Dynamics

Following the Lagrange modelling approach [36,37], we obtain the general open-chain dynamics system given by

$$\boldsymbol{\tau} = -\boldsymbol{\tau}_a + \mathbf{M}(\boldsymbol{\theta})\ddot{\boldsymbol{\theta}} + \mathbf{C}(\boldsymbol{\theta}, \dot{\boldsymbol{\theta}})\dot{\boldsymbol{\theta}} + \mathbf{G}(\boldsymbol{\theta}) \tag{17}$$

where $\boldsymbol{\tau}$ is the net torque produced at the manipulator joints by the servomotors, $\boldsymbol{\tau}_a$ is the aerodynamic torque load produced by the aircraft, $\mathbf{M}$ is the generalised inertia matrix of each link, $\mathbf{C}$ is the matrix of Coriolis and centrifugal terms, and $\mathbf{G}$ is the gravitational effect on each link. The generalised inertia matrix is given by

$$\mathbf{M} = \begin{bmatrix} m_{11} & m_{12} & 0 \\ m_{21} & m_{22} & 0 \\ 0 & 0 & m_{33} \end{bmatrix} \tag{18}$$

where

$$m_{11} = m_1 l_1^2/4 + I_1 + m_2\left(l_1^2 + l_2^2/4 + l_1 l_2 \cos\theta_2\right) + I_2 + m_a\left(l_1^2 + l_2^2 + 2l_1 l_2 \cos\theta_2\right) + I_y, \tag{19}$$

$$m_{12} = m_2\left(l_2^2/4 + l_1 l_2/2 \cos\theta_2\right) + m_a\left(l_1 l_2 \cos\theta_2 + l_2^2\right), \tag{20}$$

$$m_{21} = m_{12}, \tag{21}$$

$$m_{22} = m_2 l_2^2/4 + I_2 + m_a l_2^2 + I_y, \tag{22}$$

$$m_{33} = I_y. \tag{23}$$

The matrix of Coriolis and centrifugal terms is given by

$$\mathbf{C}(\boldsymbol{\theta}, \dot{\boldsymbol{\theta}}) = c \begin{bmatrix} 2\dot{\theta}_2 & \dot{\theta}_2 & 0 \\ \dot{\theta}_1 & 0 & 0 \\ 0 & 0 & 0 \end{bmatrix} \tag{24}$$

where $c = -(m_2/2 + m_a)l_1 l_2 \sin\theta_2$, and the vector of gravitational terms is

$$\mathbf{g}(\boldsymbol{\theta}) = \begin{bmatrix} (m_1/2 + m_2 + m_a)l_1 g \cos\theta_1 \\ (m_2/2 + m_a)l_2 g \cos\theta_2 \\ 0 \end{bmatrix}. \tag{25}$$

The air velocity is the sum of the wind tunnel air speed V_{WT}, which acts horizontally, and the aircraft velocity $(\dot{x}_a, \dot{h}_a)$, as shown in Figure 5. Thus, the air velocity in free-flight and the wind tunnel are equated so that

$$\begin{bmatrix} \dot{x}_a \\ \dot{h}_a \end{bmatrix} = \begin{bmatrix} \dot{x}_e \\ \dot{h}_e \end{bmatrix} + \begin{bmatrix} -V_{WT} \\ 0 \end{bmatrix} \tag{26}$$

giving the airspeed on the aircraft in the wind tunnel as

$$V_T = \sqrt{(\dot{x}_a + V_{WT})^2 + \dot{h}_a^2}, \tag{27}$$

and angle of attack

$$\alpha = \theta_a - \operatorname{atan2}(\dot{h}_a, \dot{x}_a + V_{WT}) \tag{28}$$

so that $\gamma = \theta_a - \alpha$. The aerodynamic forces are resolved to obtain the aerodynamic torque load:

$$\boldsymbol{\tau}_a = [\tau_{a1}, \tau_{a2}, \tau_{a3}]^T, \tag{29}$$

given by

$$\tau_{a1} = (L\cos\gamma - D\sin\gamma)(l_1\cos\theta_1 + l_2\cos\theta_2) + (L\sin\gamma + D\cos\gamma)(l_1\sin\theta_1 + l_2\sin\theta_2), \quad (30)$$
$$\tau_{a2} = (L\cos\gamma + D\sin\gamma)l_2\cos\theta_2 - (L\sin\gamma + D\cos\gamma)l_2\sin\theta_2, \quad (31)$$
$$\tau_{a3} = M. \quad (32)$$

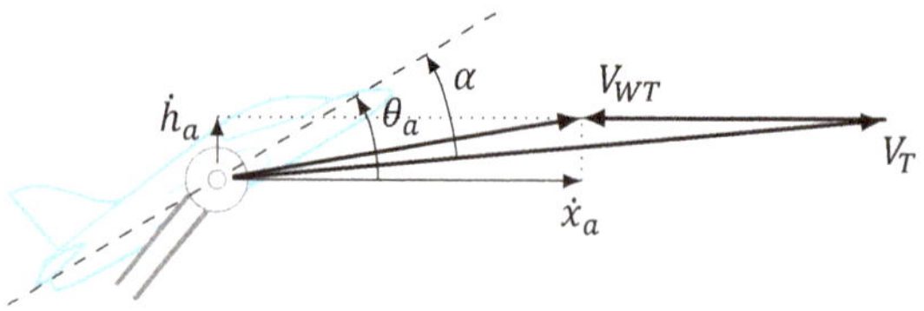

Figure 5. Air velocity as the sum of wind tunnel velocity and aircraft velocity.

3.3. *Joint Control*

The link joint angles, θ_1 and θ_2, are controlled via simple PID control, with the derivative action acting on the joint angular rates, $(\dot{\theta}_1, \dot{\theta}_2)$. The workspace of the manipulator is limited by the wind tunnel cross-section; thus, a linear controller works adequately well for the restricted range of angle demands. The joint angle reference commands, $(\theta_{\text{ref}\,1}, \theta_{\text{ref}\,2})$, are calculated from the inverse kinematics (14) and (15). Additional feedforward of the joint angular rate commands calculated from (16) is included. The controller outputs are the joint torques. It is assumed that the actuator and sensor dynamics are insignificant and can be ignored. Thus, the PID controllers are, for $i = 1, 2$,

$$\tau_i = k_{Pi}(\theta_{\text{ref}\,i} - \theta_i) + \int_0^t k_{Ii}(\theta_{\text{ref}\,i} - \theta_i)\mathrm{d}t + \tau_{\text{trim}\,i} + k_{Di}(\dot{\theta}_{\text{ref}\,i} - \dot{\theta}_i) \quad (33)$$

where $(k_{Pi}, k_{Ii}, k_{Di}), i = 1, 2$ are constant control gains and $\tau_{\text{trim}\,i}, i = 1, 2$ are the steady-state joint torques at the initial time, $t = 0$, calculated from the free-flight trim condition described in Section 2.2 and from (25)–(31). The control system architecture of each PID loop is shown in Figure 6.

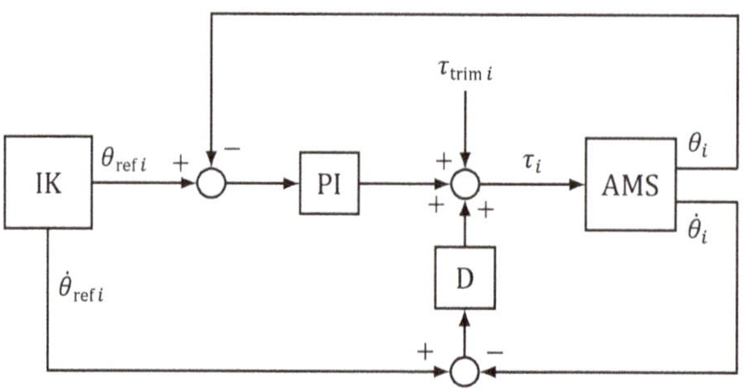

Figure 6. Block diagram showing system control architecture for the *i*th loop. The block denoted as IK represents the inverse kinematics' reference source.

4. Simulation

In order to demonstrate that the mechanism can replicate free-flight in the wind tunnel, a free-flight trajectory is simulated using the flight dynamics model of Section 2. From the inverse kinematics, the required angles and angular rates of the manipulator joints are calculated so that the aircraft in the wind tunnel experiences similar aerodynamic forces as the aircraft in the free-flight trajectory. These are passed to a simulation of the aircraft-manipulator system that is used to verify the system concept.

The equations are implemented in Simulink and the aircraft parameters are taken from [15,35] and are listed in Table 1. The controller gains were hand-tuned and are also given in Table 1. The codes for calculating the trim, the free-flight simulation, inverse kinematics, and AMS simulation are available on CORD—the Cranfield University Research Data repository [38].

Table 1. Aircraft and manipulator parameters.

Parameter	Symbol	Value	Units
Wing area	S_w	0.115	m^2
Mean aerodynamic chord	$\bar{c}$	0.161	m
Air density	ρ	1.2238	kg m^{-3}
Tailplane area	S_t	0.029	m^2
Wing body lift curve slope	$C_{Lw\alpha}$	3.72	rad^{-1}
Lift coefficient at zero α	C_{L0}	0.21	-
Tailplane lift curve slope	$C_{Lt\alpha}$	2.29	rad^{-1}
Oswald efficiency factor	e	0.70	-
Zero lift drag coefficient	C_{D0}	0.028	-
Initial pitch moment coefficient	C_{m0}	−0.050	-
Pitch damping derivative	C_q	−2.978	rad^{-1} s
Aerodynamic centre fraction	h_0	0.113	-
Centre of gravity fraction	h_{cg}	0.18	-
Tail moment arm	l_t	0.3656	m
Aircraft moment of inertia	I_y	0.219	kg m^2
Length of Link-1	l_1	0.32	m
Length of Link-2	l_2	0.32	m
Mass of Link-1	m_1	2.074	kg
Mass of Link-2	m_2	2.074	kg
Mass of aircraft	m_a	2.250	kg
Controller Gain P	$k_{Pi}, i = 1,2$	100	N m rad^{-1}
Controller Gain I	$k_{Ii}, i = 1,2$	4	N m rad^{-1} s^{-1}
Controller Gain D	$k_{Di}, i = 1,2$	200	N m rad^{-1} s

The trajectory starts at trim at the wind tunnel airspeed of $V_T = 30$ m s^{-1}, an altitude of 10 m, and $g = 9.81$ ms^{-2}. The tail angle trim is calculated as $\delta_t = -0.0621$ rad ($-3.56°$), the pitch trim is $\theta_{trim\,a} = 0.0435$ rad ($2.49°$), and the thrust $T = 2.56$ N. A perturbation in both the pitch (and angle of attack) of 0.020 rad is applied at the initial condition and the free-flight simulation trajectory is recorded. Constant tail deflection angle and thrust of the trim values are also applied.

The resulting pitch response is shown in Figure 7 for the first 5 s, where the short period mode response can be observed, and for 60 s in Figure 8, where the phugoid mode response can be clearly observed.

The reference link angles are calculated via the inverse kinematics (13)–(15), with an initial position in the wind tunnel of $x_a = 0$ and $h_a = 0.40$ m. The initial joint torques are calculated as $\tau_{trim\,1} = -16.70$ Nm and $\tau_{trim\,2} = 2.058$ Nm. The AMS system is simulated from the same initial condition of the aircraft with the initial pitch perturbation in θ_a (and subsequent angle of attack perturbation, because the wind tunnel flow is horizontal). The resulting pitch response is also shown in Figure 7, where we can see that the response closely matches the free-flight response.

The aircraft height in the wind tunnel is shown in Figure 9, along with the free-flight altitude (translated to the wind tunnel axes). For the first second, the altitude deviations for the AMS response matches the free-flight closely. As the short period mode decays, the phugoid response starts to dominate, and the difference in the responses increases. The manipulator position controller does not follow the position exactly because of the natural phase lags in the system dynamics. The difference could be reduced by increasing the controller gains and by increasing the complexity of the controller so as to not excite the high-frequency dynamics.

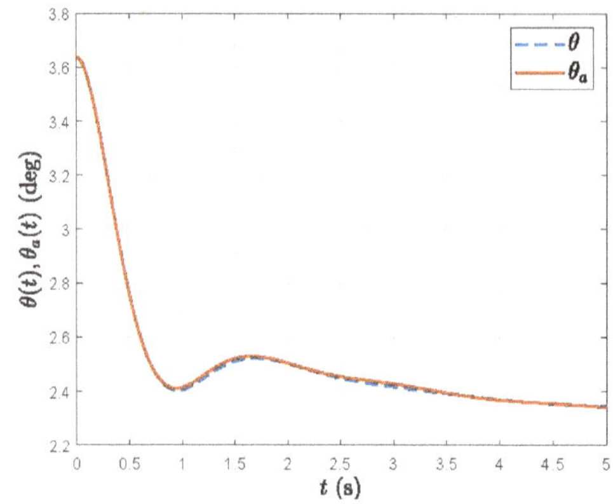

Figure 7. Short period mode pitch response of the free-flying Hawk model and the aircraft-manipulator system (AMS) model.

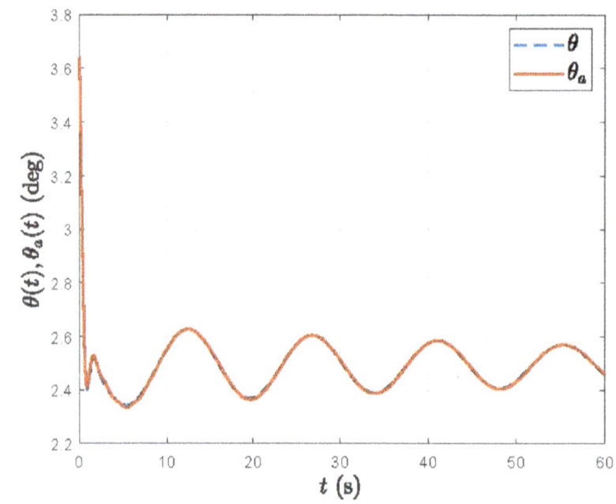

Figure 8. Phugoid mode pitch response of the free-flying Hawk model and the aircraft-manipulator system (AMS) model.

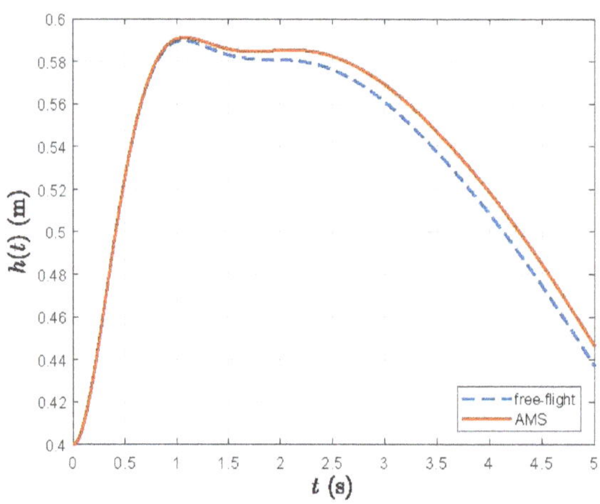

Figure 9. Short period mode altitude response of the free-flying Hawk model and the aircraft-manipulator system (AMS) model.

The altitude and horizontal positions relative to the air of the AMS simulation response are shown in Figure 10 along with the free-flight response resolved into the wind tunnel axes, that is, the response x_a calculated by integrating (26). The altitude deviation occupies nearly the entire wind tunnel working space (shown schematically in Figure 1). The altitude deviations in the AMS model response and the free-flight model response match well, but the surge distance matches less well.

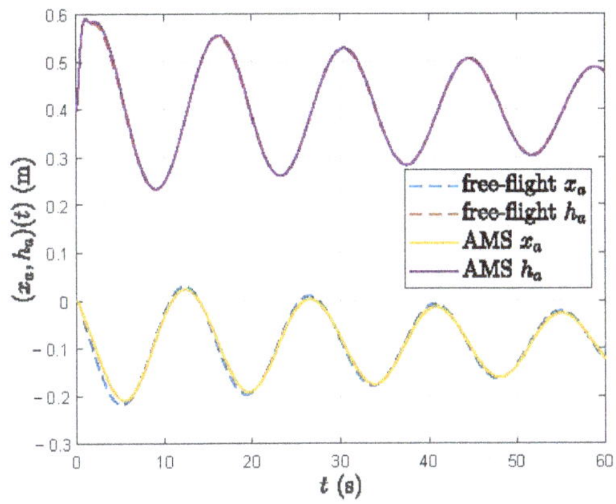

Figure 10. Phugoid mode height and lateral surge position response of the free-flying Hawk model (resolved into the wind tunnel axes) and the aircraft-manipulator system (AMS) model.

Figure 11 shows the response trajectory in the wind tunnel workspace. What can be clearly seen from Figure 11 is how the basic character of the phugoid response is reproduced. The interchange between kinetic and potential energies of the aircraft can be seen. As the aircraft climbs, it moves downstream in the wind tunnel as the speed falls, and as the height reduces due to reduced lift, the kinetic energy, and hence, speed, increases, and so the aircraft moves upstream.

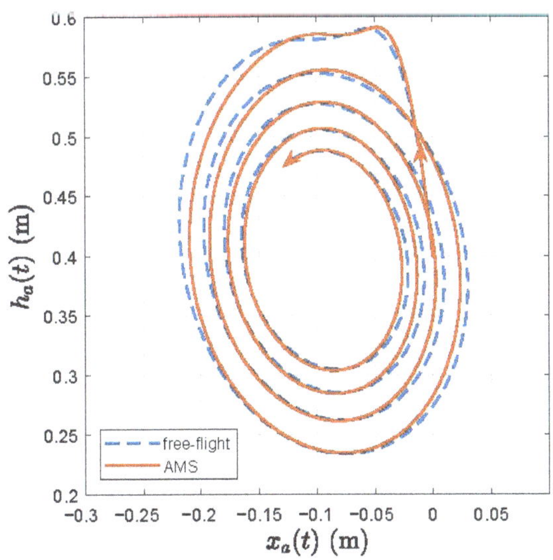

Figure 11. Phugoid mode position response of the aircraft-manipulator system (AMS) model in the wind tunnel.

5. Discussion

The results in the previous section show that the longitudinal free-flight motion can be replicated in a wind tunnel. In essence, what is happening is that the manipulator is providing the non-aerodynamic forces that a free-flying aircraft is exposed to, namely the gravitational and thrust forces, that would otherwise be absent in a wind tunnel. This gives scope for variable thrust virtual flight as well as to artificially alter the gravitational force by means of the control so that flight in, for example, a Mars environment can be recreated. Of course, the system dynamics would require scaling with respect to the dynamic pressure to perform this. Hence, the control system should be improved to not only reduce errors, but to be designed so that the controller effectively cancels the manipulator dynamics whilst introducing the gravitational and thrust forces. This would mean that the AMS system could be viewed as 'dynamically equivalent' to the free-flight model in a similar manner to, for example, [39] or [40]. Control techniques to create a dynamically equivalent system could include model matching with feedback linearisation to cancel the manipulator dynamics. Robust sliding mode control is another potential candidate. This remains for future work, as do sensitivity and robustness studies to parametric uncertainty and unmodelled dynamics.

This study considers only the feasibility from a dynamics and control perspective. Prior to building a prototype, further work is also needed on the manipulator design, which needs to be performed with respect to not only the loads, but also the aerodynamic forces on the links and joints, the aeroelastic properties of the AMS, to ensure that the rig is sufficiently stiff and that it does not laterally deflect under load. The links require aerodynamic shaping to minimize the aerodynamic load and interference of the manipulator with the flow. In addition, for a closed return wind tunnel, the coupling of the aircraft dynamics and the disturbances on the recirculating flow should be investigated. Improvements to the aerodynamics model should also be made, to include, for example, the wing lift due to pitch rate, the dependence of the pitching moment on angle of attack, and the time delay between the wing and tail. Nonlinear aerodynamics such as stall could also improve the simulation model. Effects of lower wind tunnel velocity away from the centre line could also be modelled.

For classical aircraft configurations, the lateral and longitudinal dynamics are largely decoupled; hence, this study considers only the longitudinal dynamics. A similar rig could be proposed for lateral dynamics, which may be more useful because the dutch roll mode is more dependent on the aerodynamics than the phugoid mode. However, for flexible wing aircraft and some other configurations, the lateral and longitudinal coupling is significant; therefore, a full 6-DOF virtual flight test AMS should be designed and tested in the future.

The proposed AMS can be used for a number of applications. These include flight control algorithm testing, controller implementation testing, and aircraft-in-the-loop simulation. The flow in the wind tunnel is smooth, but in free flight, aircraft often encounter gusts, turbulence, etc. A gust/turbulence generator could be inserted into the wind tunnel which would provide a cost-effective method to investigate its effect on the aircraft response. A tunnel with a good control of the airspeed could be used to increase the range of the surge variation; an analysis of this also remains for further work. This, of course, would rely on the wind tunnel speed having a sufficiently high bandwidth. The effect of the joint actuator dynamics and lags also remains for further work.

6. Conclusions

This paper proposes an aircraft-manipulator system that can replicate longitudinal free-flight in a wind tunnel. The system consists of a 1/12 scale model of a BAe Hawk attached to a 2-DOF manipulator via a pivot that allows free pitch rotation. Dynamic models of the aircraft in free-flight and of the AMS system are presented, and the feasibility of the system is investigated through simulation. The simulation results show that the proposed system can potentially provide a virtual flight test facility for longitudinal flight dynamics. The short period mode response of the aircraft is a consequence of the natural flight dynamic response of the aircraft, but the phugoid mode is imposed on the aircraft by determining the aircraft positions from a free-flight simulation response. This means that the constraints and interference of the phugoid dynamics on the aerodynamic response that would otherwise be imposed by constraining the phugoid motion of the aircraft are removed, and the response in the wind tunnel is closer to the free response, than, for example, the 4-DOF Cranfield University rig briefly described in Section 1 [2,15,16,19].

Author Contributions: Conceptualisation, A.A.I. and J.F.W.; methodology, A.A.I. and J.F.W.; software, A.A.I. and J.F.W.; validation, A.A.I. and J.F.W.; formal analysis, A.A.I. and J.F.W.; investigation, A.A.I.; writing—original draft preparation, A.A.I.; writing—review and editing, J.F.W. and G.T.; supervision, J.F.W. and G.T. All authors have read and agreed to the published version of the manuscript.

Funding: This research is partly funded by the Tertiary Educational Trust Fund (TETFUND) Nigeria, grant number TETF/ES/UNIV/OGUNSTATE/TSAS/2020. https://tetfund.gov.ng/index.php/guideline-4/ (accessed on 17 October 2024).

Institutional Review Board Statement: Not applicable.

Informed Consent Statement: Not applicable.

Data Availability Statement: The codes for calculating the trim, the free-flight simulation, inverse kinematics, and AMS simulation are on CORD—the Cranfield University research data repository doi:tbc, url: https://dspace.lib.cranfield.ac.uk/handle/1826/20712 (accessed on 17 October 2024). A Hawk CAD model is available on request from the corresponding author.

Acknowledgments: Acknowledgements to Simon Prince, Pavithra Kasula, and Elzbieta Jarzębowska for their contributions to the development and assessing the aerodynamic feasibility of the model in the wind tunnel.

Conflicts of Interest: The authors declare no conflicts of interest. The funders had no role in the design of the study; in the collection, analyses, or interpretation of data; in the writing of the manuscript; or in the decision to publish the results.

Abbreviations

The following abbreviations are used in this manuscript:

AMS	Aircraft-Manipulator System
DOF	Degrees Of Freedom
PID	Proportional Integral Derivative

References

1. Greenwell, D.I. A review of unsteady aerodynamic modelling for flight dynamics of manoeuvrable aircraft. In Proceedings of the AIAA Atmospheric Flight Mechanics Conference and Exhibit, Providence, RI, USA, 16–19 August 2004; Number AIAA 2004-5276. [CrossRef]
2. Cook, M.V. On the use of small scale aircraft models for dynamic wind tunnel investigation of stability and control. *Trans. Inst. Meas. Control* **1987**, *9*, 190–197. [CrossRef]
3. Huang, M.; Wang, Z.W. Review of wind tunnel based virtual flight testing techniques for evaluation of flight control systems. *Int. J. Aerosp. Eng.* **2015**, *2015*, 15. [CrossRef]
4. Malvestuto, F.S.; Gale, L.J.; Wood, J.H. *Compilation of Test Data on 111 Free-Spinning Airplane Models Tested in the Langley 15-Foot and 20-Foot Free-Spinning Tunnels*; NASA: Washington, DC, USA, 1947; Research Memorandum NACA-RM-L7E1: 20090025259, NACA.
5. Golovkin, M.A.; Efremov, A.A.; Kritskii, B.S.; Pavlenko, O.V.; Tsipenko, V.G. To the estimation of force and pitching moment coefficients acting on the model, full-scale aircraft and their elements at supercritical angles of attack and in a spin. *Russ. Aeronaut.* **2020**, *63*, 643–651. [CrossRef]
6. Manning, T.E.; Ratliff, C.L.; Marquart, E.J. Bridging the gap between ground and flight tests: Virtual flight testing (VFT). In Proceedings of the 1st AIAA Aircraft Engineering, Technology and Operations Congress, Los Angele, CA, USA, 19–21 September 1995; Number AIAA-95-3875. [CrossRef]
7. Ignatyev, D.D.; Sidoryuk, M.E.; Kolinko, K.A.; Khrabrov, A.N. Dynamic rig for validation of control algorithms at high angles of attack. *J. Aircr.* **2017**, *54*, 1760–1771. [CrossRef]
8. Guo, L.; Zhu, M.; Nie, B.; Kong, P.; Zhong, C. Initial virtual flight test for a dynamically similar aircraft model with control augmentation system. *Chin. J. Aeronaut.* **2017**, *30*, 602–610. [CrossRef]

9. Huang, M.; Wang, Z.W.; Guo, Z.Y.; Niu, Y.B. Design of the wind tunnel based virtual flight testing evaluation method for flight control systems. *Proc. Inst. Mech. Eng. Part G J. Aerosp. Eng.* **2018**, *232*, 17–29. [CrossRef]
10. Lu, S.; Wang, J.; Wang, Y. Research on similarity criteria of virtual flight test in low-speed wind tunnel. In Proceedings of the IEEE International Conference on Power, Intelligent Computing and Systems (ICPICS 2021), Shenyang, China, 29–31 July 2021; pp. 121–126. [CrossRef]
11. Tai, S.; Wang, L.; Yue, T.; Liu, H. Test Data Processing of Fly-by-Wire Civil Aircraft in Low-Speed Wind Tunnel Virtual Flight. In Proceedings of the 12th International Conference on Mechanical and Aerospace Engineering (ICMAE 2021), Athens, Greece, 16–19 July 2021; pp. 96–101. [CrossRef]
12. Fu, J.; Shi, Z.; Gong, Z.; Lowenberg, M.H.; Wu, D.; Pan, L. Virtual flight test techniques to predict a blended-wing-body aircraft in-flight departure characteristics. *Chin. J. Aeronaut.* **2022**, *35*, 215–225. [CrossRef]
13. Zhang, L.; Huang, Y.; Zhu, Z.; Gao, L.; Chen, F.; Wu, F.; He, M. Virtual flight test of pitch and roll attitude control based on circulation control of tailless flying wing aircraft without rudders. *Chin. J. Aeronaut.* **2023**, *36*, 52–62. [CrossRef]
14. Tai, S.; Wang, L.; Wang, Y.; Bu, C.; Yue, T. Flight dynamics modeling and aerodynamic parameter identification of four-degree-of-freedom virtual flight test. *AIAA J.* **2023**, *61*, 2652–2665. [CrossRef]
15. Hinds, H.A. The Application of a Modified Stepwise Regression (MSR) Method to the Estimation of Aircraft Stability and Control Derivatives. Ph.D. Thesis, Cranfield University, Bedford, UK, 1996.
16. Carnduff, S.D.; Erbsloeh, S.D.; Cooke, A.K.; Cook, M.V. Characterizing stability and control of subscale aircraft from wind-tunnel dynamic motion. *J. Aircr.* **2009**, *46*, 137–147. [CrossRef]
17. Pattinson, J.; Lowenberg, M.H.; Goman, M.G. Investigation of poststall pitch oscillations of an aircraft wind-tunnel model. *J. Aircr.* **2013**, *50*, 1843–1855. [CrossRef]
18. Gong, Z.; Araujo-Estrada, S.; Lowenberg, M.H.; Neild, S.A.; Goman, M.G. Experimental investigation of aerodynamic hysteresis using a five-degree-of-freedom wind-tunnel maneuver rig. *J. Aircr.* **2019**, *56*, 1029–1039. [CrossRef]
19. Pontillo, A.; Yusuf, S.; Lopez, G.; Rennie, D.; Lone, M. Investigating pitching moment stall through dynamic wind tunnel test. *Proc. Inst. Mech. Eng. Part G J. Aerosp. Eng.* **2020**, *232*, 267–279. [CrossRef]
20. Asai, K.; Konno, A.; Jiang, X.; Numata, D.; Abe, H.; Nakata, N.; Hara, T. Multi-degree-of-freedom dynamic wind-tunnel testing of a delta wing using a robotic manipulator. In Proceedings of the 28th Congress of the International Council of the Aeronautical Sciences (ICAS 2012), Brisbane, Australia, 23–28 September 2012; Number ICAS2012-3.1ST2.
21. Wei, R.; Che, B.H.; Sun, C.B.; Zhang, J.; Lu, Y.Q. A three degree of freedom manipulator used for store separation wind tunnel test. *IOP Conf. Ser. Mater. Sci. Eng.* **2018**, *372*, 012035. [CrossRef]
22. Davison, P.M.; Lowenberg, M.H.; Bernardo, M. Experimental analysis and modeling of limit cycles in a dynamic wind-tunnel rig. *J. Aircr.* **2003**, *40*, 776–785. [CrossRef]
23. Navaratna, P.D.B.; Lowenberg, M.H.; Neild, S.A. Minimally constrained flight simulation in wind tunnel. *J. Aircr.* **2019**, *56*, 1353–1366. [CrossRef]
24. Pattinson, J.; Lowenberg, M.H.; Goman, M.G. Multi-degree-of-freedom wind-tunnel maneuver rig for dynamic simulation and aerodynamic model identification. *J. Aircr.* **2013**, *50*, 551–566. [CrossRef]
25. Wang, X.; Peng, M.; Hu, Z.; Chen, Y.; Lin, Q. Feasibility investigation of large-scale model suspended by cable-driven parallel robot in hypersonic wind tunnel test. *Proc. Inst. Mech. Eng. Part G J. Aerosp. Eng.* **2017**, *231*, 2375–2383. [CrossRef]
26. Ji, Y.; Peng, M.; Lin, Q.; Yin, C. Wire-driven parallel robot suspension system for SDM in a low-speed wind tunnel. *Adv. Mech. Eng.* **2023**, *15*, 16878132231170262. [CrossRef]
27. Ahmadi, M.; Guigue, A.; Gibeault, M.; Tang, F.C. Mechatronic design of redundant robotic systems for captive trajectory simulation applications. In Proceedings of the 10th IASTED International Conference on Control and Applications (CA 2008), Quebec City, QC, Canada, 26–28 May 2008; pp. 24–29.
28. Cook, M. *Flight Dynamics Principles—A Linear Systems Approach to Aircraft Stability and Control*, 3rd ed.; Butterworth-Heinemann: Oxford, UK, 2013. [CrossRef]
29. Sinha, N.K.; Ananthkrishnan, N. *Elementary Flight Dynamics with an Introduction to Bifurcation and Continuation Methods*; CRC Press: Boca Raton, FL, USA, 2013.
30. Stengel, R.F. *Flight Dynamics*; Princeton University Press: Princeton, NJ, USA, 2004.
31. Whidborne, J.F.; Jarzębowska, E.; Agarwal, V.; Ishola, A.A. Manipulator-aircraft dynamical system dedicated for wind tunnel testing. In Proceedings of the 16th Conference on Dynamical Systems—Theory and Applications (DSTA 2021), Łódź, Poland, 6–9 December 2021; Awrejcewicz, J., Kaźmierczak, M., Mrozowski, M., Olejnik, P., Eds.; Lodz University of Technology Press: Lodz, Poland, 2021; pp. 115–116. [CrossRef]
32. Ishola, A.A.; Whidborne, J.F.; Kasula, P. Control for novel 3-DOF flight testing in a wind tunnel. In Proceedings of the 14th UKACC International Conference on Control (CONTROL 2024), Winchester, UK, 10–12 April 2024; pp. 321–322. [CrossRef]
33. Malik, I.A. The Design, Development and Evaluation of an Active Control Aircraft Model Wind Tunnel Facility. Ph.D. Thesis, Cranfield University, Bedford, UK, 1982.
34. Stevens, B.L.; Lewis, F.L. *Aircraft Control and Simulation*, 2nd ed.; John Wiley: Hoboken, NJ, USA, 2003. [CrossRef]
35. O'Gorman, D. Flight Dynamics Modelling of a 4 Degrees-of-Freedom Dynamic Test Rig. Master's Thesis, Cranfield University, Bedford, UK, 2006.
36. Yoshikawa, T. *Foundations of Robotics—Analysis and Control*; MIT Press: Cambridge, MA, USA, 1990. [CrossRef]

37. Žefran, M.; Bullo, F. Langrangian Dynamics. In *Robotics and Automation Handbook*, 1st ed.; Kurfess, T.R., Ed.; CRC Press: Boca Raton, FL, USA, 2005; Chapter 5. [CrossRef]
38. Whidborne, J.; Tang, G.; Ishola, A. *Code—Nonlinear Dynamics and Control of a Novel 3-DOF Aircraft-Manipulator for Dynamic Wind Tunnel Tests*; Cranfield Online Research Data (CORD) Repository: Bedford, UK, 2024. [CrossRef]
39. Liang, B.and Xu, Y.; Bergerman, M. Mapping a space manipulator to a dynamically equivalent manipulator. *J. Dyn. Syst. Meas. Control* **1998**, *120*, 1–7. [CrossRef]
40. Jarzębowska, E.; Kłak, M. Quaternion-based spacecraft dynamic modeling and reorientation control using the dynamically equivalent manipulator approach. In *Advances in Spacecraft Attitude Control*; Sands, T., Ed.; IntechOpen: Rijeka, Croatia, 2020; Chapter 3. [CrossRef]

Disclaimer/Publisher's Note: The statements, opinions and data contained in all publications are solely those of the individual author(s) and contributor(s) and not of MDPI and/or the editor(s). MDPI and/or the editor(s) disclaim responsibility for any injury to people or property resulting from any ideas, methods, instructions or products referred to in the content.

robotics

MDPI

Article

Quantum-Inspired Sliding-Mode Control to Enhance the Precision and Energy Efficiency of an Articulated Industrial Robotic Arm

Mehdi Fazilat and Nadjet Zioui *

Department of Mechanical Engineering, Université du Québec à Trois-Rivières, 3351 Bd des Forges, Trois-Rivières, QC G8Z 4M3, Canada; mehdi.fazilat@uqtr.ca
* Correspondence: nadjet.zioui@uqtr.ca

Abstract: Maintaining precise and robust control in robotic systems, particularly those with nonlinear dynamics and external disturbances, is a significant challenge in robotics. Sliding-mode control (SMC) is a widely used technique to tackle these issues; however, it is plagued by chattering and computational complexity, which limit its effectiveness in high-precision environments. This study aims to develop and assess a quantum-inspired sliding-mode control (QSMC) strategy to enhance the SMC's robustness, precision, and computational efficiency, specifically in controlling a six-jointed articulated robotic arm. The methodology involves creating a comprehensive kinematic and dynamic model of the robot, followed by implementing both classic SMC and the proposed Q-SMC in a comparative way. The simulation results confirm that the Q-SMC method outperforms the classic SMC, particularly in reducing chattering, improving tracking accuracy, and decreasing energy consumption by approximately 3.79%. These findings suggest that the Q-SMC technique provides a promising alternative to classical control methods, with potential applications in tasks requiring high precision and efficient robotic manipulations.

Keywords: industrial robotic manipulator arm; kinematics modeling; nonlinear dynamics; sliding-mode control; quantum-inspired sliding-mode control; energy efficiency

1. Introduction

1.1. Context of the Study

Robust control is a key component in robotics, particularly in controlling the complexities of nonlinear dynamics and external disturbances that arise when operating articulated robotic arms. Sliding-mode control (SMC) is well known for its robustness and precision, particularly in managing the nonlinear dynamics and external disturbances encountered when controlling robotic arms. Its ability to maintain stability and performance despite the system's uncertainties makes it particularly ideal for articulated robotic arms with large degrees of freedom [1–4]. SMC accomplishes this by shifting the system's state to a predefined sliding surface, where it can effectively handle variations in the robot's dynamics and external forces applied to tasks such as trajectory tracking, path planning, and force control, ensuring that the robotic arm can execute precise and reliable movements even under challenging conditions [5–7]. However, traditional SMC techniques have substantial limitations, such as chattering and computing complexity, which limit their practical implementation in high-precision and dynamic situations [8–10]. To address these challenges, the current study provides a robust sliding-mode controller with chattering rejection capabilities and suggests a quantum-inspired sliding-mode control approach designed for a six-degree-of-freedom articulated robotic arm. The work advances the field by constructing a thorough kinematic and dynamic model of the robot using precise CAD designs from SolidWorks software 2024 SP4.0 to extract mass properties required for correct path planning and trajectory execution and evaluating the practice's performance parameters [11]. A unique quantum control algorithm employing multiple qubit operators is also developed, which improves the robustness of the control strategy. This novel approach improves the robustness and precision of the control system, considerably boosting the robot's energy efficiency performance, as evidenced by rigorous testing. Integrating the quantum principles into SMC is a novel advancement in robotic arm control, opening new avenues for overcoming the constraints of traditional approaches to create more efficient and adaptive robotic systems.

1.2. Related Works

The integration of backstepping terminal sliding-mode control with radial basis function neural networks, as demonstrated by Vijay and Jena [12], highlights the application of SMC in controlling specific objects of a robot manipulator with three degrees of freedom (DOF) in an overhead transmission; however, challenges such as parameter tuning and computational complexity have not been solved. Similarly, Adhikary and Mahanta [13] introduced an adaptive backstepping SMC with time delay estimation, enhancing trajectory tracking and disturbance rejection in two-DOF robotic manipulators, though real-time implementation poses challenges. Norsahperi and Danapalasingam [14] advanced the field by proposing an improved optimal integral SMC to reduce the tracking error and energy consumption in robotic manipulators. This has been validated through simulations on a two-DOF manipulator, with significant potential for industrial applications. Nguyen et al. [15] developed a backstepping global fast terminal sliding-mode control, addressing chattering and enhancing transient response in a two-DOF robotic manipulator, although uncertainty estimation remains challenging. Baek et al. [16] contributed with their widely and stable adaptive SMC, focusing on a two-link planar robot manipulator, demonstrating adaptability with challenges in tuning and convergence. Further advancing SMC, Baek and Kwon [17] introduced a strong and stable adaptive SMC, enhancing disturbance rejection and minimizing chattering in robotic manipulators, particularly in dynamic uncertainty environments. Feng et al. [18] addressed chattering mitigation through full-order SMC with time-varying gains applied to a two-DOF robotic manipulator. At the same time, Zhai and Li [19] focused on high-speed and high-precision applications through fast-exponential SMC, integrating a super-twisting controller with a high-order sliding-mode observer. Soriano et al. [20] shifted the focus to energy efficiency, proposing an optimized SMC using a bat algorithm to reduce energy consumption in a SCARA robot, emphasizing the importance of sustainability in industrial robotics. The integration of neural networks with SMC has also seen considerable advancements, with Yen et al. [21] combining recurrent fuzzy wavelet neural networks with adaptive SMC to enhance tracking accuracy and stability in industrial robots. At the same time, Jung [22] used radial basis function-like neural networks in neuro-sliding-mode control for a three-link rotary robot manipulator, refining SMC gain selection. Gambhire et al. [23] provided a broader perspective by examining the evolution of SMC techniques, including integrating intelligent control strategies such as neural networks, emphasizing the need for robust control mechanisms. Yu et al. [24] extended the discussion with a comprehensive overview of terminal SMC, suggesting an integration with artificial intelligence techniques to enhance adaptability and robustness. Finally, Yin et al. [25] introduced a compensation SMC with a nonlinear disturbance observer for machining robotic manipulators, significantly improving tracking accuracy and robustness, particularly in industrial applications. The literature on SMC techniques in robotics indicates a clear trend toward more adaptive, intelligent, and energy-efficient control methods, with ongoing research focusing on optimizing real-time implementation and integrating advanced computational techniques to address persistent challenges such as chattering, uncertainty estimation, and energy consumption.

Quantum-inspired SMC denotes a substantial upgrade in control techniques. It aims to manage the limitations of the classic SMC, such as chattering, robustness against disturbances, and computational efficiency. Incorporating quantum principles into SMC offers new possibilities for enhancing the precision and robustness of science and engineering, especially in robotic systems, making it a promising area for prospective investigation.

Early applications of quantum methods in robotics demonstrate the potential of quantum SMC to make fundamental transformations in control systems. For example, Gan et al. [26] integrated quantum-behaved particle swarm optimization with SMC to improve control systems for unmanned underwater vehicles, focusing on enhancing robustness in complex underwater environments. Similarly, Fazilat et al. [27] developed a quantum-based kinematic model for industrial robotic arms, such as the ABB IRB140, seriously reducing computational demands and facilitating real-time processing. Zioui et al. [28] further contributed by modeling rigid body orientation using quantum spins, a crucial aspect of robotics that simplifies spatial orientation modeling and bridges classical and quantum control systems. The development of quantum algorithms and their application in robotics has shown notable promise. Boudjoghra et al. [29] introduced a quantum computing-based solution using the Harrow–Hassidim–Lloyd (HHL) algorithm to address state-domain equations in control theory. This approach is particularly beneficial for dynamic systems in robotics, reducing computational intricacy. Singh and Sloth [30] developed an evolving type 2 quantum fuzzy neural network for robotic manipulators, integrating quantum fuzzy logic with traditional neural networks to enhance adaptability and stability. State-of-the-art applications of quantum control in robotics are beginning to emerge, showcasing the potential of these methods to enhance performance in problematic environments. Zheng and Su [31] used QPSO to enhance SMC for electro-hydraulic servo systems, achieving significant improvements in tracking accuracy and setting a benchmark for optimizing control in uncertain robotic environments. Qu et al. [32] introduced a novel integral SMC for helicopter systems, integrating quantum information techniques to improve control accuracy and disturbance rejection, which is crucial for dynamic robotic systems like helicopters. In another investigation, Zioui et al. [33] extended quantum computing applications in robotic kinematics by developing a quaternion model for robotic arm positioning, demonstrating the feasibility of quantum models in practical robotics and paving the way for future Q-SMC strategies. The impact of quantum-inspired control methods on robotics is increasingly evident as researchers explore their adaptability and efficiency. Sivak et al. [34] proposed a model-free quantum control approach using reinforcement learning, enhancing the adaptability and performance of quantum-based control methods in environments where precise models are challenging to obtain. Quantum computing's potential to revolutionize robotics is further highlighted by Petschnigg et al. [35], who synthesized the current state of quantum computing and proposed its application to complex robotic challenges like AI, machine learning, and kinematics. Niu et al. [36] involved quantum control through deep reinforcement learning to optimize quantum systems, offering insights into adapting these methods for robotic applications that require real-time decision-making under uncertainty. Specialized quantum control strategies for robotics continue to advance the field. Reshetnikov and Ulyanov [37] explored the application of quantum fuzzy controllers in robotic systems like mobile manipulators, demonstrating marked control accuracy and robustness improvements. Tavanaei-Sereshki and Ramezani-al [38] developed a quantum genetic algorithm-based SMC for autonomous underwater vehicles, showing superior performance in nonlinear, dynamic surroundings and highlighting the broader applicability of quantum-inspired control strategies in other robotic systems. The study by Xi et al. [39] addresses the significant challenge of controlling robot manipulators in industrial environments characterized by high uncertainties and nonlinear dynamics. Their robust adaptive SMC system integrates an adaptive sliding-mode disturbance observer with backstepping techniques, demonstrating enhanced precision and stability in uncertain environments. The reviewed studies collectively illustrate the transformative potential of quantum SMC in various aspects of intelligent mechanisms and robotics. By addressing challenges in traditional control methods, from high-dimensional optimization to real-time adaptation in dynamic environments, these studies contribute to a growing body of knowledge that could significantly influence overcoming the limitations of classical methods, enhancing the precision, robustness, and computational efficiency of robotic control systems.

1.3. Problem Formulation and Contribution

While SMC has proven to be a robust solution for managing the nonlinear dynamics and external disturbances in robotic arms, significant limitations such as chattering and computational complexity persist. These issues hinder the practical application of SMC in high-precision, dynamic environments, particularly in robotics systems with high degrees of freedom. More adaptive, precise, and computationally efficient control strategies still need to be met, especially in scenarios requiring real-time response and energy efficiency. It is essential to investigate filling this gap by exploring the potential of quantum-inspired sliding-mode control to examine the probability of overcoming these intrinsic limitations.

The primary purpose of the current examination is to develop and validate a novel quantum-enhanced sliding-mode control strategy, particularly for a six-degree-of-freedom articulated robotic arm and perform a comparative study between the performance of classic SMC and a quantum version of sliding-mode control. It aims to enhance SMC's robustness, precision, and computational efficiency by integrating quantum principles into the control strategy, focusing on addressing the persistent issues of chattering, computational complexity, and robustness against disturbances, which are vital for achieving high-performance robotic control to improve the control system's energy efficiency and adaptability, ultimately contributing to more reliable and efficient robotic arm manipulations in dynamic environments.

The effectiveness of this study lies in its possibility of enhancing control systems in robotics by introducing quantum-inspired sliding-mode control as a practicable alternative to classic methods. Incorporating quantum principles into SMC could increase robotic systems' performance and energy efficiency by addressing the evolution of computational methodologies. It offers a more robust and precise control strategy that can be applied in applications, particularly in the adaptability and effectiveness of robotic systems in real-world scenarios where precision, speed, and reliability are paramount.

The present study compares two control strategies, the classical sliding-mode control and its quantum-inspired sliding-mode control counterpart. The primary objective was to evaluate the integration of quantum principles into control methodologies and assess its potential to enhance performance. In this comprehensive case study, we developed a robust SMC-based control framework for our robotic arm and extended it to include quantum-inspired elements. While acknowledging the effectiveness of other advanced control strategies such as Model Predictive Control, reinforcement learning-based methods, Adaptive Control, Fractional Order Control, and H-infinity Robust Control, we notice the significance of exploring these approaches to broaden the comparative scope of our research. However, for this study, we focused on a singular, well-established control strategy and its quantum-inspired enhancement to facilitate a concentrated and stringent analysis of their respective performance.

The current research presents a comprehensive study of robust control of an industrial manipulator robotic arm incorporating quantum-inspired sliding-mode control for robotic arms. Section 2 explores the kinematic modeling of the ABB IRB140 robot, emphasizing an advanced approach to developing a precise model for motion planning and performance evaluation. This section also details the CAD design of the robotic arm, underscoring the critical importance of accurately obtaining mass properties. Furthermore, it outlines the design of a robust SMC strategy, including techniques for reducing chattering and introducing a novel quantum-inspired sliding-mode control algorithm employing multiple qubit operators. Section 3 presents the experimental results, demonstrating the superior performance of the quantum-enhanced SMC in managing the manipulator robot arm. Finally, Section 4 discusses the implications of these findings and suggests directions for future research in the control of robotics and quantum computing.

2. Methodology

2.1. Robotic Arm Presentation

The study focuses on the ABB IRB 140 robot, illustrated in Figure 1. This six-axis articulated robot is widely employed in different industrial applications. According to ABB's technical specifications, it provides flexible mounting options, such as floor, wall, and inverted positions, to accommodate different working environments. The IRB 140 robot is commonly utilized for arc welding, assembly, material handling, machine tending, cleaning, and spraying, packing, and deburring. With a weight of approximately 98 kg, it can support an end-effector with a payload capacity of up to 5 kg. The robot's reach extends to about 810 mm at its mounting flange, and it can bear up to 1.5 kg of equipment on its upper arm. The joint limits offer a significant functional workspace, as outlined in Table 1 [11].

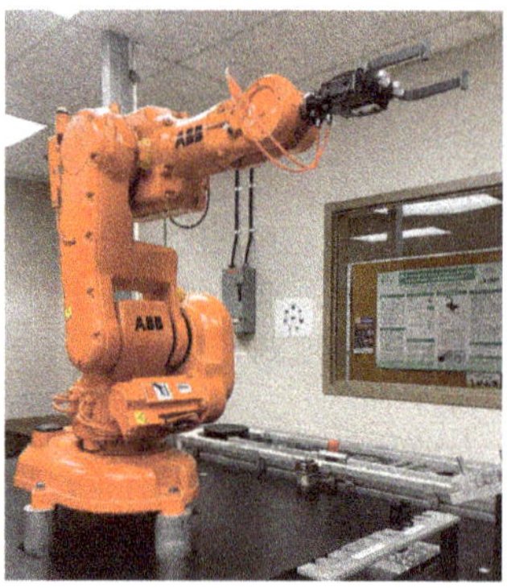

Figure 1. The ABB IRB 140 robot located in the UQTR automation laboratory.

Table 1. Joint limits of the ABB IRB 140 robot.

Joints	Type of the Joint	Limits (°)
1	R	+180 to −180
2	R	+110 to −90
3	R	+50 to −230
4	R	+200 to −200
5	R	+120 to −120
6	R [1]	+400 to −400

[1] R stands for rotational or revolute.

The robotic arm features an IRC5 advanced controller designed to handle multiple robots, optimizing their performance for shorter cycle times and precise movements. It also incorporates RobotWare (Robot Studio), allowing ABB robots to be programmed from a workstation without disrupting active production processes. This configuration includes the ABB Virtual Controller, a representation of the production-level software that enables program development. Robot Studio presents highly realistic simulations, utilizing simple robot programs and configuration files that accurately reflect real-world operations [11].

For the present research, the ABB IRB 140 robot was utilized in its original configuration, strictly following the manufacturer's specifications. The robot's structure and system remained unchanged, with no custom modifications. This approach ensures that our study's results and insights accurately reflect the standard performance of the ABB IRB 140 as commonly observed in industrial settings. Additionally, it provides a baseline for evaluating the robot's efficiency and dynamics in typical operational scenarios.

2.2. Mathematical Model of the Robot

The evaluation of the ABB IRB-140 robotic arm at the UQTR mechatronic laboratory began by inputting joint-specific data to generate trajectories, which served as a foundation for implementing kinematic models. These models were developed using Denavit–Hartenberg parameters (Table 2) to define the position and orientation of the end-effector. The robot's joint motions were generated using fifth-order polynomial equations and transformation matrices, allowing for a detailed description of the potential positions and orientations. This kinematic analysis was a prototype of dynamic modeling, which employed the Euler–Lagrange method to explore the robot's dynamics, focusing on joint torque calculations and energy consumption. The dynamic model was further enhanced by incorporating inertia and mass center point data from detailed CAD/CAM designs created using SolidWorks software. This phase seamlessly transitioned into computer-aided optimization (CAO), enabling comprehensive simulations representing various model fidelity levels. Integrating kinematic and dynamic models facilitated a comprehensive analysis, allowing precise estimation of the robot's energy needs through torque profiles.

Table 2. Denavit–Hartenberg Parameters of the ABB IRB 140 [11,28].

Link	a (mm)	α (°)	d (mm)	q (°)
1	$a_1 = 70$	−90	$d_1 = 352$	q_1
2	$a_2 = -360$	0	0	$q_2 + 90$
3	0	−90	0	q_3
4	0	90	$d_4 = 380$	q_4
5	0	−90	0	q_5
6	0	0	$d_6 = 65$	q_6

After that, the inverse kinematics was developed. The model involves determining the joint angles that achieve a specific end-effector position. This model is crucial for maintaining safe and reliable robot operations but also allows for explicit control over the robot's posture. Additionally, it offers a computationally efficient method for determining joint angles, making them particularly beneficial in real-time control scenarios where rapid computation is essential.

The differential kinematics was also developed to define how the angular velocities of a robot's joints relate to its end-effector's linear and angular velocities. By analyzing velocities and static forces, the Jacobian matrix J of the manipulator is derived. This matrix plays a key role in examining and controlling robotic motion, identifying singularities and redundancy, formulating inverse kinematic equations, and characterizing the manipulability of velocity and force [40]. The Jacobian matrix is specifically adapted to the unique joint configurations of each robot, greatly enhancing motion planning and control, which are essential for executing precision tasks. It also addresses singularities and redundancies, improving the robot's operational efficiency and safety.

Finally, a dynamic model is developed to enable the analysis of a robot's performance regarding joint acceleration forces and torques. The Euler–Lagrange method is commonly employed to establish such a dynamic model. The first three proximal joints are fundamental as they play a significant role in assessing the mechanical loads experienced by the mechanical structure of the robot during operation, which is a key factor in the dynamic modeling and assumptions made in the model. The dynamic behavior of a robotic arm with n joints can be described by relation (1) [11].

$$M\ddot{q} + V + G = \tau \tag{1}$$

In this context, $\ddot{q}$ represents the joint acceleration vector, M is the inertia matrix, V corresponds to the Coriolis vector, G denotes the gravitational vector, and τ is the force and torque vector. In our study, the elements of the inertia matrix and the positions of the mass centers were determined using SolidWorks software. The uniform density assumption for each link was applied across all models. It also considered key values related to mass and other physical properties, such as the mass center positions and inertia matrices, represented within their respective reference frames for the three proximal links. The precision of a dynamic model relies heavily on accurately determining mass centers and inertia matrices. To obtain these necessary data in engineering, straightforward dimensional specifications, and scientific methods, including CAD modeling, Experimental Modal Analysis, and Inertia Measurement Units, are utilized. CAD modeling provides detailed information on dimensions and mass distribution, while Experimental Modal Analysis and Inertia Measurement Units offer direct measurements of inertia characteristics. The mass of each link can be calculated assuming constant and uniform density. SolidWorks software was utilized to determine the volume of each link. The mass of each link is estimated by multiplying the ratio of an individual link's volume to the total robot volume by the total robot mass.

2.3. CAD Designs of the Robot

Employing SolidWorks, we performed a high degree of precision in modeling each robotic arm component. A determined purpose of accuracy and steady state to our conceptual design parameters depicted our methodology. This introductory phase has specified a solid foundation for a robotic arm balanced to enhance the capabilities within industrial automation, mainly characterized by its superior functionality. During the CAD design process, we make the simplifying assumption that the robot's components have a uniform density. While this assumption simplifies the calculations, it may result in inaccuracies since it must account for the material variations in the real robot. Additionally, ergonomics and safety were essential throughout the design iterations, driven by an iterative process. This process concerned rigorous stress examination, evaluation of energy consumption patterns, and comprehensive persistence testing. These steps were required to establish the arm's mechanical robustness and stable reliability, ensuring its appropriateness for reinforcing industrial application. The precise, detailed model depicted in Figure 2 is fundamental for the simulations that require high fidelity and detailed analysis. This model reproduces the robot's configuration with maximum accuracy, making it ideal for investigating elaborate dynamics and interactions within the real robot's mechanism. Mass and inertia values are established on the presumed material properties and the model's geometry. These values are essential for dynamic simulations, but they may not fully reflect the actual robot due to potential manufacturing variations and inconsistencies in material properties [11].

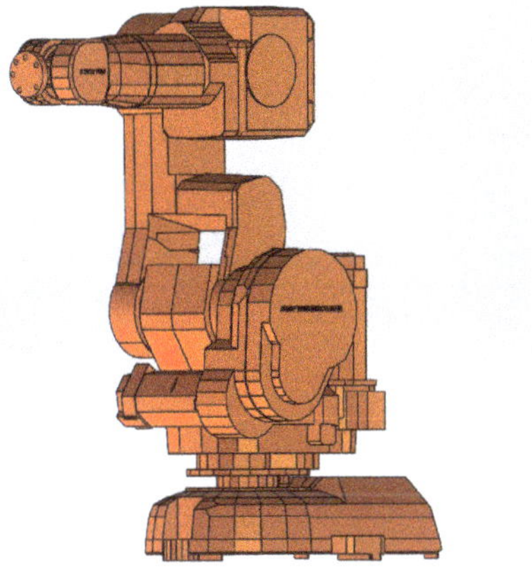

Figure 2. Detailed SolidWorks model of the ABB IRB 140 robotic arm [11].

The specifics of the model and the results for the proximal links obtained using the mass properties tool are outlined in Table 3 [11].

Table 3. Mass property results of each model calculated using SolidWorks software [11].

ABB IRB 140	Parameters (Unit)	Link 1	Link 2	Link 3
Mass Properties	*Weight* (kg)	35	25	18
	Xc (mm)	277.87	218.29	−24.56
	Yc	373.12	229.73	−219.9
	Zc	−199.03	112.43	−25.86
	Ixx (kg·m^2)	6.5	0.9	2.5
	Ixy	1.1	−0.03	−0.001
	Ixz	3.05	0.1	0.09
	Iyy	2.02	1.3	2.7
	Iyz	5.07	−0.01	−0.8

2.4. Robot Performance Assessment

To evaluate the accuracy of the three models' predictions, we analyzed the energy consumption by the three proximal joints and the robot's total energy consumption over the same duration and path of movement. In the proposed modeling approach, the energy consumption of each joint at a specific time can be calculated from the joint torque and angular velocity using Equation (2). The robot's integrated energy consumption is assumed to be the sum of the energy consumption values of all the joints.

$$E_i = \int_{t_0}^{t_f} \tau_i(t) \cdot \dot{q}_i(t) \, dt \tag{2}$$

We employ a theoretical approach to evaluate the energy consumption of robotic arms. This approach centers on dynamic models that simulate each joint's torque τ_i and angular velocity $\dot{q}_i$ Detailed explanations of how these parameters are simulated are provided in the methodology section. The simulated values are then used in Equation (2) to calculate the energy consumption of each joint. The theoretical method offers a comprehensive analysis of energy consumption, avoiding the practical challenges and complexities associated with the installation and calibration of physical sensors on the robotic arm.

Focusing on a theoretical and simulation-based approach contributes significantly to understanding energy dynamics in robotic arms, especially in scenarios where direct measurement is impractical or impossible. This approach also aligns with current trends in employing computational models to analyze complex system contributions to robotics fields.

2.5. Sliding-Mode Control Strategy

One method of robust control technique for controlling a complicated and nonlinear mechanism like a manipulator robotic arm is called sliding-mode control methodology, a type of variable structure control system [4,10,41]. The most crucial feature of the sliding-mode control is the complete insensitivity to parametric uncertainty and external disturbances during the sliding process. The variable structure control system utilizes a high-speed switching-control law for two purposes. First of all, it forces the nonlinear system's form trajectory along a user-defined surface in the state space, named the sliding or switching surface [42,43]. The control approach has one gain if the state trajectory of the mechanism is above the surface and a different gain if the controlling object, such as trajectory in robotics, drops below the surface and because of this named sliding surface. Secondly, it keeps the mechanism state control object on this surface by following the time [44,45]. During the controlling process, the control system's structure differs from one to another and thus it donates the name variable structure control. This model also permits the elimination of interactions among the joints of the manipulator [46,47]. A general equation of the motion can be represented in the space state by the following [48]:

$$x = f\ (x,\ t) + g\ (x,\ t)\cdot\ u \tag{3}$$

where u is the control input, x is the state vector also considered as the output, and the functions $f\ (x,\ t)$ and $g\ (x,\ t)$ are nonlinear functions.

The control input variable is defined in the following:

$$u_i(x,t) = \begin{cases} u_i^+(x,t) & if\ \ S_i(x,t) > 0 \\ u_i^-(x,t) & if\ \ S_i(x,t) < 0 \end{cases} \tag{4}$$

where u_i, is the ith component of u, and $S_i(x,t) = 0$ is the ith component-switching hypersurfaces $S(x, t) = 0$, $S \in R^m$.

According to the presented rules with discontinuous control, the system is named a variable structure system since the controller switches alternatively based on the state of the mechanism. The sliding mode appears on a switching surface $S(x) = 0$, which pushes the machine to behave as a linear-time uniform system, which can be assumed to be stable. For it to be linear, the surfaces can be written as:

$$s_i(x) = x_n + \sum_{i=1}^{n} \lambda_i \cdot x_i \tag{5}$$

The condition for the sliding mode to exist on the ith surface is provided by the following equation:

$$\lim_{s_i \to 0^+} \dot{S} > 0 \qquad \text{and} \ \lim_{s_i \to 0^-} \dot{S} < 0 \tag{6}$$

This is when $S\dot{S} < 0$ is too close to $S_i(x) = 0$, when all the trajectories shift towards the switching surface. In the perfect sliding mode on S_i, the related control is the equal control issued from Equation (3) and given by the equation for $\dot{S} = 0$:

$$u_{eq} = g^{-1}(x,t)\left[\dot{x}(t) - f(x,t)\right] \tag{7}$$

So, the discontinuous control input presented in relation (4) can be noted as follows:

$$u_i = \begin{cases} u^*_{ieq} + \Delta u_i^+ & if \ S_i > 0 \\ u^*_{ieq} + \Delta u_i^- & if \ S_i < 0 \end{cases} \quad (8)$$

where u_{eq} illustrates the low-frequency control component or the steady state equivalent control signal, and Δu presents the high-frequency discontinuous term. For the functional case, the control equation is known by the evaluated value due to error modulization and variation in the parameters as follows:

$$u^*_{eq} = u_{eq} + \Delta u_{eq} \quad (9)$$

This last formula is equivalent to the discontinuous control input in relation (8). The term of high-frequency Δu can be represented differently, such as the equation based on the classical reaching law, which is one of the methods reported in the literature for alleviating chattering in sliding mode. Classical reaching law can express in four principal subcategories that are represented as the following:

Constant reaching law:

$$\dot{s} = -\varepsilon \cdot sgn(s), \qquad \varepsilon > 0 \quad (10)$$

Exponential reaching law:

$$\dot{s} = -\varepsilon \cdot sgn(s) - ks, \qquad \varepsilon > 0 \quad k > 0 \quad (11)$$

Power-rate reaching law:

$$\dot{s} = -k\,|s^\alpha| \cdot sgn(s), \qquad 0 < \alpha < 1 \quad k > 0 \quad (12)$$

General reaching law:

$$\dot{s} = -\varepsilon \cdot sgn(s) - f(s)\,,\ \varepsilon > 0 \ \text{ where } f\ (0) = 0 \text{and } sf(s) > 0 \text{when s } \neq 0 \quad (13)$$

To obtain a robust sliding-mode control based on reaching law, consider the general equation motion as below:

$$\ddot{x} = f(x) + g(x)u + d(t) \quad (14)$$

where $f(x)$ and $g(x)$ are unknown equations and $g(x) > 0$ and $d(t)$ are the terms of disturbance. As sliding surface and derivative of the sliding surface, the combination of error of models considered satisfy the Hurwitz condition and can be described as follows:

$$s = \dot{e} + ce, c > 0 \quad (15a)$$

$$e = r - x(t) \quad (15b)$$

$$\dot{e} = \dot{r} - \dot{x}(t) \quad (15c)$$

For the derivative of the sliding-surface equation considering the effect of external disturbance as $d(t)$:

$$\dot{s} = \ddot{e} + c\dot{e} = \ddot{r} - \ddot{x} + c(\dot{r} - \dot{x}) = \ddot{r} - f(x) - g(x)u - d(t) + c(\dot{r} - \dot{x}) \quad (16)$$

To obtain the robust control sliding mode based on the exponential reaching law from the relations of (12) and (16):

$$\begin{array}{c}\ddot{r}-f(x)-g(x)u-d(t)+c(\dot{r}-\dot{x})=-\varepsilon\cdot sgn(s)-ks\\ u=\frac{1}{g(x)}(\ddot{r}-f(x)-d(t)+c(\dot{r}-\dot{x})+\varepsilon\cdot sgn(s)+ks\end{array} \quad (17)$$

The derivative of the sliding-surface equation can also be considered with (15) described with the disturbance term as follows:

$$\dot{s}=-\varepsilon\cdot sgn(s)-ks+d_c-d \quad (18)$$

The disturbance term d_c must satisfy the conditions for reaching the sliding surface, and the term d should be limited. dl and du are the lower and upper terms of disturbance, respectively, as:

$d_l \le d(t) \le d_u$, when s(t) > 0, $\dot{s}=\varepsilon-ks+d_c-d$, we want $\dot{s}$(t) < 0, so let $d_c=d_l$.

When s(t) < 0, $\dot{s}=-\varepsilon-ks+d_c-d$, we want $\dot{s}$(t) > 0, so let $d_c=d_u$.

Therefore, if we define $d_1=\frac{d_u-d_l}{2}, d_2=\frac{d_u+d_l}{2}$, then we can obtain the following:

$$d_c=d_2-d_1\cdot sgn(s) \quad (19)$$

The discontinuity of the sign function will generate chattering in the closed loop system. For this reason, the sign function is usually substituted by a saturation function sat (s/ε), where $sat(.)$ is described as follows:

$$sat(x)=\begin{cases}x & if\ |x|\le 1\\ sgn\ (x) & if\ |x|>1\end{cases} \quad (20)$$

To mitigate chattering, the study employs an exponential reaching law, which adjusts the conventional reaching law to achieve a smoother transition as the system state approaches the sliding surface. This is accomplished by adding a term, $-k\cdot s$, which gradually decreases the convergence rate to the sliding surface, thereby reducing the rapid switching responsible for chattering. Additionally, the discontinuous sign function $sgn(s)$ is replaced with a saturation function sat (s/ϵ), which introduces a boundary layer around the sliding surface. This change smooths the control action, significantly curbing chattering by preventing abrupt changes in the control input. By adjusting the thickness of this boundary layer, the system can strike an optimal balance between reducing chattering and maintaining precise control, enhancing the robustness and applicability of SMC in high-precision environments.

Employing this alternate will present a tracking error. The trade-off between the tracking error and control bandwidth will be created by setting the boundary layer properly. As mentioned before, the position of the robot's end-effector in this case study depends on the first three joints and links. For this reason, the control strategy implements the first three joints of the robot. Generally, for the three links, the robot's sliding-mode control can be described as follows:

$$s=\dot{e}+ce \quad (21)$$

For example, $e=\theta_d-\theta$.

This will lead to $\dot{s}=\ddot{e}+c\dot{e}=\ddot{\theta}_d-\ddot{\theta}+c\dot{e}$ and

$$\dot{s}=-\varepsilon\ sgn(s) \quad (22)$$

The combination of Equations (21) and (22) will result in the following:

$$\ddot{\theta} = \ddot{\theta}_d + c\dot{e} + \varepsilon \, sgn\ (s) \tag{23}$$

The general equation of the robot relies on the dynamics of the robot described as relation (1), which can be rewritten in terms of accelerations as the following:

$$\ddot{\theta} = M^{-1}(\tau - V - G) \tag{24}$$

With relations (23) and (24), we obtain the main equation of sliding-mode control as follows:

$$\tau = M\left(\ddot{\theta}_d + c\dot{e} + \varepsilon \, sgn(s)\right) + V + G \tag{25}$$

Assuming the presence of the disturbances for the robot in the working space to determine and track of end-effector position and considering inverse kinematics and dynamics of the robot manipulator, we can achieve the following equation for controlling in the sliding-mode technique:

$$\tau = M{\cdot}J^{-1}\left(\ddot{X}_d + c\dot{e} + \varepsilon \, sgn(s) - \dot{J}(\theta)\dot{\theta}\right) + V + G \tag{26}$$

2.6. Quantum Computing Basics

Quantum computing operates on a different principle compared to classical computing, utilizing quantum bits, or qubits, to encode and process information. A qubit state, denoted as $|q\rangle$, can be expressed as a superposition of the classical binary states 0 and 1 [49,50]. Mathematically, this is represented as:

$$|q\rangle = \alpha|0\rangle + \beta|1\rangle \tag{27}$$

Here, α and β are complex coefficients that correspond to the probability amplitudes of the qubit being in the states $|0\rangle$ and $|1\rangle$, respectively. These probabilities can be interpreted such that $|\alpha|^2$ gives the likelihood of the qubit being in the $|0\rangle$ state, while $|\beta|^2$ gives the probability of it being in the $|1\rangle$ state. In the context of vector space, the states $|0\rangle$ and $|1\rangle$ can be represented as the vectors $|0\rangle \equiv \begin{pmatrix} 1 \\ 0 \end{pmatrix}$ and $|1\rangle \equiv \begin{pmatrix} 0 \\ 1 \end{pmatrix}$, respectively [49,50]. Thus, a qubit state $|q\rangle$ can be depicted in vector form as $\begin{pmatrix} \alpha \\ \beta \end{pmatrix}$. Quantum operations, known as quantum gates, can be applied to qubits to alter their states. These operations are often represented by Hamiltonian matrices [28,33]. The fundamental quantum gates that act on a single qubit include the identity, X, Y, and Z gates, which correspond to the Pauli matrices $\sigma_0, \sigma_x, \sigma_y$, and σ_z, respectively, as defined by the following matrices [50]:

$$\sigma_0 = \begin{pmatrix} 1 & 0 \\ 0 & 1 \end{pmatrix} \tag{28}$$

$$\sigma_x = \begin{pmatrix} 0 & 1 \\ 1 & 0 \end{pmatrix} \tag{29}$$

$$\sigma_y = \begin{pmatrix} 0 & -i \\ i & 0 \end{pmatrix} \tag{30}$$

$$\sigma_z = \begin{pmatrix} 1 & 0 \\ 0 & -1 \end{pmatrix} \tag{31}$$

Other single-qubit quantum gates can be expressed as a linear combination of the Pauli gates, such as the Hadamard gate depicted in Equation (32) and the three basic rotation gates illustrated in Equations (33)–(35) [51,52].

$$H = \frac{\sqrt{2}}{2}\begin{pmatrix} 1 & 1 \\ 1 & 1 \end{pmatrix} = \frac{\sqrt{2}}{2}(\sigma_0 + \sigma_x) \tag{32}$$

$$R_x(\theta) = \begin{pmatrix} cos\theta & -i\ sin\theta \\ -i\ sin\theta & cos\theta \end{pmatrix} = cos\theta\ \sigma_0 - i\ sin\theta\ \sigma_x \tag{33}$$

$$R_y(\theta) = \begin{pmatrix} cos\theta & -sin\theta \\ sin\theta & cos\theta \end{pmatrix} = cos\theta\ \sigma_0 - i\ sin\theta\ \sigma_y \tag{34}$$

$$R_z(\theta) = \begin{pmatrix} e^{-i\theta} & 0 \\ 0 & e^{i\theta} \end{pmatrix} = cos\theta\ \sigma_0 - i\ sin\theta\ \sigma_z \tag{35}$$

2.6.1. Developing the Quantum Comparator

The quantum comparator is an innovative computational tool that harnesses quantum principles to enhance precision and efficiency in comparison tasks. It integrates two primary components: a quantum subtractor and a quantum sign detector [50].

The quantum subtractor computes the difference between two real numbers. Operating within the quantum framework, it offers higher parallelism and potentially faster speeds than classical subtractors. This enables it to prepare the data for the next step by providing the relative magnitude of the two numbers. Once the subtraction is complete, the result is passed to the quantum sign detector. This component determines the sign of the computed difference, indicating whether the first number is more significant than, less than, or equal to the second number. By leveraging quantum superposition and entanglement principles, the quantum sign detector identifies the sign accurately and efficiently, completing the comparison. These components work together to enable the quantum comparator to perform comparisons with greater accuracy and speed than classical methods, making it a valuable tool in quantum computing applications [53–55].

2.6.2. The Quantum Subtractor

The quantum subtractor for two real numbers relies on the tensor product between two real qubit states, $q_1 = C_{\theta_1}|0\rangle + S_{\theta_1}|1\rangle$ and $q_2 = C_{\theta_2}|0\rangle + S_{\theta_2}|1\rangle$. These qubit states, q_1 and q_2, are derived by applying a quantum rotation around the y-axis, as described by the following equations:

$$q_1 = R_y(\theta_1)|0\rangle \tag{36}$$

$$q_2 = R_y(\theta_2)|0\rangle \tag{37}$$

The tensor product between q_1 and q_2 yields the coefficients of the eigenstates:

$$q_1 \otimes q_2 = C_{\theta_1}C_{\theta_2}|00\rangle + C_{\theta_1}S_{\theta_2}|01\rangle + S_{\theta_1}C_{\theta_2}|10\rangle + S_{\theta_1}S_{\theta_2}|11\rangle \tag{38}$$

The coefficient $S_{\theta_1}C_{\theta_2}$ can be obtained by measuring the system $q_1 \otimes q_2$ in the state $|10\rangle$. This coefficient can be rewritten using the trigonometric identity:

$$S_{\theta_1}C_{\theta_2} = sin\left(\frac{\alpha-\beta}{2}\right)cos\left(\frac{\alpha+\beta}{2}\right) = \frac{1}{2}(sin(\alpha) - sin(\beta)) \tag{39}$$

where $\frac{\alpha-\beta}{2} = \theta_1$ and $\frac{\alpha+\beta}{2} = \theta_2$, with $\alpha = \theta_1 + \theta_2$ and $\beta = \theta_2 - \theta_1$.

Thus, the subtraction of two real numbers $x = sin(\alpha)$ and $y = sin(\beta)$ can be computed through the following steps:

Step 1: Compute $\alpha = \arcsin(x)$ and $\beta = \arcsin(y)$.

Convert the input numbers x and y into angles α and β, which will be used for quantum operations.

Step 2: Determine θ_1 as $\frac{\alpha-\beta}{2}$ and θ_2 as $\frac{\alpha+\beta}{2}$.

This calculates the rotation angles θ_1 and θ_2, encoding the difference and sum of the input numbers.

Step 3: Initialize the qubits q_1 and q_2 to $|0\rangle$.

This prepares the qubits in a known starting state before any quantum operations are applied.

Step 4: Apply the quantum rotations $R_y(\theta_1)$ to q_1 and $R_y(\theta_2)$ to q_2.

This performs quantum rotations on the qubits using the calculated angles, encoding the input numbers into the qubit states.

Step 5: Measure the system in the state $|10\rangle$. The coefficient should be calculated on the state vector, yielding half of the subtracted result, which can be doubled by applying a gain. However, the sign of the subtracted result is required for creating a comparator, and it is the same as the sign of its half. Consequently, doubling the result is unnecessary. This method involves measuring the quantum system to obtain a coefficient related to the difference.

2.6.3. The Quantum Sign Detector

The quantum sign detector is inspired by the Boolean subtraction operation, particularly focusing on the concept of the borrow, which is illustrated in the truth table. The borrow, denoted as r, is equal to 1 only when the minuend a is 0 and the subtrahend b is 1. The logical expression for the borrow can be represented as $r = \bar{a} \cdot b$. This expression indicates that a borrow occurs, meaning r equals 1, only if a is less than b. The quantum sign detector is inspired by the expression of the borrow of the Boolean subtraction, as described in the truth table depicted in Table 4.

Table 4. Truth table of the subtraction between two Boolean numbers.

a	b	$s = a - b$	r **(Borrow)**
0	0	0	0
0	1	1	1
1	0	1	0
1	1	0	0

In quantum computing, classical logic operations are translated into quantum gate operations. The purpose of the quantum sign detector is to implement the logic of the borrow operation using quantum gates, effectively detecting whether the result of a subtraction would require a borrow, which in classical terms, would indicate a negative result. Two key quantum gates are involved in this operation: the X gate (quantum NOT) and the CCNOT gate (Toffoli gate). The X gate is the quantum analogue of the classical NOT gate. It flips the state of a qubit; for instance, if the input qubit is in the $|0\rangle$ state, applying an X gate changes it to $|1\rangle$, and vice versa. In the context of the quantum sign detector, the X gate is used to invert the qubit representing a, producing $|\bar{a}\rangle$, which corresponds to the classical negation of a.

The CCNOT gate, or Toffoli gate, is a controlled-controlled-NOT gate. It performs a NOT operation on a target qubit only if the two control qubits are both in the $|1\rangle$ state. In the quantum sign detector, the CCNOT gate, takes $|\bar{a}\rangle$ and $|b\rangle$ as inputs and operates on an ancillary qubit initialized to $|0\rangle$. This operation effectively implements the logical AND between $\bar{a}$ and b, which corresponds to the classical borrow operation.

The quantum circuit for the sign detector operates as follows: Start by preparing qubits that represent the binary values a and b, along with an additional ancillary qubit initialized to $|0\rangle$. The qubit representing a is then passed through an X gate to obtain $|\bar{a}\rangle$. Subsequently, the CCNOT gate is applied to $|\bar{a}\rangle$ and $|b\rangle$, with the ancillary qubit as the target. The state of the ancillary qubit will be flipped to $|1\rangle$ if both $|\bar{a}\rangle = 1$ and $|b\rangle = 1$, thereby implementing the borrow logic. The final state of the ancillary qubit indicates the result of the quantum sign detection. If the ancillary qubit is in the $|1\rangle$ state, it corresponds to a borrow in the classical operation, signifying that the subtraction of b from a would result in a negative value. This quantum implementation of the borrow operation not only mirrors the classical logic but also leverages the principles of quantum mechanics, such as parallelism and quantum efficiency. Figure 3 depicts the quantum sign detector in a quantum circuit.

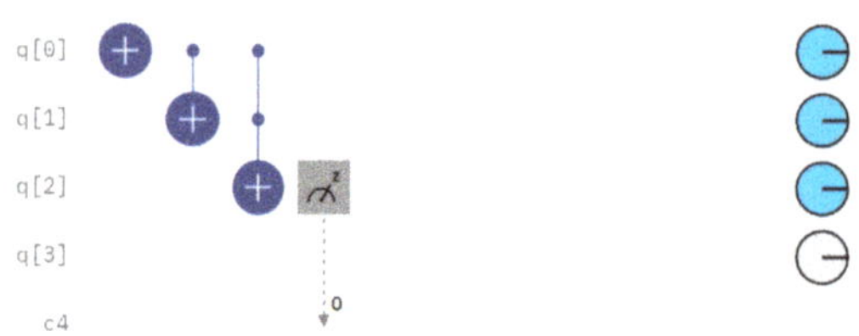

Figure 3. The quantum sign detector circuit [56].

2.6.4. The Quantum Adder

To effectively implement the hysteresis function, a subtractor is required, which can be realized using an adder and a sign detector. The necessary components for the sign detection have already been developed in the context of the comparator function. Therefore, the remaining task is to develop the quantum adder. The addition of two real numbers, x and y, is achieved using trigonometric identities as illustrated in the following steps. This process is grounded in the principles of quantum mechanics, specifically leveraging the tensor product and quantum state measurements. The tensor product between quantum states q_1 and q_2 yields the coefficients of the eigenstates presented in Equation (38), and to focus on the addition process, we measure the system q_1q_2 in the state $|01\rangle$. This measurement can be reformulated using the following trigonometric identity:

$$S_{\theta_1}C_{\theta_2} = cos\left(\frac{\alpha-\beta}{2}\right)sin\left(\frac{\alpha+\beta}{2}\right) = \frac{1}{2}(sin(\alpha) + sin(\beta)) \quad (40)$$

Here, $\alpha = \theta_1 + \theta_2$ and $\beta = \theta_2 - \theta_1$. Therefore, the addition of two real numbers x and y, where $x = sin(\alpha)$ and $y = sin(\beta)$, is computed as follows:

Step 1: Compute $\alpha = \arcsin(x)$ and $\beta = \arcsin(y)$.

The real numbers x and y are first converted into angles α and β using the arcsine function, which is crucial for preparing the inputs for subsequent quantum operations.

Step 2: Calculate $\theta_1 = \frac{\alpha-\beta}{2}$ and $\theta_2 = \frac{\alpha+\beta}{2}$.

Using the computed angles α and β, the intermediary angles θ_1 and θ_2 are calculated and will define the quantum rotations applied to the qubits.

Step 3: Initialize quantum states q_1 and q_2 to 0.

The qubits q_1 and q_2 are initialized to the ground state $|0\rangle$. This initialization provides a known reference state for the quantum operations.

Step 4: Perform quantum rotations $R_y(\theta_1)$ on q_1 and $R_y(\theta_2)$ on q_2.

The rotations $R_y(\theta_1)$ and $R_y(\theta_2)$ are performed on the qubits q_1 and q_2, respectively. These rotations adjust the quantum states to encode the information about the original real numbers.

Step 5: Measure the system at the state $|01\rangle$. The measurement yields the coefficient of the state vector, representing half of the sum $x + y$. While the full addition result typically requires multiplying this coefficient by 2, in this context, only the sign of the result is necessary for constructing the hysteresis function. Hence, the multiplication by 2 can be omitted, as the sign of the result remains unchanged.

Developing a quantum adder is required for implementing advanced quantum functions. This process harnesses key quantum abilities such as superposition, interference, and measurement. The quantum adder can efficiently and simultaneously operate on multiple states, yielding precise and optimized outcomes that are often unachievable with classical computing methods. The quantum system's capability to compute the sign of the sum without needing a full-scale addition underscores quantum computing's potential to simplify and enhance resource-intensive operations.

2.6.5. Proposed Quantum Algorithm

The quantum error e_Q is derived using a series of quantum operations that replace the classical error calculation. Let P denote the desired position and P_3 the actual position of the end-effector. The quantum error e_Q is calculated as follows:

For each axis i, compute the angles α_i and β_i corresponding to the components of P and P_3:

$$\alpha_i = arcsin(P_i) \tag{41}$$

$$\beta_i = arcsin(P_{3i}) \tag{42}$$

Next, calculate the rotation angles θ_{1i} and θ_{2i} as:

$$\theta_{1i} = \frac{\alpha_i - \beta_i}{2} \tag{43}$$

$$\theta_{2i} = \frac{\alpha_i + \beta_i}{2} \tag{44}$$

Two qubits q_{1i} and q_{2i} are initialized in the state $|0\rangle$ and the quantum rotations $Ry(\theta_{1i})$ and $Ry(\theta_{2i})$ are applied to these qubits, respectively:

$$q_{1i} = cos(\theta_{1i})|0\rangle + sin(\theta_{1i})|1\rangle \tag{45}$$

$$q_{2i} = cos(\theta_{2i})|0\rangle + sin(\theta_{2i})|1\rangle \tag{46}$$

The tensor product of these qubits is computed, and the system is measured in the state $|10\rangle$ to yield the quantum error component:

$$e_{Q_i} = k \cdot (q_{1i} \otimes q_{2i} \otimes q_{3i}) \tag{47}$$

Here the symbol $\otimes$ represents the tensor product, and k is a parametric term that can be adjusted to scale the quantum error component as needed for the specific requirements of the quantum control algorithm.

The derivative of the quantum error de_Q is computed using the quantum subtractor. Considering dP as the desired angular velocity and dP_Q as the quantum-calculated angular velocity obtained through the R_y gate, the derivative error de_Q is determined by the following relation:

$$de_Q = Quantum\ Subtractor\ (dP, dP_Q) \tag{48}$$

The quantum sliding surface $s_{quantum}$ is formed to approximate the classical sliding surface using quantum gates. First, the quantum error e_Q is scaled by a constant vector c:

$$scaled\ error = c \cdot e_Q \tag{49}$$

Then, the scaled quantum error and the quantum derivative error are added using quantum rotations. The resulting quantum sliding surface is expressed as:

$$s_{quantum} = n\left(sin\left(\frac{\theta_{c\cdot e}}{2}\right) + sin\left(\frac{\theta_{deQ}}{2}\right)\right) \tag{50}$$

Here, n is a parameter that can be tuned according to the specific requirements of the control system normalization, providing more flexibility in how the quantum sliding surface is scaled, and θ_{ce} and θ_{de} are the rotation angles for the scaled error and derivative error, respectively. The sign of the quantum sliding surface $s_{quantum}$ is detected using quantum computational techniques. The quantum state $|s\rangle$ representing the sliding surface is prepared as:

$$|s\rangle = cos(\theta)\,|0\rangle + sin(\theta)\,|1\rangle \tag{51}$$

where θ is calculated by the relation:

$$\theta = arcsin\left(\frac{s(t)}{max(|s(t)|)}\right) \tag{52}$$

The quantum sign detector then applies the X gate (quantum NOT gate) and the Toffoli gate (CCNOT gate) to determine the sign of the sliding surface. The outcome of the measurement after applying these gates indicates the sign of the sliding surface, with the ancillary qubit's state corresponding to +1 or -1.

The quantum control law u_Q is formulated by integrating the quantum sliding surface and the sign detection results. The control variable V is computed using the quantum sliding surface as:

$$V = J^{-1} \cdot \left(\ddot{P} + c \cdot de_Q + q \cdot Sign(s_Q) - \dot{J} \cdot \dot{q}\right) \tag{53}$$

where J is the Jacobian matrix, $\ddot{P}$ represents the desired acceleration, and $\dot{J} \cdot \dot{q}$ accounts for the effects of dynamic changes in the system.

The final control input u_Q is then calculated as:

$$u_Q = M \cdot V + B + G \tag{54}$$

So, M is the inertia matrix, B represents the Coriolis/centripetal forces, and G denotes the gravitational forces.

3. Results and Discussion

The following Simulink model is employed as the implementation algorithm for the carried-out simulation of the motion control of the robotic arm manipulator. Simulink allows creating blocks that have all the features and capabilities of any type of built-in function. The block function of the plant implemented all equations for the dynamic equations of motion, such as the inertia, gravity, and Coriolis centrifugal parameters, to obtain the torque and force equation of the robot presented in the kinematics and dynamic models of the robot in the methodology section of the current study and the mass properties of the robot, which consist of mass center points and inertia matrixes for the first three links presented in the section on CAO design and Table 3. A classic sliding-mode controller with the expositional reaching law approach based on the presented method is implemented in the controller block function, and the schematic diagram of the controller model is represented in Figure 4. Other Simulink models based on the quantum approach incorporating the quantum operators to handle the quantum version of the sliding-mode controller for the robot manipulator are designed and illustrated in Figure 5.

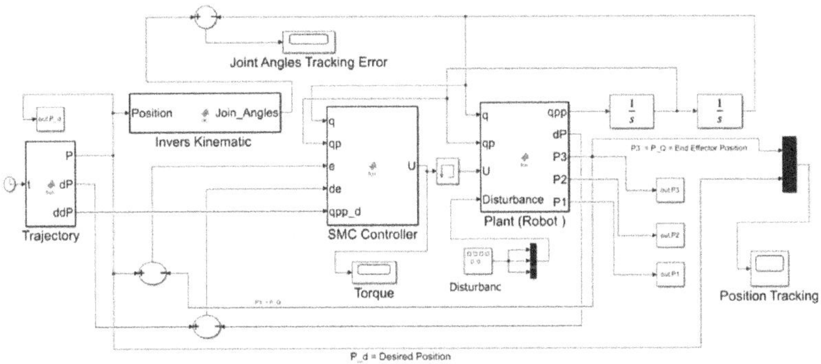

Figure 4. Simulink trajectory model of the robot manipulator for SMC.

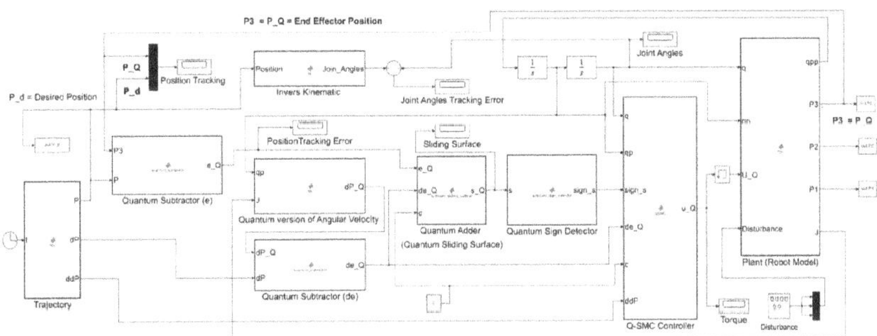

Figure 5. Simulink trajectory model of the robot manipulator for Q-SMC.

The sliding-mode controller algorithm is used for motion control based on a design with and without disturbances to evaluate the model's robustness. The value of disturbances applied based on the sine and cosine trajectory of the joint variable is predefined as a percentage of the input signal to examine the robustness of the designed controller. The implemented algorithm examines thoroughly a specific trajectory to verify the performance and behavior of the designed sliding-mode controllers of the robot to execute tasks undertaking the controllers. A circular trajectory is defined in the robot's working space considering avoiding singularity to perform the robot's task and estimate the chosen controller's execution. The motion of the end-effector begins at the same point for both controllers, positioned somewhere within the working space but outside the circular trajectory. Upon initiating the simulation, the robot attempts to reach the desired circular path, perform a circular motion along the defined trajectory, and maintain its position according to the specified parameters. The successful transition from an initial position outside the defined path to accurately following the specified circular trajectory within the robot's workspace confirms the correct operation of the controllers. Figure 6 illustrates the robot performing the assigned task under the SMC and Q-SMC controllers.

The Q-SMC aligns closely with the desired trajectory, guiding the robotic arm to precise coordinates, as the red dotted line shows. In contrast, the SMC controller, represented by the blue dotted line, exhibits delayed response and reduced accuracy, resulting in the arm deviating more noticeably from the intended path when reaching the coordinates.

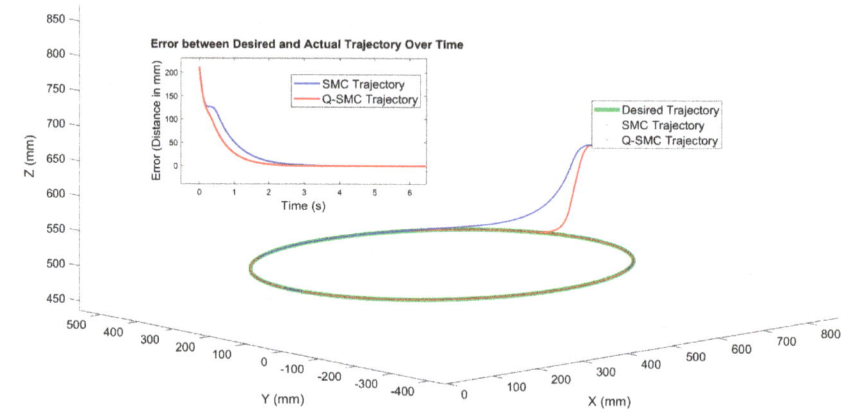

Figure 6. Projection of X–Y–Z trajectory of robot manipulator executed by controllers.

Figures 7–9 illustrate the comparative position-tracking performance of the robotic arm's end-effector along the X, Y, and Z axes, employing both classic sliding-mode control and quantum-inspired sliding-mode control. The Q-SMC demonstrates superiority over the SMC in both transient and steady-state performance. As highlighted in the zoom-in inset, it achieves faster convergence to the desired trajectory with reduced overshoot. This enhancement is attributed to quantum-inspired innovations that facilitate smoother control actions and improved management of nonlinearities and disturbances.

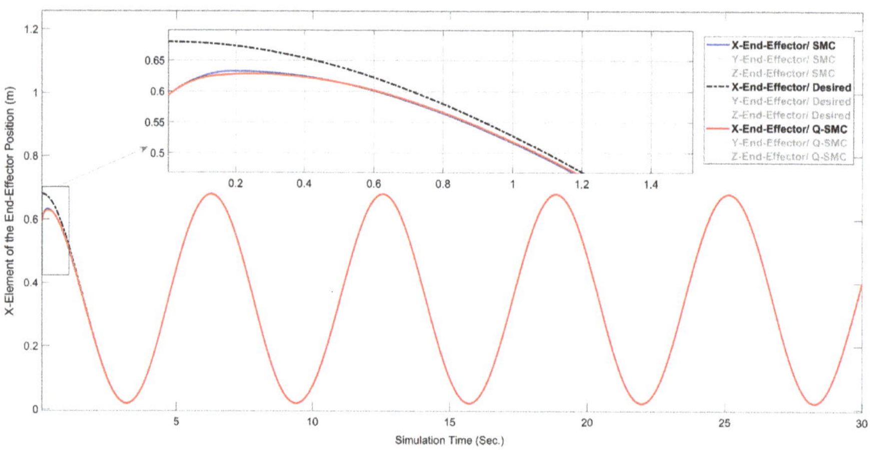

Figure 7. Comparison of position tracking (X-component) for the robot end-effector.

Furthermore, Q-SMC maintains a closer adherence to the desired trajectory throughout the simulation, exhibiting exceptional tracking accuracy and robustness. The results along the *Y*-axis further underscore the benefits of Q-SMC, which delivers precise and smooth trajectory tracking. Consistently, Q-SMC outperforms SMC in terms of quicker convergence and reduced overshoot. The enhanced transient response and accurate path alignment are evident throughout the simulation. These improvements stem from the proposed controller's capacity to effectively mitigate uncertainties and disturbances, resulting in smoother and more dependable control actions.

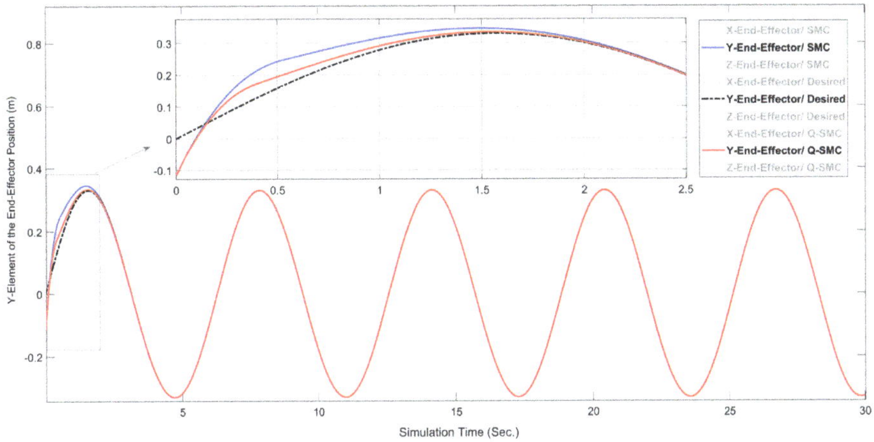

Figure 8. Comparison of position tracking (Y–component) for the robot end-effector.

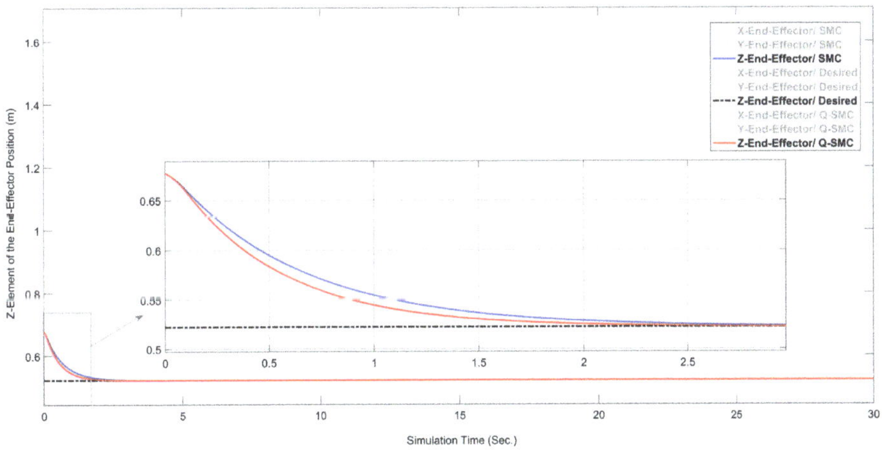

Figure 9. Comparison of position tracking (Z-component) for the robot end-effector.

In contrast, SMC displays slightly greater deviations from the desired trajectory, particularly during the transient phase, highlighting Q-SMC's superior precision and robustness. The quantum-inspired enhancements significantly reduce overshoot and oscillations, as depicted in the magnified transient response. Although both controllers ultimately achieve the target position, Q-SMC consistently provides better precision and stability throughout the simulation. The reduced chattering observed with Q-SMC decreases abrupt control actions, enhancing energy efficiency and preserving the mechanical integrity of the system. These findings reaffirm Q-SMC as a robust control strategy for applications requiring smooth and accurate trajectory tracking.

Figures 10–12 illustrate the tracking error of the robot's end-effector under both classical SMC and Q-SMC controllers. The results indicate that Q-SMC achieves a particularly lower steady-state error compared to SMC, showing improved tracking precision. While both controllers exhibit rapid error convergence, Q-SMC stabilizes more quickly with minimal oscillations, reflecting its enhanced robustness and smoother control actions. These findings underscore the effectiveness of the Q-SMC approach in maintaining trajectory accuracy, even in dynamic conditions.

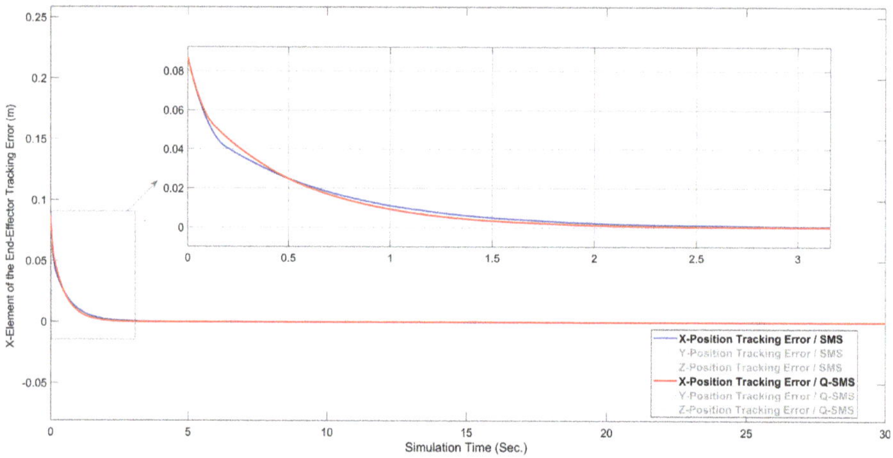

Figure 10. Comparison of tracking error (X-component) for the robot end-effector.

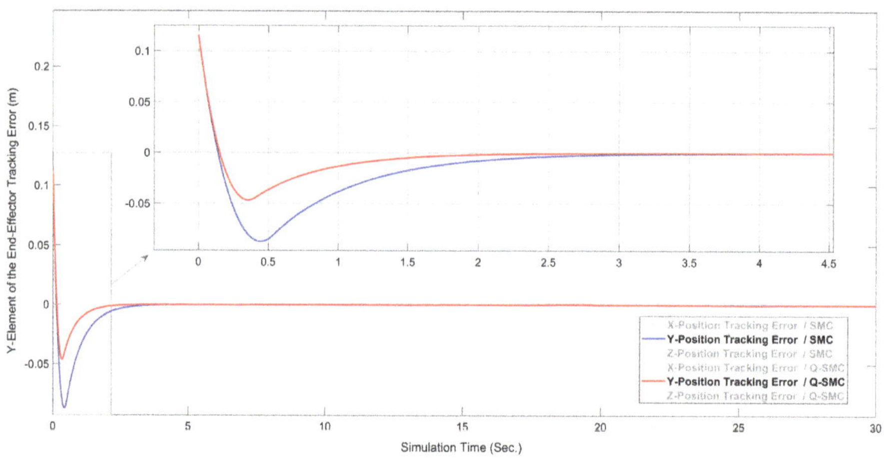

Figure 11. Comparison of tracking error (Y-component) for the robot end-effector.

Additionally, Q-SMC's reduced chattering and optimized control actions further validate it as a robust and precise control strategy for robotic systems. The classical SMC shows a notable initial overshoot in the Y-position, highlighting its greater sensitivity to sudden changes in system dynamics. In contrast, Q-SMC exhibits better stability, faster error convergence, and reduced fluctuations, resulting in a more consistent response over time. This difference in robustness allows Q-SMC to handle dynamic variations more efficiently and makes its smoother trajectory control particularly suitable for precision applications, solidifying its reputation as an advanced and effective control method for robotic systems.

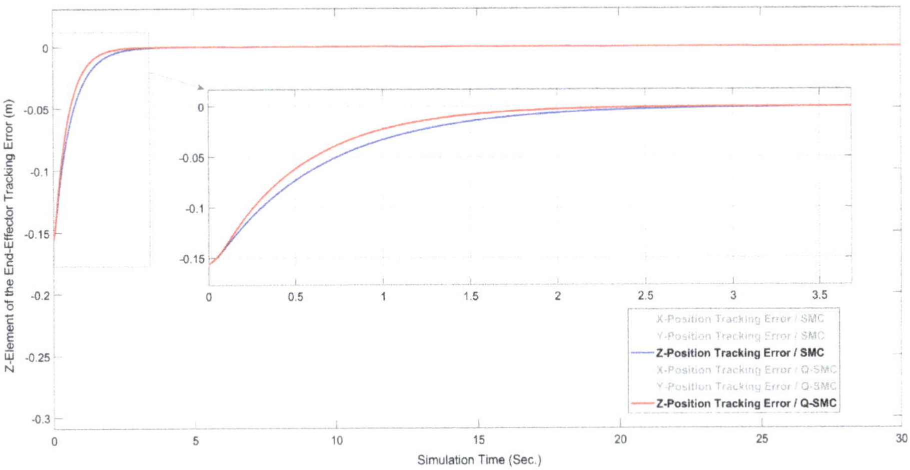

Figure 12. Comparison of tracking error (Z-component) for the robot end-effector.

The tracking performance for the Z-position of the robot's end-effector reveals that both controllers undergo a transient phase. However, Q-SMC achieves quicker convergence to near-zero errors and maintains a smoother trajectory. While classical SMC shows effectiveness, it experiences slight oscillations during stabilization, indicating a less refined response to system dynamics. In contrast, Q-SMC's ability to stabilize rapidly while managing smoother tracking errors underlines its precision and robustness, especially in addressing nonlinearities. These results further confirm the practicality of Q-SMC for applications that require high accuracy and reliability in robotic motion control.

Table 5 reviews the results of the classic and quantum sliding-mode controller performances. The comparison shows that the performances of both controllers are nearly identical. The evaluation of each controller's performance considers key metrics such as steady-state error, response speed, rise time, and settling time, addressing both time- and frequency-domain requirements. Considering all the measured parameters for both controllers when following the same trajectory, the Q-SMC model demonstrated superior performance.

Table 5. Performance of angular position for the different controllers.

Performances	Rising Time (s)	Settling Time (s)	Overshoot (%)	Steady-State Error (%)
		SMC		
Arm 1	0.301	0.42	1.76	0.088
Arm 2	0.297	0.79	2.09	0.076
Arm 3	0.302	0.53	1.97	0.066
		Q-SMC		
Arm 1	0.283	0.383	1.32	0.071
Arm 2	0.276	0.565	1.41	0.055
Arm 3	0.295	0.497	1.25	0.042

The controllers' ability to withstand modeling inaccuracies and unmodeled dynamics can be determined from their performance under disturbance conditions, albeit implicitly. In practical applications, the models used for controller design are usually approximations, making a controller's capability to maintain its performance despite such inaccuracies crucial. A control system's capacity to respond promptly and effectively to anticipated and unforeseen changes, including disturbances, is vital. This is particularly crucial in dynamic systems, where delays can result in significant errors or instability. The controllers' robustness is evaluated by analyzing their responses to disturbances, particularly when exposed to a sinusoidal disturbance set at 35% of the input signal. The performance response of the controllers under disturbance demonstrates satisfactory and appropriate behavior, as detailed in Table 6.

Table 6. Performance of angular position for the different controllers under disturbance.

Performances	Rising Time (s)	Settling Time (s)	Overshoot (%)	Steady-State Error (%)
		SMC		
Arm 1	0.525	0.579	1.85	0.0999
Arm 2	0.662	0.799	2.03	0.0807
Arm 3	0.515	0.598	1.97	0.0794
		Q-SMC		
Arm 1	0.454	0.691	1.39	0.0785
Arm 2	0.479	0.659	1.48	0.0551
Arm 3	0.463	0.623	1.28	0.0510

Upon reviewing the data in Tables 5 and 6, it is evident that the system's performance with and without disturbances is quite similar. However, in the presence of disturbances, the steady-state error increased to 10.71% for the quantum sliding-mode controller and 12.13% for the classical sliding-mode controller. The overshoot remained unchanged, while the rise times increased by an average of 0.2 s. Similarly, in the scenario without disturbances, the controllers displayed comparable response and reaching times under disturbance conditions for the same trajectory execution and initial conditions.

Both controllers display worthy robustness in the presence of disturbances, maintaining low tracking errors even under substantial disturbances. The analysis of the response plots highlights several required characteristics relevant to the design and assessment of control systems. Notably, the transient response analysis indicates that Q-SMC outperforms SMC by achieving a faster settling time with fewer instabilities, suggesting that the improved damping characteristics of Q-SMC enable it to bring the system to a steady state more efficiently. Additionally, Q-SMC consistently minimizes steady-state error, ensuring greater accuracy in tracking the desired trajectory. This feature is advantageous in precision engineering applications, where performance and implementation complexity are key in real-world implementations such as robotics; the selection or design of controllers must consider these factors. Moreover, despite being often overlooked, energy efficiency is vital, especially in systems that operate continuously or under power constraints. The smoother control action and reduced oscillations observed in Q-SMC suggest it is more energy-efficient than conventional SMC.

Figures 13–16 represent the torque control signals for individual robotic arm joints and the robot's total torque, providing essential insights into the performance and efficiency of the evaluated control strategies under 35% of input signal disturbances. Outcomes show how the controllers, SMC and Q-SMC, manage the dynamic requirements of individual joints under defined trajectories, recalling the smoothness, oscillations, and magnitude of the torque values that indicate the control algorithms' efficiency in handling nonlinearities and disturbances. The total torque across all joints offers a close view of the robotic arm's overall dynamic load and energy exertion, which is crucial for comparing the total effort required by SMC versus Q-SMC to achieve the same task and conditions. These figures are important for performance evaluation, as the torque signals indicate the system's ability to handle nonlinear dynamics, ensure smooth control actions, and resist chattering issues typically associated with classical SMC. The data can further enable energy efficiency analysis by linking torque values directly to the robot's energy consumption, showcasing how well the control system manages resources. Additionally, the formations accentuate the robustness of Q-SMC under disturbance scenarios, highlighting its capability to preserve stable arrangements without significant oscillations or overshoot.

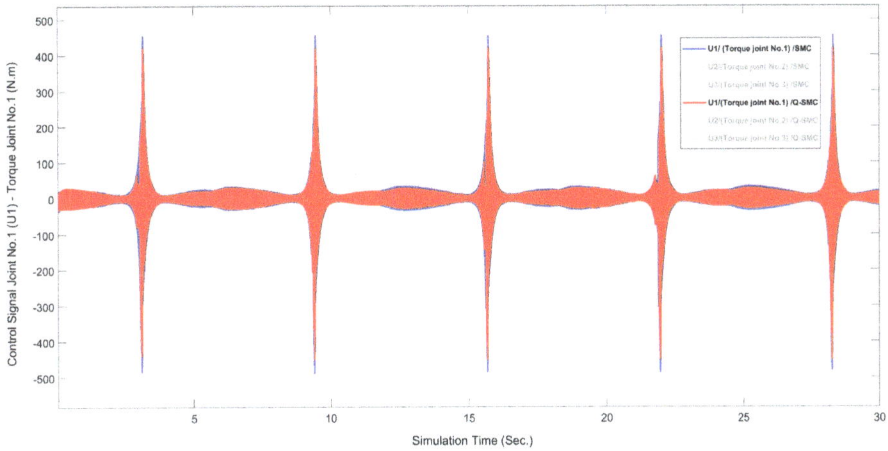

Figure 13. Control signals for joint 1 for SMC and Q-SMC controllers under disturbance.

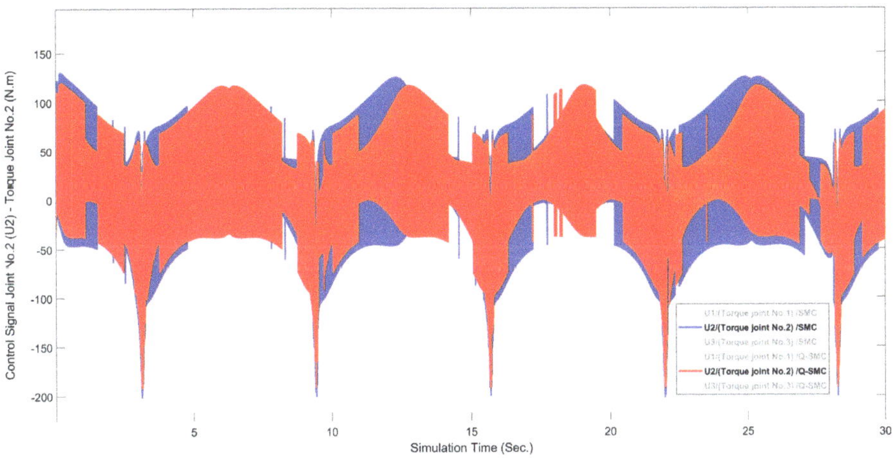

Figure 14. Control signals for joint 2 for SMC and Q-SMC controllers under disturbance.

These advancements improve the precision and stability of the robotic manipulator while minimizing mechanical wear and stress, ultimately extending the operational lifespan of the robotic components. As a result, both approaches are particularly well-suited for enhancing trajectory tracking precision in high-precision industrial applications and complex robotic systems. The findings emphasize the superior robustness and adaptability of Q-SMC, showcasing its potential to excel in high-performance dynamic environments.

In terms of total torque profiles, the Q-SMC consistently outperforms classical SMC by generating more stable and efficient control signals that effectively reject disturbances while maintaining system stability. Collectively, these results demonstrate Q-SMC's enhanced performance in overcoming the limitations of classical SMC, offering improved stability, precision, and efficiency. Its ability to effectively surpass chattering positions Q-SMC as a promising advancement for robust control in industrial automation and other high-performance sectors in dynamic and disturbance-prone environments.

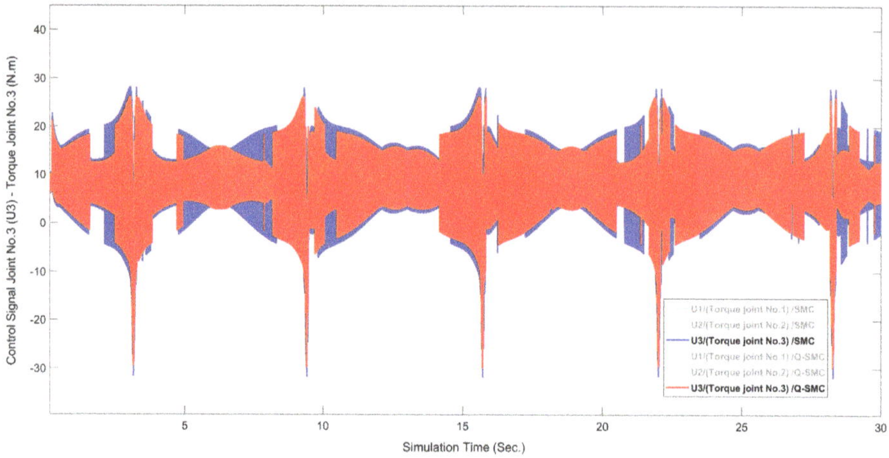

Figure 15. Control signals for joint 3 for SMC and Q-SMC controllers under disturbance.

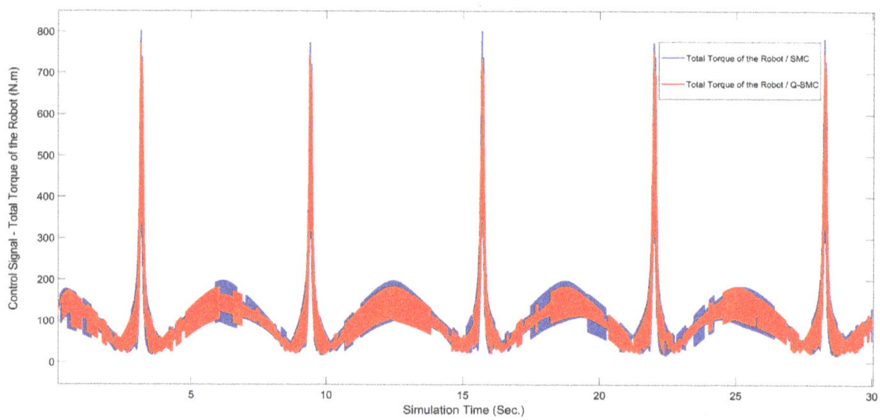

Figure 16. Control signals for the robot under SMC and Q-SMC controllers under disturbance.

Estimating the energy consumption of robotic systems across various controllers is essential for assessing the efficiency and effectiveness of these control strategies. By analyzing the total energy drawn from the robot's torque profile needed to perform identical trajectories, we can gain valuable insights into the effectiveness of each controller in managing the complex dynamics of robotic systems. Energy consumption is directly related to the operational demands placed on the controller, including the forces and torques required for precise movements, especially when faced with disturbances. A control strategy that minimizes energy usage while preserving or enhancing system performance indicates superior efficiency, contributing to the robot's performance and reliability. This approach provides a comprehensive framework for considering the balance between control precision, robustness, and energy efficiency, establishing a clear benchmark for optimizing robotic implementation.

Figure 17 shows the total energy consumption of the robotic system under disturbance conditions operated by both the SMC and Q-SMC based on the robot performance assessment presented in relation (2). The illustration proves that the Q-SMC provides a more stable energy profile and decreases total energy consumption compared to the classical SMC. Particularly, the robot under the Q-SMC controller consumed approximately 3.79% less energy than the classical SMC controller. This reduction is noteworthy as it underlines the quantum approach's capability to enhance energy efficiency while maintaining or even enhancing control accuracy. These findings indicate that the Q-SMC effectively reduced the effects of disturbances and optimized energy usage, leading to a more sustainable and reliable control strategy. This advancement in energy management is required for the long-term operation of robotic systems, as it suggests reduced wear on mechanical components and a more environmentally tolerable approach to robotic control. The results highlight the potential of quantum-inspired control methods in advancing the field of robotics, particularly in applications where energy efficiency is as essential as precision and robustness.

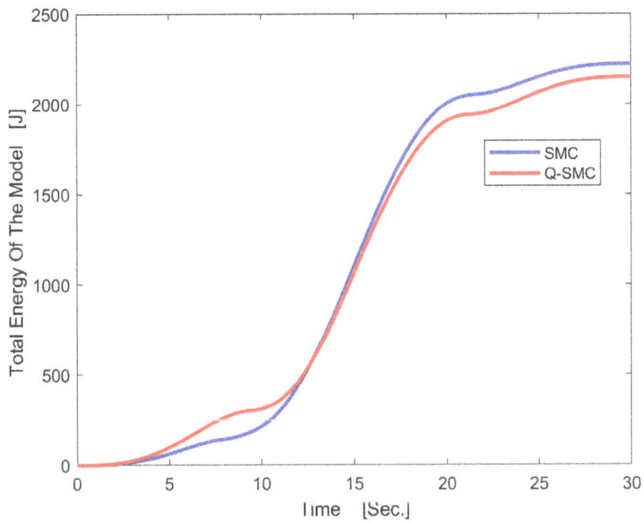

Figure 17. Total energy of the robot run by controllers under disturbance.

Q-SMC has demonstrated superior energy efficiency compared to SMC. This is particularly advantageous for battery-powered robots, allowing longer operational durations without recharging. Furthermore, reducing energy consumption leads to cost savings and a decrease in heat generation in industrial environments, ultimately extending the lifespan of robotic components. This enhanced energy efficiency also promotes environmental sustainability by reducing the dependence on non-renewable energy sources. It plays a significant role in ensuring the overall reliability and longevity of robotic systems, especially in high-precision applications where maintaining mechanical integrity is critical.

In a comprehensive and overarching manner, the principle of superposition facilitates the simultaneous representation of multiple potential system states, thereby increasing the control algorithm's capacity to respond to dynamic changes. Within the Q-SMC framework, superposition is utilized to encode the robotic end-effector's desired and actual states into a unified quantum state. The quantum error computation detailed in Equations (41)–(47) exemplifies this principle, as it allows for concurrent analysis of multiple input trajectories, enabling rapid and precise error evaluation. This comprehensive error assessment mechanism enhances trajectory tracking, promoting faster convergence to the desired path and mitigating transient overshoot. As evidenced in Figures 7–12 and Tables 5 and 6, Q-SMC outperforms classical SMC, demonstrating superior tracking precision and smoother control transitions, affirming superposition's efficacy in optimizing control dynamics with or without disturbances.

Entanglement establishes a foundational relation between interdependent control variables, such as error signals and their derivatives, ensuring seamless synchronization for dynamic responsiveness. In the Q-SMC framework, this principle is operationalized through the quantum comparator and sign detector presented in Sections 2.6.1–2.6.3, enabling the real-time alignment of quantum error and its derivative. This synchronization ensures that adjustments to the sliding surface accurately mirror dynamic changes in the robotic system, resulting in minimizing control response delays. Accordingly, Q-SMC consistently delivers precise and stable control actions characterized by reduced trajectory deviations and improved steady-state accuracy. The benefits of entanglement's influence are shown in Figures 9–12, where the Q-SMC exhibits robust stability during transient phases, effectively accommodating dynamic variations and reinforcing its advanced adaptability for complex control scenarios.

The computational efficiency of Q-SMC derives from the strategic utilization of quantum gates, including Hadamard and rotation gates, which enable intricate mathematical operations such as error scaling and derivative computation. These gates manipulate the intrinsic parallelism of quantum mechanics, allowing the controller to process high-dimensional data in real-time with minimal computational load. For instance, the quantum subtractor in Equations (36)–(39) adeptly computes trajectory differences, generating precise and responsive control signals. This computational optimization translates directly into the observed smoother control transitions and significantly reduced delays, as illustrated in Figures 13–16, emphasizing the practical benefits of integrating quantum gates into the control framework.

Chattering, a general challenge in classical SMC, is effectively reduced in Q-SMC by involving the exponential reaching law combined with a saturation function. This methodology establishes a boundary layer around the sliding surface and smoothens the transitions in control inputs, thereby minimizing the abrupt variations that cause chattering. This refinement, drawing stimulation from quantum error correction, enhances the system's energy efficiency and preserves the robotic components' mechanical integrity. As depicted in Figures 13–16, the torque profiles produced by Q-SMC exhibit considerably smoother characteristics compared to those generated by classical SMC. Additionally, the system's enhanced energy efficiency is quantified in Figure 17, where Q-SMC displays a 3.79% reduction in total energy consumption, emphasizing its superior performance in energy-sensitive and precision-demanding applications.

4. Conclusions

The present study aimed to evaluate the effectiveness of quantum-inspired sliding-mode control in enhancing the robustness, accuracy, and computational efficiency of control methods for articulated robotic arms, focusing specifically on a six-degree-of-freedom robotic manipulator. By integrating quantum principles into the conventional sliding-mode control framework, the research addressed persistent issues such as chattering, computational complexity, and robustness against disturbances. The methodology involved the development of a comprehensive kinematic and dynamic model of the robotic arm, followed by the implementation and comparison of both classic SMC and Q-SMC through extensive simulations. The findings provide valuable insights into the potential of quantum-inspired approaches in advancing robotic control systems.

The results revealed several significant findings. Most notably, Q-SMC outperformed the classic SMC in key areas such as precision, robustness, and energy efficiency. Q-SMC effectively mitigated the chattering phenomenon, a common issue in classic SMC, resulting in smoother and more precise control of the robotic arm. Additionally, Q-SMC confirmed quicker response times and lower steady-state errors, showcasing its improved capability to handle the nonlinear dynamics and external disturbances inherent in robotic systems. The torque profile and energy consumption analysis further highlighted the efficiency of Q-SMC, with the robotic arm consuming approximately 3.79% less energy under Q-SMC compared to classic SMC.

These findings have important implications for both theoretical and practical applications in the field of robotics and control systems. Theoretically, this study contributes to the existing body of knowledge by introducing a novel application of quantum principles to sliding-mode control, advancing our understanding of how quantum computing techniques can enhance control system performance. This opens new avenues for the design and optimization of robust controllers. Practically, implementing Q-SMC could lead to technological advancements in robotic systems, particularly in applications requiring high precision and reliability, such as industrial automation, medical robotics, and aerospace. Furthermore, the reduced energy consumption associated with Q-SMC suggests potential benefits for developing more sustainable and efficient robotic systems.

However, it is important to acknowledge certain limitations of the study, primarily due to its execution in a simulated environment. While the models employed were comprehensive, they may not fully capture the complexities of real-world scenarios. Additionally, the application of quantum-inspired algorithms was constrained by current computational capabilities, which may limit the generalizability of the findings to other types of robotic systems or more complex environments. These limitations suggest that further validation through experimental setups is necessary to confirm the effectiveness and relevance of Q-SMC in real-world applications.

Recognizing the crucial importance of experimental validation, we are committed to bridging the gap between simulations and real-world applications. According to the promising simulation results presented in this study, our future work will focus on incorporating other advanced strategies; we prioritized depth over breadth in this initial study, validating Q-SMC for high-precision tasks such as trajectory tracking and energy-efficient path execution under varying loads and disturbances. To ensure comparability, we will replicate simulation conditions and evaluate real-world performance using a hybrid classical–quantum framework, where computationally intensive components are executed on available quantum platforms. Performance metrics include chattering reduction, trajectory tracking accuracy, and energy efficiency. Beyond the specific case study examined here, we aim to expand Q-SMC's applicability to diverse robotic platforms and tasks, including industrial applications like assembly and welding, to explore scalability and versatility.

In conclusion, the findings underscore the robust control capabilities of both conventional sliding-mode control and quantum-inspired sliding-mode control for robotic arms. While SMC is well known for its robustness, the proposed Q-SMC demonstrates superior accuracy, precision, and an enhanced ability to address common challenges like chattering. Q-SMC significantly improves the stability and precision of the control system, particularly in dynamic, disturbance-prone environments. Its smoother control actions contribute to the overall better performance of the robotic arm, resulting in faster response times, reduced steady-state errors, and lower energy consumption, making it a more practical and effective technique for achieving high-performance robotic control.

Author Contributions: M.F. contributed to conceptualization, methodology, investigation, formal analysis, writing and editing of the original draft, and visualization. N.Z. contributed to providing resources, supervision, project administration, formal analysis, review and editing of the original draft, funding acquisition, and visualization. All authors have read and agreed to the published version of the manuscript.

Funding: This work was financially supported by NSERC Canada.

Data Availability Statement: The data supporting the findings of this study are not publicly available as they are part of ongoing research and future work. Data may be shared upon reasonable request after the completion of future studies.

Conflicts of Interest: The authors declare no conflicts of interest.

Abbreviations

The following abbreviations are used in this manuscript:

SMC	Sliding-Mode Control
QSMC	Quantum Sliding-Mode Control
CAD	Computer-Aided Design
CAO	Computer-Aided Optimization
CAM	Computer-Aided Manufacturing
CCNOT	Controlled-Controlled-Not
DH	Denavit–Hartenberg

References

1. Anh, H.P.H.; Van Kien, C.; Son, N.N.; Nam, N.T. New approach of sliding mode control for nonlinear uncertain pneumatic artificial muscle manipulator enhanced with adaptive fuzzy estimator. *Int. J. Adv. Robot. Syst.* **2018**, *15*, 1729881418773204. [CrossRef]
2. Azeez, M.I.; Abdelhaleem, A.M.M.; Elnaggar, S.; Moustafa, K.A.F.; Atia, K.R. Optimized sliding mode controller for trajectory tracking of flexible joints three-link manipulator with noise in input and output. *Sci. Rep.* **2023**, *13*, 12518. [CrossRef]
3. Ajwad, S.A.; Iqbal, J.; Islam, R.U.; Alsheikhy, A.; Almeshal, A.; Mehmood, A. Optimal and robust control of multi DOF robotic manipulator: Design and hardware realization. *Cybern. Syst.* **2018**, *49*, 77–93. [CrossRef]
4. Liu, Z.; Peng, K.; Han, L.; Guan, S. Modeling and control of robotic manipulators based on artificial neural networks: A review. *Iran. J. Sci. Technol. Trans. Mech. Eng.* **2023**, *47*, 1307–1347.
5. Wang, X.; Wang, D.; Du, M.; Song, K.; Ni, Y.; Li, Y. A two-layer trajectory tracking control scheme of manipulator based on elm-smc for autonomous robotic vehicle. *IEEE Trans. Autom. Sci. Eng.* **2023**, *21*, 2337–2348. [CrossRef]
6. Ravandi, A.K.; Khanmirza, E.; Daneshjou, K. Hybrid force/position control of robotic arms manipulating in uncertain environments based on adaptive fuzzy sliding mode control. *Appl. Soft Comput.* **2018**, *70*, 864–874. [CrossRef]
7. Kumar, R.; Kumar, K. Design and control of a two-link robotic manipulator: A review. *AIP Conf. Proc.* **2021**, *2358*, 050020.
8. Abdelmaksoud, S.I.; Al-Mola, M.H.; Abro, G.E.M.; Asirvadam, V.S. In-Depth Review of Advanced Control Strategies and Cutting-Edge Trends in Robot Manipulators: Analyzing the Latest Developments and Techniques. *IEEE Access* **2024**, *12*, 47672–47701. [CrossRef]
9. Abbas, N.; Abbas, Z.; Zafar, S.; Ahmad, N.; Liu, X.; Khan, S.S.; Foster, E.D.; Larkin, S. Survey of Advanced Nonlinear Control Strategies for UAVs: Integration of Sensors and Hybrid Techniques. *Sensors* **2024**, *24*, 3286. [CrossRef] [PubMed]
10. Zaihidee, F.M.; Mekhilef, S.; Mubin, M. Robust speed control of PMSM using sliding mode control (SMC)—A review. *Energies* **2019**, *12*, 1669. [CrossRef]
11. Fazilat, M.; Zioui, N. The Impact of Simplifications of the Dynamic Model on the Motion of a Six-Jointed Industrial Articulated Robotic Arm Movement. *J. Robot. Control* **2024**, *5*, 173–186. [CrossRef]
12. Vijay, M.; Jena, D. Backstepping terminal sliding mode control of robot manipulator using radial basis functional neural networks. *Comput. Electr. Eng.* **2018**, *67*, 690–707. [CrossRef]
13. Adhikary, N.; Mahanta, C. Sliding mode control of position commanded robot manipulators. *Control Eng. Pract.* **2018**, *81*, 183–198. [CrossRef]
14. Norsahperi, N.; Danapalasingam, K. An improved optimal integral sliding mode control for uncertain robotic manipulators with reduced tracking error, chattering, and energy consumption. *Mech. Syst. Signal Process.* **2020**, *142*, 106747. [CrossRef]
15. Truong, T.N.; Vo, A.T.; Kang, H.-J. A backstepping global fast terminal sliding mode control for trajectory tracking control of industrial robotic manipulators. *IEEE Access* **2021**, *9*, 31921–31931. [CrossRef]
16. Baek, J.; Kwon, W.; Kang, C. A new widely and stably adaptive sliding-mode control with nonsingular terminal sliding variable for robot manipulators. *IEEE Access* **2020**, *8*, 43443–43454. [CrossRef]

17. Baek, J.; Kwon, W. Practical adaptive sliding-mode control approach for precise tracking of robot manipulators. *Appl. Sci.* **2020**, *10*, 2909. [CrossRef]
18. Feng, Y.; Zhou, M.; Yu, X.; Han, F. Full-order sliding-mode control of rigid robotic manipulators. *Asian J. Control* **2019**, *21*, 1228–1236. [CrossRef]
19. Zhai, J.; Li, Z. Fast-exponential sliding mode control of robotic manipulator with super-twisting method. *IEEE Trans. Circuits Syst. II Express Briefs* **2021**, *69*, 489–493. [CrossRef]
20. Soriano, L.A.; Rubio, J.d.J.; Orozco, E.; Cordova, D.A.; Ochoa, G.; Balcazar, R.; Cruz, D.R.; Meda-Campaña, J.A.; Zacarias, A.; Gutierrez, G.J. Optimization of sliding mode control to save energy in a SCARA robot. *Mathematics* **2021**, *9*, 3160. [CrossRef]
21. Yen, V.T.; Nan, W.Y.; Van Cuong, P. Recurrent fuzzy wavelet neural networks based on robust adaptive sliding mode control for industrial robot manipulators. *Neural Comput. Appl.* **2019**, *31*, 6945–6958. [CrossRef]
22. Jung, S. Improvement of tracking control of a sliding mode controller for robot manipulators by a neural network. *Int. J. Control Autom. Syst.* **2018**, *16*, 937–943. [CrossRef]
23. Gambhire, S.J.; Kishore, D.R.; Londhe, P.S.; Pawar, S.N. Review of sliding mode based control techniques for control system applications. *Int. J. Dyn. Control* **2021**, *9*, 363–378. [CrossRef]
24. Yu, X.; Feng, Y.; Man, Z. Terminal sliding mode control—An overview. *IEEE Open J. Ind. Electron. Soc.* **2020**, *2*, 36–52. [CrossRef]
25. Yin, F.; Wen, C.; Ji, Q.; Zhang, H.; Shao, H. A compensation sliding mode control for machining robotic manipulators based on nonlinear disturbance observer. *Trans. Inst. Meas. Control* **2022**, *44*, 2336–2349. [CrossRef]
26. Gan, W.; Zhu, D.; Ji, D. QPSO-model predictive control-based approach to dynamic trajectory tracking control for unmanned underwater vehicles. *Ocean Eng.* **2018**, *158*, 208–220. [CrossRef]
27. Fazilat, M.; Zioui, N.; St-Arnaud, J. A novel quantum model of forward kinematics based on quaternion/Pauli gate equivalence: Application to a six-jointed industrial robotic arm. *Results Eng.* **2022**, *14*, 100402. [CrossRef]
28. Zioui, N.; Mahmoudi, A.; Tadjine, M. Representing quantum spins in different coordinate systems for modelling rigid body orientation. *Karbala Int. J. Mod. Sci.* **2023**, *9*, 11. [CrossRef]
29. Boudjoghra, M.E.A.; Daimellah, S.A.S.; Zioui, N.; Mahmoudi, Y.; Tadjine, M. State-Domain Equations and Their Quantum Computing Solution Based HHL Algorithm. *Math. Model. Eng. Probl.* **2022**, *9*, 879–886. [CrossRef]
30. Singh, R.; Sloth, C. Characterizing Manipulator Motion Using an Evolving Type 2 Quantum Fuzzy Neural Network. In Proceedings of the 2024 IEEE/SICE International Symposium on System Integration (SII), Ha Long, Vietnam, 8–11 January 2024.
31. Zheng, X.; Su, X. Sliding mode control of electro-hydraulic servo system based on optimization of quantum particle swarm algorithm. *Machines* **2021**, *9*, 283. [CrossRef]
32. Qu, Q.; Chen, F.; Jiang, B.; Tao, G. Integral sliding mode control for helicopter via disturbance observer and quantum information technique. *Math. Probl. Eng.* **2015**, *2015*, 938246. [CrossRef]
33. Zioui, N.; Mahmoudi, Y.; Mahmoudi, A.; Tadjine, M.; Bentouba, S. A novel quantum-computing-based quaternions model for a robotic arm position. *Int. J. Comput. Intell. Control* **2021**, *13*, 71–77.
34. Sivak, V.V.; Eickbusch, A.; Liu, H.; Royer, B.; Tsioutsios, I.; Devoret, M.H. Model-free quantum control with reinforcement learning. *Phys. Rev. X* **2022**, *12*, 011059. [CrossRef]
35. Petschnigg, C.; Brandstötter, M.; Pichler, H.; Hofbaur, M.; Dieber, B. Quantum computation in robotic science and applications. In Proceedings of the 2019 International Conference on Robotics and Automation (ICRA), Montreal, QC, Canada, 20–24 May 2019.
36. Niu, M.Y.; Boixo, S.; Smelyanskiy, V.N.; Neven, H. Universal quantum control through deep reinforcement learning. *Npj Quantum Inf.* **2019**, *5*, 33. [CrossRef]
37. Reshetnikov, A.; Ulyanov, S. Quantum Algorithm of Imperfect KB Self-organization. Pt II: Robotic Control with Remote Knowledge Base Exchange. *Artif. Intell. Adv.* **2021**, *3*, 44–70. [CrossRef]
38. Tavanaei-Sereshki, Z.; Ramezani-Al, M.R. Quantum genetic sliding mode controller design for depth control of an underwater vehicle. *Meas. Control* **2018**, *51*, 336–348. [CrossRef]
39. Xi, R.-D.; Xiao, X.; Ma, T.-N.; Yang, Z.-X. Adaptive sliding mode disturbance observer based robust control for robot manipulators towards assembly assistance. *IEEE Robot. Autom. Lett.* **2022**, *7*, 6139–6146. [CrossRef]
40. Haviland, J.; Corke, P. Manipulator Differential Kinematics: Part I: Kinematics, Velocity, and Applications. *IEEE Robot. Autom. Mag.* **2023**, *31*, 149–158. [CrossRef]
41. Zaare, S.; Soltanpour, M.R.; Moattari, M. Adaptive sliding mode control of n flexible-joint robot manipulators in the presence of structured and unstructured uncertainties. *Multibody Syst. Dyn.* **2019**, *47*, 397–434. [CrossRef]
42. Ranjbar, E.; Suratgar, A.A.; Menhaj, M.B.; Prasad, M. Design of a fuzzy adaptive sliding mode control system for MEMS tunable capacitors in voltage reference applications. *IEEE Trans. Fuzzy Syst.* **2021**, *30*, 1838–1852. [CrossRef]
43. Wu, L.; Liu, J.; Vazquez, S.; Mazumder, S.K. Sliding mode control in power converters and drives: A review. *IEEE/CAA J. Autom. Sin.* **2021**, *9*, 392–406. [CrossRef]
44. Zhao, Y.; Wang, J.; Cao, G.; Yuan, Y.; Yao, X.; Qi, L. Intelligent control of multilegged robot smooth motion: A review. *IEEE Access* **2023**, *11*, 86645–86685. [CrossRef]

45. Costa-Castello, R.; Carrero, N.; Dormido, S.; Fossas, E. Teaching, analyzing, designing and interactively simulating sliding mode control. *IEEE Access* **2018**, *6*, 16783–16794. [CrossRef]
46. Marques, F.; Flores, P.; Claro, J.C.P.; Lankarani, H.M. A survey and comparison of several friction force models for dynamic analysis of multibody mechanical systems. *Nonlinear Dyn.* **2016**, *86*, 1407–1443. [CrossRef]
47. Truong, T.N.; Vo, A.T.; Kang, H.-J. Neural network-based sliding mode controllers applied to robot manipulators: A review. *Neurocomputing* **2023**, *562*, 126896. [CrossRef]
48. Sciavicco, L.; Siciliano, B. *Modelling and Control of Robot Manipulators*; Springer Science & Business Media: Berlin/Heidelberg, Germany, 2012.
49. Feraoun, H.; Fazilat, M.; Dermouche, R.; Bentouba, S.; Tadjine, M.; Zioui, N. Quantum maximum power point tracking (QMPPT) for optimal solar energy extraction. *Syst. Soft Comput.* **2024**, *6*, 200118. [CrossRef]
50. Reda, D.; Talaoubrid, A.; Fazilat, M.; Zioui, N.; Tadjine, M. A quantum direct torque control method for permanent magnet synchronous machines. *Comput. Electr. Eng.* **2025**, *122*, 109994. [CrossRef]
51. Ahmadpour, S.-S.; Nooralllahzadeh, M.; Al-Khafaji, H.M.R.; Darbandi, M.; Navimipour, N.J.; Javadi, B.; Ain, N.U.; Hosseinzadeh, M.; Yalcin, S. A new energy-efficient design for quantum-based multiplier for nano-scale devices in internet of things. *Comput. Electr. Eng.* **2024**, *117*, 109263. [CrossRef]
52. Ahmadpour, S.-S.; Navimipour, N.J. A new nano-design of 16-bit carry look-ahead adder based on quantum technology. *Phys. Scr.* **2023**, *98*, 125108. [CrossRef]
53. Orts, F.; Ortega, G.; Cucura, A.C.; Filatovas, E.; Garzón, E.M. Optimal fault-tolerant quantum comparators for image binarization. *J. Supercomput.* **2021**, *77*, 8433–8444. [CrossRef]
54. Yuan, Y.; Wang, C.; Wang, B.; Chen, Z.-Y.; Dou, M.-H.; Wu, Y.-C.; Guo, G.-P. An improved QFT-based quantum comparator and extended modular arithmetic using one ancilla qubit. *New J. Phys.* **2023**, *25*, 103011. [CrossRef]
55. Ahmadpour, S.-S.; Navimipour, N.J.; Kerestecioglu, F. A new nano-design of an efficient synchronous full-adder/subtractor based on quantum-dots. *Eurasia Proc. Sci. Technol. Eng. Math.* **2023**, *22*, 81–86. [CrossRef]
56. IBM Quantum Composer. 2024. Available online: https://quantum.ibm.com/composer/files/new (accessed on 26 January 2025).

Disclaimer/Publisher's Note: The statements, opinions and data contained in all publications are solely those of the individual author(s) and contributor(s) and not of MDPI and/or the editor(s). MDPI and/or the editor(s) disclaim responsibility for any injury to people or property resulting from any ideas, methods, instructions or products referred to in the content.

robotics

MDPI

Article

Upper-Limb Robotic Rehabilitation: Online Sliding Mode Controller Gain Tuning Using Particle Swarm Optimization

Deira Sosa Méndez [1,*], David Bedolla-Martínez [2], Maarouf Saad [2], Yassine Kali [3], Cecilia E. García Cena [4] and Ángel L. Álvarez [1]

1 Escuela de Ingeniería de Fuenlabrada, Universidad Rey Juan Carlos, 28942 Madrid, Spain
2 Electrical Engineering, École de Technologie Supérieure, Montreal, QC H3C 1K3, Canada
3 DIFIA Laboratory, School of Engineering, Université du Québec en Abitibi-Témiscamingue, Rouyn-Noranda, QC J9X 5E4, Canada
4 Escuela Técnica Superior de Ingeniería y Diseño Industrial, Center for Automation and Robotics, UPM-CSIC, Universidad Politécnica de Madrid, 28012 Madrid, Spain
* Correspondence: deira.sosa.mendez@urjc.es or sosam.deira@gmail.com

Abstract: Two primary challenges in controlling robotic rehabilitation devices are the uncertainties in dynamic models and, more importantly, the need for controllers capable of adapting to external disturbances due to human–robot interaction. To address these issues, this paper proposes the particle swarm optimization (PSO) algorithm for the real-time gain tuning in the sliding mode controller (SMC) based on the exponential reaching law (ERL). The proposed approach was designed for a seven-degrees-of-freedom (DOF) robotic exoskeleton used in upper-limb physical rehabilitation. The optimization algorithm aims to minimize tracking errors in rehabilitation exercises through the robust ERL controller applied to nonlinear systems with external disturbances. The proposed method was validated through experimental tests conducted on two healthy subjects, and the outcomes indicated a reduction of over 20% in tracking errors compared to heuristically tuned gains. Mathematical analyses of dynamic modeling and algorithm convergence are shown.

Keywords: exoskeleton; exponential reaching law; particle swarm optimization algorithm; sliding mode

1. Introduction

According to the World Health Organization in 2019 [1], 2.4 billion people experienced conditions that could benefit from rehabilitation services (1 in 3 impaired people globally). Between 1990 and 2019, there was a 69.4% rise in the population living with disabilities. Musculoskeletal disorders and strokes are among the leading causes of disability worldwide [2]. These conditions often result in limited functional capacity, particularly in terms of mobility.

One of the most common ways to support mobility recovery in individuals is through rehabilitation services, where physical rehabilitation plays a fundamental role. These services are patient-centered and aim to promote independence. Within these treatments, robotic-assisted rehabilitation has proven to be efficient because this method allows for personalized, precise, and repetitive movements, increasing the intensity of the treatment [3,4]. Such devices include exoskeletons, which are robotic systems designed based on bio-inspired models (similar in shape and functions to the human body) that are externally attached to the user [5,6].

The main challenges in robotic rehabilitation with exoskeletons are (a) those that come from their physical characteristics and (b) those that come from their application. The former addresses engineering design aspects for the physical components, workspace, and robot kinematic/kinetic models. The latter contemplates the nature of rehabilitation treatments, such as precision (personalized treatments), physical assistance by the physiotherapist (resistive or assisted therapy), and coupling between the robot and the patient (generates highly nonlinear systems with changing dynamic models), among others [7,8].

These latter aspects present a significant challenge for developers as they require the implementation of automated control strategies that ensure compliance while also providing security to users. A key aspect in the design of control strategies is the tuning of controller gains. Typically, this tuning is performed heuristically or based on the biomechanical characteristics of a particular patient population. However, this approach presents the following drawbacks: (a) the process is slow and tedious [8], and (b) its application is limited to a small group of users. Therefore, it is essential to develop approaches for automatic controller gain tuning that account for system complexities, model uncertainties, and external disturbances (such as human–exoskeleton interaction). The following section provides a brief literature review on these approaches.

2. Literary Review: Controllers and Gain Tuning Methods

Due to the nature of exoskeleton applications, it is crucial to implement controllers that ensure optimal performance, as these systems interact directly with the user and are exposed to external disturbances. This review focuses on analyzing the most commonly used controllers in exoskeletons and the techniques employed for gain tuning, covering both classical and more recent approaches. Table 1 provides a brief overview of several controllers main characteristics, along with examples of studies where they have been applied.

As shown in Table 1, most controllers combine different approaches to achieve good performance in the application. However, the Proportional–Integral–Derivative (PID) controller stands out as the most widely used due to its simplicity in implementation and tuning, as well as its effectiveness in linear systems. It is followed by sliding mode control (SMC), neural networks (NNs), fuzzy logic (FL), and supertwisting control (ST).

In terms of robustness against uncertainties and disturbances, SMC and ST controllers are particularly noteworthy, with the latter also being more accurate in complex, nonlinear systems. On the other hand, NN- and FL-based approaches are also capable of effectively handling uncertainty and achieve high accuracy, particularly when trained and properly designed. The choice of controller depends on system complexity, the nature of disturbances, and the required level of precision or robustness.

In addition to selecting the type of controller, another crucial factor for its efficiency is the choice of the gain tuning method, as this directly influences the control system stability and performance. For this purpose, various approaches are employed, which differ in complexity and effectiveness. Table 2 presents some of the most commonly used gain tuning methods, ranging from traditional techniques, such as heuristic tuning, to advanced approaches, including optimization algorithms and machine learning.

It should be noted that in most of the reviewed works, the controller gains are presented as constant values over time, without specifying how these values were assigned. In these studies, only the effectiveness of the proposed controller is demonstrated.

Table 1. Controller comparison.

Controller	Advantages	Disadvantages	Works
PID, PD and PI	• Easy to understand and implement. • Effective on linear systems.	• Do not handle nonlinear systems, uncertainties, or large disturbances. • Require manual tuning.	PD: 3-DOF LLE [9] (Sim), 5-DOF ULE S [10] (Exp). PI: 3-DOF ULE Fuzzy-PI [11] (Exp-4 HS). PID: 1-DOF ULE [12] (Exp-6 HS), 1-DOF ULE Fuzzy PID [13] (Exp-5 HS), 2-DOF LLE PID with fuzzy precompensator [14] (Sim with human gait dataset), 2-DOF LLE- robust PID adaptive [15] (Sim and Exp-3 HS), 2-DOF active and passive hybrid hydraulic ankle prosthesis [16] (Sim-Exp), 2-DOF LLE [17] (Sim), 3-DOF LLE [18,19] (Sim), 5-DOF LLE [20] (Sim), 9-DOF LLE online adaptive PID [21] (Sim)
Sliding Mode Control (SMC)	• Robust against uncertainties, external disturbances, and variations in system parameters. • Adjustable nonlinear control for complex dynamic systems.	• It uses high-frecuency switching. • It exhibits the chattering phenomenon. • Dificult to adjust due to the high nonlinearity of the control system.	2-DOF ULE [22,23] (Sim), 2-DOF ULE New model free terminal SMC [24] (Sim), 2-DOF ULE Fuzzy SMC [25] (Sim), 2-DOF ULE robust neural adaptive integral SMC [26] (Exp-2 HS), 3-DOF ULE [27] (Sim and Exp), 3-DOF pediatric LLE robust SMC [28] (Sim), 5-DOF ULE adaptive finite-time robust SMC [29] (Sim), 6-DOF ULE adaptive SMC [30] (co-simulation and Exp-1 HS), 7-DOF ULE new adaptive reaching law [31] (Exp- 1 HS), 7-DOF iReHave ULE fractional-order ultra-local model-based neural network SMC [32] (7-DOF co-simulation and 2-DOF Exp).
Supertwisting (ST)	• Robust against disturbances and inaccurate modeling. • It implements a two-stage control, which makes the switching less abrupt.	• It requires a precise parameter adjustment. • It is complex to design and implement for multiple degrees of freedom (DOF).	1-DOF ULE 2nd order SM-ST [33] (Exp), 3-DOF ULE [34] (Sim and Exp-2 HS).
Backstepping	• It is designed to stabilize a special class of nonlinear systems called strict-feedback systems. • Guarantees system stability.	• It is sensitive to variations in the system parameters. • In practice, it requires intensive calculations and it may exhibit the chattering phenomenon.	2-DOF ULE [35,36] (Sim), 2-DOF LLE Backstepping with NN [37] (Sim).
Neural Networks (NNs)	• Adapt well to highly nonlinear systems and capable of managing uncertainties. • Learn and improve their performance over time.	• Require large volumes of data for training. • Their design and calibration are complex.	2-DOF ULE [26] (Exp-2 HS), 2-DOF LLE [17,38] (Sim).
Fuzzy Logic (FL)	• Flexible to address uncertainties, disturbances, or inaccurate systems. • It does not require precise mathematical modeling.	• Dificult to optimize and design for extremely complex systems. • At times, it is less precise than other controllers if not tuned correctly.	Hand [39] (Exp-6 HS), 1-DOF ULE elbow [40–42](Exp).

Table 2. Gain tuning methods comparison.

Method	Advantages	Disadvantages	Works
Tuning by trial and error, manually or pre-tuned.	• Flexible and suitable for a wide variety of systems. • It is commonly used in nonlinear systems or difficult model systems.	• It is slow for high-dimensional systems. • It does not guarantee optimal performance without significant operator experience.	2-DOF ULE: [22] (Sim), [36] (Sim).
Ziegler–Nichols (ZN)	• Widely used for tuning PID controllers. • Easy to apply and useful for the allocation of initial gains.	• Empirical formulas are used to adjust the parameters. • It may not be optimal in terms of robustness and response to disturbances.	PID: 3-DOF LLE [18] (Sim), [19] (Sim).
Variable or adaptive gain method	• The controller parameters are tuned dynamically during operation in response to changes in the nonlinear system or disturbances. • Greater robustness against variations in the system's dynamics.	• The implementation is more complex and requires precise mathematical models or advanced algorithms.	1-DOF ULE applied adaptative PID [12] (Exp-6 HS), 2-DOF LLE applied a robust PID adaptive controller [15] (Sim and Exp-3 HS), 3-DOF LLE applied an optimal PID [19] (Sim), 3-DOF ULE applied fuzzy logic [11] (Exp-4 HS), 5-DOF ULE applied an adaptive finite-time robust SMC [29] (Sim), 9-DOF LLE applied an adaptive PID [21] (Sim).
Neural network-based control (learning-based tuning)	• Controls a nonlinear system by learning from collected data. • Ability to adapt to highly nonlinear systems and manage unmodeled disturbances.	• It requires a large training dataset and is difficult to interpret and manually adjust. • The controller may need to be retrained if the system undergoes significant changes.	2-DOF ULE [26] (EXp-2 HS), 3-DOF LLE [18] (Offline, Sim), 5-DOF LLE [20] (Sim), 7-DOF iReHave ULE [32] (7-DOF Co-simulation and 2-DOF Exp).
Nonlinear model predictive control (NMPC)	• It uses a nonlinear system model to predict its future behavior and optimizes the control signal based on those predictions.	• Computationally intensive (involves solving an optimization problem in real time).	7-DOF ULE robust MPC with an integral sliding mode (Exp- 3 HS) [43].
Heuristic optimization (evolutionary, genetic, or particle swarm algorithms)	• It handles nonlinear systems with a large number of parameters. • Suitable when search space is complex and there are multiple objectives to optimize, such as performance against disturbances and stability. • Explores a broad solution space and automatically tunes the controller parameters.	• It can be slow and require high computational resource consumption. • It finds solutions that are very close to optimal.	PSO: 2-DOF ULE PID [35] (offline and Sim), 2-DOF LLE PID with fuzzy precompensator [14] (Sim with human gait dataset), 2-DOF LLE robust PID adaptive controller [15] (Sim and Exp- 3 HS), 3-DOF LLE PD [9] (Offline and Sim), 3-DOF ULE [34] (Online Sim and Exp-2 HS), 9-DOF LLE online adaptive PID controller [21] (Sim).

According to Table 2, for linear systems, methods such as Ziegler–Nichols (the most common for parameter initialization) and tuning by trial and error (either manually or pre-tuned) tend to be effective and easy to implement. However, in nonlinear systems, which are inherently susceptible to uncertainties and disturbances, the most effective methods include heuristic optimization, robust control, and adaptive control. This is because neural networks require considerable time to process each input and target data sample due to the size of each training set.

Over the years, nature has inspired the development of algorithms to solve complex real-world problems. However, there is no universal applicable heuristic method for optimizing the gains of a nonlinear controller in the presence of disturbances, as the effectiveness of each algorithm depends on the type of nonlinear system, the nature of the disturbances, and the specific requirements of the control problem. Some of the most common heuristic methods used for these types of problems include genetic algorithms (GAs), particle swarm optimization (PSO) [8,9,14–16,19,21,35], simulated annealing (SA), ant colony optimization (ACO), cuckoo search (CS) algorithm, and differential evolution (DE) algorithms.

For optimizing gains in a nonlinear controller in the presence of disturbances, genetic algorithms and PSO are the most widely used and effective due to their flexibility and ability to identify suitable solutions in nonlinear problems with multiple local optima. However, when rapid convergence is required or there are computational limitations, PSO is an excellent choice, as it is an algorithm that is part of swarm intelligence, a significant branch of artificial intelligence [44,45]. Conversely, if robustness against the possibility of getting trapped in local optima is desired and more computational time is available, genetic algorithms or differential evolution are more appropriate options.

In the context of exoskeletons for rehabilitation, where there is physical interaction with users, methods that require precise knowledge of the mathematical model are generally not used, especially if the system is of high order and exhibits nonlinearities or external disturbances [29,46–48]. Therefore, in these applications, it is essential to have a method that adjusts the controller parameters in real time, adapting to the evolution of the system and changes in user characteristics. Designing such solutions are complex and may require specialized hardware and software.

As a result, it is necessary to implement control approaches based on metaheuristic optimization that adapt in real time to different users. These algorithms identify efficient configurations for the controller compared to traditional methods. By adopting these robust approaches, the efficiency of rehabilitation tasks is improved.

Optimization-based approaches overcome the drawbacks of those that do not employ it, so the key steps of this approach are outlined below:

1. Establish an objective function: The aim is to meet specific criteria while considering the associated cost, whether minimum or maximum. This can be achieved through one or more objective functions, or by using a weighted objective function.
2. Optimizer selection: Direct methods, such as the response surface method and gradient descent, as well as swarm-based methods like evolutionary algorithms (EAs), are employed. Direct methods are sensitive to noise, which can reduce their performance. Additionally, they typically provide solutions based on a single criterion, tend to converge to local optima, and may encounter issues related to an unidentified search space. In contrast, swarm-based methods have demonstrated superior performance compared to these traditional approaches [8,44].

Lately, the particle swarm (PS) algorithm has emerged as one of the EAs utilized for optimizing controller parameters in exoskeletons, due to the following characteristics [19,21,49]: (1) its simplicity and high convergence speed; (2) it does not need any assumptions about the problem to be optimized; (3) it explores extensive solution spaces; (4) it is capable of handling intricate complex nonlinear systems with a high number of dimensions and challenges in dynamic optimization across diverse domains; (5) it does not demand a precise dynamic model or accurate system parameters beforehand; (6) a limited number of parameters require tuning; and (7) it exhibits a high likelihood and efficiency in discovering global optima, among others.

Despite the merits of the PS algorithm, it also has some disadvantages [15,16,19,21]: (1) the time required for convergence might be extended, potentially leading to undesirable chattering phenomena in a control context; (2) the potential problem of early convergence could hinder the ability to adapt to sudden changes in the system and the environment; and (3) there is a risk of early convergence, leading to entrapment in local optima, among others.

In this case, due to the application objectives, the PS algorithm was chosen to optimize the gains of the sliding mode controller. This technique is a robust and well-established control method, designed to handle uncertain dynamics, provide a rapid response to changes, offer robustness against parameter variations, and facilitate implementation [23,27,28,30]. However, its main disadvantage is the occurrence of oscillations. To mitigate this problem and reduce convergence time, an alternative approach is proposed that incorporates an exponential function as the reaching law, which preserves the robustness of SMC [28,31,50,51]. This enables the controller to adapt in real time to changes in the morphology and motor abilities of exoskeleton users.

To the best of our knowledge, the main contributions of this study involve the following:

- Online gain tuning using the exponential reaching law (ERL) and the PSO algorithm on a highly nonlinear system is proposed for the first time.
- This is the first real-time implementation of the robust PSO-ERL algorithm on a 7 DOF exoskeleton for online gain tuning for trajectory tracking.
- It presents the findings from the experimental assessment of gain tuning among healthy subjects exhibiting diverse physiological characteristics.

The work is structured as follows: Section 3 covers the PSO algorithm's mathematical aspects, the exoskeleton's dynamical model (nonlinear considering external disturbances), and the controller (features, stability analysis, etc.). Section 4 details the implementation conditions, experimental results, and analyses performed. The last section concludes and suggests several future study directions.

3. Mathematical Aspects

In this section, we address the main concepts considered for the development of this work.

3.1. Exoskeleton's Uncertain Dynamic Model

During physical therapy treatments, patients wear the exoskeleton for purposes of rehabilitation and/or assistance. Due to this, there are coupled systems with two different dynamics (human and exoskeleton) which must be considered in the real application.

An adaptive controller is required for nonlinear systems that adapt to model uncertainties and external disturbances. So, the dynamics of the ETS-MARSE robot are presented in joint space as follows [43]:

$$M(\theta)\ddot{\theta} + C(\theta,\dot{\theta})\dot{\theta} + G(\theta) + F(\dot{\theta}) = \tau_o + \tau_u \quad (1)$$

where $\theta \in \mathbb{R}^{n\times 1}$ contains the joint angular position, $\dot{\theta} \in \mathbb{R}^{n\times 1}$ vector contains the joint angular velocity, $\ddot{\theta} \in \mathbb{R}^{n\times 1}$ vector contains the joint angular acceleration, $M(\theta) \in \mathbb{R}^{n\times n}$ is the inertial matrix, $C(\theta,\dot{\theta}) \in \mathbb{R}^{n\times n}$ is the centrifugal and Coriolis terms, $G(\theta) \in \mathbb{R}^{n\times 1}$ is the gravitational forces, $F(\dot{\theta}) \in \mathbb{R}^{n\times 1}$ characterizes nonlinear Coulomb friction, $\tau_o \in \mathbb{R}^{n\times 1}$ denotes the generalized torque vector, and $\tau_u \in \mathbb{R}^{n\times 1}$ represents the vector of unknown disturbing forces originating from the patient with n equal to 7 (number of joints). Consider the following relations:

$$M = M_o + M_u \tag{2}$$
$$C = C_o + C_u \tag{3}$$
$$G = G_o + G_u \tag{4}$$

where the terms with subscript "o" represent the nominal part and terms with subscript "u" represent the unknown part for M, C, and G.

Isolating $\ddot{\theta}$ from Equation (1), Equation (5) is obtained:

$$\ddot{\theta} = M_o^{-1}(\theta)[\tau_o - C_o(\theta,\dot{\theta})\dot{\theta} - G_o(\theta)] + U_u \tag{5}$$

where U_u includes the unknown variables shown in Equation (6), and $M_o(\theta)$ is a symmetric matrix that is positive definite, ensuring the availability of $M_o^{-1}(\theta)$.

$$U_u = M_o^{-1}(\theta)[\tau_u - M_u(\theta)\ddot{\theta} - C_u(\theta,\dot{\theta})\dot{\theta} - G_u(\theta) - F(\dot{\theta})] \tag{6}$$

A compensatory torque derived from the nominal components of (1) is as follows:

$$\tau_o = M_o(\theta)v(t) + C_o(\theta,\dot{\theta})\dot{\theta} + G_o(\theta) \tag{7}$$

where $v(t)$ to be designed later and it represents the virtual control that guides the system toward the control goal. Substituting Equation (7) in Equation (5), the following uncertain linear system is obtained.

$$\ddot{\theta} = v(t) + U_u \tag{8}$$

3.2. Proposed Controller

The initial step involves selecting the sliding surface S based on the tracking error, as expressed in Equation (9). This indicates that upon reaching the sliding surface, the tracking error decreases to zero. The rate of convergence is linked to the value of Λ_i.

$$S_i = \Lambda_i e_i + \dot{e}_i \tag{9}$$

where the tracking error is calculated as $e_i = \theta_{di} - \theta_i$, where θ_{di} denotes the desired trajectory, and θ_i represents the measured angular position.

The subsequent phase includes choosing the virtual control v that facilitates the error convergence toward the sliding surface. To achieve this, the following condition must be fulfilled:

$$S_i\dot{S}_i < 0 \qquad \forall t$$

A controller based on sliding modes with ERL was chosen for nonlinear systems, whose typical reaching law is shown in Equation (10):

$$\dot{S}_i = -\frac{K_i}{D(S_i)}\operatorname{sign}(S_i) \tag{10}$$
$$D(S_i) = \varsigma_i + (1-\varsigma_i)e^{-\rho_i|S_i|^{h_i}}$$

$$\text{sign}(S_i) = \begin{cases} 1, & \text{for } S_i > 0 \\ 0, & \text{for } S_i = 0 \\ -1, & \text{for } S_i < 0 \end{cases}$$

where K_i is a strictly positive gain, ς_i is a strictly positive offset less than one ($0 < \varsigma_i < 1$), h_i is a positive integer greater than zero ($h_i > 0$), and ρ_i is also a positive integer greater than zero ($\rho_i > 0$).

Relation (10) has the following features:

- In the event of an increase in $|S_i|$, $D(S_i) \to \varsigma_i$, leading to the convergence of $K_i/D(S_i)$ toward K_i/ς_i. Consequently, during the reaching phase, $K_i/D(S_i)$ increases, resulting in a faster attraction toward the sliding surface.
- In the case of a decrease in $|S_i|$, $D(S_i) \to 1$, causing $K_i/D(S_i)$ to converge to K_i. Consequently, $K_i/D(S_i)$ gradually decreases, thereby mitigating chattering.

Thus, the ERL does not impact the stability of control through sliding modes since $D(S_i)$ remains strictly positive. Additionally, it enables the controller to dynamically adapt to changes in the sliding surface by allowing the variation in $K_i/D(S_i)$ within the range of K_i to K_i/ς_i.

It is crucial to emphasize that the switching term $K_i sign(S_i)$ in Equation (10) frequently results in heightened control activity, commonly referred to as chattering (an undesirable phenomenon). To address this concern, the paper employs a smoothed fragmented term in the control input, as illustrated in Equation (11):

$$\dot{S}_i = -\frac{K_i}{D(S_i)}\text{sat}\left(\frac{S_i}{\psi_i}\right) \qquad \forall t, K_i > 0 \tag{11}$$

where

$$\text{sat}\left(\frac{S_i}{\psi_i}\right) = \begin{cases} 1, & \text{for } S_i \geq \psi_i \\ \frac{S_i}{\psi_i}, & \text{for } -\psi_i \leq S_i \leq \psi_i, \forall t, 0 < \psi_i \ll 1 \\ -1, & \text{for } S_i \leq \psi_i \end{cases}$$

By employing this substitution, the system's convergence is restricted to a boundary layer surrounding the sliding surface. The size of this neighborhood is directly determined by the parameter ψ_i. Therefore, Equation (11) effectively addresses chattering issues and enhances tracking performance.

In accordance with Equations (5), (9), and (11), we obtain v_i:

$$v_i - \ddot{\theta}_{di} + \Lambda_i(\dot{\theta}_{di} - \dot{\theta}_i) + \frac{K_i}{D(S_i)}\text{sat}\left(\frac{S_i}{\psi_i}\right) \tag{12}$$

The online tuning process will determine the optimal gain values K_i and Λ_i, which adjust to changes during the trajectory tracking.

3.2.1. Controller Stability Analysis

To assess the controller stability, Equation (13) is chosen as the Lyapunov function.

$$H(S_i) = \frac{1}{2}S_i^2 \tag{13}$$

Hence, if $\dot{H} < 0$, it indicates $\dot{S}_i < 0$ for $S_i > 0$ and $\dot{S}_i > 0$ for $S_i < 0$ (refer to Equation (14)). This leads to the emergence of a switching phenomenon to uphold the condition $S_i\dot{S}_i < 0$.

$$\dot{H}(S_i) = S_i\dot{S}_i \tag{14}$$

where

$$\dot{S}_i = \Lambda_i\dot{e}_i + \ddot{e}_i \tag{15}$$

$$\ddot{e}_i = \ddot{\theta}_{di} - \ddot{\theta}_i \tag{16}$$

Replacing Equations (12), (15), and (16) into (14), we obtain the following:

$$\dot{H}(S_i) = S_i\left(\frac{-K_i}{D(S_i)}\text{sat}\left(\frac{S_i}{\psi_i}\right) - U_{ui}\right) \tag{17}$$

To ensure asymptotic stability, the following inequality must be satisfied:

$$|U_{ui}| < \frac{K_i}{D(S_i)} \tag{18}$$

where U_{ui} represents the unknown dynamics (external disturbances and model uncertainties), which is assumed to be locally continuous and limited by $Umax_i$ (Equation (19)):

$$0 <|U_{ui}| \leq Umax_i < \infty \tag{19}$$

3.3. Particle Swarm Optimization Algorithm

Kennedy and Eberhart introduced the conventional PSO algorithm in 1995. This metaheuristic draws inspiration from the collaborative behavior observed in fish and birds, relying on the cooperation of agents through the information sharing. Within the PSO algorithm, every agent is regarded as a particle, functioning as a potential solution in an optimization problem [52,53].

The fundamental model involves the initialization of a population with randomly selected solutions within the search space. The objective is to identify the optimal solution, with each particle continuously refining its behavior over iterations, leveraging its own experiences and insights gleaned from the top-performing particles within the swarm [8,15]. Every particle is defined by vectors representing its position and velocity (Equation (20b)).

$$X_i(t+1) = X_i(t) + V_i(t+1) \tag{20a}$$

$$V_i(t+1) = \omega V_i(t) + c_1s_1[P_b(t) - X_i(t)] + c_2s_2[P_g(t) - X_i(t)] \tag{20b}$$

where X_i denotes the particle position, V_i denotes the particle velocity, P_b denotes the best individual position of each particle i, P_g stands for the entire swarm's best global position, and ω denotes the inertia weight assigned to each particle; c_1 and c_2 denote the cognitive and social acceleration coefficients specific to each particle, where s_1 and s_2 denote two random numbers chosen independently from the interval [0, 1], respectively.

The main three parameters of the PSO algorithm are (1) inertial weight (ω), (2) the cognitive acceleration parameter (c_1), and (3) the social acceleration (c_2).These parameters impact the algorithm's ability to conduct both global and local searches, and its summarization is as follows: (1) the global search is enhanced with a large inertial weight, whereas the local search is enhanced with a small inertial weight; (2) if $c_1 > c_2$ then the global search is facilitated, and (3) if $c_2 > c_1$ then the local search is improved.

3.3.1. Convergence Analysis

As the PSO is a stochastic algorithm, it is imperative to provide a convergence analysis overview. To this end, this subsection considers its deterministic version and presents its convergence analysis based on the discrete-time dynamic system theory [52,53].

In this case, the random numbers are replaced by the average (0.5), so Equation (20b) is written as below:

$$X_i(t+1) = X_i(t) + V_i(t+1) \tag{21a}$$
$$V_i(t+1) = \omega V_i(t) + c[P(t) - X_i(t)] \tag{21b}$$

where

$$P(t) = \frac{c_1 P_b(t) + c_2 P_g(t)}{c_1 + c_2} \tag{22a}$$
$$c = \frac{c_1 + c_2}{2} \tag{22b}$$

Equations (21a) and (21b) are reformulated in matrix form as follows:

$$\begin{bmatrix} X_i(t+1) \\ V_i(t+1) \end{bmatrix} = A \begin{bmatrix} X_i(t) \\ V_i(t) \end{bmatrix} + BP(t) \tag{23}$$

$$A = \begin{bmatrix} 1-c & \omega \\ -c & \omega \end{bmatrix}, B = \begin{bmatrix} c \\ c \end{bmatrix}$$

where $P(t)$ is the external input, while A and B correspond to the dynamical matrix and input matrix, respectively.

So, the time-dependent behavior of the PSO algorithm relies on the dynamic matrix A's eigenvalues. These eigenvalues are computed using Equation (24).

$$\det(\eta I - A) = 0 \tag{24}$$

The result of Equation (24) is shown in Equation (25):

$$\eta^2 + (c - 1 - \omega)\eta + \omega = 0 \tag{25}$$

The eigenvalues $\eta_{1,2}$ are shown in Equation (26):

$$\eta_{1,2} = \frac{\omega + 1 - c \pm \sqrt{\Delta}}{2} \tag{26}$$

where $\Delta = (\omega + 1 - c)^2 - 4\omega$. Therefore, the algorithm's effectiveness and convergence rely on the values assigned to the parameters ω and c.

The conditions derived from the eigenvalues given in Equation (26) are as follows: (1) $\omega < 1$, (2) $c > 0$, and (3) $2\omega - c + 2 > 0$.

The convergence region is illustrated in the (ω, c) plane, as depicted in Figure 1a. Regardless of the initial position and velocity, the particle will converge to its equilibrium position, as defined by Equations (22a) and (32), only if the algorithm parameters fall within this triangular region.

Before the convergence, the particle may exhibit the following behaviors:

1. When the eigenvalues of matrix A take on complex values, harmonic oscillations manifest around the equilibrium point. This equivalence is represented by Equation (27), and its domain in the plane is illustrated in Figure 1b.

$$\omega^2 + c^2 - 2\omega c - 2\omega - 2c + 1 < 0 \tag{27}$$

2. The oscillating pattern resembling zigzagging emerges near the equilibrium point when there is at least one eigenvalue of matrix A with a negative real part, whether it is a real or complex value. This relationship is expressed by either Equation (28) or (29), and its region in the plane is illustrated in Figure 1c.

$$\omega < 0 \tag{28}$$

$$\omega - c + 1 < 0 \tag{29}$$

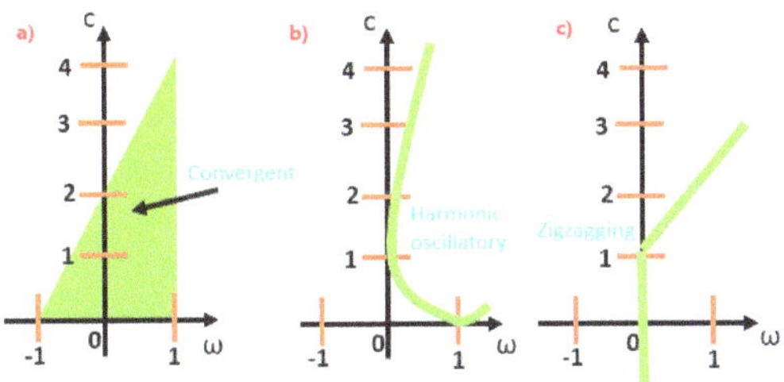

Figure 1. Regions of dynamic behavior within the parameter space (ω, c). (**a**) Convergence region, (**b**) harmonic oscillatory behavior, and (**c**) zigzagging behavior. Information taken from [53].

3.3.2. Equilibrium Point

The particle's initial state is typically not in a state of equilibrium. In practice, it is crucial to determine whether the particle will eventually reach equilibrium, signifying the optimization algorithm's convergence and the trajectory it will traverse in the state space while exploring for optimal points.

Equation (23) is written as follows:

$$Y_{(k+1)} = AY_k + BP(t) \tag{30}$$

where $Y_k = [X_k, V_k]^T$.

For an equilibrium point to exist, Equation (31) must be satisfied for any k.

$$Y^{eq}_{(k+1)} = Y^{eq}_k \tag{31}$$

In the deterministic analysis, the particle must possess zero velocity and be positioned at the attraction point P (Equation (22a)). Consequently, Equation (32) is obtained:

$$Y^{eq} = [P, 0]^T \tag{32}$$

It means $X^{eq} = P$ and $V^{eq} = 0$. Therefore, the equilibrium point is stable if and only if both eigenvalues of matrix A (real or complex) have magnitudes less than 1.

4. Results: Real-Time Implementation

This study performs gain tuning (K_i and Λ_i) of the ERL controller on a highly nonlinear exoskeleton robot, subject to external disturbances, such as initial offsets and user variations. The problem is formulated as an optimization task and addressed using the PSO algorithm.

4.1. Exoskeleton Description

The controller is applied to the ETS-MARSE (École de Technologie Supérieure—Motion Assistive Robotic-exoskeleton for Superior Extremity) with 7 DOF (see Figure 2). This exoskeleton facilitates rehabilitation by assisting movements for individuals with impaired upper extremities. Its design takes into account the upper extremity alignment, featuring 3 degrees of freedom (DOF) for the shoulder (S), 1 DOF for the elbow (E), and 3 DOF for the wrist (W). The modified Denavit–Hartenberg parameters (D-H) for the exoskeleton are detailed in Table 3.

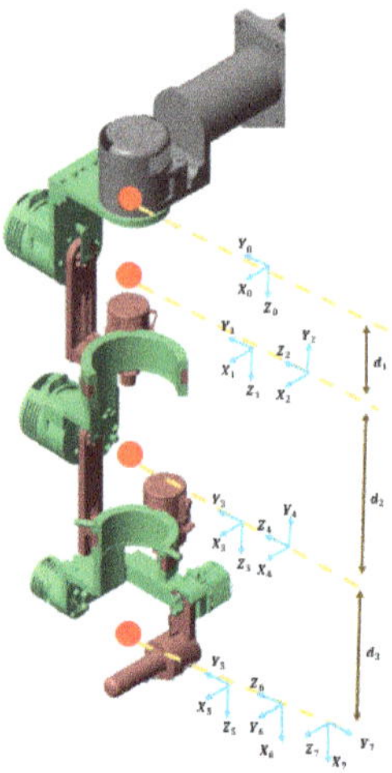

Figure 2. ETS MARSE: exoskeleton.

Table 3. Modified D-H parameters.

Movement	θ_i	a_{i-1}	α_{i-1}	d_i	Range [deg]
S: Horizontal Flex-Ext	θ_1	0	0	d_1	−20 to 70
S: Vertical Flex-Ext	θ_2	0	$-\frac{\pi}{2}$	0	−5 to 120
S: Int-Ext rot	θ_3	0	$+\frac{\pi}{2}$	d_2	−85 to 80
E: Ext-Flex	θ_4	0	$-\frac{\pi}{2}$	0	−5 to 115
W: Pron-sup	θ_5	0	$+\frac{\pi}{2}$	d_3	−85 to 85
W: Ext-Flex	$\theta_6 - \frac{\pi}{2}$	0	$-\frac{\pi}{2}$	0	−25 to 20
W: Ulnar radial deviation	θ_7	0	$-\frac{\pi}{2}$	0	−55 to 60

The exoskeleton's real-time system consists of three processing units, detailed as follows:

- Host PC (Intel Core i7-4770 CPU @3.4 GHz, and 16 GB RAM): facilitates the transmission of higher-level controls to the exoskeleton via the human–machine interface (developed in LabView 2017).
- A real-time PC (NI PXI-8108, Intel dual-core @2.53 GHz processor and 8 GB RAM): operates the top-level control and manages the exoskeleton dynamics with a sampling time of 1 ms.
- FPGA (NI PXI-7813R): utilized for handling analog and digital inputs and outputs to the actuators and sensors, executing the low-level control (PI) current control loop with a sampling time of 50 µs.

The robot utilizes brushless DC motors, specifically Maxon EC-45 and Maxon EC-90, in combination with harmonic drives. Motors 1 and 2 have a gear ratio of 120:1, while motors 3–7 have a gear ratio of 100:1.

4.2. Tests Description

In this section, the tests to be conducted are described, with the following considerations:

1. The experiments were carried out by donning the exoskeleton on two healthy subjects (one at a time, as shown in Table 4 and Figure 3).
2. A trajectory for passive rehabilitation was executed that encompasses the movement of all joints, taking into account the modified D-H parameters, as detailed in Table 3. This trajectory starts with the user's elbow flexed at 90°.
3. During the experiment, the upper limb of the subjects remained in a passive state while the exoskeleton drives the user's extremity.

Table 4. Users' features.

User	Gender	Age (Years Old)	Weight [kg]	Height [cm]
$User_1$	Male	33	75	160
$User_2$	Female	33	54	154

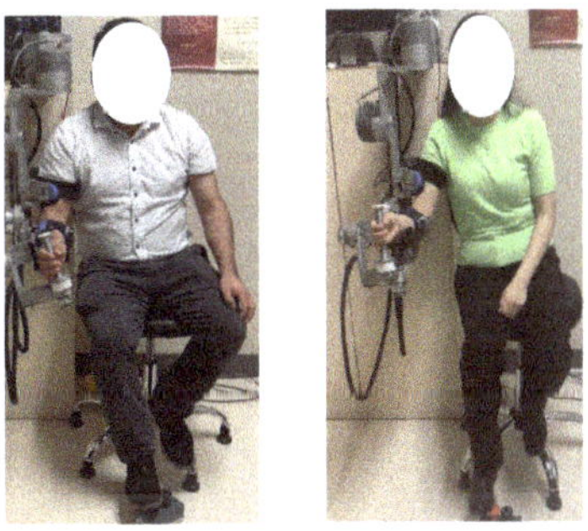

(a) (b)

Figure 3. Exoskeleton with users. (**a**) User 1. (**b**) User 2.

To demonstrate the efficiency of the PSO algorithm when tuning the ERL controller gains, the following tests were performed:

1. Assess the ERL performance controller under pre-tuned gains, denoted as PT conditions.
2. Assess the ERL controller's real-time performance through online tuning using PSO, denoted as PSO conditions.
3. Assess the ERL controller's performance using the globally tuned gains obtained after applying the PSO algorithm, denoted as PSOG conditions.

4.2.1. First Test

The gains were chosen heuristically and theirs values are shown in Table 5.

Table 5. ERL: Pre-tuned gains.

Metric	q_1	q_2	q_3	q_4	q_5	q_6	q_7
K_i	50.0	20.0	90.0	60.0	250.0	500.0	450.0
Λ_i	90.0	40.0	70.0	20.0	25.0	10.0	10.0
ς_i	0.5	0.5	0.5	0.5	0.5	0.5	0.5

Table 5. *Cont.*

Metric	q_1	q_2	q_3	q_4	q_5	q_6	q_7
ρ_i	2.0	2.0	2.0	2.0	2.0	2.0	2.0
h_i	2.0	2.0	2.0	2.0	2.0	2.0	2.0
ψ_i	0.5	0.5	0.5	0.5	0.5	0.5	0.5

4.2.2. Second Test

The ERL controller parameters vary over time and are adaptively tuned online. This flexibility allows for efficient tracking of trajectories, even when confronted with external disturbances like patient forces or physiotherapist assistance. The control scheme is depicted in Figure 4.

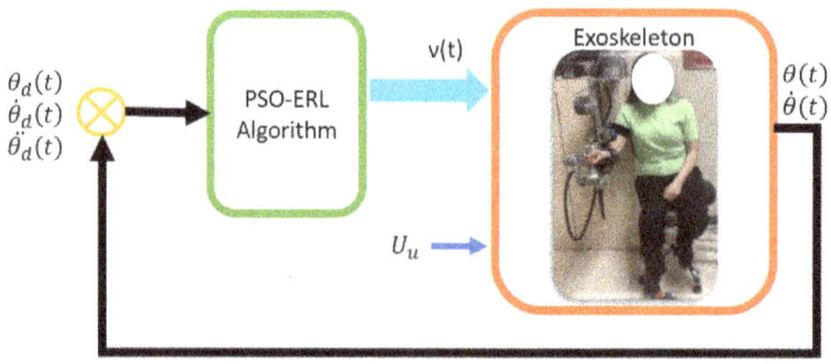

Figure 4. Control scheme.

Commonly, to address the optimization problem, a single objective function is used that encompasses all DOF. In this work, a weighted objective function is employed: it includes position and velocity errors for each degree of freedom (DOF), where the position error is prioritized. So, the function targeted as the objective in the PSO algorithm is presented in Equation (33).

$$f(e, \dot{e}) = \alpha||e|| + \beta||\dot{e}|| \quad (33)$$

Here, $\alpha + \beta = 1$, with α and β constrained to the range 0 to 1.

In this scenario, each particle comprises the following two gains, K_i and Λ_i. The goal is to dynamically identify the optimal particle in real time, minimizing the objective function $f(e, \dot{e})$. Therefore Algorithm 1 introduces the proposed robust PSO-ERL algorithm.

Algorithm 1 Proposed robust PSO-ERL algorithm.

Define the number of particles in the swarm, n.
Initialize the swarm with random values.
i ← 1
repeat
  Insert a particle i (K_i, Λ_i)
  Compute ν using the ERL approach Equation (12)
  Calculate $\tau_0(t)$ using Equation (7).
  Utilize τ_0 as the input for the system.
  Compute the objective function f using Equation (33).
  Store the value of f for particle i.
  i ← i + 1
until i > m
Determine $P_i(t)$ and $P_g(t)$.
Resolve Equation (20b).
GOTO 4

In this case, Equation (20a) represents the gain value (K_i or Λ_i), and Equation (20b) represents the corresponding gain change rate. The particle's initial values (K_i and Λ_i) are randomly generated within their respective search space, as defined in Table 6. Subsequently, the objective function is calculated in each iteration to assess each particle, iteratively guiding the PSO-ERL to find the optimal solution. The particle exhibiting the objective function minimum value corresponds to the best global gain.

Table 6. Search space.

Gains Constraints	q_1	q_2	q_3	q_4	q_5	q_6	q_7
K_{min}	25	10	70	40	200	460	430
K_{max}	70	60	130	80	320	540	550
Λ_{min}	70	30	60	2	20	5	1550
Λ_{max}	100	80	110	28	70	40	1950

The remaining parameters for the PSO algorithm and the controller's experimental conditions are detailed in Table 7.

Table 7. Experimental conditions (online gain tuning with PSO).

Metric	Value
Initial offset (each joint)	5 [deg]
External disturbances (see Table 4)	2 users
Number of particles (m)	30.0
ω (inertial factor of PSO)	0.9
c_1 (personal acceleration parameter of PSO)	0.1
c_2 (group acceleration parameter of PSO)	0.3
α (objective function, f)	0.7
β (objective function, f)	0.3
ς (controller parameter, ERL)	0.5
ρ (controller parameter, ERL)	2.0
h (controller parameter, ERL)	2.0
ψ (controller parameter, ERL)	0.5

To select the parameters in Table 7, we considered the following:

- $\omega \approx 1$: Promotes global exploration.
- $c_2 > c_1$: Global optimum is prioritized.
- $\alpha > \beta$: Prioritizing position error minimization.

Once the second test was completed (applying the PSO algorithm to determine the gains K_i and Λ_i of the controller), the values of the global gains were obtained for each user, which are shown in Table 8.

Table 8. Global gains tuned with ERL + PSO.

Metric	q_1	q_2	q_3	q_4	q_5	q_6	q_7
K_{User_1}	52.1	47.4	101.3	68.6	289.8	460.0	550.0
K_{User_2}	25.0	50.5	70.0	63.5	253.4	492.9	503.0
Λ_{User_1}	88.4	37.6	79.5	8.4	46.5	26.7	1654.7
Λ_{User_2}	99.9	80.0	94.1	17.4	24.9	10.4	1664.6

4.2.3. Third Test

It consists in executing the ERL controller with the gain values shown in Table 8.

So, in the next section, we perform a comparative analysis of the results obtained in the three experiments.

4.3. Experimental Results and Comparative Analysis

Figure 5 shows the results of the trajectory tracking, tracking error, control signals, and cartesian tracking and error graphs of user 1, respectively. Furthermore, Figure 6 corresponds to user 2. In each figure, there are three signals, each one corresponding to the experiments carried out (PT, PSO, and PSOG).

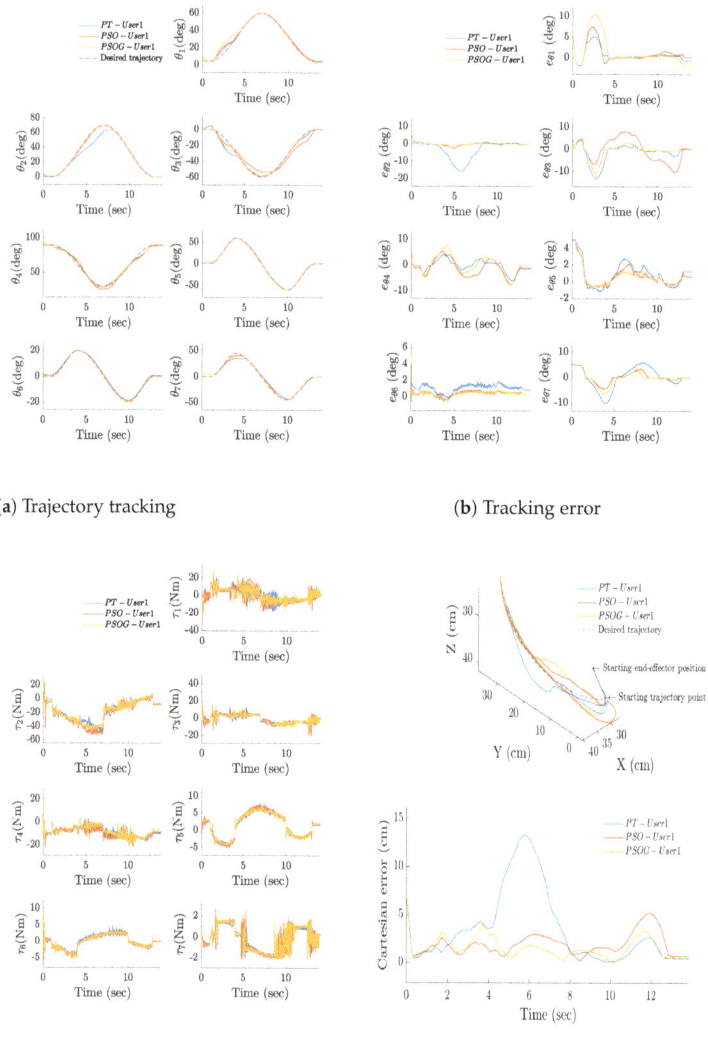

(**a**) Trajectory tracking (**b**) Tracking error

(**c**) Control signal (**d**) Cartesian tracking and error

Figure 5. User 1. (**a**) Trajectory tracking. (**b**) Tracking error. (**c**) Control signal. (**d**) Cartesian tracking and error.

To evaluate the PSO algorithm's behavior, Figure 7 presents the evolution of the values of K and λ of a particle, showing an oscillatory and convergent behavior. Choosing the parameters ω, c_1, c_2 guarantees the PSO algorithm's deterministic convergence, whose eigenvalues of Equation (26) are equal to $\eta_{1,2} = 0.85 \pm j0.42$.

According to the results obtained, the average RMSE (root mean square error) for both users in the first test was $[0.05, 0.07]rad$ and the average RMSE for the same users in the third test was $[0.03, 0.05]rad$. This shows that the proposed approach reduces the average RMSE of user 1 by 28.3% and by 23.5% for user 2.

It should be noted that chattering is not eliminated entirely, however, the average RMST (root mean square torque) for the same users in the first test was $[7.33, 7.21]$ and for the third test was $[7.36, 7.33]$. It is concluded that the RMST in the third experiment increased by 0.4% and 1.6% compared to the first test, which means a small increase in the control activity while greatly improving the tracking error.

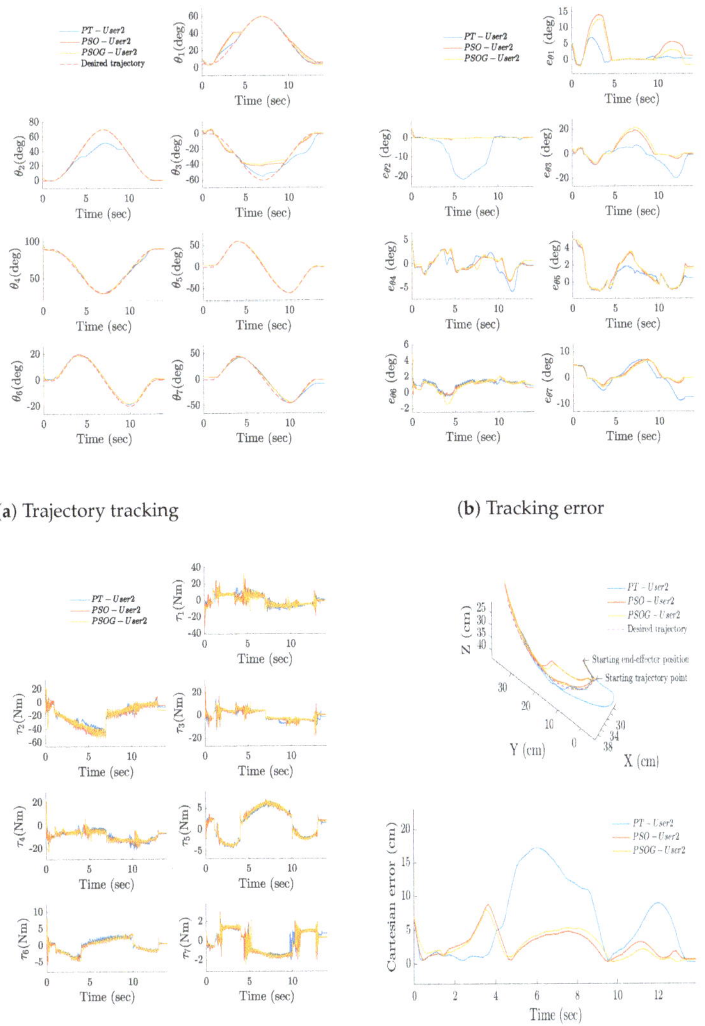

(**a**) Trajectory tracking (**b**) Tracking error

(**c**) Control signal (**d**) Cartesian tracking and error

Figure 6. User 2. (**a**) Trajectory tracking. (**b**) Tracking error. (**c**) Control signal. (**d**) Cartesian tracking and error.

Tables 9 and 10 show the users' results for the RMSE and RMST of each joint, as well as the average for the first and third tests.

Table 9. Results: root mean square error (RMSE).

Joint	$User_1$			$User_2$		
	PT	**PSOG**	**%**	**PT**	**PSOG**	**%**
q_1	0.03	0.06	+110.0	0.03	0.08	+109.5
q_2	0.10	0.01	−88.1	0.17	0.00	−94.8
q_3	0.07	0.05	−27.6	0.13	0.16	25.6
q_4	0.03	0.06	+52.4	0.03	0.02	−22.0
q_5	0.03	0.02	−23.4	0.02	0.03	23.3
q_6	0.02	0.00	−55.3	0.02	0.02	−1.7
q_7	0.07	0.04	−38.7	0.08	0.05	−33.0
Mean	0.05	0.03	−28.3	0.07	0.05	−23.4

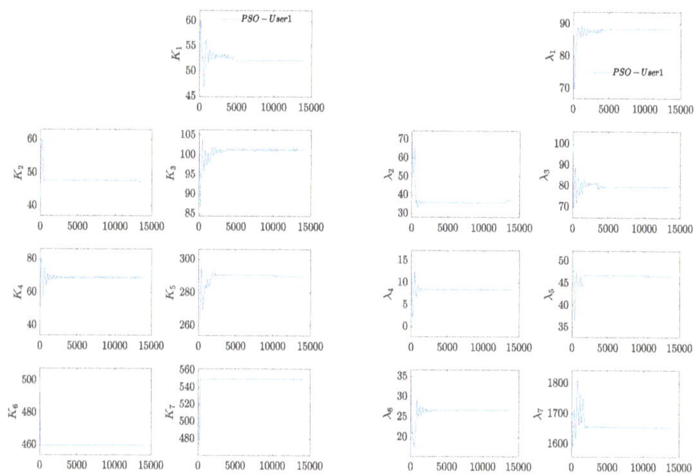

(a) K_i (b) Λ_i

Figure 7. Global gain evolution. (**a**) K_i. (**b**) Λ_i

Table 10. Results: root mean square torque (RMST).

Joint	$User_1$			$User_2$		
	PT	**PSOG**	**%**	**PT**	**PSOG**	**%**
q_1	7.45	7.24	−2.7	7.56	6.47	−14.4
q_2	22.66	22.89	+1.0	22.05	24.36	+10.4
q_3	4.58	4.91	+7.2	4.75	4.20	−11.7
q_4	9.86	9.35	−5.1	9.52	9.54	+0.1
q_5	3.60	3.72	+3.5	3.51	3.59	+2.2
q_6	2.08	2.18	+4.7	2.01	1.99	−0.9
q_7	1.11	1.21	+9.2	1.10	1.16	+5.2
Mean	7.33	7.36	+0.3	7.21	7.33	+1.5

Additionally, it is worth noting that the elapsed time for the first and third experiments was around 238 µs, while for the second experiment it was around 263 µs, representing an 11% increase.

5. Discussion

Rehabilitation exoskeletons are high-order systems with nonlinearities and are subject to external disturbances [29,46–48]. To optimize their performance, it is essential to develop controllers that account for user interaction and allow real-time dynamic adjustment of their parameters.

In most studies, controllers use constant gains that ensure adequate performance in experimental tests, enabling trajectory tracking adapted to a specific group of users [23,54–56]. However, online adaptive control is a promising alternative for improving system response to disturbances [12,15,19,21,29,55,57].

This study implements a robust control approach with dynamic gain adjustment, based on mathematical formulations that consider modeling uncertainties and disturbances [23,27,28,30]. A sliding mode controller with an exponential reaching law was used [31,50], which simultaneously reduced chattering and convergence time without compromising system robustness. Additionally, it provides a quick response to system changes, resistance to parameter variations, and ease of implementation.

To optimize the gains of the nonlinear controller in the presence of disturbances, the PSO algorithm was employed due to its ability to find optimal solutions in problems with multiple local minima, its low computational cost, and its adaptability to various applications [15,44,45].

To the best of our knowledge, this is the first study to experimentally apply this method to a 7 DOF exoskeleton for online gain adjustment in a sliding mode controller. The results obtained with healthy subjects of different morphologies showed an improvement of over 20% in trajectory tracking, along with a significant reduction in chattering.

This work presents a promising solution for tuning robust controllers in dynamically coupled systems. However, controller performance depends on the correct selection of gains within the search space, defined according to the system's physical characteristics. If the exoskeleton lacks dynamic stability and energy efficiency, the algorithm alone will not guarantee significant improvements.

6. Conclusions

This work addresses the challenge of dynamically optimizing the parameters of an exoskeleton in real time for its application in physical rehabilitation, successfully providing unique and optimal parameters for each patient, which improved movement performance. Consequently, a promising solution was presented for tuning robust controllers in coupled and continuously varying systems. It is important to note that the controller's performance is limited by the gains within the search space, which depend on the exoskeleton's physical characteristics. Thus, the efficacy of the proposed algorithm in enhancing control performance is contingent upon the exoskeleton's capacity for robust dynamic stability and energy efficiency.

Obtaining gains from the exponential reaching law controller via the particle swarm optimization algorithm reduced the error in trajectory tracking by more than 20% in two users with different morphologies, opening the path for its applications on different users with different motor conditions. Furthermore, the proposed controller demonstrates the capacity to attenuate the chattering phenomenon, even when the tracking error is enhanced, while concurrently maintaining a low execution time. For future work, an improved version of the PSO algorithm is proposed to further optimize trajectory tracking and reduce energy consumption.

Author Contributions: Conceptualization, D.S.M. and D.B.-M.; Investigation, D.S.M.; Methodology, D.S.M.; Formal analysis, D.S.M. and D.B.-M. (controller part); Implementation, D.S.M. and D.B.-M.; Validation, D.S.M. and D.B.-M.; Writing—original draft, D.S.M.; Reviewing, D.B.-M., M.S., Y.K., C.E.G.C. and Á.L.Á.; Supervision, M.S. All authors have read and agreed to the published version of the manuscript.

Funding: This research is partially supported by grant PDC2023-145812-I00 (Project SAMPL2D), which is funded by MICIU/AEI/10.13039/501100011033 and by "Next Generation EU/PRTR".

Data Availability Statement: Data will be made available on request.

Acknowledgments: The first and second authors would like to thank CONAHCYT (Mexican National Council of Humanities, Science and Technology) for the support under grants 795353 and 739833, respectively. CONAHCYT was previously named CONACYT (Mexican National Council of Science and Technology).

Conflicts of Interest: The authors declare that they have no known competing financial interests or personal relationships that could have appeared to influence the work reported in this paper.

Abbreviations

The following abbreviations are used in this manuscript:

ACO	Ant colony optimization
CS	Cuckoo search
DE	Differential evolution
DOF	Degree of fredom
E	Elbow
Exp	Experimental
FL	Fuzzy logic
GA	Genetic algorithm
HS	Healthy subject
LLE	Lower limb exoskeleton
NN	Neural network
PID	Proportional–integral–derivative
PSO	Particle swarm optimization
S	Shoulder
SA	Simulated annealing
Sim	Simulation
SMC	Sliding mode control
ST	Supertwisting
ULE	Upper limb exoskeleton
W	Wrist

References

1. Cieza, A.; Causey, K.; Kamenov, K.; Hanson, S.W.; Chatterji, S.; Vos, T. Global estimates of the need for rehabilitation based on the Global Burden of Disease study 2019: A systematic analysis for the Global Burden of Disease Study 2019. *Lancet* **2020**, *396*, 2006–2017. [CrossRef]
2. World Health Organization. Musculoskeletal Health. July 2022. Consult: December 2023. Available online: https://www.who.int/news-room/fact-sheets/detail/musculoskeletal-conditions (accessed on 22 May 2024) .
3. Moulaei, K.; Bahaadinbeigy, K.; Haghdoostd, A.A.; Nezhad, M.S.; Sheikhtaheri, A. Overview of the role of robots in upper limb disabilities rehabilitation: A scoping review. *Arch. Public Health* **2023**, *81*, 84. [CrossRef] [PubMed]

4. Choutri, K.; Fareh, R.; Rahman, M.H.; Bettayeb, M.; Fadloun, S.; Lagha, M. Reinforcement Learning Fractional Order PID Controller For Upper Limb Rehabilitation Robot. In Proceedings of the 2023 International Conference on Fractional Differentiation and Its Applications (ICFDA), Ajman, United Arab Emirates, 14–16 March 2023; pp. 1–6. [CrossRef]
5. Rocon, E.; Pons, J.L. *Exoskeletons in Rehabilitation Robotics: Tremor Suppression*; Springer Science & Business Media: Berlin/Heidelberg, Germany, 2011; Volume 69.
6. Pons, J.L. *Wearable Robots: Biomechatronic Exoskeletons*; John Wiley & Sons Ltd.: Chichester, UK, 2008.
7. Gull, M.A.; Bai, S.; Bak, T. A review on design of upper limb exoskeletons. *Robotics* **2020**, *9*, 16. [CrossRef]
8. Wang, J.; Tang, B.; Pang, M.; Xiang, K.; Ju, Z. Self-adaptive Particle Swarm Optimization with Human-in-the-loop for Ankle Exoskeleton Control. *Sens. Mater.* **2021**, *33*, 3227. [CrossRef]
9. de La Rosa-Hernández, G.A.; Sernaque-Julca, J.C.; Quiroz-Compeán, G.; Rodríguez-Liñan, J.Á; Torres-Treviño, L.M. Tuning of a Control Scheme for an Exoskeleton Using Swarm Intelligence. In Proceedings of the 2023 IEEE EMBS R9 Conference, Guadalajara, Mexico, 5–7 October 2023; IEEE: New York, NY, USA, 2023; pp. 1–4.
10. Sosa Méndez, D.; García Cena, C.E.; Bedolla-Martínez, D.; Martín González, A. Innovative Metaheuristic Optimization Approach with a Bi-Triad for Rehabilitation Exoskeletons. *Sensors* **2024**, *24*, 2231. [CrossRef]
11. Habiba, K.N.; Arifin, A.; Babgei, A.F.; Risciawan, A.; Zazuli, M.I. Design of Fuzzy-PI Controller for Shoulder Exoskeleton with Motoric Progress of Rehabilitation Subject Consideration. In Proceedings of the 2022 International Conference on Computer Engineering, Network, and Intelligent Multimedia (CENIM), Surabaya, Indonesia, 22–23 November 2022; pp. 32–37. [CrossRef]
12. Safira, L.A.; Arifin, A.; Kusuma, H.; Risciwan, A.; Zazuli, M.I. Adaptive PID Controller Based on Sliding Surface for Controlling Elbow Joint Robot Rehabilitation. In Proceedings of the 2023 International Seminar on Intelligent Technology and Its Applications (ISITIA), Surabaya, Indonesia, 26–27 July 2023; pp. 316–321. [CrossRef]
13. Sidabalok, S.M.; Arifin, A.; Pramudijanto, J.; Kusuma, H.; Risciwan, A.; Zazuli, M.I. Development of Elbow Joint Exoskeleton Control System Using Fuzzy Pid Control Method for Post Stroke Rehabilitation. In Proceedings of the 2023 International Seminar on Intelligent Technology and Its Applications (ISITIA), Surabaya, Indonesia, 26–27 July 2023; pp. 310–315. [CrossRef]
14. de Medeiros, R.B.; Muñoz, D.M. Tuning of FP-PID Controller based on PSO Algorithm Applied to a Human Gait. In Proceedings of the 2022 Latin American Robotics Symposium (LARS), 2022 Brazilian Symposium on Robotics (SBR), and 2022 Workshop on Robotics in Education (WRE), São Bernardo do Campo, Brazil, 18–21 October 2022; pp. 1–6. [CrossRef]
15. Belkadi, A.; Oulhadj, H.; Touati, Y.; Khan, S.A.; Daachi, B. On the robust PID adaptive controller for exoskeletons: A particle swarm optimization based approach. *Appl. Soft Comput.* **2017**, *60*, 87–100. [CrossRef]
16. Han, Y.; Liu, C.; Xiu, H.; Li, Z.; Shan, S.; Wang, X.; Ren, L.; Ren, L. Trajectory Control of an Active and Passive Hybrid Hydraulic Ankle Prosthesis Using an Improved PSO-PID Controller. *J. Intell. Robot. Syst.***2022**, *105*, 48. [CrossRef]
17. Belov, M.P.; Truong, D.D.; van Tuan, P. Self-Tuning PID Controller Using a Neural Network for Nonlinear Exoskeleton System. In Proceedings of the 2021 II International Conference on Neural Networks and Neurotechnologies (NeuroNT), Saint Petersburg, Russia, 16 June 2021; pp. 6–9. [CrossRef]
18. Al-Waeli, K.H.; Ramli, R.; Haris, S.M.; Zulkoffli, Z.B.; Amiri, M.S. Offline ANN-PID Controller Tuning on a Multi-Joints Lower Limb Exoskeleton for Gait Rehabilitation. *IEEE Access* **2021**, *9*, 107360–107374. [CrossRef]
19. Amiri, M.S.; Ramli, R.; Ibrahim, M.F.; Wahab, D.A.; Aliman, N. Adaptive Particle Swarm Optimization of PID Gain Tuning for Lower-Limb Human Exoskeleton in Virtual Environment. *Mathematics* **2020**, *8*, 2040. [CrossRef]
20. Belov, M.P.; Truong, D.D.; Khoa, T.D. Self-Tuning Subordinate Control System Based on Neural Network for Nonlinear Electric Drivers of Lower Limbs of Exoskeleton. In Proceedings of the 2022 Conference of Russian Young Researchers in Electrical and Electronic Engineering (ElConRus), Saint Petersburg, Russian, 25–28 January 2022; pp. 549–553. [CrossRef]
21. Liu, J.; Fang, H.; Xu, J. Online Adaptive PID Control for a Multi-Joint Lower Extremity Exoskeleton System Using Improved Particle Swarm Optimization. *Machines* **2021**, *10*, 21. [CrossRef]
22. Dali, Hassen, M.; Laamiri, I.; Bouguila, N. A Robust Adaptive Non-Singular Terminal Sliding Mode Control: Application to an Upper-Limb Exoskeleton with Disturbances and Uncertain Dynamics. *Inf. Technol. Control* **2024**, *53*, 171–186. [CrossRef]
23. Mahmoud, I.; Saidi, I. Trajectory Tracking Control of Upper-Limb Rehabilitation Exoskeleton Based on Robust Control. In Proceedings of the 2022 5th International Conference on Advanced Systems and Emergent Technologies (IC ASET), Hammamet, Tunisia, 22–25 March 2022; pp. 330–335. [CrossRef]
24. Bembli, S.; Haddad, N.K.; Belghith, S. An exoskeleton – upper limb system control using a robust Model free terminal sliding mode with EMG signal. In Proceedings of the 2021 International Conference on Control, Automation and Diagnosis (ICCAD), Grenoble, France, 3–5 November 2021; pp. 1–8. [CrossRef]
25. Hassen, M.D.; Jouirou, R.; Bouguila, N. Robust Fuzzy Terminal Sliding Mode Control for Passive Control of Upper-Limb Exoskeleton. In Proceedings of the 2024 International Conference on Control, Automation and Diagnosis (ICCAD), Paris, France, 15–17 May 2024; pp. 1–6. [CrossRef]
26. Jebri, A.; Madani, T.; Djouani, K.; Benallegue, A. Robust adaptive neuronal controller for exoskeletons with sliding-mode. *Neurocomputing* **2020**, *399*, 317–330. [CrossRef]

27. Silawatchananai, C.; Howimanporn, S. Robust control design of arm exoskeleton based on sliding mode control. In Proceedings of the 2020 9th International Congress on Advanced Applied Informatics (IIAI-AAI), Kitakyushu, Japan, 1–15 September 2020; pp. 542–547. [CrossRef]
28. Narayan, J.; Bharti, R.R.; Dwivedy, S.K. Robust Sliding Mode Control with Reaching Laws for a Pediatric Lower-Limb Exoskeleton System. In Proceedings of the 2022 Second International Conference on Power, Control and Computing Technologies (ICPC2T), Raipur, India, 1–3 March 2022; pp. 1–6. [CrossRef]
29. Ratiba, F.; Mohamed, G.; Mustapha, H.; Noura, A. Adaptive Finite-Time Robust Sliding Mode Controller For Upper Limb Exoskeleton Robot. In Proceedings of the 2022 19th International Multi-Conference on Systems, Signals & Devices (SSD), Sétif, Algeria, 6–10 May 2022; pp. 1255–1260. [CrossRef]
30. Zhang, G.; Wang, J.; Yang, P.; Guo, S. A learning control scheme for upper-limb exoskeleton via adaptive sliding mode technique. *Mechatronics* **2022**, *86*, 102832. [CrossRef]
31. Brahmi, B.; El-Monajjed, K.; Rahman, M.H.; Ahmed, T.; El-Bayeh, C.; Khan, M.R.; Saad, M. Novel Adaptive Reaching Law for Sliding Mode Control of an Upper Limb Exoskeleton Robot. In Proceedings of the 2020 IEEE Region 10 Symposium (TENSYMP), Dhaka, Bangladesh, 5–7 June 2020; pp. 1432–1437. [CrossRef]
32. He, D.; Wang, H.; Tian, Y.; Guo, Y. A Fractional-Order Ultra-Local Model-Based Adaptive Neural Network Sliding Mode Control of n -DOF Upper-Limb Exoskeleton with Input Deadzone. *IEEE/CAA J. Autom. Sin.* **2024**, *11*, 760–781. [CrossRef]
33. Fazli, E.; Rakhtala, S.M.; Mirrashid, N.; Karimi, H.R. Real-time implementation of a super twisting control algorithm for an upper limb wearable robot. *Mechatronics* **2022**, *84*, 102808. [CrossRef]
34. Tiaiba, H.; Daachi, M.E.H.; Madani, T. Real-time adaptive super twisting algorithm based on PSO algorithm: Application for an exoskeleton robot. *Robotica* **2024**, *42*, 1816–1841. [CrossRef]
35. Aichaoui, M.; Ikhlef, A. Adaptive Backstepping Control for Upper Limb Rehabilitation Robot using PSO Tuning. In Proceedings of the 2022 19th International Multi-Conference on Systems, Signals & Devices (SSD), Sétif, Algeria, 6–10 May 2022; pp. 601–608. [CrossRef]
36. Dong, J.; Jia, Z.; Li, E.; Lv, Q. AAN Controller with Adaptive Gain for Upper Limb Exoskeleton. *IEEE Access* **2024**, *12*, 112767–112775. [CrossRef]
37. Xia, P.; Yang, Y.; Jin, S.; Liu, X.; Dong, X. Neural Networks Iterative Learning Impedance Control of Lower Limb Exoskeleton for the Later Stage of Rehabilitation. In Proceedings of the 2022 IEEE 11th Data Driven Control and Learning Systems Conference (DDCLS), Chengdu, China, 3–5 August 2022; pp. 250–255. [CrossRef]
38. Huang, P.; Yuan, W.; Li, Q.; Feng, Y. Neural Network-Based Optimal Control of a Lower-limb Exoskeleton Robot. In Proceedings of the 2021 6th IEEE International Conference on Advanced Robotics and Mechatronics (ICARM), Chongqing, China, 3–5 July 2021; pp. 154–159. [CrossRef]
39. Agnanto, D.; Arifin, A.; Babgei, A.F. Multi-input Multi-output Fuzzy Logic Controller for Hybrid Exoskeleton and Functional Electrical Stimulation for Hand Movements Rehabilitation of Hemiparesis Patients. In Proceedings of the 2021 International Seminar on Intelligent Technology and Its Applications (ISITIA), Surabaya, Indonesia, 21–22 July 2021; pp. 272–277. [CrossRef]
40. Sangeetha, T.S.; Soman, S.; Sivanandan, K.S.S.; Parameswaran, A.P.; Baiju, T. Intelligent Control of Exoskeletons for Human Limbs using Knowledge-Based Fuzzy Inference System. In Proceedings of the 2023 IEEE International Conference on Distributed Computing, VLSI, Electrical Circuits and Robotics (DISCOVER), Mangalore, India, 13–14 October 2023; pp. 173–178. [CrossRef]
41. Dan, S.; Cheng, H.; Zhang, Y.; Liu, H. A Fuzzy Indrect Adaptive Robust Control for Upper Extremity Exoskeleton Driven by Pneumatic Artificial Muscle. In Proceedings of the 2022 IEEE International Conference on Mechatronics and Automation (ICMA), Guilin, Guangxi, China, 7–10 August 2022; pp. 839–846. [CrossRef]
42. Soman, S.; Sangeetha, T.S.; Sivanandan, K.S.S.; Parameswaran, A.P.; Baiju, T. Personalized Estimation and Modification of Elbow Angular Displacement for Upper Limb Exoskeletons:A Fuzzy Logic-Based Approach. In Proceedings of the 2023 IEEE International Conference on Distributed Computing, VLSI, Electrical Circuits and Robotics (DISCOVER), Mangalore, India, 13–14 October 2023; pp. 179–184. [CrossRef]
43. Bedolla-Martinez, D.; Kali, Y.; Saad, M.; Ochoa-Luna, C.; Rahman, M.H. Learning human inverse kinematics solutions for redundant robotic upper-limb rehabilitation. *Eng. Appl. Artif. Intell.* **2023**, *126*, 106966. [CrossRef]
44. Samala, R.K. Particle Swarm Optimization. In *Swarm Intelligence-Recent Advances and Current Applications*; IntechOpen: London, UK, 2023.
45. Gad, A.G. Particle Swarm Optimization Algorithm and Its Applications: A Systematic Review. *Arch. Comput. Methods Eng.* **2022**, *29*, 2531–2561. [CrossRef]
46. Fitzsimons, K.; Kalinowska, A.; Dewald, J.P.; Murphey, T.D. Task-based hybrid shared control for training through forceful interaction. *Int. J. Robot. Res.* **2020**, *39*, 1138–1154. [CrossRef]
47. Saveriano, M.; Abu-Dakka, F.J.; Kramberger, A.; Peternel, L. Dynamic movement primitives in robotics: A tutorial survey. *Int. J. Robot. Res.* **2023**, *42*, 1133–1184. [CrossRef]

48. Dehio, N.; Smith, J.; Wig, D.L.; Mohammadi, P.; Mistry, M.; Steil, J.J. Enabling impedance-based physical human–multi–robot collaboration: Experiments with four torque-controlled manipulators. *Int. J. Robot. Res.* **2022**, *41*, 68–84. [CrossRef]
49. Sreejeth, M.; Kumar, R.; Tripathi, N.; Garg, P. Tuning A PID Controller using Metaheuristic Algorithms. In Proceedings of the 2023 8th International Conference on Communication and Electronics Systems (ICCES), Coimbatore, India, 1–3 June 2023; pp. 276–282. [CrossRef]
50. Komurcugil, H.; Bayhan, S.; Guler, N.; Abu-Rub, H. A New Exponential Reaching Law Approach to the Sliding Mode Control: A Multilevel Multifunction Converter Application. *IEEE Trans. Ind. Electron.* **2023**, *70*, 7557–7568. [CrossRef]
51. Fallaha, C.J.; Saad, M.; Kanaan, H.Y.; Al-Haddad, K. Sliding-Mode Robot Control with Exponential Reaching Law. *IEEE Trans. Ind. Electron.* **2011**, *58*, 600–610. [CrossRef]
52. Gopal, A.; Sultani, M.M.; Bansal, J.C. On stability analysis of particle swarm optimization algorithm. *Arab. J. Sci. Eng.* **2020**, *45*, 2385–2394. [CrossRef]
53. Trelea, I.C. The particle swarm optimization algorithm: Convergence analysis and parameter selection. *Inf. Process. Lett.* **2003**, *85*, 317–325. [CrossRef]
54. Palazzi, E.; Luzi, L.; Dimo, E.; Meneghetti, M.; Vicario, R.; Luzia, R.F.; Vertechy, R.; Calanca, A. An affordable upper-limb exoskeleton concept for rehabilitation applications. *Technologies* **2022**, *10*, 22. [CrossRef]
55. Aole, S.; Elamvazuthi, I.; Waghmare, L.; Patre, B.; Bhaskarwar, T.; Prasetyo, T. ADRC for Upper Limb Exoskeleton: A Simulation Study. In Proceedings of the 2022 IEEE 5th International Symposium in Robotics and Manufacturing Automation (ROMA), Malacca, Malaysia, 6–8 August 2022; IEEE: Piscataway, NJ, USA, 2022; pp. 1–6.
56. Qureshi, M.U.; Mudassir, M. Robust Control Design For 3 Degree Of Freedom Fully Actuated Upper Limb Exoskeleton. In Proceedings of the 2021 16th International Conference on Emerging Technologies (ICET), Islamabad, Pakistan, 22–23 December 2021; IEEE: Piscataway, NJ, USA, 2021; pp. 1–6.
57. Zhao, Y.; Wu, H.; Zhang, M.; Mao, J.; Todoh, M. Design methodology of portable upper limb exoskeletons for people with strokes. *Front. Neurosci.* **2023**, *17*, 1128332. [CrossRef]

Disclaimer/Publisher's Note: The statements, opinions and data contained in all publications are solely those of the individual author(s) and contributor(s) and not of MDPI and/or the editor(s). MDPI and/or the editor(s) disclaim responsibility for any injury to people or property resulting from any ideas, methods, instructions or products referred to in the content.

robotics

MDPI

Article

Minimum-Energy Trajectory Planning for an Underactuated Serial Planar Manipulator

Domenico Dona' [1,2,*], Jason Bettega [1], Iacopo Tamellin [3], Paolo Boscariol [1] and Roberto Caracciolo [1]

[1] Dipartimento di Tecnica e Gestione dei Sistemi Industriali, Università degli Studi di Padova, 36100 Vicenza, Italy; jason.bettega@unipd.it (J.B.); paolo.boscariol@unipd.it (P.B.); roberto.caracciolo@unipd.it (R.C.)
[2] Dipartimento di Psicologia Generale, Università degli Studi di Padova, 35131 Padova, Italy
[3] Dipartimento di Ingegneria per la Medicina di Innovazione, Università degli Studi di Verona, 37134 Verona, Italy; iacopo.tamellin@univr.it
* Correspondence: domenico.dona@unipd.it

Abstract: Underactuated robotic systems are appealing for industrial use due to their reduced actuator number, which lowers energy consumption and system complexity. Underactuated systems are, however, often affected by residual vibrations. This paper addresses the challenge of generating energy-optimal trajectories while imposing theoretical null residual (and yet practical low) vibration in underactuated systems. The trajectory planning problem is cast as a constrained optimal control problem (OCP) for a two-degree-of-freedom revolute–revolute planar manipulator. The proposed method produces energy-efficient motion while limiting residual vibrations under motor torque limitations. Experiments compare the proposed trajectories to input shaping techniques (ZV, ZVD, NZV, NZVD). Results show energy savings that range from 12% to 69% with comparable and negligible residual oscillations.

Keywords: minimum-energy; underactuated; point-to-point motion

1. Introduction

Ensuring an efficient use of resources is the key element that defines the profitability of any manufacturing process. One key element is cost reduction, which is inevitably linked to the cost of energy, which can vary sensibly over time and without a predictable pattern. Beyond direct economic costs, any manufacturing process is also associated with an environmental cost, which is proportional in part to its energy expenditure. This fact has also been recognized at the political level, as demonstrated by the adoption of the Sustainable Development Goals (SDGs) by the EU [1]. In particular, energy reduction is central in both SDG12 and SDG9. The effort to push cleaner production through SDGs is, however, just a part of a bigger and long-lasting effort towards energy efficiency that started 40 years ago [2].

The literature on methods to improve the energy efficiency of automation and robotic systems, i.e., two staples of modern energy production, is rather extended, as testified by the review work [3] that analyzes several methods to achieve the goal of a greener mechatronics [4]. An energy-efficient automatic system is one that implements some strategy to reduce the electrical energy intake. This feature can be enforced at the design stage, by means of a lightweight design [5] or by a careful selection of the motor–reducer set [6,7] that overcomes the traditional approach based on inertia matching [8]. Another interesting and effective energy reduction technique is the exploitation of natural motion,

https://doi.org/10.3390/robotics14070098

which consists of tuning the motion characteristics with the elastic properties of the systems, so that it can be moved by relying minimally on the actuation effort [9]. This approach has been tested in several works [10–13] with good results, but similar results can be obtained by carefully designing an elastic element to reduce the energy consumption in a rest-to-rest motion [14,15].

The focus on motion properties as a relevant factor in the determination of the energy consumption is indeed not only limited to natural motion: a large body of studies has investigated the conditions that make a trajectory or a motion profile energy optimal. The alteration of the motion profile is often the least intrusive solution, as it generally does not require any physical alteration to the system [3], and, hence, it is a virtually 'free', but still effective, solution.

The generation of an energy-efficient motion profile is usually the result of some optimization technique based on a more or less detailed model of the system. One large group of studies focuses on the optimization performed on the basis of standard motion profiles [16], whose simple parametrization is well fitted to the determination of optimal motion conditions, as proven analytically in [17], or experimentally in [18]. The limitation to standard motion profiles, however, restricts the manifold in which the feasible solutions are located, given the usually very limited number of degrees of freedom that characterize the solution space. Some improvements can be found by designing a motion profile with a more efficient parametrization that is specifically tailored for the purpose, as in the work [19] that uses Chebyshev polynomials to build a rest-to-rest motion profile. Another option is the modulated cycloidal motion employed in [20] to generate energy-efficient motion profiles with null residual oscillation in one- and two-link flexible manipulators.

The two approaches just mentioned can, however, also be seen as direct approaches to an optimal control problem [21]. The generation of a motion profile can indeed be cast as a minimization problem constrained to some kinematic quantities (such as initial and final positions) and to the dynamics of the system [22]. If the cost function is the consumed energy, its minimization along a trajectory that connects the initial and final position/velocity within the respect of the system dynamics is precisely the 'true' energy-optimal solution [23].

However, application of the aforementioned techniques has been limited in the context of underactuated robotic systems. Underactuated systems are ubiquitous in robotics and mechatronics [24], as many systems of wide practical use do belong to this class. Underactuation, i.e., the presence of less actuated degrees of freedom than the overall number of degrees of freedom, appears whenever some sort of flexibility is present in the system. This happens virtually in all flexible systems, such as in flexible link robots or in industrial robots, where some form of joint flexibility is often present. Overhead cranes [25] and underactuated cable-driven robots [26] do also belong to the class of underactuated systems, just to mention two common applications. The 2-DOFs RR planar manipulator used for the experimental test can therefore be used as a representative model to test novel control and planning techniques, due to its nonlinear dynamics and underactuation properties.

This work proposes the formulation of a constrained optimal control problem solution to generate a motion profile for underactuated systems that is characterized by minimum energy expenditure, that enforces arbitrary kinematic conditions at the boundaries and limited motor torque, and that results in theoretically null residual oscillation. The method is based on the development of an accurate nonlinear dynamic model, which accounts for the electromechanical dynamics of the manipulator under investigation. The latter is a 2-DOFs RR planar manipulator with just one actuated joint.

The contribution of this paper is to experimentally assess the benefits of an optimal control-based planner for generating minimum-energy point-to-point motion for underactuated systems, with the additional requirement of suppressing residual oscillations.

This work includes a description of the setup and its analytical dynamic model, then covers the method used to set up and solve the optimization problem. The resulting motion profiles are then tested experimentally on a custom lab setup and the results are compared, in terms of residual oscillations amplitude and in terms of absorbed electric energy, with some standard planning techniques based on input shaping.

2. Dynamic Model

The system under investigation is a planar two-link manipulator with revolute joints. A sketch of the studied manipulator is presented in Figure 1. The first joint is actuated by a motor, while the second joint is passive and equipped with a torsional spring that generates a restoring torque. The second revolute joint is also equipped with a rotary encoder that is, however, not used for the experiment. The system is underactuated, since it has two degrees of freedom and just one actuator.

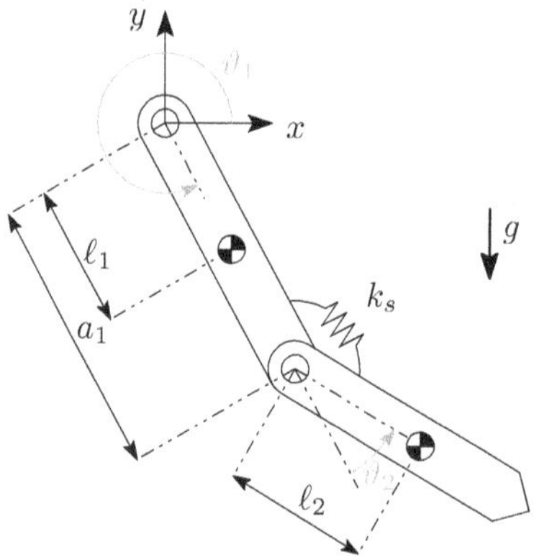

Figure 1. Sketch of the 2-DOFs underactuated planar manipulator.

The dynamics of the manipulator are described by the following equation (see for example [27])

$$\begin{bmatrix} \tau_1 \\ 0 \end{bmatrix} = \mathbf{M}(\mathbf{q})\ddot{\mathbf{q}} + \mathbf{C}(\mathbf{q}, \dot{\mathbf{q}})\dot{\mathbf{q}} + \mathbf{g}(\mathbf{q}) + \mathbf{K}\mathbf{q} + \mathbf{F}_v\dot{\mathbf{q}} + \mathbf{F}_c \,\mathrm{sign}(\dot{\mathbf{q}}), \tag{1}$$

where $\mathbf{q} = [q_1, q_2]^\top$ is the vector of joint angle coordinates, τ_1 is the torque applied through the first joint, $\mathbf{M}(\mathbf{q})$ is the (generalized) mass matrix, $\mathbf{C}(\mathbf{q}, \dot{\mathbf{q}})$ is the Coriolis matrix, $\mathbf{g}(\mathbf{q})$ is the gravitational torque vector, $\mathbf{K} = \mathrm{diag}([0, k_s])$ is the stiffness matrix with k_s being the torsional spring constant, and $\mathbf{F}_v$ and $\mathbf{F}_c$ are the viscous and Coulomb friction coefficient matrices, respectively. The mass matrix is given by

$$\mathbf{M}(\mathbf{q}) = \begin{bmatrix} J_1 + J_2 + J_m + (m_2 + m_{\mathrm{enc}})a_1^2 + 2m_2 a_1 \ell_2 \cos q_2 & J_2 + m_2 a_1 \ell_2 \cos q_2 \\ J_2 + m_2 a_1 \ell_2 \cos q_2 & J_2 \end{bmatrix}, \tag{2}$$

where m_1, m_2 are the link masses, m_{enc} is the mass of the encoder and its mounting, J_1, J_2 are the link inertia referred to the joint axes, J_m is the motor inertia, ℓ_1, ℓ_2 are the link center-of-mass positions, and a_1 is the length of the first link.

The Coriolis and centrifugal matrix is

$$\mathbf{C}(\mathbf{q},\dot{\mathbf{q}}) = \begin{bmatrix} h\dot{q}_2 & h(\dot{q}_1+\dot{q}_2) \\ -h\dot{q}_1 & 0 \end{bmatrix}, \tag{3}$$

where $h = -m_2 a_1 \ell_2 2\sin(q_2)$. The gravitational torque vector is

$$\mathbf{g}(\mathbf{q}) = \begin{bmatrix} [m_1\ell_1 + (m_2+m_{\text{enc}})a_1]g\cos q_1 + m_2 g\ell_2\cos(q_1+q_2) \\ m_2 g\ell_2\cos(q_1+q_2) \end{bmatrix}, \tag{4}$$

where g is the gravitational acceleration. The forward dynamics can be derived by solving Equation (1) for $\ddot{\mathbf{q}}$:

$$\ddot{\mathbf{q}} = \mathbf{M}^{-1}(\mathbf{q})\left(\begin{bmatrix}\tau_1 \\ 0\end{bmatrix} - \mathbf{C}(\mathbf{q},\dot{\mathbf{q}})\dot{\mathbf{q}} - \mathbf{g}(\mathbf{q}) - \mathbf{K}\mathbf{q} - \mathbf{F}_v\dot{\mathbf{q}} - \mathbf{F}_c\,\text{sign}(\dot{\mathbf{q}})\right) = \mathbf{f}_{\text{D}}(\mathbf{q},\dot{\mathbf{q}},\tau_1), \tag{5}$$

where $\mathbf{f}_{\text{D}}(\cdot)$ denotes the forward dynamics map.

To enforce higher-order constraints, the time derivative of the acceleration (i.e., the jerk) is computed using the chain rule:

$$\dddot{\mathbf{q}} = \frac{\partial \mathbf{f}_{\text{D}}}{\partial \mathbf{q}}\dot{\mathbf{q}} + \frac{\partial \mathbf{f}_{\text{D}}}{\partial \dot{\mathbf{q}}}\ddot{\mathbf{q}} + \frac{\partial \mathbf{f}_{\text{D}}}{\partial \tau_1}\dot{\tau}_1 = \mathbf{j}_{\text{D}}(\mathbf{q},\dot{\mathbf{q}},\ddot{\mathbf{q}},\tau_1,\dot{\tau}_1), \tag{6}$$

where $\mathbf{j}_{\text{D}}(\cdot)$ denotes the jerk dynamics map.

The complete system dynamics can be written in state-space form. Define the state vector and control input as

$$\mathbf{x} = \left[\mathbf{q}^\top,\ \dot{\mathbf{q}}^\top,\ \ddot{\mathbf{q}}^\top,\ \tau_1\right]^\top, \tag{7}$$

$$u = \dot{\tau}_1. \tag{8}$$

The state-space dynamics is then given by

$$\dot{\mathbf{x}} = \frac{\mathrm{d}}{dt}\begin{bmatrix}\mathbf{q} \\ \dot{\mathbf{q}} \\ \ddot{\mathbf{q}} \\ \tau_1\end{bmatrix} = \begin{bmatrix}\dot{\mathbf{q}} \\ \ddot{\mathbf{q}} \\ \mathbf{j}_{\text{D}}(\mathbf{q},\dot{\mathbf{q}},\ddot{\mathbf{q}},\tau_1,u) \\ u\end{bmatrix} = \mathbf{f}(\mathbf{x},u), \tag{9}$$

where $\mathbf{f}(\mathbf{x},u)$ denotes the overall state-space dynamics of the system.

Note that the map $\mathbf{j}_{\text{D}}$ in Equation (9) can be substituted with any underactuated manipulator model. The proposed approach is intended to be general, and the 2-DOFs system is adopted here primarily for a practical experimental validation.

3. Minimum-Energy Planning

3.1. Requirement of the Trajectory

The goal of this work is to plan a point-to-point trajectory for the system presented in the previous section, but similar considerations are valid for many other underactuated systems. First of all, the initial and final configurations must be defined: they will serve as the kinematics boundary conditions. Since the system is underactuated, only one of the joint coordinates can be directly imposed. In this work, we choose to impose a value for q_1.

To determine the corresponding value of q_2, we require the system to be in static equilibrium, meaning both joint velocities and accelerations are zero. Given a specified value of q_1, this condition can be enforced by solving the following root-finding problem

$$0 = g_2(\mathbf{q}) + k_s q_2 = e_q(q_2), \tag{10}$$

which is derived by considering the second row of Equation (1) under the assumption $\dot{\mathbf{q}} = \ddot{\mathbf{q}} = \mathbf{0}$. Here, g_2 denotes the second component of the gravity vector $\mathbf{g}$ and e_q is the equilibrium condition function. Once Equation (10) is solved for both the initial and final point, this results in the initial and final configurations $\mathbf{q}_0$ and $\mathbf{q}_f$.

In addition to reaching the desired configurations, the trajectory must satisfy specific boundary conditions to ensure stable motion. Specifically, the system should start and end at rest, meaning that the joint velocities must be zero at both the initial and final times. Moreover, zero acceleration is required at the final time to prevent residual oscillations and thus ensure that the system remains at the target configuration.

These requirements can be expressed mathematically as:

$$\begin{cases} \mathbf{q}(0) = \mathbf{q}_0, \\ \mathbf{q}(t_f) = \mathbf{q}_f, \\ \dot{\mathbf{q}}(0) = \mathbf{0}, \\ \dot{\mathbf{q}}(t_f) = \mathbf{0}, \\ \ddot{\mathbf{q}}(t_f) = \mathbf{0}, \end{cases} \quad \rightarrow \quad \begin{cases} \mathbf{A}_0 \mathbf{x}(0) = \mathbf{b}_0, \\ \mathbf{A}_f \mathbf{x}(t_f) = \mathbf{b}_f, \end{cases} \tag{11}$$

where t_f is the final time, and $\mathbf{A}_0$, $\mathbf{A}_f$, $\mathbf{b}_0$, and $\mathbf{b}_f$ are appropriate matrices and vectors used to compactly express the boundary conditions in matrix form.

3.2. Objective Function

To plan a minimum-energy trajectory, we must define an appropriate objective function. In this system, only the first joint is actuated, and it is driven by a direct-drive DC motor. As a result, the motor torque is directly related to the armature current through

$$i_a = \frac{\tau_1}{k_t}, \tag{12}$$

where i_a is the armature current and k_t is the motor's torque constant.

Using the standard electrical model of a DC motor, the armature voltage can be expressed as

$$v_a = R_a i_a + L_a \frac{\mathrm{d}i_a}{\mathrm{d}t} + k_v \dot{q}_1, \tag{13}$$

where v_a is the armature voltage, R_a is the armature resistance, L_a is the armature inductance, and k_v is the back-EMF constant. In this case, the inductance term has to be considered, as the system does not exhibit constant inertia [17].

The instantaneous electrical power consumed by the motor is then given by

$$\mathcal{P} = v_a i_a = R_a i_a^2 + L_a i_a \frac{\mathrm{d}i_a}{\mathrm{d}t} + k_v \dot{q}_1 i_a, \tag{14}$$

where $\mathcal{P}$ denotes the electrical power input to the motor.

Substituting Equation (12) into the expression above, and assuming $k_v = k_t$ (as we are considering DC motors), we obtain

$$\mathcal{P} = \frac{R_a}{k_t^2} \tau_1^2 + \frac{L_a}{k_t^2} \tau_1 \dot{\tau}_1 + \dot{q}_1 \tau_1, \tag{15}$$

highlighting how the electrical power depends on the system states.

Finally, the total energy consumed by the motor during the task is given by

$$\mathcal{E} = \int_0^{t_f} \mathcal{P}\ \mathrm{d}t, \tag{16}$$

where t_f is the prescribed task duration and $\mathcal{E}$ represents the total energy consumption, which serves as the optimization objective.

3.3. Optimal Control Problem

This section formulates the minimum-energy trajectory planning task as an optimal control problem. Since the optimization variables are time-dependent functions rather than finite-dimensional vectors, the resulting formulation is infinite-dimensional, a class of problems commonly referred to as optimal control problems [28].

Using Equations (9), (11) and (16), the problem can be stated as

$$\begin{aligned}
\underset{\mathbf{x}(\cdot),\, u(\cdot)}{\text{minimize}} \quad & \mathcal{E} = \int_0^{t_f} \mathcal{P}(\mathbf{x}, u)\,\mathrm{d}t && \text{(17a)}\\
\text{subject to:} \quad & \dot{\mathbf{x}}(t) = \mathbf{f}(\mathbf{x}(t), u(t)) && \text{(17b)}\\
& \mathbf{A}_0\mathbf{x}(0) = \mathbf{b}_0 && \text{(17c)}\\
& \mathbf{A}_f\mathbf{x}(t_f) = \mathbf{b}_f && \text{(17d)}\\
& |\tau_1(t)| \le \tau_{\text{lim}}. && \text{(17e)}
\end{aligned}$$

Here, τ_{lim} denotes the limit torque that the motor can exert. Since the torque τ_1 is part of the system state, the constraint in (17e) constitutes a state constraint. Consequently, the problem in Equation (17) is a nonlinear optimal control problem with state constraints. To solve such problems, numerical methods are typically employed. In particular, direct methods are preferred, as indirect methods often struggle to handle state constraints effectively [29].

The problem formulated in Equation (17) can be solved using standard direct-method-based solvers. In this work, the Rockit framework is employed for this purpose [30]. The solver is not in general real-time capable, as solving large nonlinear constrained optimization problems remains an open research problem.

4. Results

4.1. Experimental Setup

The experimental setup is composed by a two-link planar manipulator actuated only on the first joint by a "Speeder motion line—MB057DG218" motor. The second is passive and a torsional spring is made from two linear springs in parallel. The experimental setup is shown in Figure 2.

The system is controlled via Simulink Real-Time using a National Instruments PCIe-6321 data I/O board. The motor driver operates in current control mode.

Reference tracking is implemented through a standard position feedback architecture combining PID control with feedforward compensation, running at a control frequency of 1 kHz. The PID weights have been manually tuned to ensure minimal trajectory tracking error. The motion of the first and second joint coordinates is tracked using a Vicon 3D motion capture system, operating at a sampling frequency of 400 Hz. The electrical power consumed by the DC motor is computed as the product of the measured armature current and voltage. The total energy consumption is then obtained by numerical integration over time. The main physical parameters of the system are summarized in Table 1.

Figure 2. Experimental setup: the 2-DOFs underactuated manipulator.

Table 1. Data of the two-link underactuated serial manipulator studied in this work.

Parameter	Unit	Value
m_1	kg	0.237
m_2	kg	0.021
m_{enc}	kg	0.10
a_1	m	0.172
a_2	m	0.154
ℓ_1	m	0.086
ℓ_2	m	0.077
J_1	kg m^2	3.601×10^{-3}
J_m	kg m^2	2.700×10^{-5}
J_2	kg m^2	1.660×10^{-4}
$f_{v,1}$	Nms/rad	3.913×10^{-3}
$f_{v,2}$	Nms/rad	1.949×10^{-4}
$f_{c,1}$	Nm	3.431×10^{-3}
$f_{c,2}$	Nm	6.455×10^{-5}
k_s	Nm/rad	0.1949
R_a	Ω	1.7
L_a	H	3.39×10^{-3}
k_t	Nm/A	0.071

Two different test cases are studied to investigate the proposed optimal control based planner. Test case I consists of moving the the manipulator from the stable equilibrium point to a case where the $\vartheta_{1,f} = 7\pi/4$, while test case II consists of a swing between symmetric points, i.e., $\vartheta_{1,0} = 5\pi/4$ and $\vartheta_{1,f} = 7\pi/4$. The data concerning the two test-cases are summarized in Table 2.

Table 2. Test cases trajectories data.

Quantity	Unit	Test-Case I	Test-Case II
$\vartheta_{1,0}$	rad	$3\pi/2$	$7\pi/4$
$\vartheta_{1,f}$	rad	$5\pi/4$	$7\pi/4$
t_f	s	1.0	1.5

4.2. Test Case I

The first test case involves the execution of a rest-to-rest motion from the stable equilibrium position, i.e., from $\vartheta_1 = 3/2\pi$ rad to $\vartheta_1 = 7/4\pi$ rad. The performance of the energy-optimal motion profile designed according to the method outlined in Section 3 is assessed by a comparison with some shaped polynomial motion profile of degree 5. A fifth-order polynomial profile is chosen as it allows to simply enforce position, speed, and acceleration at the two boundaries. It must be pointed out that the execution of this motion by the first link of the robot would inevitably generate pronounced residual oscillations; therefore, the basic poly5 motion is filtered using input shaping. Input shaping consists of the alteration of a reference profile by convolving it with a sequence of a finite number of impulses with defined timing and amplitude, with the aim of achieving null residual oscillations. Input shapers are widely adopted for their simple implementation and their simple design, which requires just to measure the frequency and the damping factor of the oscillation mode to be suppressed [31,32].

The most basic and popular implementation of input shaping is the Zero Vibration (ZV) shaper, which achieves null residual vibration by placing the second pulse half of the damped oscillation period after the first one. A less common alternative is the Negative Zero Vibration (NZV) shaper, which allows for a reduced delay between consecutive pulses [33]. One drawback of the ZV and the ZVD shaper is their limited capability of coping with model uncertainties, so that any model-plant mismatch significantly affects the amount of residual oscillations. There are indeed some shaping solutions that are specifically designed to be more robust to model-plant mismatches, such as the Zero Vibration and Derivative (ZVD) shaper and the Negative Zero Vibration and Derivative (NZVD). These two solutions are quite convenient when model-plant mismatches are significant, as in the case of the uncertainty in the determination of oscillation modes or in the presence of significant model nonlinearities [34]. The latter is the case under consideration here, for which the determination of the modal properties is conducted by a linearization around the stable equilibrium point of the model of Equation (9).

The results are reported in Figures 3, 4, 5, 6, and 7, corresponding to the optimal trajectory, and the ZV-, ZVD-, NZV-, and NZVD-filtered trajectories, respectively.

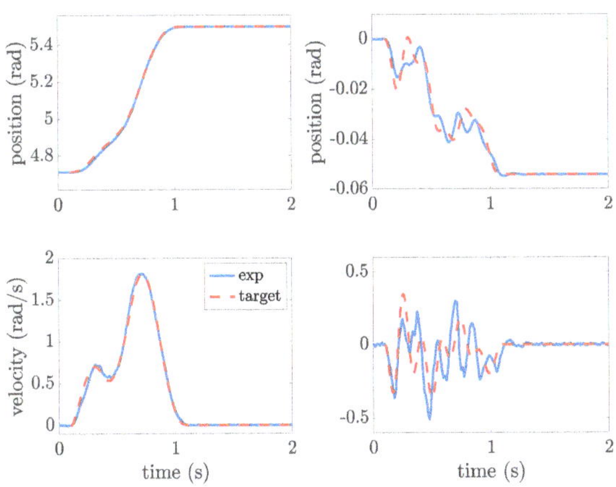

Figure 3. Test case I: optimal trajectory.

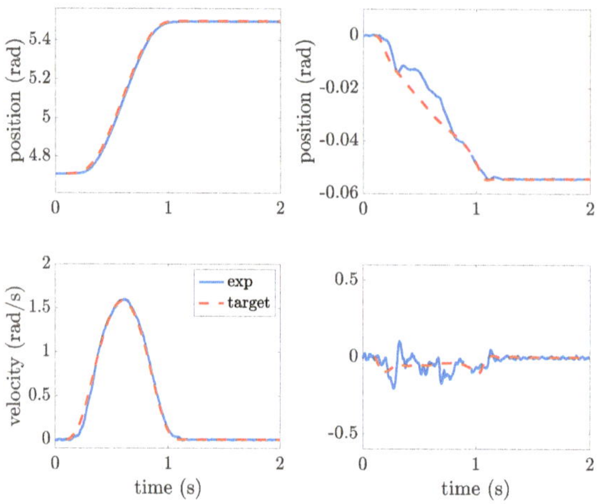

Figure 4. Test case I: ZV trajectory.

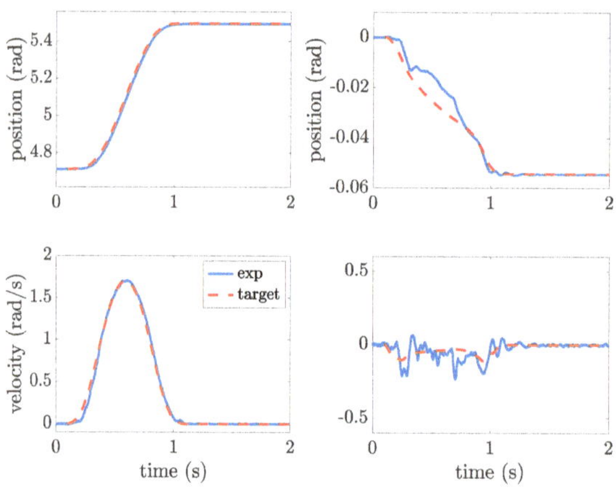

Figure 5. Test case I: ZVD trajectory.

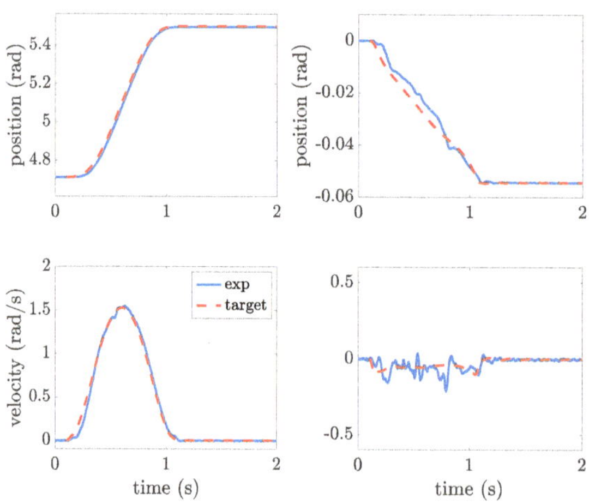

Figure 6. Test case I: NZV trajectory.

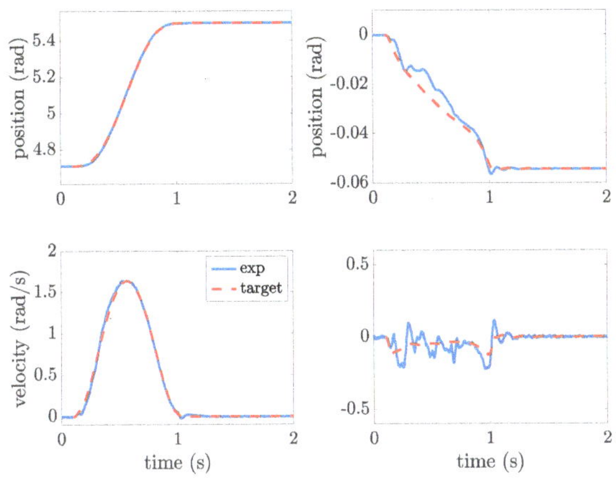

Figure 7. Test case I: NZVD trajectory.

From the energy point-of-view, it is worth noticing that the proposed trajectory allows a significant saving when compared to one of the other trajectories tested in test case I. In particular the evolution of the cumulative energy absorbed by the motor during the planned motion is depicted in Figure 8.

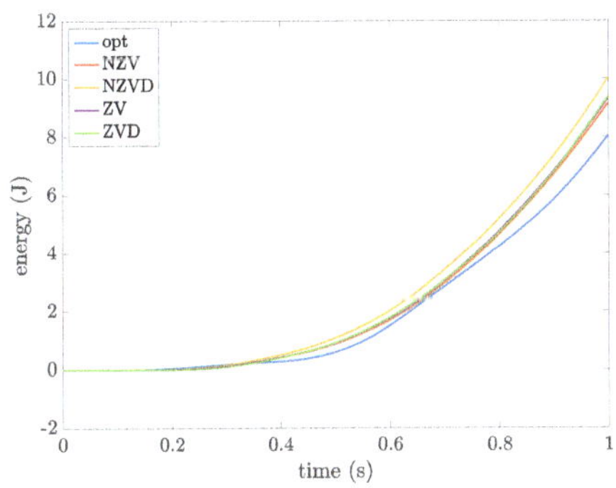

Figure 8. Test case I: cumulative energy expenditure over different tested trajectories.

Furthermore, a quantitative comparison in terms of energy expenditure and residual oscillations is resumed in Table 3.

Table 3. Test case I: comparison of energy consumption and residual oscillations.

Trajectory Type	Energy Consumption (J)	Oscillations (rad)
optimal	8.044	3×10^{-4}
ZV	9.161; (+13.89%)	5×10^{-4}; (+66.67%)
ZVD	10.048; (+24.91%)	7×10^{-4}; (+133.33%)
NZV	9.332; (+16.1%)	10×10^{-4}; (+233.33%)
NZVD	9.391; (+16.75%)	7×10^{-4}; (+133.33%)

Notably, the proposed trajectory is comparable to the other methods in terms of peak residual oscillations, which remain quite limited in their order of magnitude. At the same time, using a non-optimized motion profile affects the energy expenditure quite significantly, more specifically in the range from +13.89% to +16.75%. The data show, therefore, the improved performance brought by the proposed solution.

4.3. Test Case II

Test case II involves the motion between two symmetrical positions, in this case between $\vartheta_{1,0} = 5\pi/4$ rad and $\vartheta_{1,f} = 7\pi/4$ rad. As for the previous test case, the experimental results are provided by evaluating the position and speed of both links, as well as the electric energy intake, when executing the optimized motion and the shaped motion profiles as well. The results of the experimental trials are displayed in Figures 9–14 and in Table 4.

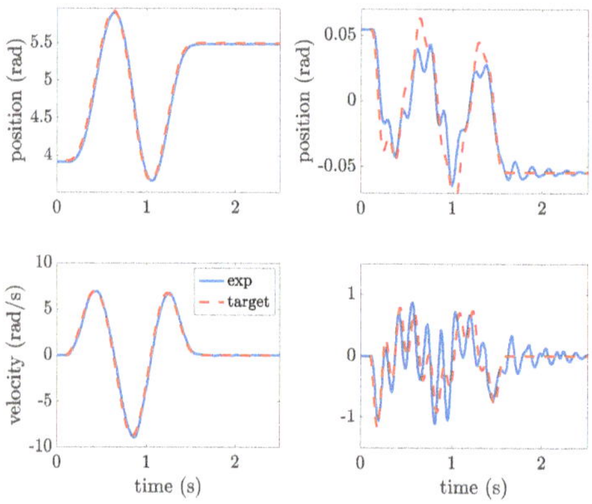

Figure 9. Test case II: execution of the energy optimal trajectory.

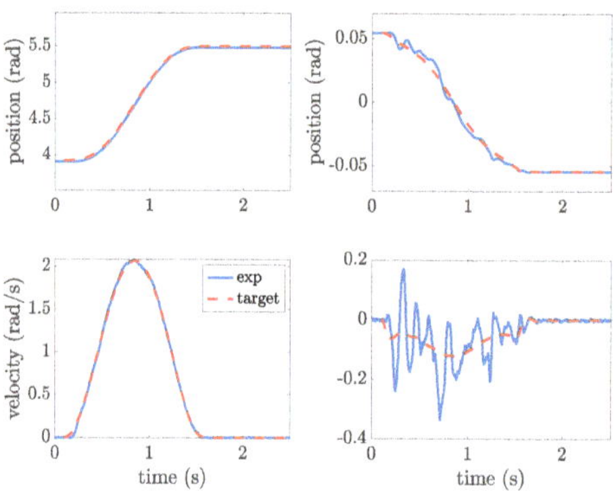

Figure 10. Test case II: execution of the ZV trajectory.

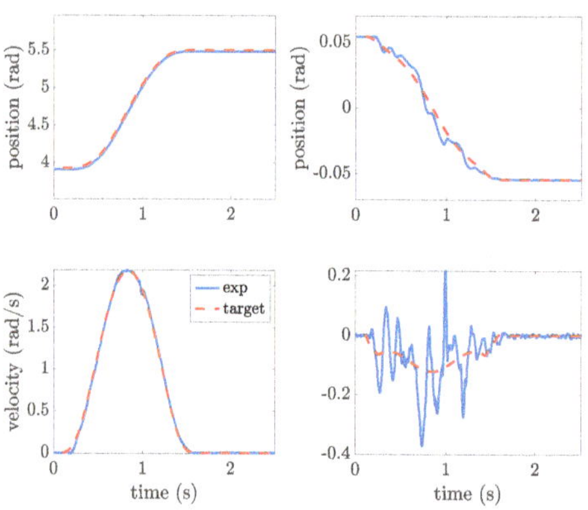

Figure 11. Test case II: execution of the ZVD trajectory.

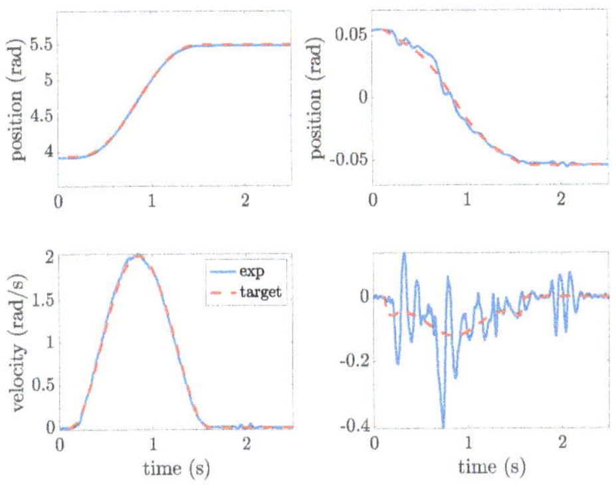

Figure 12. Test case II: execution of the NZV trajectory.

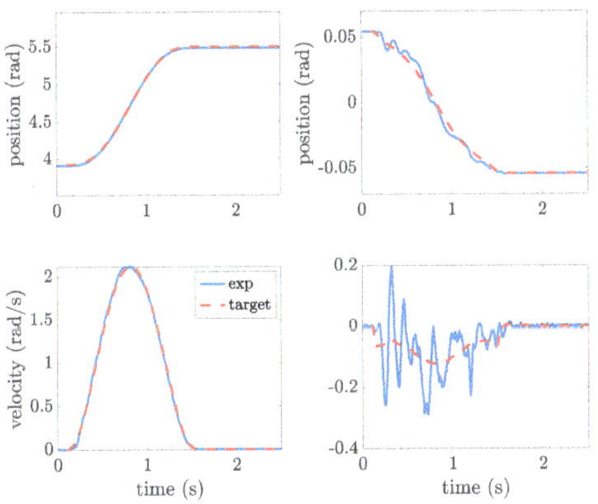

Figure 13. Test case II: execution of the NZVD trajectory.

From the energy point-of-view, it is worth noticing that the proposed trajectory allows a very significant saving, as all the others trajectories require at least 3 times more energy, as shown in terms of the evolution of the cumulative energy absorbed by the motor in Figure 14 and as summarized in Table 4.

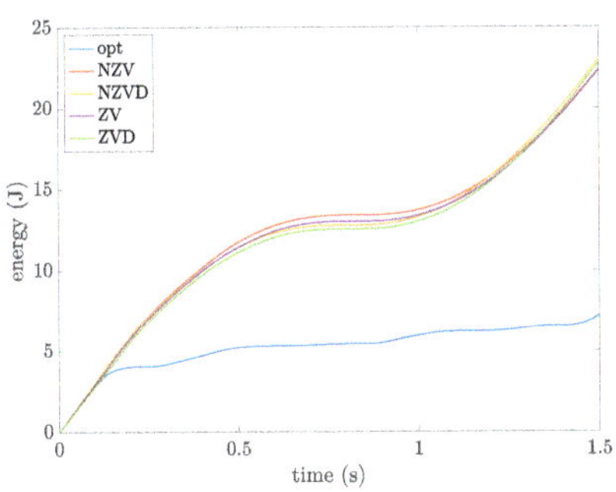

Figure 14. Test case II: cumulative energy expenditure over different tested trajectories.

Table 4. Test case II: comparison of energy consumption and residual oscillations

Trajectory Type	Energy Consumption (J)	Peak Oscillation (rad)
optimal	7.211	8.0×10^{-3}
ZV	22.404; (+210.69%)	2.5×10^{-3}; (−68.75%)
ZVD	23.002; (+218.98%)	3.0×10^{-4}; (−96.25%)
NZV	22.363; (+210.12%)	1.2×10^{-3}; (−85%)
NZVD	22.802; (+216.21%)	2.0×10^{-4}; (−75%)

Looking at the residual oscillations, however, the proposed optimal trajectory results in higher residual vibrations. This can be attributed to the significantly higher acceleration content of the proposed trajectory, which increases the sensitivity to unmodeled dynamics and is harder to track by the control device. Nevertheless, the residual oscillations remain an order of magnitude smaller than the total displacement and they are quickly damped, so they provide a minimal detrimental effect to the quality of the overall motion.

Compared to the ZV filter (another non-robust method), the proposed trajectory achieves residual vibrations below 2×10^{-3} rad in 0.5 s, whereas the ZV filter reaches the same level in 0.4 s. The remaining filters suppress the oscillations almost instantaneously.

5. Conclusions

This work presents an optimal-control-based planner for generating energy-efficient trajectories for underactuated manipulators. The formulation accommodates torque constraints and explicitly enforces oscillation suppression at the final time. The trajectory optimization problem is solved using an open-source solver.

The approach has been validated experimentally on a planar two-degree-of-freedom manipulator with a passive second joint. Experimental results demonstrate significant energy savings while maintaining low residual oscillations.

The experimental validation demonstrates robustness to model mismatches—such as non-ideal friction and nonlinear stiffness—highlighting the potential of the approach for deployment in more complex and realistic scenarios.

The method has been benchmarked against common input shaping techniques (ZV, ZVD, NZV, and NZVD), resulting in comparable residual oscillations. Future work will focus on extending the proposed approach to other robotic systems.

Author Contributions: Conceptualization, D.D. and P.B.; methodology, D.D. and P.B.; software, D.D., J.B. and I.T.; validation, D.D. and J.B.; formal analysis, D.D. and P.B.; investigation, D.D. and P.B.; resources, J.B. and I.T.; data curation, D.D. and P.B.; writing—original draft preparation, D.D. and P.B.; writing—review and editing, D.D. and P.B.; visualization, D.D.; supervision, P.B. and R.C.; project administration, R.C.; funding acquisition, P.B. All authors have read and agreed to the published version of the manuscript.

Funding: This study was carried out within the PNRR research activities of the consortium iNEST funded by the European Union Next-GenerationEU (Piano Nazionale di Ripresa e Resilienza (PNRR)—Missione 4 Componente 2, Investimento 1.5—D.D. 1058 23/06/2022, ECS_00000043). This manuscript reflects only the authors' views and opinions; neither the European Union nor the European Commission can be considered responsible for them.

Data Availability Statement: The original contributions presented in this study are included in the article. Further inquiries can be directed to the corresponding author.

Acknowledgments: During the preparation of this manuscript/study, the authors used ChatGPT 4o for the purposes of revising the text from typos and grammatical errors. The authors have reviewed and edited the output and take full responsibility for the content of this publication.

Conflicts of Interest: The authors declare no conflicts of interest.

References

1. Sachs, J.D.; Schmidt-Traub, G.; Mazzucato, M.; Messner, D.; Nakicenovic, N.; Rockström, J. Six transformations to achieve the sustainable development goals. *Nat. Sustain.* **2019**, *2*, 805–814. [CrossRef]
2. Gonzalez-Torres, M.; Bertoldi, P.; Castellazzi, L.; Pérez-Lombard, L. Review of EU product energy efficiency policies: What have we achieved in 40 years? *J. Clean. Prod.* **2023**, *421*, 138442. [CrossRef]
3. Carabin, G.; Wehrle, E.; Vidoni, R. A review on energy-saving optimization methods for robotic and automatic systems. *Robotics* **2017**, *6*, 39. [CrossRef]
4. Hehenberger, P.; Habib, M.; Bradley, D. *EcoMechatronics*; Springer: Berlin/Heidelberg, Germany, 2023.
5. Kroll, L.; Blau, P.; Wabner, M.; Frieß, U.; Eulitz, J.; Klärner, M. Lightweight components for energy-efficient machine tools. *CIRP J. Manuf. Sci. Technol.* **2011**, *4*, 148–160. [CrossRef]
6. Meoni, F.; Carricato, M. Optimal selection of the motor-reducer unit in servo-controlled machinery: A continuous approach. *Mechatronics* **2018**, *56*, 132–145. [CrossRef]
7. Boscariol, P.; Richiedei, D. Energy optimal design of servo-actuated systems: A concurrent approach based on scaling rules. *Renew. Sustain. Energy Rev.* **2022**, *156*, 111923. [CrossRef]
8. Pasch, K.A.; Seering, W. On the drive systems for high-performance machines. *J. Mech. Trans. Autom. Des.* **1984** , *106* , 102–108. [CrossRef]
9. Barreto, J.P.; Schöler, F.J.F.; Corves, B. The concept of natural motion for pick and place operations. In *Proceedings of the New Advances in Mechanisms, Mechanical Transmissions and Robotics: Proceedings of The Joint International Conference of the XII International Conference on Mechanisms and Mechanical Transmissions (MTM) and the XXIII International Conference on Robotics (Robotics' 16), Aachen, Germany, 26–27 October 2016*; Springer: Berlin/Heidelberg, Germany, 2017; pp. 89–98.
10. Scalera, L.; Palomba, I.; Wehrle, E.; Gasparetto, A.; Vidoni, R. Natural motion for energy saving in robotic and mechatronic systems. *Appl. Sci.* **2019**, *9*, 3516. [CrossRef]
11. Palomba, I.; Wehrle, E.; Carabin, G.; Vidoni, R. Minimization of the energy consumption in industrial robots through regenerative drives and optimally designed compliant elements. *Appl. Sci.* **2020**, *10*, 7475. [CrossRef]
12. Bettega, J.; Richiedei, D.; Tamellin, I.; Trevisani, A. Reducing energy consumption and driving torque in an underactuated robotic arm through natural motion. In Proceedings of the International Workshop IFToMM for Sustainable Development Goals, Bilbao, Spain, 22–23 June 2023; Springer: Berlin/Heidelberg, Germany, 2023; pp. 89–96.
13. Bruzzone, L.; Verotti, M.; Fanghella, P. Natural Motion of the RR-4R-R Manipulator: Effects of Trajectory Types and Parameters. In Proceedings of the International Workshop IFToMM for Sustainable Development Goals, Lamezia Terme, Italy, 9–11 June 2025; Springer: Berlin/Heidelberg, Germany, 2025; pp. 238–245.
14. Richiedei, D.; Trevisani, A. Optimization of the energy consumption through spring balancing of servo-actuated mechanisms. *J. Mech. Des.* **2020**, *142*, 012301. [CrossRef]
15. Scalera, L.; Carabin, G.; Vidoni, R.; Wongratanaphisan, T. Energy efficiency in a 4-DOF parallel robot featuring compliant elements. *Int. J. Mech. Control* **2019**, *20*, 49–57.
16. Biagiotti, L.; Melchiorri, C. *Trajectory Planning for Automatic Machines and Robots*; Springer Science & Business Media: Berlin/Heidelberg, Germany, 2008.
17. Richiedei, D.; Trevisani, A. Analytical computation of the energy-efficient optimal planning in rest-to-rest motion of constant inertia systems. *Mechatronics* **2016**, *39*, 147–159. [CrossRef]
18. Carabin, G.; Vidoni, R. Energy-saving optimization method for point-to-point trajectories planned via standard primitives in 1-DoF mechatronic systems. *Int. J. Adv. Manuf. Technol.* **2021**, *116*, 331–344. [CrossRef]
19. Van Oosterwyck, N.; Vanbecelaere, F.; Knaepkens, F.; Monte, M.; Stockman, K.; Cuyt, A.; Derammelaere, S. Energy optimal point-to-point motion profile optimization. *Mech. Based Des. Struct. Mach.* **2024**, *52*, 239–256. [CrossRef]
20. Abe, A. An effective trajectory planning method for simultaneously suppressing residual vibration and energy consumption of flexible structures. *Case Stud. Mech. Syst. Signal Process.* **2016**, *4*, 19–27. [CrossRef]
21. Von Stryk, O.; Bulirsch, R. Direct and indirect methods for trajectory optimization. *Ann. Oper. Res.* **1992**, *37*, 357–373. [CrossRef]
22. Dona', D.; Lenzo, B.; Rosati, G. Planning real-time energy efficient trajectories for a two degrees of freedom balanced serial manipulator. In Proceedings of the International Workshop IFToMM for Sustainable Development Goals, Bilbao, Spain, 22–23 June 2023; Springer: Berlin/Heidelberg, Germany, 2023; pp. 81–88.
23. Dona', D.; Lenzo, B.; Boscariol, P.; Rosati, G. A mixed direct/indirect method for generating energy-efficient motion laws for an inverted pendulum. In Proceedings of the IFToMM World Congress on Mechanism and Machine Science, Tokyo, Japan, 5–10 November 2023; Springer: Berlin/Heidelberg, Germany, 2023; pp. 322–331.
24. De Luca, A.; Book, W.J. Robots with flexible elements. In *Springer Handbook of Robotics*; Springer: Berlin/Heidelberg, Germany, 2016; pp. 243–282.

25. Lu, B.; Fang, Y.; Sun, N. Sliding mode control for underactuated overhead cranes suffering from both matched and unmatched disturbances. *Mechatronics* **2017**, *47*, 116–125. [CrossRef]
26. Piva, G.; Richiedei, D.; Trevisani, A. Model inversion for trajectory control of reconfigurable underactuated cable-driven parallel robots. *Nonlinear Dyn.* **2025**, *113* , 8697–8712. [CrossRef]
27. Siciliano, B.; Sciavicco, L.; Villani, L.; Oriolo, G. *Robotics: Modelling, Planning and Control*; Springer: Berlin/Heidelberg, Germany, 2009; Volume 0, pp. 1–623.
28. Liberzon, D. *Calculus of Variations and Optimal Control Theory: A Concise Introduction*; Princeton University Press: Princeton, NJ, USA, 2011.
29. Bryson, A.E. *Applied Optimal Control: Optimization, Estimation and Control*; Routledge: London, UK, 2018.
30. Gillis, J.; Vandewal, B.; Pipeleers, G.; Swevers, J. Effortless modeling of optimal control problems with rockit. In Proceedings of the 39th Benelux Meeting on Systems and Control, Elspeet, The Netherlands, 10–12 March 2020.
31. Singhose, W. Command shaping for flexible systems: A review of the first 50 years. *Int. J. Precis. Eng. Manuf.* **2009**, *10*, 153–168. [CrossRef]
32. Boscariol, P.; Richiedei, D.; Tamellin, I. Residual vibration suppression in uncertain systems: A robust structural modification approach to trajectory planning. *Robot. Comput.-Integr. Manuf.* **2022**, *74*, 102282. [CrossRef]
33. Singhose, W.; Ooten Biediger, E.; Chen, Y.H.; Mills, B. Reference command shaping using specified-negative-amplitude input shapers for vibration reduction. *J. Dyn. Sys. Meas. Control* **2004**, *126*, 210–214. [CrossRef]
34. Vaughan, J.; Yano, A.; Singhose, W. Comparison of robust input shapers. *J. Sound Vib.* **2008**, *315*, 797–815. [CrossRef]

Disclaimer/Publisher's Note: The statements, opinions and data contained in all publications are solely those of the individual author(s) and contributor(s) and not of MDPI and/or the editor(s). MDPI and/or the editor(s) disclaim responsibility for any injury to people or property resulting from any ideas, methods, instructions or products referred to in the content.

robotics

MDPI

Article

Event-Based Closed-Loop Control for Path Following of a Purcell's Three-Link Swimmer

Cristina Nuevo-Gallardo [1,*], Luis Mérida-Calvo [2], Inés Tejado [1,*], Blas M. Vinagre [1] and Vicente Feliu-Batlle [3]

1 Escuela de Ingenierías Industriales, Universidad de Extremadura, 06006 Badajoz, Spain; bvinagre@unex.es
2 Instituto de Investigaciones Energéticas y Aplicaciones Industriales, Universidad de Castilla-La Mancha, 13071 Ciudad Real, Spain; luis.merida@uclm.es
3 Escuela Técnica Superior de Ingeniería Industrial de Ciudad Real, Universidad de Castilla-La Mancha, 13071 Ciudad Real, Spain; vicente.feliu@uclm.es
* Correspondence: cnuevog@unex.es (C.N.-G.); itejbal@unex.es (I.T.); Tel.: +34-924489767 (I.T.)

Abstract

Purcell's three-link swimmers, characterised by segments connected through one-degree-of-freedom joints, exhibit a difficulty in following precise paths. This is attributed to their motion primitives, which do not inherently generate displacement in a singular, predictable direction. To overcome this limitation, this paper proposes a closed-loop control strategy on the basis of event-based control. This control approach enables the robot to perform a specific motion primitive when the deviation from the desired trajectory exceeds a predefined threshold. In other words, an asynchronous strategy is used to adjust the motion of the swimmer, thereby ensuring tracking of the desired path with a limited error. The effectiveness of this closed-loop control strategy is demonstrated through experiments with a motor-driven 30 cm-length prototype. These tests show that this event-based control strategy allows the swimmer to follow specific paths with a tracking error of less than 30% of its length.

Keywords: Reynolds number; Purcell's swimmer; modelling; prototype; event-based control; path following

1. Introduction

With promising potential for diverse applications, autonomous swimming robots are set to revolutionise aquatic environments. They can assist with surveillance and protection around marine infrastructure, perform vital search and rescue missions, and even handle maintenance operations within complex pipe systems [1,2]. Inspired by the movements of biological swimmers like eels and water snakes, a leading approach in this field involves articulated snake-like robots, which navigate intricate underwater environments with remarkable adaptability. Snake-like robots intended for these applications can already be found in the literature [3,4], demonstrating the practical viability of this approach. These bio-inspired systems offer significant advantages through their undulating movement, which adapts to irregular shapes while minimising environmental disturbance in sensitive ecological environments and confined spaces.

Within this broader context of snake-like swimming robots, the Purcell's swimmer represents a fundamental model designed to simulate the behaviour of biological swimmers in fluid environments. Originally intended for navigation at low Reynolds number (*Re*) regimes, where fluid dynamics are dominated by viscous forces rather than inertial ones, this system was introduced by Edward M. Purcell as the simplest swimmer capable of navigating these regimes [5]. The Purcell's swimmer consists of three segments and two joints, making it a simplified version of more complex snake-like robots. This design allows it to achieve net movement by rotating its lateral segments in asymmetric sequences, known as motion primitives or gaits, which define their angular positions.

Research in viscosity-dominated regimes has established a solid theoretical foundation for understanding the behaviour of the swimmer, with its kinematics and dynamics being the most widely studied aspects. Researchers have extensively developed and analysed two-dimensional dynamic models, investigating various parameters that influence swimmer displacement. These studies have explored critical aspects such as swimmer geometry [6–8], motion primitives [9], and its asymmetry and stability [10]. Complementing two-dimensional approaches, other research efforts have focused on three-dimensional models of swimmers [11,12]. Some studies have taken a more generalised approach, first examining the dynamics of N-link systems and then attempting to approximate these models to sperm cell swimmers, with specific attention to the three-link case [13]. Concerning motion primitives, the literature presents traditional gaits such as square and circular configurations, which have been implemented and comparatively analysed in several studies [11,14]. Additionally, researchers have proposed innovative methodologies for designing novel motion primitives, as documented in a range of publications [7,9,15–21].

Regarding actuator types for rotating lateral links, the literature predominantly features two primary approaches: motorised systems and magnetic field-based actuation. Motorised prototypes have been extensively explored, with two notable servomotor-actuated swimmers developed in [14,22]. Another motorised prototype was introduced in [23], although experimental results were not presented. Magnetic field-based actuation represents an alternative approach, with significant research focused on magnetic Purcell's swimmers. Researchers have comprehensively investigated these systems in studies such as [24–27]. A particularly noteworthy experimental contribution was the creation and testing of a magnetic prototype spanning a few centimetres, as detailed in [26].

Complementing these actuator strategies, some researchers have conducted mathematical analyses exploring the implications of passive and active elastic joints [23,28], providing additional theoretical insights into swimmer locomotion mechanisms. Moreover, ionic polymer-metal composites (IPMCs) have emerged as innovative materials for developing and simulating advanced swimming mechanisms. In [29], researchers explored the potential of IPMCs in designing a three-link Purcell's swimmer, demonstrating the versatility of this material in biomimetic locomotion systems. Building upon this approach, a recent work successfully fabricated an IPMC-based Purcell's swimmer prototype in which the joints were fabricated by this material, offering experimental results that validate the design [30].

While Purcell's swimmer has shown promise in viscosity-dominated environments, there exists a notable gap in understanding its behaviour and applications in inertia-dominated regimes ($Re > 1$). Extending this concept beyond its original theoretical framework is crucial for its practical application in marine environments, where higher Re are typical. Despite its simple design, the Purcell's swimmer offers significant potential for real-world applications. Its long and slender design makes it an ideal tool for specialised subsea inspections, such as around offshore wind farms. This allows it to reach remote and confined underwater spaces that are otherwise inaccessible by conventional methods, much like other articulated robotic systems [3]. In broader aquatic settings such as lakes, reservoirs, and shallow seas, these robots, equipped with appropriate tools and sensors, could aid in ecological inspections, habitat monitoring, or even rescue missions for trapped species. In the same way as snake-like robots, their biologically mimetic behaviours enable them to blend seamlessly with the surrounding environment [31].

Nevertheless, effective deployment in these applications requires trajectory-following capabilities, which remain relatively unexplored for Purcell's swimmers. Notably, in [32], the author identifies distinct gaits, described as piecewise functions, enabling the swimmer to trace square and circular trajectories through an open-loop control strategy that eliminates the need for feedback mechanisms. Complementing this research, an open-loop control approach is proposed in [14], which focuses on estimating swimmer displacement and rotation primitives. The study further advanced the understanding of trajectory generation by analytically determining the optimal number of primitive repetitions required to achieve the desired movement path. Despite this, no closed-loop control strategies have been applied to the Purcell's swimmer for the purpose of following given trajectories. Furthermore, its unique locomotion, driven by specific motion primitives, requires that any control strategy explicitly account for these fundamental gaits to achieve effective navigation.

Given the characteristics of this robot, event-based control is a suitable closed-loop strategy for enhancing its path-following performance. This approach includes various methods that reduce resource use by executing control actions only when needed. Among these, event-triggered control has the widest adoption, whereby control updates occur when a system-dependent condition, such as a state or output error, exceeds a threshold [33,34]. Conversely, self-triggered control predicts the subsequent triggering instant based on the present state, thereby reducing the necessity for continuous monitoring. This feature is particularly advantageous in systems with limited sensing or computational resources. More recently, adaptive and learning-based event-triggered control has emerged as a promising direction, enabling controllers to adjust triggering conditions in real time based on environmental disturbances or system uncertainties, thereby improving robustness in dynamic settings [35]. Each approach has its own set of trade-offs in terms of implementation complexity, performance, and resource efficiency, making them suitable for different classes of systems and application domains. Several examples of application of event-based methods in controlling other categories of mobile robots can be found in [36,37], as well as robotic arms in [38,39]

In this context, the aim of this paper is twofold. Firstly, it involves the kinematic and dynamic study of the swimmer, alongside the fabrication of a 30 cm-length motor-driven prototype. Secondly, it proposes an event-based closed-loop control strategy for path following. This strategy employs a threshold-based logical condition that considers both position error and its rate of change to initiate new events. Its operation switches between translation and rotation primitives based on trajectory error, allowing real-time path correction when the swimmer deviates from the target path. Moreover, experimental validation using the motor-driven prototype confirmed the effectiveness of the strategy.

Thus, the main contributions of this paper, all contextualised within inertia-dominated environments, include the following:

1. The design, modelling, and fabrication of a three-link Purcell's swimmer prototype;
2. The proposal and experimental validation of a closed-loop control strategy for path following.

This document is organised as follows. Section 2 provides the definition and kinematic modelling of a Purcell's swimmer, alongside the theoretical movement of the classical swimmer and the basis of event-based control. Section 3 outlines the methodology employed in this work, detailing the mechanical design of the fabricated motor-driven Purcell's swimmer prototype, the dynamic modelling of such swimmers, and the designed control strategy for path following. The results of both simulations and experiments are presented and discussed in Section 4. Finally, conclusions and future works are drawn in Section 5.

2. Background

This section is devoted to the description of a Purcell's swimmer concerning its geometry and kinematics, followed by the fundamentals of event-based control.

2.1. Generalities of Purcell's Swimmers

2.1.1. Geometry and Kinematics

The Purcell's swimmer consists of three links connected by one degree-of-freedom (DOF) joints, as illustrated in Figure 1. The segments are designated from 0 to 2, being their lengths l_0, l_1, and l_2, while the rotational joints are designated as j_1 and j_2. A ratio calculated by $\eta = l_0/l$ relates the lengths of the links, being l the total length of the swimmer. The lateral links will be supposed of equal length.

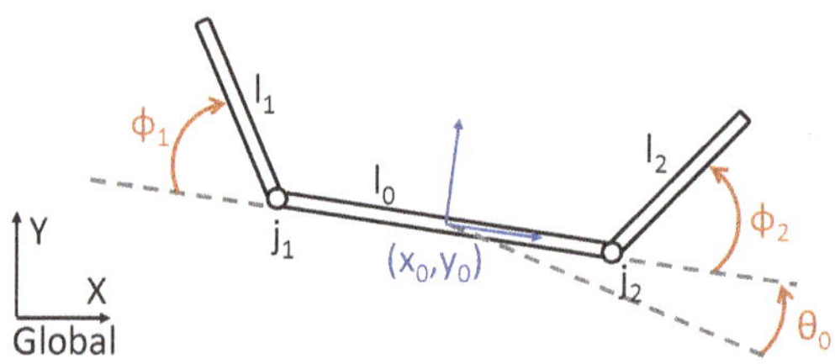

Figure 1. General scheme of Purcell's swimmer.

The angular position of i-link with respect to the global X axis is represented by θ_i. The rotation of the lateral links is dictated by a motion primitive (or gait), a function that defines the angles ϕ_1 and ϕ_2 over time. These local gait angles are related to the global angular positions through the following equations: $\theta_1 = \phi_1 - \theta_0$ and $\theta_2 = \phi_2 + \theta_0$.

The literature presents several motion primitives, often categorised into those for translation and those for rotation. Translation primitives enable the swimmer to advance along the X axis of its body-fixed reference frame, whereas rotation primitives induce a rotation of the central segment about the Z axis. Furthermore, these primitives are typically designated according to their graphical representation in the ϕ_1 and ϕ_2 plane. Among the translation primitives identified in the literature, this work employs the most frequently utilised one, known as the square primitive, as depicted in Figure 2a. Regarding the rotation primitive, a gait exhibiting a double-square form with central symmetry about the origin of the coordinate system has been adopted, as illustrated in Figure 2b. Their mathematical definitions can be found in Appendix A.

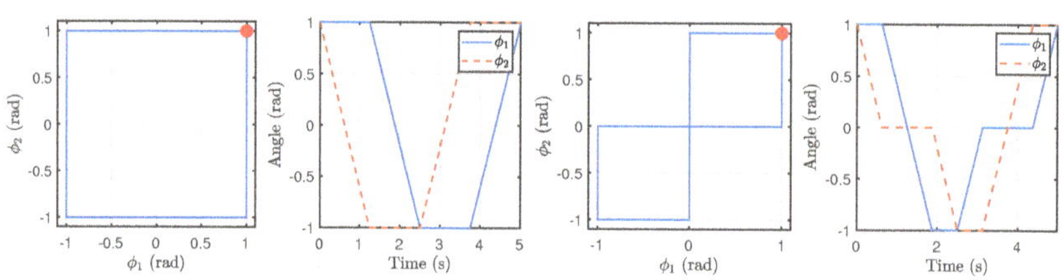

(a) (b)

Figure 2. Motion primitives applied to the Purcell's swimmer, defined with unitary amplitude: (**a**) square (translation primitive); (**b**) bi-square (rotation primitive). The red circular mark represents the initial point of the gait.

When assessing the dynamics of the swimmer, the angles ϕ_1 and ϕ_2 fully define the movement of links l_1 and l_2 relative to the central link. However, the central link position is undetermined. Considering the mathematical development in [30] and defining the position of the centre of i-link as $\mathbf{X}_i = [x_i \quad y_i \quad \theta_i]^T$, the linear and angular velocities of the links can be expressed as follows [8,17,22]:

$$\dot{\mathbf{X}}_i = \mathbf{A}_i\dot{\mathbf{X}}_0 + \mathbf{B}_i\dot{\mathbf{\Phi}} \tag{1}$$

where $\mathbf{\Phi} = [\phi_1 \quad \phi_2]^T$, with $i = \{0,1,2\}$, referring subscript 0 to the central link of the Purcell's swimmer. Matrices $\mathbf{A}_i$ and $\mathbf{B}_i$, defined in [17,30], vary depending on the link for which velocity is being calculated. Further details can be found in Appendix B.1.

Regarding the acceleration of i-link, it can be obtained through the derivative of $\dot{\mathbf{X}}_i$ and can be expressed, in matrix form, as follows:

$$\ddot{\mathbf{X}}_i = \mathbf{C}_i\ddot{\mathbf{X}}_0 + \mathbf{D}_i\dot{\mathbf{X}}_0 + \mathbf{E}_i\ddot{\mathbf{\Phi}} \tag{2}$$

being matrices $\mathbf{C}_i$, $\mathbf{D}_i$, and $\mathbf{E}_i$ defined in Appendix B.2.

Moreover, the squared velocity will be used to calculate environment forces, so its expression should be also obtained. The squared velocity of i-link can be expressed, in terms of the velocity of the central link and the gait angles, as follows:

$$\dot{\mathbf{X}}_i^2 = \mathbf{G}_i\dot{\mathbf{X}}_0^2 + \mathbf{H}_i\dot{\mathbf{X}}_0 + \mathbf{K}_i\dot{\mathbf{\Phi}}^2 \tag{3}$$

where matrices $\mathbf{G}_i$, $\mathbf{H}_i$, and $\mathbf{K}_i$ are also detailed in Appendix B.1.

2.1.2. Classical Results

The Purcell's swimmer was initially conceived to navigate in viscosity-dominated environments. This implies that the dynamic model of the swimmer only takes into account the viscous forces present in the interaction between the fluid and the swimmer, resulting in a straightforward model that has been outlined in previous studies and facilitated the analysis of its movement in these environments [30,40].

The findings indicate that classical motion primitives, such as the aforementioned square, generate a net displacement of the swimmer along the X axis, thereby enabling forward movement in the fluid environment. The displacement of the midpoint of the central segment of the swimmer along each of its axes, as well as the rotation of the central segment, are shown in Figure 3 for a millimetre-length swimmer. As is evident, despite a larger X-displacement, non-null movement along the Y axis and rotation of the central segment are observed. This suggests that, by repeatedly applying the square primitive, the swimmer will move forward on the X axis while deflecting slightly on the Y axis. This hypothesis is supported by Figure 4, which depicts the XY trajectory of the swimmer in the same conditions as Figure 3.

On another note, it is possible to achieve a rotation of the central segment of the swimmer to modify its orientation by considering other types of primitives, such as the bi-square primitive that was introduced above. The results subsequent to the implementation of this gait are also plotted in Figure 3. Similar to the square motion primitive, the bi-square gait produces non-null net motion along the other axes, thus resulting in the deviation of the swimmer in both the X and Y directions during the application of the primitive.

With regard to the trajectory of the Purcell's swimmer, Figure 4 illustrates how the central segment traces a loop or figure-eight trajectory while implementing the square gait. This trajectory, which is characteristic of such a swimmer within viscosity-dominated environments, has been obtained both theoretically and experimentally [14,41].

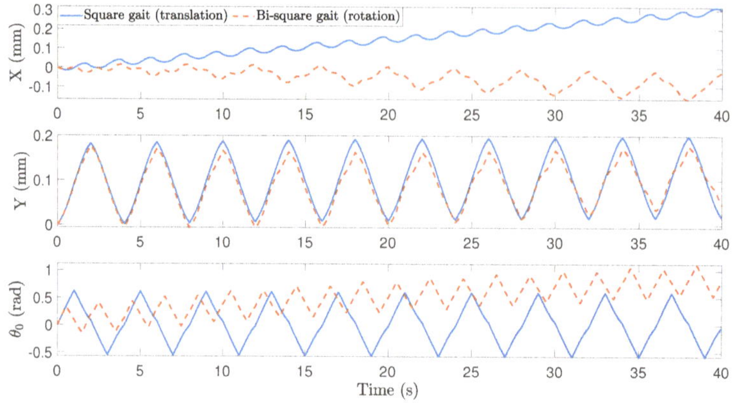

Figure 3. Displacement of a millimetre-length Purcell's swimmer navigating through a viscosity-dominated regime applying 10 repetitions of the translation and rotation gaits.

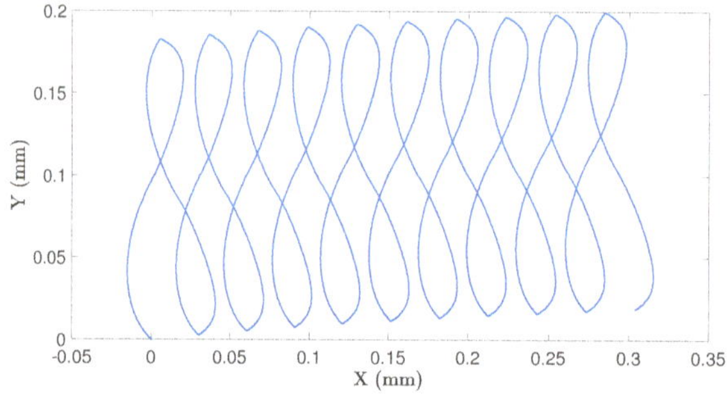

Figure 4. Trajectory of a millimetre-length Purcell's swimmer navigating through a viscosity-dominated regime applying 10 repetitions of the translation and rotation gaits.

2.2. Generalities of Event-Based Control

The event-driven control, as the name suggests, is based on the activation of a controller when an event occurs, that is, the triggering of an event determines the calculation of the control action [42]. An event is usually triggered by a logical condition that, in a generic form, can be expressed as follows:

$$(\text{logical condition IS true}) \text{ OR } (h_{without} \geq h_{max}) \tag{4}$$

This event-based condition determines that an event occurs when the logical condition becomes true or when the elapsed time without triggering the event, $h_{without}$, is equal or higher than a set time period, h_{max}. This condition has two terms: an asynchronous term (on the left), involving the logical condition, and a synchronous part (on the right), which is a safety condition that triggers the event. The safety condition is included to trigger the event when the logical condition never becomes true.

A basic scheme of an event-based controller would include a controller, the system, a sensor, and an event detector. The controller receives data from the event detector when a new event takes place, while the controller calculates the control action and sends it to the system. Finally, the sensor measures the system output every sampling period, h_{sensor}, and sends it to the event detector, in order to evaluate the logical condition. Concerning the activation of each element, the sensor and event detector are activated periodically in order to detect if a new event occurs. On the contrary, the controller is only active when the event detector registers an event.

The event-triggering condition defined in the event detector and the activation of each element will determine the functioning of the control loop. The main criteria to define the event-triggering condition can be found in [42–44], of which the three most commonly used are as follows:

1. Immediate triggering, which means that the data are read or sent to the next element in the control loop just when it arrives.
2. Periodic triggering, whereby the data are read or sent at every sampling period h.
3. Logical condition-based triggering, which employs several criteria, such as threshold and absolute deadband, to initiate events. In the threshold condition, for example, an event occurs when the measured data surpass a specific fixed value, represented by Δ.

3. Methodology

This section deals with the methodology followed throughout this work. Firstly, details of the prototype design are given, followed by the description of the dynamic model of such a swimmer and the definition of the control strategy for path following.

3.1. Purcell's Swimmer Prototype

The Purcell's swimmer prototype fabricated in this work, shown in Figure 5, is composed of two parts, namely, the floating and submerged parts, which have different functions. On the one hand, the submerged part corresponds to the three segments that make up the swimmer, where the central one is immobile and the lateral links can rotate thanks to the actuators, DC motors in this case. The connection between the lateral segments and the motor shaft is done by an intermediate component and plastic screws. Due to geometrical constraints, the lateral segments can only rotate within the range $-\pi/2 < \phi_i < \pi/2$ rad. The three segments were designed with rectangular cross-section for better manufacturing.

(a) (b)

Figure 5. Purcell's swimmer motor-driven prototype: (**a**) design in SolidWorks 2018; (**b**) fabricated prototype.

The floating section, however, not only ensures a constant depth of the swimmer segments during experiments but also incorporates a sealed housing. This housing protects all electronic components and other elements susceptible to water damage. A press-fitted cover on the housing contains several markers used for tracking the movement of the robot during the experiments. The key electrical components are as follows:

1. DC motors and driver: the lateral segments are rotated by 6 V low-power micro metal gearmotors from Pololu Robotics and Electronics(Pololu Corporation, Las Vegas, NV, USA).These motors, detailed in Table 1, feature a 100:1 gearbox and a built-in incremental encoder. A Toshiba TB6612FNG driver (Toshiba Electronic Devices & Storage Corporation, Tokyo, Japan) powers these DC motors.

2. Microcontroller: an Arduino Nano 33 IoT (Arduino AG, Lugano, Switzerland) serves as microcontroller, managing all its movements and functionalities. Its WiFi+Bluetooth module, along with its numerous digital pins (usable for interrupts) and pulse width modulation (PWM) pins, made it suitable for this application.
3. Batteries: two 3.7 V batteries provide power to the robot.
4. LEDs and buttons: several LEDs and push buttons were also included inside and outside the housing of the robot for diverse purposes. External indicators allow to switch the robot on/off, change or identify its operating mode, and check the WiFi connection status. Internally, push buttons function as limit switches, essential for initialising the motor position.

Table 1. Technical specifications of DC motors used for the prototype.

Technical Specifications	Value	Units	Technical Specifications	Value	Units
Rated voltage	6	V	Rated torque	0.7	kg·cm
Gear ratio	100.37:1	-	Rated speed	90	rpm
Speed at no load	155	rpm	Instantaneous torque	1.5	kg·cm
Current at no load	60	mA			

Concerning materials, the prototype housing, the lateral links, and the mechanical parts were mainly fabricated with polylactic acid (PLA), a material used for additive manufacturing in 3D printers, although tough resin was also used for the fabrication of certain pieces that required better mechanical properties.

The choice of segment lengths in Purcell's swimmer has been the subject of prior optimisation studies, where the lateral segments were sized relative to the central segment and a specific motion primitive under viscosity-dominated conditions. These studies aimed to maximise metrics such as relative displacement, efficiency, or both, per cycle. In the present work, the length of the central link was fixed at 40.5 mm due to mechanical constraints: the DC motors were housed within this segment, and the distance between them could not be reduced. However, the overall length of the swimmer could still be adjusted by modifying the length of the lateral segments, offering greater design flexibility.

For the experiments conducted in this work, a greater length was chosen for the lateral segments (147.64 mm). This decision was mainly driven by the need to achieve larger absolute displacements, thus facilitating the observation, quantification, and swimmer motion analysis in the experimental setup. Furthermore, at this scale, factors such as the resolution of motion capture systems, interaction with the surrounding medium, and the physical limitations of the test bench make it more practical to work with a larger swimmer. Finally, a longer segment length also contributes to greater robustness of the system against small inaccuracies in fabrication or control, thereby improving the reproducibility of the experiments.

3.2. *Modelling of a Purcell's Swimmer*

This section begins with some preliminaries regarding initial hypotheses and notation. Next, the environmental forces that arise from the interaction between the swimmer and the fluid are introduced. Finally, the dynamic model of Purcell's three-link swimmer is developed.

3.2.1. Preliminaries

Let consider the following assumptions [45]:

1. The fluid is viscid, incompressible, and irrotational in the inertial frame.
2. The swimmer incorporates a floatation element designed to maintain the underwater components at a constant depth.

3. The flow field is defined by a constant, irrotational fluid velocity.
4. Boundary effects are considered negligible.
5. The swimmer navigates within an inertia-dominated regime.

Let us consider the following notation: the fluid velocities in X and Y axes are denoted as $V_{f,x}$ and $V_{f,y}$, respectively; $V_{r,x,i}$ and $V_{r,y,i}$ are the relative linear velocities of i-link with respect to the fluid in X and Y directions; $\dot{V}_{r,x,i}$ and $\dot{V}_{r,y,i}$ represent the relative linear accelerations of i-link; and relative angular velocity and acceleration of i-link are denoted as $\dot{\Theta}_{r,i}$ and $\ddot{\Theta}_{r,i}$, respectively.

3.2.2. Environment Interaction

The interaction between swimming objects and fluid environments leads to the appearance of forces that oppose to the movement. Mainly, two types of hydrodynamic forces can be found in these regimes: added-mass (or virtual-mass) forces and drag (or viscous) forces. Hereafter, these forces will be described considering their application to a Purcell's three-link swimmer.

The added-mass forces are opposed to the movement of the swimmer and represent the effective mass of the fluid that surrounds the swimmer and must be accelerated with it. These forces depend on the relative acceleration of the swimmer through the following expression [45,46]:

$$\begin{bmatrix} f_{a,x,i} \\ f_{a,y,i} \\ \tau_{a,i} \end{bmatrix} = - \begin{bmatrix} c_{a,i}^{\parallel} \cos\theta_i & -c_{a,i}^{\perp} \sin\theta_i & 0 \\ c_{a,i}^{\parallel} \sin\theta_i & c_{a,i}^{\perp} \cos\theta_i & 0 \\ 0 & 0 & c_{a,i}^{\circ} \end{bmatrix} \begin{bmatrix} \dot{V}_{r,x,i} \\ \dot{V}_{r,y,i} \\ \ddot{\Theta}_{r,i} \end{bmatrix} \tag{5}$$

where $f_{a,x,i}$, $f_{a,y,i}$, and $\tau_{a,i}$ are the added-mass forces in the X and Y axes and the generated torque, respectively. The added-mass coefficients of the i-link in the tangential and perpendicular direction have been named as $c_{a,i}^{\parallel}$ and $c_{a,i}^{\perp}$, respectively, while the added-mass torque coefficient is defined by $c_{a,i}^{\circ}$. These coefficients only depend on the body geometry [47].

The relative acceleration of the swimmer can be obtained, for each link, as follows [45]:

$$\begin{bmatrix} \dot{V}_{r,x,i} \\ \dot{V}_{r,y,i} \\ \ddot{\Theta}_{r,i} \end{bmatrix} = \begin{bmatrix} \cos\theta_i & \sin\theta_i & 0 \\ -\sin\theta_i & \cos\theta_i & 0 \\ 0 & 0 & 1 \end{bmatrix} \begin{bmatrix} \ddot{x}_i \\ \ddot{y}_i \\ \ddot{\theta}_i \end{bmatrix} + \dot{\theta}_i \begin{bmatrix} -\sin\theta_i & \cos\theta_i & 0 \\ -\cos\theta_i & -\sin\theta_i & 0 \\ 0 & 0 & 0 \end{bmatrix} \begin{bmatrix} \dot{x}_i - V_{f,x} \\ \dot{y}_i - V_{f,y} \\ \dot{\theta}_i \end{bmatrix} \tag{6}$$

Notice that the influence of the flow field is incorporated in Equation (6) by subtracting the fluid velocity from the swimmer velocity, which is a common and straightforward method for modelling the effect of ocean currents on underwater robots [48,49].

Substituting this expression into (5), leads to the following:

$$\begin{aligned} \begin{bmatrix} f_{a,x,i} \\ f_{a,y,i} \\ \tau_{a,i} \end{bmatrix} = & - \begin{bmatrix} c_{a,i}^{\parallel} \cos^2\theta_i + c_{a,i}^{\perp} \sin^2\theta_i & \left(c_{a,i}^{\parallel} - c_{a,i}^{\perp}\right) \sin\theta_i \cos\theta_i & 0 \\ \left(c_{a,i}^{\parallel} - c_{a,i}^{\perp}\right) \sin\theta_i \cos\theta_i & c_{a,i}^{\parallel} \sin^2\theta_i + c_{a,i}^{\perp} \cos^2\theta_i & 0 \\ 0 & 0 & c_{a,i}^{\circ} \end{bmatrix} \begin{bmatrix} \ddot{x}_i \\ \ddot{y}_i \\ \ddot{\theta}_i \end{bmatrix} \\ & - \dot{\theta}_i \begin{bmatrix} -\left(c_{a,i}^{\parallel} - c_{a,i}^{\perp}\right) \sin\theta_i \cos\theta_i & c_{a,i}^{\parallel} \cos^2\theta_i + c_{a,i}^{\perp} \sin^2\theta_i & 0 \\ -c_{a,i}^{\parallel} \sin^2\theta_i - c_{a,i}^{\perp} \cos^2\theta_i & \left(c_{a,i}^{\parallel} - c_{a,i}^{\perp}\right) \sin\theta_i \cos\theta_i & 0 \\ 0 & 0 & 0 \end{bmatrix} \begin{bmatrix} \dot{x}_i - V_{f,x} \\ \dot{y}_i - V_{f,y} \\ \dot{\theta}_i \end{bmatrix} \end{aligned} \tag{7}$$

In order to simplify the equation, the matrices will be denoted as follows:

$$\mathbf{M}_i = \begin{bmatrix} c_{a,i}^{\parallel} \cos^2\theta_i + c_{a,i}^{\perp} \sin^2\theta_i & \left(c_{a,i}^{\parallel} - c_{a,i}^{\perp}\right) \cos\theta_i \sin\theta_i & 0 \\ \left(c_{a,i}^{\parallel} - c_{a,i}^{\perp}\right) \cos\theta_i \sin\theta_i & c_{a,i}^{\perp} \cos^2\theta_i + c_{a,i}^{\parallel} \sin^2\theta_i & 0 \\ 0 & 0 & c_{a,i}^{o} \end{bmatrix}$$

$$\mathbf{N}_i = \begin{bmatrix} -\left(c_{a,i}^{\parallel} - c_{a,i}^{\perp}\right) \dot{\theta}_i \cos\theta_i \sin\theta_i & c_{a,i}^{\parallel} \dot{\theta}_i \cos^2\theta_i + c_{a,i}^{\perp} \dot{\theta}_i \sin^2\theta_i & 0 \\ -c_{a,i}^{\perp} \dot{\theta}_i \cos^2\theta_i - c_{a,i}^{\parallel} \dot{\theta}_i \sin^2\theta_i & \left(c_{a,i}^{\parallel} - c_{a,i}^{\perp}\right) \dot{\theta}_i \cos\theta_i \sin\theta_i & 0 \\ 0 & 0 & 0 \end{bmatrix}$$

And the equation of added-mass forces for i-link can be written as follows:

$$\mathbf{F}_{a,i} = -\mathbf{M}_i \ddot{\mathbf{X}}_i - \mathbf{N}_i \left(\dot{\mathbf{X}}_i - \mathbf{V}_f\right) \tag{8}$$

where $\mathbf{F}_{a,i} = \begin{bmatrix} f_{a,x,i} & f_{a,y,i} & \tau_{a,i} \end{bmatrix}^T$ and $\mathbf{V}_f = \begin{bmatrix} V_{f,x} & V_{f,y} & 0 \end{bmatrix}^T$.

The drag or viscous forces typically consist of two components, encompassing both linear and nonlinear effects: the linear effects depend only on the relative velocity of each link, while the nonlinear ones depend on the squared relative velocity.

The linear drag forces can be obtained from the resistive force theory (RFT) by means of the following expression:

$$\begin{bmatrix} f_{v,x,i}^{l} \\ f_{v,y,i}^{l} \\ \tau_{v,i}^{l} \end{bmatrix} = -\begin{bmatrix} c_{v,i}^{\parallel} \cos\theta_i & -c_{v,i}^{\perp} \sin\theta_i & 0 \\ c_{v,i}^{\parallel} \sin\theta_i & c_{v,i}^{\perp} \cos\theta_i & 0 \\ 0 & 0 & c_{v,l}^{\circ} \end{bmatrix} \begin{bmatrix} V_{r,x,i} \\ V_{r,y,i} \\ \dot{\Theta}_{r,i} \end{bmatrix} \tag{9}$$

being $f_{v,x,i}^{l}$ and $f_{v,y,i}^{l}$ the linear drag forces, $\tau_{v,i}^{l}$ the linear drag torque, $c_{v,i}^{\parallel}$ and $c_{v,i}^{\perp}$ the drag coefficients of the i-link in the tangential and perpendicular direction, respectively (both common to linear and nonlinear effects), and $c_{v,l}^{\circ}$ the drag torque parameter for linear effects. The relative velocity can be obtained, for each link, as follows [45]:

$$\begin{bmatrix} V_{r,x,i} \\ V_{r,y,i} \\ \dot{\Theta}_{r,i} \end{bmatrix} = \begin{bmatrix} \cos\theta_i & \sin\theta_i & 0 \\ -\sin\theta_i & \cos\theta_i & 0 \\ 0 & 0 & 1 \end{bmatrix} \begin{bmatrix} \dot{x}_i - V_{f,x} \\ \dot{y}_i - V_{f,y} \\ \dot{\theta}_i \end{bmatrix} \tag{10}$$

Simplifying terms and joining forces and velocities in matrices, the total drag forces and torque can be calculated through the following [8]:

$$\mathbf{F}_{v,i}^{l} = -\mathbf{R}_i^{l} \left(\dot{\mathbf{X}}_i - \mathbf{V}_f\right) \tag{11}$$

where $\mathbf{F}_{v,i}^{l} = \begin{bmatrix} f_{v,x,i}^{l} & f_{v,y,i}^{l} & \tau_{v,i}^{l} \end{bmatrix}^T$ and $\mathbf{R}_i^{l}$, which is called the resistance tensor, is defined by the following:

$$\mathbf{R}_i^{l} = \begin{bmatrix} c_{v,i}^{\perp} \sin^2\theta_i + c_{v,i}^{\parallel} \cos^2\theta_i & \left(c_{v,i}^{\parallel} - c_{v,i}^{\perp}\right) \cos\theta_i \sin\theta_i & 0 \\ \left(c_{v,i}^{\parallel} - c_{v,i}^{\perp}\right) \cos\theta_i \sin\theta_i & c_{v,i}^{\perp} \cos^2\theta_i + c_{v,i}^{\parallel} \sin^2\theta_i & 0 \\ 0 & 0 & c_{v,l}^{\circ} \end{bmatrix}$$

Concerning nonlinear drag forces, they depend on the squared velocity of the swimmer unlike linear ones, and they can be calculated as follows [45]:

$$\begin{bmatrix} f_{v,x,i}^{II} \\ f_{v,y,i}^{II} \\ \tau_{v,i}^{II} \end{bmatrix} = -\begin{bmatrix} c_{v,i}^{\parallel}\text{sgn}(V_{r,x,i})\cos\theta_i & -c_{v,i}^{\perp}\text{sgn}(V_{r,y,i})\sin\theta_i & 0 \\ c_{v,i}^{\parallel}\text{sgn}(V_{r,x,i})\sin\theta_i & c_{v,i}^{\perp}\text{sgn}(V_{r,y,i})\cos\theta_i & 0 \\ 0 & 0 & c_{v,nl}^{\circ} \end{bmatrix} \begin{bmatrix} \dot{V}_{r,x,i}^{2} \\ \dot{V}_{r,y,i}^{2} \\ \ddot{\Theta}_{r,i}^{2} \end{bmatrix} \tag{12}$$

where $f_{v,x,i}^{II}$ and $f_{v,y,i}^{II}$ are the nonlinear drag forces, $\tau_{v,i}^{II}$ is the nonlinear drag torque, and $c_{v,nl}^{\circ}$ is the drag torque parameter for nonlinear effects. Substituting the squared relative velocity and expressing in matrix form, the nonlinear drag forces can be obtained as follows:

$$\mathbf{F}_{v,i}^{II} = -\mathbf{R}_i^{II}\left(\dot{\mathbf{X}}_i - \mathbf{V}_f\right)^2 \tag{13}$$

where $\mathbf{F}_{v,i}^{II} = \begin{bmatrix} f_{v,x,i}^{II} & f_{v,y,i}^{II} & \tau_{v,i}^{II} \end{bmatrix}^T$ and matrix $\mathbf{R}_i^{II}$ is defined as follows:

$$\mathbf{R}_i^{II} = \begin{bmatrix} c_{v,i}^{\parallel}\text{sgn}(V_{r,x,i})\cos\theta_i\cos 2\theta_i + c_{v,i}^{\perp}\text{sgn}(V_{r,y,i})\sin\theta_i\sin 2\theta_i & c_{v,i}^{\parallel}\text{sgn}(V_{r,x,i})\cos\theta_i\sin 2\theta_i - c_{v,i}^{\perp}\text{sgn}(V_{r,y,i})\sin\theta_i\cos 2\theta_i & 0 \\ c_{v,i}^{\parallel}\text{sgn}(V_{r,x,i})\sin\theta_i\cos 2\theta_i - c_{v,i}^{\perp}\text{sgn}(V_{r,y,i})\cos\theta_i\sin 2\theta_i & c_{v,i}^{\parallel}\text{sgn}(V_{r,x,i})\sin\theta_i\sin 2\theta_i + c_{v,i}^{\perp}\text{sgn}(V_{r,y,i})\cos\theta_i\cos 2\theta_i & 0 \\ 0 & 0 & c_{v,nl}^{\circ} \end{bmatrix}$$

3.2.3. Dynamic Model

Considering an inertia-dominated regime, both added-mass and drag forces must be taken into account in the environment interaction. According to second Newton law, the force balance for each link is given by the following:

$$m\,\ddot{\mathbf{X}}_0 = \sum_{i=0}^{2}\left(\mathbf{F}_{a,i} + \mathbf{F}_{v,i}^{I} + \mathbf{F}_{v,i}^{II}\right) \tag{14}$$

being m the mass of the robot [45]. Recalling expressions (8), (11), and (13) and substituting them into (14), the force balance equation can be rewritten as follows:

$$m\,\ddot{\mathbf{X}}_0 = \sum_{i=0}^{2}\left[-\mathbf{M}_i\ddot{\mathbf{X}}_i - \mathbf{N}_i\left(\dot{\mathbf{X}}_i - \mathbf{V}_f\right) - \mathbf{R}_i^{I}\dot{\mathbf{X}}_i - \mathbf{R}_i^{II}\left(\dot{\mathbf{X}}_i - \mathbf{V}_f\right)^2\right] \tag{15}$$

Substituting the expressions of $\dot{\mathbf{X}}_i$, $\dot{\mathbf{X}}_i^2$, and $\ddot{\mathbf{X}}_i$ and solving for $\ddot{\mathbf{X}}_0$, the acceleration of the centre of the central link can be estimated as follows:

$$\ddot{\mathbf{X}}_0 = \frac{\mathbf{P}_D\dot{\mathbf{X}}_0 + \mathbf{Q}_D\dot{\mathbf{\Phi}} + \mathbf{Q}_{DD}\ddot{\mathbf{\Phi}} + \mathbf{N}_i\mathbf{V}_f - \sum_{i=0}^{2}\mathbf{R}_i^{II}\left(\mathbf{A}_i\dot{\mathbf{X}}_0 + \mathbf{B}_i\dot{\mathbf{\Phi}} - \mathbf{V}_f\right)^2}{\mathbf{P}_{DD}} \tag{16}$$

where the matrices are defined as follows:

$$\mathbf{P}_D = -\sum_{i=0}^{2}\left[\mathbf{M}_i\mathbf{D}_i + \left(\mathbf{N}_i + \mathbf{R}_i^{I}\right)\mathbf{A}_i\right]$$

$$\mathbf{P}_{DD} = \sum_{i=0}^{2}(m + \mathbf{M}_i\mathbf{C}_i)$$

$$\mathbf{Q}_D = -\sum_{i=0}^{2}\left(\mathbf{N}_i + \mathbf{R}_i^{I}\right)\mathbf{B}_i$$

$$\mathbf{Q}_{DD} = -\sum_{i=0}^{2}\mathbf{M}_i\mathbf{E}_i$$

3.3. Control Strategy for Path Following

This section details the closed-loop control strategy for path following, specifically addressing the control problem associated with Purcell's swimmers.

3.3.1. Control Problem Formulation

In the reviewed literature, only primitives for translation and rotation of the centre of the central link of the Purcell's swimmer have been found. This implies that any movement that the swimmer needs to make or any trajectory to be followed must be performed by executing such gaits.

Following straight paths with no inclination, while seemingly simple, is challenging because translation gaits inherently cause drift along the Y axis. Similarly, complex curved paths with varying curvatures and dimensions cannot be followed by relying solely on X-axis movement. The persistent Y-axis drift further complicates trajectory tracking, causing the swimmer to progressively deviate from its intended path. It is also important to note that all primitives must be executed completely from start to finish, meaning the swimmer must wait for one gait to conclude before initiating another. Finally, external factors like environmental disturbances or inertia can cause the swimmer to deviate from its path more significantly or earlier than anticipated during experiments.

Given this context, a closed-loop control strategy should be proposed that overcomes all these issues. The requirements that the designed control strategy should have are as follows:

1. To correct deviations of the path followed by the robot with respect to the desired one in order to compensate possible drifts.
2. To allow switching between different types of primitives.

Among the existing control strategies, event-based control allows the control action to be modified according to the fulfilment of a logical condition, so that it is possible to change, in this way, the motion primitive to be applied to the swimmer. Other control strategies provide control laws that do not allow to change the motion primitive, which is not useful for this application. Several examples of application of event-based methods in controlling other categories of mobile robots can be found in [36,37], as well as robotic arms in [38,39].

In this case, the logical condition of the event-driven control depends on the tracking error and its derivative to keep the robot on its path. If the error exceeds a set threshold, the motion primitive is adjusted to correct the trajectory and reduce deviations from drift or disturbances. This control also facilitates the use of the two types of primitives seen above: one when the tracking error is below the threshold, and the other when it is exceeded. Moreover, a key advantage is that the strategy allows for waiting for the current primitive to complete before recalculating the tracking error and deciding if a gait modification is needed.

3.3.2. Proposed Control Strategy

The proposed strategy for tracking a trajectory with the Purcell's swimmer is an event-based control according to the scheme shown in Figure 6, where the triggering of the logical condition depends on two variables: the tracking error, better known as position error (e_p), and its derivative ($\dot{e}_p$). Basically, the strategy consists of implementing a motion primitive for translation, when the swimmer is following or approaching the path, combined with the execution of a primitive for rotation, when it is further than a fixed distance and it is moving away from the trajectory. In other words, the proposed strategy switches between translation and rotation primitives depending on a logical function of e_p and $\dot{e}_p$.

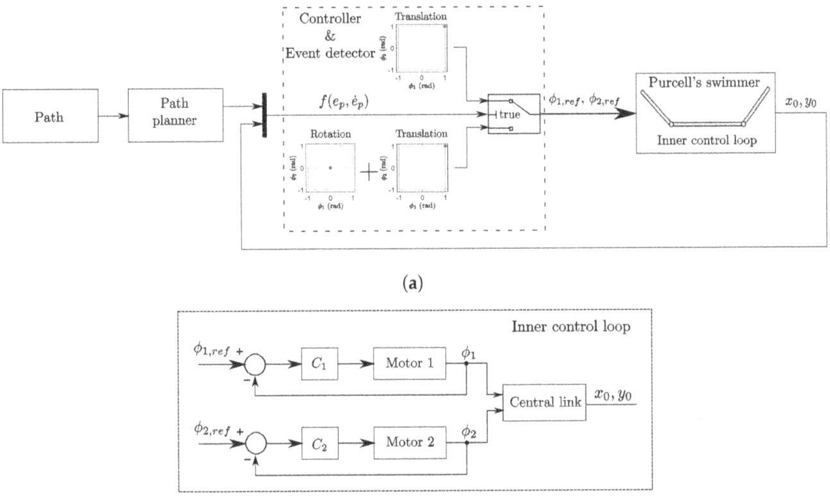

(a)

(b)

Figure 6. Event-driven control in closed-loop for path following of a Purcell's swimmer: (**a**) outer control loop (path following); (**b**) details of inner control loop (actuators).

The first issue to be considered is the type of path, namely, straight or curved, to be followed by the swimmer. Due to the fact that the swimmer is only able to move in a rectilinear direction, the curvature of the path is important because, if the path is curved, it should be divided into a certain number of straight segments so that the swimmer can follow it. The number of segments into which the curved path is divided will depend on the precision desired for the movement of the swimmer. This task will be performed by the path planner.

Secondly, the event detector takes part and evaluates the following triggering condition:

$$f(e_p, \dot{e}_p) = ((|e_p| \geq \Delta) \text{ AND } (\dot{e}_p > 0)) \text{ OR new segment} \tag{17}$$

where Δ is the threshold. According to condition (17), a new event will occur when any of the following situations is met:

- The absolute value of e_p is equal or higher than Δ and its derivative is positive. In this situation, the event detector analyses if the swimmer is moving away from the trajectory, and both conditions concerning e_p and $\dot{e}_p$ must be true for a new event to be detected. Should any of the aforementioned conditions not be met, that is, the swimmer is in proximity to the trajectory and within the threshold ($|e_p| < \Delta$) or if it is approaching the trajectory, thus leading to a reduction in error ($\dot{e}_p < 0$), then any event occurs. The event triggering condition uses the error term (e_p) to ensure the robot remains within the specified Δ of the trajectory. However, successive applications of rotation primitives, though necessary, can induce slight deviations that may cause the swimmer to drift significantly. By considering the derivative of the error ($\dot{e}_p$), the strategy can opt to maintain translational movement when the swimmer is outside Δ but approaching the trajectory, allowing it to naturally converge and re-enter the defined limits without unnecessary and potentially detrimental rotational adjustments.
- A new segment of the path must be followed, in order to redirect the swimmer to the direction of the new segment. This situation is necessary for those paths that are composed of multiple straight segments, such as compound or curved paths divided into straight segments.

The data sent to the event detector are the position of the centre of the central link of the swimmer in the XY plane ($\mathbf{X}_0$), and the event detector calculates the position error e_p as the perpendicular distance between $\mathbf{X}_0$ and the path. Given that all the motion primitives have the same duration (T_g), the logical condition is evaluated periodically, after a motion primitive finishes. If the logical condition is not met, the controller proceeds with executing the translation primitive, as it assumes that the orientation of the swimmer is adequate and, therefore, the swimmer follows the desired path. On the contrary, if the logical condition is met, the controller applies a rotation primitive to adjust the swimmer orientation and rectify its motion in accordance with the desired path.

For comparison purposes and to validate the control strategy, both the tracking error and the mean square error (MSE) have been taken as performance indices, where the latter was given by the following definition:

$$\text{MSE} = \frac{1}{n}\sum_{k=1}^{n} e_{p,k}^2 \tag{18}$$

where n is the number of samples.

In between two events, any data are sent to the controller. Nevertheless, the lateral links of the Purcell's swimmer should be rotating at every instant, as they are implementing the motion primitive. To solve this, two control loops have been considered, as shown in Figure 6. The outer loop (Figure 6a) is the event-based controller, and determines the primitive that the swimmer should implement to follow the trajectory. The inner loop (Figure 6b) is a proportional-derivative (PD) controller that works at every instant to control the rotation of the lateral links, to ensure that the swimmer is implementing a motion primitive.

Concerning the inner control loop, the position of each of the DC motors was firstly identified as a second order system defined as follows:

$$G_p(s) = \frac{K}{s(\tau s + 1)} \tag{19}$$

being τ and K the time constant and the DC gain, respectively.

Secondly, a PD controller of the following form:

$$C(s) = K_P(1 + T_D s) \tag{20}$$

where K_P and T_D are the proportional and the derivative time constants, respectively, was tuned using the root locus method to a settling time of about 0.5 s with no overshoot as design specifications for a step response of $\pi/2$ rad because of the geometrical constraints of the lateral links. The parameters of the system and the controller are indicated in Table 2, where M1 and M2 refer to the motor that rotates l_1 and l_2, respectively. The responses of both motors applying the PD controllers are shown in Figure 7a, for a step reference, and in Figure 7b, for a ramp one. As can be observed, the design specifications are fulfilled.

Table 2. Identification and controller parameters for both actuators of the motor-driven prototype. M1 refers to the motor that rotates segment l_1, while M2 rotates l_2.

Parameters	M1	M2
K	0.2935	0.2730
τ	0.0655	0.068
K_P	19.5	20.0
T_D	0.02	0.02

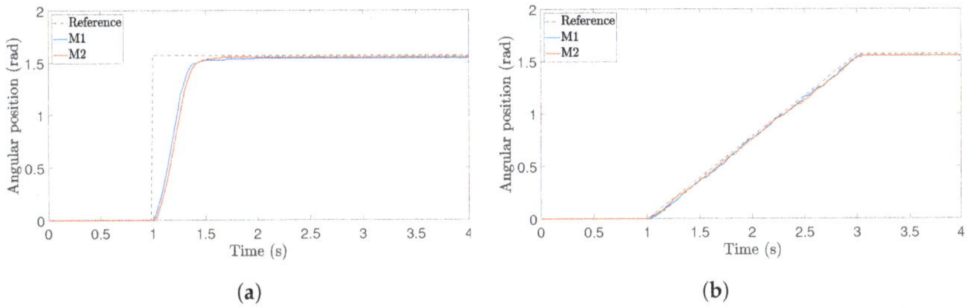

Figure 7. Response of the DC motors of the prototype: (**a**) controlled output for a step reference; (**b**) controlled output for a ramp reference. M1 refers to the motor that rotates l_1 while M2 rotates l_2.

4. Results

This section covers the results obtained in both simulations and experiments carried out with the motor-driven prototype.

4.1. Simulations

To conduct open-loop simulations of the Purcell's swimmer, dynamic model (14) was simulated in MATLAB ® in its R2022b version by solving the differential equation through the Runge–Kutta method. The simulation parameters indicated in Table 3 were considered for the fluid, geometry of the swimmer, and motion primitives. In addition, the drag coefficients were estimated through COMSOL Multiphysics® version 5.5 as detailed in [50], while the added-mass coefficients were approximated to those of a slender body, defined as follows [47]:

$$c^{\parallel}_{a,i} = 0; \quad c^{\perp}_{a,i} = \frac{1}{4}\pi\rho l_i^2; \quad c^{\circ}_{a,i} = \frac{1}{128}\pi\rho l_i^4$$

The added mass of a slender body in the longitudinal direction, i.e., X axis, can be neglected in comparison to the body mass, so the added mass coefficient in this direction was approximated to zero [45,47].

Table 3. Parameters used for motor-driven prototype simulations and experiments.

Water		Swimmer		Gaits	
Parameter	**Value**	**Parameter**	**Value**	**Parameter**	**Value**
Density (ρ)	1000 kg/m^3	Total length (l)	335.78 mm	Amplitude (ϵ)	$\pi/3$ rad
Dynamic viscosity (μ)	1.002·10^{-3} kg/m·s	Relation between links (η)	0.1206	Period (T_g)	4 s
		Mass of the robot (m)	0.479 kg		

The simulation results implementing the clockwise square gait are shown in Figure 8, where the displacement in X and Y axes and the trajectory followed by the centre of the central link have been plotted. The data in Figure 8a corroborate the idea that a positive net displacement on the X axis is consistently achieved. The total displacement achieved is 5.75 m along the X axis, while the displacement with a single gait repetition is 0.19 m. Additionally, an oscillatory motion along the Y axis, typical of motion primitives, is evident. The amplitude of these oscillations, which is dependent on the dimensions of the swimmer, attains approximately 0.12 m in this case, aligning with its dimensions.

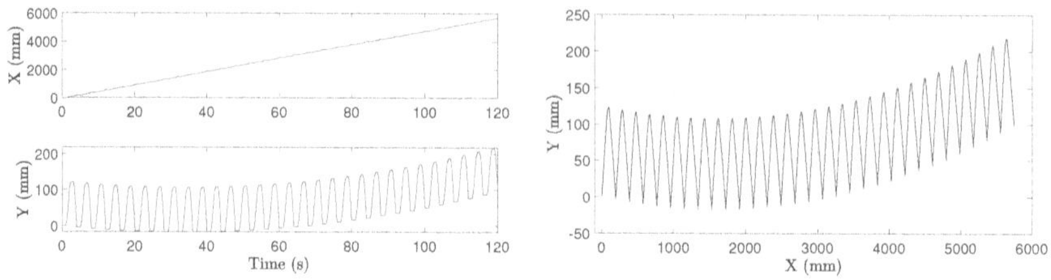

(a) (b)

Figure 8. Simulated displacement of the centre of the central link of Purcell's swimmer navigating within an inertia-dominated regime, considering null fluid velocity and the geometry of the motor-driven prototype, and applying the clockwise square gait with amplitude $\epsilon = 1.0472$ rad: (**a**) displacement in X and Y directions; (**b**) trajectory in the XY plane.

Concerning the trajectory observed in Figure 8b, it deviates from that characteristic of viscosity-dominated regimes. Under these conditions, the swimmer typically traces distinctive figure-eight loops (as depicted in Figure 4). In the present case, however, the loops exhibit a greater spatial extent and fail to close upon completion of the motion primitive, resulting in a trajectory resembling a sawtooth pattern.

Finally, it is evident from Figure 8b that the mean trajectory deviates from the $Y = 0$ axis instead of following a straight line. This behaviour is consistent with results observed in viscosity-dominated regimes, which were considered in the development of the closed-loop path following strategy. For this specific experiment, the final positive Y-axis drift amounts to 10 cm, although the direction and magnitude of the drift vary throughout the simulation period.

In order to assess how external disturbances (specifically, the presence of a uniform flow field) affect the displacement and trajectory of the swimmer, several open-loop simulations under different fluid velocities and directions were conducted. The results are presented in Figure 9 and Table 4. A noticeable impact of the fluid flow on the net displacement and trajectory of the swimmer is shown in Figure 9 in comparison with Figure 8b, with the extent and direction of the deviation depending on the orientation of the flow relative to the motion of the swimmer. Notably, although the selected fluid velocity (0.01 m/s) may appear small in absolute terms, it is considerably high when compared to the size and mass of the swimmer. Nevertheless, the characteristic sawtooth-shaped trajectory remains qualitatively preserved in all cases, indicating that the locomotion pattern is robust to moderate flows.

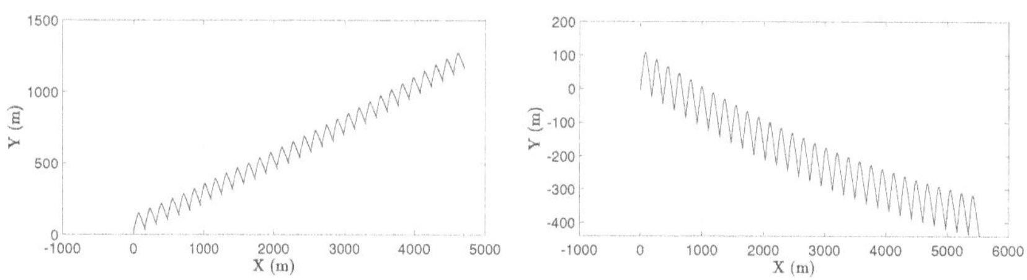

(a) (b)

Figure 9. Simulated trajectory of the centre of the central link of Purcell's swimmer navigating within an inertia-dominated regime under a fluid velocity of 0.01 m/s applying the clockwise square gait with amplitude $\epsilon = 1.0472$ rad: (**a**) fluid velocity in X direction; (**b**) fluid velocity in Y direction.

Table 4 shows a comparison of the displacement and amplitude of oscillations between the case with null fluid velocity and the simulations performed. Focusing on the displacement along the X-axis (since the applied primitive corresponds to translation), it can be observed that, in all cases where $V_f \neq 0$, the net X-displacement decreases compared to the reference case ($V_f = 0$), with reductions ranging from 4% to 22%. Regarding the Y-axis, the displacement increases consistently across all flow conditions, indicating that the swimmer deviates more significantly when exposed to external disturbances. Moreover, the amplitude of the characteristic sawtooth oscillations in the Y direction also increases, from values around 120 mm in the reference case to up to 152 mm under flow. These findings highlight the importance of implementing closed-loop control strategies to effectively regulate the trajectory of the swimmer and compensate for deviations caused by environmental disturbances.

Table 4. Comparison of the simulation results considering different fluid velocities and directions.

$V_{f,x}$ (m/s)	$V_{f,y}$ (m/s)	Δx_0 (mm)	Reduction in Δx_0 with Respect to Reference Case	Δy_0 (mm)	Amplitude of Y Oscillations (mm)
0	0	5749.8	-	99.09	120
−0.01	0	4703.7	18.2%	1165.8	119–152
0	−0.01	5522.6	4.0%	−440.3	111–132
−0.01	−0.01	4483.1	22.0%	623.1	122–137

4.2. Experiments

The experimental procedures and findings derived from testing the motor-driven prototype are covered in this section.

4.2.1. Types of Experiments

This section details the experimental procedures performed with the motor-driven prototype. Specifically, two distinct categories of experiments were conducted:

1. Open-loop experiments: The first experiments carried out with the motor-driven prototype consisted of implementing the translation and rotation primitives that will be used for path following, with the aim of verifying that the direction of the swimmer displacement corresponds to that observed in simulations. Specifically, the square and bi-square primitives from Figure 2 were implemented for translation and rotation, respectively, applying them in clockwise or counterclockwise to obtain displacements in different directions. Hereafter, the translation primitives that provide positive displacement in X axis will be named as positive translation primitives, while those that produce a counterclockwise increase in the swimmer orientation will be called positive rotation primitives, and vice versa. These gaits were repeatedly applied a total of 30 times.
2. Closed-loop experiments: The second type of experiments were carried out to verify the validity of the path following control algorithm. The square and bi-square motion primitives were implemented for translation and rotation of the robot, respectively. Concerning the path to be followed, three types of straight paths were considered to check that the robot was able to follow the trajectories, which were as follows:
    (a) A simple trajectory with no inclination, where the robot only has to change direction if it deviates.
    (b) A 45° inclined trajectory, for which the robot has to make an initial turn and position itself in the same direction as the path to be followed, and then implement the path following control algorithm in the same way as for the trajectory with no inclination.
    (c) A path consisting of two straight segments through a combination of the two previous ones, i.e., a first inclined segment and a second segment with zero

slope, in order to check the transition from one segment to the other at different angles of inclination.

4.2.2. Equipments

Figure 10 shows the setup used for the experiments with the motor-driven prototype. As can be observed, it consists of the following:

- A pool filled with water, as observed in Figure 10a. Due to the dimensions of the prototype, it was necessary to carry out the experiments in a large tank that would allow the robot to move without any possible interference from nearby walls. To this end, the facilities at the University of Castilla-La Mancha (Spain) were used, specifically a pool measuring approximately 3 × 5 metres, large enough to allow the robot to move freely. The height of the pool, approximately 1 m, is also suitable so that the bottom does not interfere with the rotation of the lateral segments of the swimmer when the pool is fully or partially filled.
- A motion capture system to detect the position of the robot at each stage of the experiment. For this purpose, a four-camera system from Qualisys (Qualisys AB, Gothenburg, Sweden) was deployed, as visualised in Figure 10a, which is capable of detecting the position of the markers placed in the prototype cover, as seen in Figure 10b. The software that allows to capture, visualise and record the position of the markers in real time is Qualisys Track Manager (QTM). The acquired position can also be sent in real time to other softwares, such as LabVIEW or MATLAB®, facilitating the development of closed-loop experiments. In this case, LabVIEW 2020 was used to communicate with the robot in real time.
- A computer to run QTM version 2020.3 and LabVIEW 2020 softwares as seen in Figure 10c. In addition, the computer was used to process the data collected in the experiments using MATLAB®, which was also installed on the computer.

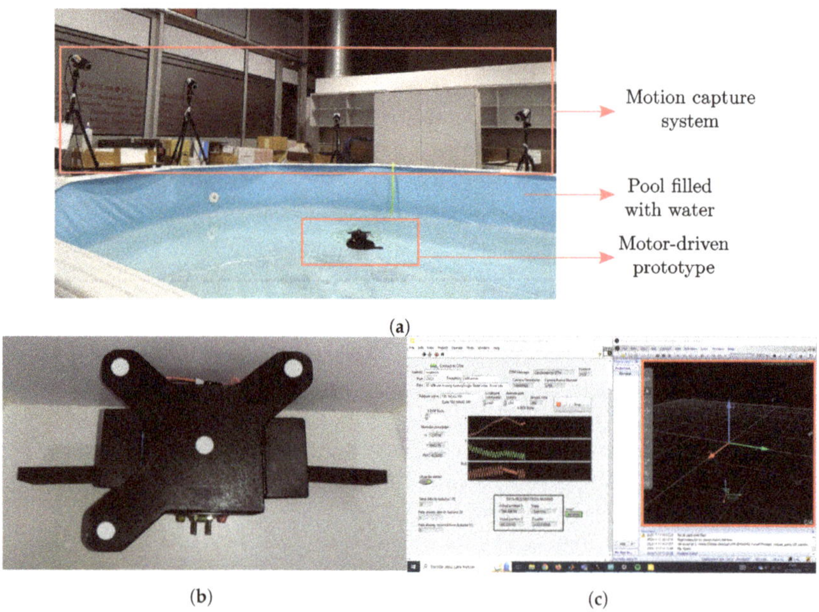

Figure 10. Setup of the experiments carried out with the motor-driven prototype: (**a**) motion capture cameras and pool; (**b**) cover with markers; (**c**) computer with LabVIEW and QTM softwares.

A communication protocol was developed to enable closed-loop experiments and transmit the position of the robot, as detected by the motion capture system, to the robot. This protocol, represented in Figure 11, consisted of three phases: cameras-QTM, QTM-LabVIEW, and LabVIEW-Arduino. Firstly, the cameras communicated with the QTM software using the precision time protocol (PTP) and an Ethernet connection. Then, QTM communicated in real time with LabVIEW via the transmission control protocol/internet protocol (TCP/IP). Lastly, the communication between the computer and the robot was done through LabVIEW. To do this, it was necessary to integrate the exchange of data with both QTM and the robot in the same LabVIEW file. This communication was performed through the user data protocol (UDP) via WiFi.

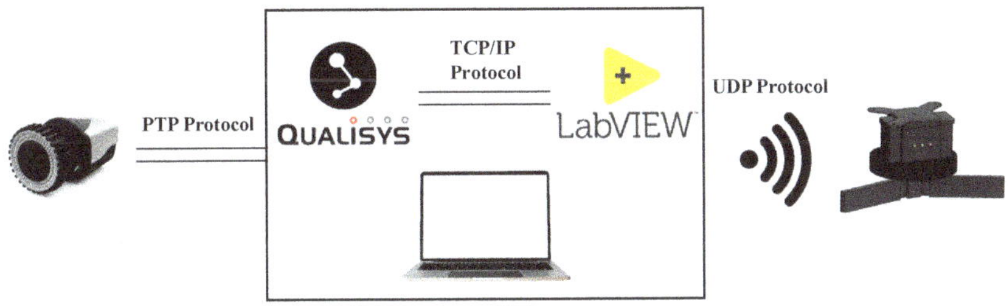

Figure 11. Scheme of the communication protocols developed for the motor-driven prototype experiments.

To ensure reliable communication, a crucial step was selecting the optimal frequency for data exchange between QTM and LabVIEW. A 10 Hz frequency was chosen to prevent data loss or buffer accumulation, which could lead to the control strategy operating incorrectly. Higher frequencies tested resulted in communication delays due to LabVIEW processing limitations. Thus, 10 Hz proved to be the maximum viable frequency for these specific experiments to avoid such drawbacks and ensure the correct execution of the control strategy.

4.2.3. Motion Primitives Experiments

The linear and angular displacements over time of the central link for the four primitives implemented in these experiments are plotted in Figure 12, while the net displacements are tabulated in Table 5. Similar to the simulations results, the swimmer does not trace the eight-shape loop of the viscosity-dominated case. Instead, the trajectory followed by the centre of the central link is composed of upward and downward movements similar to a sawtooth pattern, as already observed in simulations. The amplitude of these movements, although it differs throughout the experiments, achieved approximately 10 cm and is consistent with the dimensions of the swimmer.

In the case of the translation primitives shown in Figure 12a,b, it can be observed that the direction of the displacement in the X axis coincides with that obtained with the simulated model, i.e., the primitive for positive translation coincides with that applied theoretically, which is the clockwise square gait, while the primitive for negative translation is the counterclockwise square gait. Moreover, it can be seen that, in both cases, there is a drift in the Y axis, as already observed in the simulations, as well as a slight change in the orientation of the central segment.

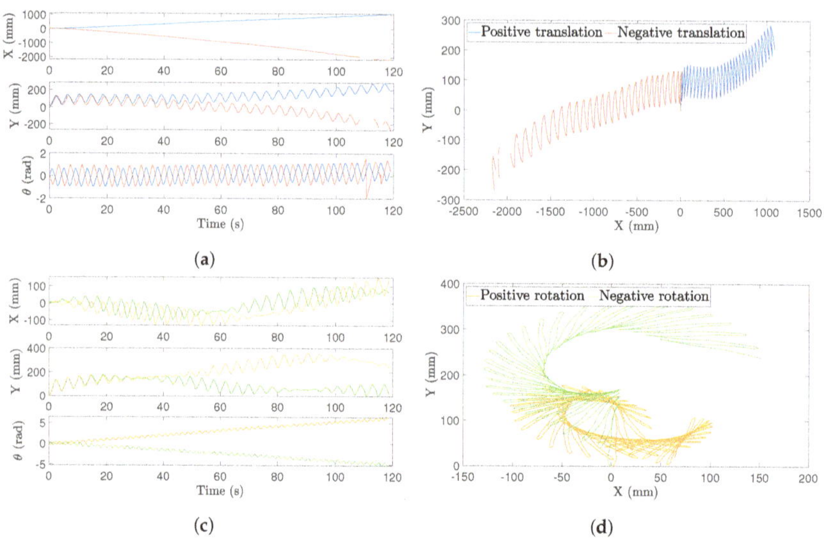

Figure 12. Experimental displacement of motor-driven prototype implementing translation and rotation gaits: (**a**) displacement in three axes implementing translation gaits; (**b**) trajectory implementing translation gaits; (**c**) displacement in three axes implementing rotation gaits; (**d**) trajectory implementing rotation gaits.

However, the amplitude of the displacement is not consistent with the model or between the experiments themselves: since the primitives are the same but applied in opposite directions, it would be expected that the displacements would be also the same, but in opposite directions. Nevertheless, this is not reflected in the results, where it can be seen that the robot moves twice as much in the X axis with the negative translation primitive than with the positive translation gait (see Table 5). This asymmetry could be likely caused by small fabrication inaccuracies in the prototype, particularly a non-uniform mass distribution across the swimmer, which may shift the centre of mass and lead to direction-dependent inertial effects. Such asymmetries are difficult to avoid in physical implementations, especially at this scale, and are amplified under open-loop conditions where no corrective feedback is applied. These results highlight the limitations of open-loop execution and motivate the use of a closed-loop strategy to correct trajectory deviations caused by structural imbalances or external disturbances.

Regarding the rotation primitives, whose results are illustrated in Figure 12c,d, it can be seen that the positive rotation primitive causes a positive change of orientation of the central segment of the robot, and the opposite occurs for the negative rotation primitive. As for the amplitude of the angular displacement, in this case it is similar for both primitives, around 5–6 rad in absolute values. It is also observed that there is a drift in X and Y axes, positive in both cases and of greater amplitude for the negative rotation primitive.

Table 5. Experimental net displacement for translation and rotation gaits, extracted from Figure 12.

Gait	Δx_0 (mm)	Δx_0/gait (mm)	Δy_0 (mm)	Δy_0/gait (mm)	$\Delta \theta_0$ (rad)	$\Delta \theta_0$/gait (rad)
Positive translation	1091.50	36.38	204.95	6.83	0.33	0.011
Negative translation	−2149.95	−71.67	−268.25	−8.94	0.48	0.016
Positive rotation	64.18	2.14	19.19	0.64	6.24	0.208
Negative rotation	151.50	5.05	238.55	7.95	−4.94	−0.16

In view of the results obtained for the translation and rotation primitives, it is worth clarifying the following:

1. With respect to the translation primitives, the above results do not affect path following, since the control strategy should be able to correct the direction of the robot movement regardless of how far it moves in the XY plane and its angular position. What is important in this case is that there is a net displacement in the X axis that is greater than that in the other axes.
2. For rotation primitives, considering the dimensions of the robot and the angular displacement achieved, the drifts in X and Y axes can be neglected and will not affect, to a large extent, path following experiments.

4.2.4. Path Following Experiments

The results of the closed-loop experiments are depicted in Figure 13, where the swimmer trajectory has been represented in blue colour and the red marks correspond to the event detector activation. Evidently, this was not performed after the completion of each gait. These and other modifications to the original strategy were conducted and are indicated below:

- To optimise data exchange between the interacting elements, the control strategy evaluation was not performed after each individual gait execution. Instead, it was determined to wait until four repetitions of the motion primitives were completed, to prevent saturation of the information exchange between the motion capture system and the robot.
- Two threshold values were considered for the experiments: $\Delta_1 = l/3.35 = 100$ mm and $\Delta_2 = l/1.68 = 200$ mm, which will also be referred to as case 1 and 2, respectively. The rationale for selecting these specific threshold values stems from the observed deviations in both simulations and physical experiments. The Y-axis drift per motion primitive exhibits variability between these two contexts. In simulations, this drift ranges from 0.1 mm in the middle of the simulations to 10.41 mm at the end, suggesting a maximum potential cumulative drift of 41.64 mm over four consecutive primitive executions, as planned for the experiments. Notably, the experimental open-loop application of the square primitive reveals even larger deviations, reaching up to 11 mm per primitive, which extrapolates to 44 mm over four repetitions. Consequently, selecting a threshold below 44 mm would likely trigger a new control event and necessitate the application of the rotation primitive at each evaluation of the control strategy. Consequently, thresholds exceeding this critical value, specifically ranging from approximately two to five times the 44 mm-drift, were chosen to avoid excessive and potentially destabilising activation of the rotation primitive.

Figure 13 shows case 1 results in left column and case 2 in the right column. As can be observed, the following conclusions can be drawn:

- Path with no inclination (Figure 13a,b): The results indicate that a lower Δ led to a higher frequency of robot rotations. This is attributed to the earlier exceedance of Δ, necessitating more frequent reorientations towards the desired path. Specifically, case 1 (Figure 13a) exhibited a total of four rotations, whereas case 2 (Figure 13b) involved three rotations. The second rotation in case 2 was required because the initial reorientation was insufficient to maintain the trajectory of the swimmer, leading to further deviation and a subsequent need for correction (evident in the X range of 600–800 mm in Figure 13b).
- Inclined path (in Figure 13c,d): The robot successfully followed the inclined path for both Δ values, with highly similar trajectories observed in both cases. However, in case 2 (Figure 13d), the swimmer executed one additional rotation compared to case 1.

This supplementary rotation occurred near the end of the trajectory due to a deviation away from the desired path. For the remaining rotations along the inclined paths, their timing was notably consistent across both Δ values.

- Combined path (see Figure 13e,f): The swimmer exhibited superior performance in case 2, as depicted in Figure 13f. Initially, the robot rotated at the beginning of the first inclined segment to align its angular orientation and achieve a slope comparable to the desired trajectory. Subsequently, it continued with translational motion until e_p exceeded Δ, at which point it rotated again to reduce the deviation. For the majority of the path, the swimmer remained within the $\pm\Delta$ error bounds until a deviation occurred in the final zero-slope segment, prompting a further rotation to move downwards towards the intended trajectory. Case 1 (Figure 13e) showed unexpected results, with significant swimmer deviation in the range $1000 < X < 1300$ mm, and, although corrective rotations were implemented, the deviation remained considerable. Nevertheless, the robot achieved complete path tracking. The final zero-slope segment involved multiple rotations due to the swimmer orientation exceeding $\pi/2$ rad while targeting a 0 rad slope, requiring repeated adjustments.

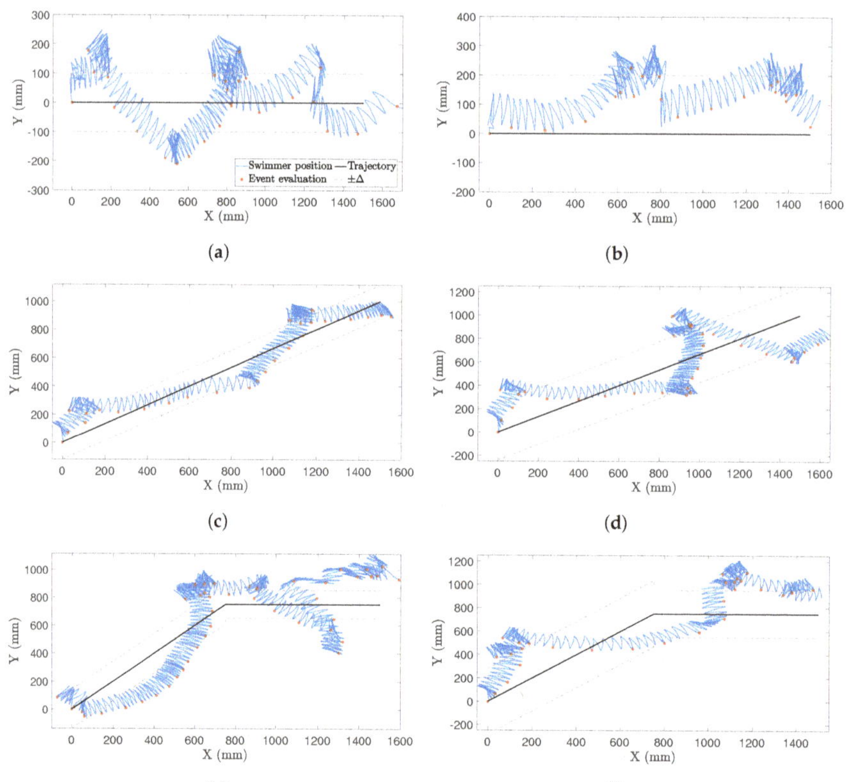

Figure 13. Closed-loop control for path following of straight paths with the motor-driven prototype considering as thresholds $\Delta_1 = 100$ mm and $\Delta_2 = 200$ mm: (**a**) not inclined and Δ_1; (**b**) not inclined and Δ_2; (**c**) inclined and Δ_1; (**d**) inclined and Δ_2; (**e**) combined and Δ_1; (**f**) combined and Δ_2. Red marks (designated as "event evaluation") refer to the event detector activation, i.e., those instants when the triggering condition in the event-based control was evaluated during experiments.

For comparison purposes, open-loop experiments for not inclined and inclined paths were also performed (the combined path was not tested because of the poor results obtained for the inclined one). The results are shown in Figure 14. As can be seen, the swimmer deviated to a large extent from the desired path, so closed-loop control is essential to reduce deviation.

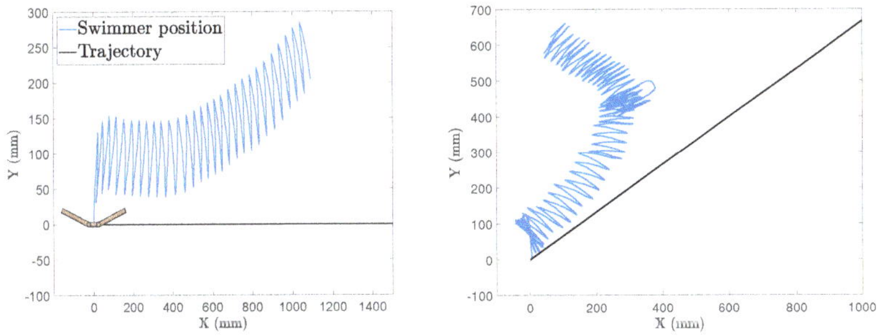

(a) (b)

Figure 14. Experimental open-loop control for path following of straight paths with the motor-driven prototype: (**a**) not inclined; (**b**) inclined.

A schematic of the robot with its actual dimensions has been included in Figure 14a to show the amplitude of the robot movement compared to its size. It is worth noting that, at first glance, the amplitude of the Y-movements appears to be much larger than the size of the robot, but there are two factors that influenced this. On the one hand, the inertia of the robot helped it to move further, so the movements were wider than those observed in the simulations. The upward motion of the robot involved a sequential rotation of its links, first one and then the other, with a similar sequence occurring during downward motion. This coordinated rotation of both links in each vertical movement cycle resulted in a larger amplitude of displacement along the Y axis.

With regard to e_p, it has been calculated for each path, for open- and closed-loop, and for each Δ, and the results are plotted in Figure 15. The time axis has been normalised to t/T_f, with T_f being the final time of the experiment, to improve result visualisation. As can be observed, e_p for open-loop tracking (see Figure 15a) increases progressively until the end of the experiment, as expected from the results shown in Figure 14. Regarding the closed-loop tracking (see Figure 15b,c), it is evident that, for both values of Δ, the robot detected that the threshold had been exceeded and changed its direction of movement to reduce the error. Therefore, the results indicate that, when e_p increases above Δ, it immediately decreases again towards values below the threshold. For the case 1 (see Figure 15b), an increase of the error well above the threshold is observed for $t/T_f \approx 0.7$, which corresponds to the deviation experienced by the swimmer in the range $1000 < X < 1300$ mm in Figure 13e.

For a better comparison, the MSE for each experiment has been calculated and tabulated in Table 6. The data reveal a direct correlation between the Δ value and the MSE across all paths, with the lowest Δ yielding the smallest MSE and thus minimal trajectory deviation. For the path with no inclination, only minor differences are observed between the MSE of the open-loop control and the smallest Δ. This is likely attributable to the shorter duration of the open-loop experiment, which does not cover the entirety of the path (as evident in Figure 14a, where the final displacement is approximately 1100 mm compared to the total path length of 1500 mm). To sum up, it can be concluded that path following is more accurate for lower Δ values in the proposed control strategy.

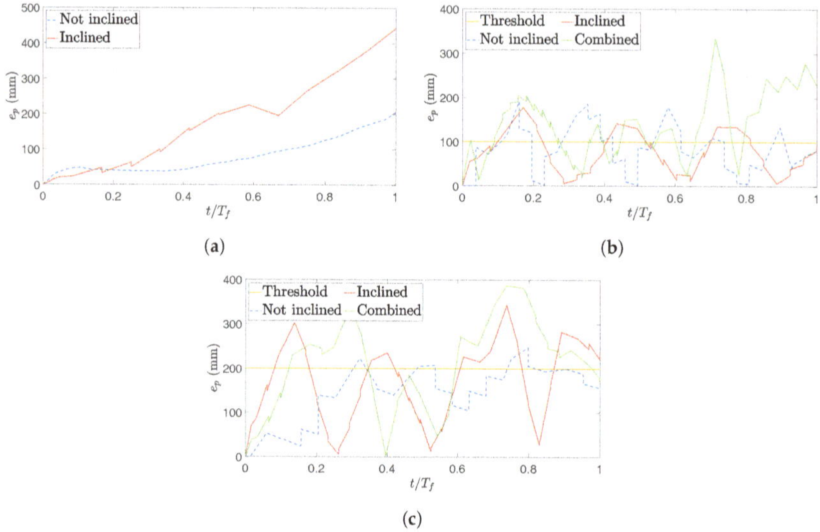

Figure 15. Position errors of path following experiments of straight paths: (**a**) open-loop experiments; (**b**) closed-loop and $\Delta_1 = 100$ mm; (**c**) closed-loop and $\Delta_2 = 200$ mm.

Table 6. MSE ($\times 10^3$) calculated for each path followed by the motor-driven prototype for two values of threshold (Δ).

Path	Open-Loop	Closed-Loop	
		$\Delta_1 = 100$ mm	$\Delta_2 = 200$ mm
Not inclined	9.32	9.05	22.76
Inclined	54.55	6.37	30.30
Combined	-	21.03	47.79

4.3. Discussion

This section includes a brief discussion with a comparison between the simulated and experimental results of the motor-driven prototype.

Several similarities can be found regarding the open-loop experiments and the simulations. First of all, the amplitude of the swimmer movement on the Y axis during the implementation of a motion primitive is similar for both cases (around 10 cm in experiments and 12 cm in simulations), and the loops that the swimmer performs in the XY plane when navigating through viscosity-dominated environments are not observed in any of the results, showing instead a sawtooth pattern.

However, regarding the results, several differences are found in their magnitude. Firstly, the displacement in X is almost six times greater in the simulations than in the experiments, indicating that, for a single repetition of the primitive, the swimmer displaces 19 cm and 3.6 cm in simulations and experiments, respectively. Secondly, differences are also observed in the Y-drift, indicating that the swimmer deviates 10 cm in simulations and 20.5–26.8 cm in experiments, that is, the difference between both ranges from 2.05 to 2.68 times. Thus, the simulations show a larger longitudinal displacement along the X axis, but the experiments reveal a greater Y-drift.

In light of the presented results, several factors were identified that may have influenced the differences between simulations and experiments. Firstly, although the size of the pool should have minimised confinement effects, the enclosed environment might have introduced unaccounted-for forces in the dynamic model. Wall proximity could have influenced robot motion, and fluid oscillations from wall interactions might have affected displacement. Moreover, while maintaining constant depth and protecting electronics, the float itself could have influenced robot dynamics through unmodelled water surface drag forces.

Regarding the dynamic model, although the drag coefficients had been calculated via COMSOL Multiphysics® simulations, they could have deviated from actual values, impacting environmental drag forces and the swimmer displacement. Concerning added-mass coefficients, these were derived from theoretical expressions and might not have accurately reflected real-world values. Discrepancies would have affected added-mass forces and, consequently, the robot motion. Furthermore, the complexity of the model and MATLAB® implementation could have introduced minor discrepancies. Finally, the idealised representation of the fluid environment and hydrodynamic forces within the dynamic model omitted potentially relevant effects. As an example, the oscillatory motion of the swimmer caused the float to sway, resulting in its partial submersion in the fluid, which may have increased the drag.

In the area that the path-following control strategy concerns, the results have shown its effectiveness. However, alternatives or improvements could be proposed in terms of the triggering condition or the implementation of the strategy. Given the dissimilarities between simulation results and experimental data under the conditions explored in this work, it is inadvisable to employ model-dependent triggering criteria like linear predictor-based deadband and model-based approaches for path following. These methods, relying on inaccurate model predictions, would likely yield unsatisfactory control performance. However, promising alternative triggering strategies could be developed using absolute or integral deadband criteria, which assess the rate of deviation from the trajectory by comparing current and past data points.

For enhanced implementation, minimising communication delay and packet loss in the tracking system is crucial for accurate path following. Ideally, the robot should receive its position immediately after each primitive execution via fast communication. A significant advancement would be utilising the onboard positioning system of the robot, eliminating the reliance on external cameras for position detection and transmission.

5. Conclusions

This paper has presented a closed-loop control strategy for path following of Purcell's three-link swimmers on the basis of event-based control. The strategy has been validated through experiments with a 30 cm-length motor-driven Purcell's swimmer prototype within an inertia-dominated regime. The theoretical modelling of the Purcell's swimmer was undertaken, succeeded by a description of the fabricated prototype. Following this, the simulations and experiments conducted were detailed, culminating in a discussion of the findings.

A comparison between simulation and experimental outcomes indicated both similarities and differences. Notably, both approaches showed consistent swimmer direction and overall displacement along the X axis. Furthermore, the extent of upward and downward motion observed in Y direction displayed a sawtooth pattern and similar amplitudes, aligning with the physical dimensions of the prototype. The trajectory followed by the swimmer showed differences from the ideal case at low Reynolds number (Re) conditions (viscosity-dominated regimes), as the eight-shape loops were not traced in this case.

Concerning experimental results, the prototype managed to displace and rotate in the desired directions with translation and rotation primitives, respectively. The closed-loop strategy was tested experimentally for path following with two values of threshold (Δ) and three types of straight paths, comparing with the open-loop alternative by means of the mean square error (MSE). The results showed that the strategy is appropriate for this type of swimmer, as it was able to follow all path types. Moreover, MSE results showed that, the smaller the Δ, the more accurate the tracking.

Future research should focus on refining experimental conditions by minimising communication delays and integrating onboard positioning systems to improve path-following accuracy. Additionally, exploring the robot performance with diverse and more intricate trajectories would be a valuable direction for future investigation. Moreover, future implementations may also incorporate adaptive mechanisms to improve the response to external disturbances. In particular, the integration of adaptive thresholds or disturbance observers could be explored to improve control robustness in environments with variable flow conditions or near-wall effects. In addition, future work may consider the integration of intelligent control techniques, such as fuzzy logic or neural networks, to enhance adaptability in the presence of unmodelled dynamics.

Author Contributions: Conceptualization, I.T. and B.M.V.; methodology, C.N.-G., I.T. and B.M.V.; software, C.N.-G. and L.M.-C.; validation, C.N.-G.; formal analysis, C.N.-G.; investigation, C.N.-G.; resources, I.T., B.M.V. and V.F.-B.; data curation, C.N.-G. and L.M.-C.; writing—original draft preparation, C.N.-G. and I.T.; writing—review and editing, C.N.-G., L.M.-C., I.T., B.M.V. and V.F.-B.; visualization, C.N.-G.; supervision, I.T. and B.M.V.; project administration, I.T. and B.M.V.; funding acquisition, I.T. and B.M.V. All authors have read and agreed to the published version of the manuscript.

Funding: This work has been partially supported by the Agencia Estatal de Investigacion (Ministerio de Ciencia e Innovacion) through the project PID2022-141409OB-C22/AEI/10.13039/501100011033/FEDER, UE, by the Consejeria de Economia e Infraestructuras (Junta de Extremadura) through the grants "Ayuda a Grupos de Investigacion de Extremadura" no. GR21168 and GR18159 and the project IB18109, and by the European Regional Development Fund (FEDER) "A way to make Europe". Cristina Nuevo-Gallardo would like to thank Universidad de Extremadura for its support through the scholarships "Plan de Iniciación a la Investigación, Desarrollo Tecnológico e Innovación" in the 2018 and 2019 editions.

Institutional Review Board Statement: Not applicable.

Informed Consent Statement: Not applicable.

Data Availability Statement: The data will be available under request.

Acknowledgments: Special thanks to Instituto de Investigaciones Energéticas y Aplicaciones Industriales (Universidad de Castilla-La Mancha, Spain) for providing the equipment for the development of the experiments with the designed prototype.

Conflicts of Interest: The authors declare no conflicts of interest.

Abbreviations

The following abbreviations are used in this manuscript:

DOF	Degree-of-freedom
IPMC	Ionic polymer-metal composite
LED	Light-emitting diode
MSE	Mean square error
PD	Proportional-derivative
PLA	Polylactic acid
PTP	Precision time protocol
PWM	Pulse width modulation
QTM	Qualisys Track Manager

Re	Reynolds number
RFT	Resistive force theory
TCP/IP	Transmission control protocol/internet protocol
UDP	User data protocol

Appendix A. Motion Primitives for Translation and Rotation of the Purcell's Swimmer

This appendix includes the definitions of the motion primitives for displacement in X axis and rotation. The unscaled angles s_1 and s_2 for these primitives in their clockwise version are defined as piecewise functions by the following equations. T_g is the gait period and the segments are of equal duration, thus, $t_i - t_{i-1} = t_{i+1} - t_i$.

Square gait:

$$s_1(t) = \begin{cases} 1, & t \in (0, t_1] \\ 1 - \frac{2}{t_2 - t_1}(t - t_1), & t \in (t_1, t_2] \\ -1, & t \in (t_2, t_3] \\ -1 + \frac{2}{T_g - t_3}(t - t_3), & t \in (t_3, T_g] \end{cases}, \quad s_2(t) = \begin{cases} 1 - \frac{2}{t_1} t, & t \in (0, t_1] \\ -1, & t \in (t_1, t_2] \\ -1 + \frac{2}{t_3 - t_2}(t - t_2), & t \in (t_2, t_3] \\ 1, & t \in (t_3, T_g] \end{cases} \tag{A1}$$

Bi-square gait:

$$s_1(t) = \begin{cases} \frac{-1}{t_1} t, & t \in (0, t_1] \\ -1, & t \in (t_1, t_2] \\ -1 + \frac{1}{t_3 - t_2}(t - t_2), & t \in (t_2, t_3] \\ 0, & t \in (t_3, t_4] \\ 0, & t \in (t_4, t_5] \\ \frac{1}{t_6 - t_5}(t - t_5), & t \in (t_5, t_6] \\ 1, & t \in (t_6, t_7] \\ 1 - \frac{1}{T_g - t_7}(t - t_7), & t \in (t_7, T_g] \end{cases}, \quad s_2(t) = \begin{cases} 0, & t \in (0, t_1] \\ \frac{-1}{t_2 - t_1}(t - t_1), & t \in (t_1, t_2] \\ -1, & t \in (t_2, t_3] \\ -1 + \frac{1}{t_4 - t_3}(t - t_3), & t \in (t_3, t_4] \\ \frac{1}{t_5 - t_4}(t - t_4), & t \in (t_4, t_5] \\ 1, & t \in (t_5, t_6] \\ 1 - \frac{1}{t_7 - t_6}(t - t_6), & t \in (t_6, t_7] \\ 0, & t \in (t_7, T_g] \end{cases} \tag{A2}$$

Appendix B. Kinematic Variables

This section develops the expressions for the velocity and acceleration of the i-link, as well as the variables that define these expressions for the central, left (l_1) and right (l_2) segments.

Appendix B.1. Velocity

Regarding the linear and angular velocities of the links, they can be expressed as follows [8,17,22]:

$$\dot{\mathbf{X}}_i = \mathbf{A}_i \dot{\mathbf{X}}_0 + \mathbf{B}_i \dot{\mathbf{\Phi}} \tag{A3}$$

where matrices $\mathbf{A}_i$ and $\mathbf{B}_i$ are defined in [17] as follows:

- Central link: $\mathbf{A}_0 = \mathrm{I}_3$ and $\mathbf{B}_0 = 0_{3\times 2}$
- Left link:

$$\mathbf{A}_1 = \begin{bmatrix} 1 & 0 & \frac{l_0}{2}\sin\theta_0 - \frac{l_1}{2}\sin(\phi_1 - \theta_0) \\ 0 & 1 & -\frac{l_0}{2}\cos\theta_0 - \frac{l_1}{2}\cos(\phi_1 - \theta_0) \\ 0 & 0 & 1 \end{bmatrix}; \ \mathbf{B}_1 = \begin{bmatrix} \frac{l_1}{2}\sin(\phi_1 - \theta_0) & 0 \\ \frac{l_1}{2}\cos(\phi_1 - \theta_0) & 0 \\ -1 & 0 \end{bmatrix}$$

- Right link:

$$\mathbf{A}_2 = \begin{bmatrix} 1 & 0 & -\frac{l_0}{2}\sin\theta_0 - \frac{l_2}{2}\sin(\phi_2+\theta_0) \\ 0 & 1 & \frac{l_0}{2}\cos\theta_0 + \frac{l_2}{2}\cos(\phi_2+\theta_0) \\ 0 & 0 & 1 \end{bmatrix}; \ \mathbf{B}_2 = \begin{bmatrix} 0 & -\frac{l_2}{2}\sin(\phi_2+\theta_0) \\ 0 & \frac{l_2}{2}\cos(\phi_2+\theta_0) \\ 0 & 1 \end{bmatrix}$$

Likewise, the squared velocity of i-link has also been used for the definition of nonlinear drag forces. It can be expressed, in terms of the velocity of the central link and the gait angles, as follows:

$$\dot{\mathbf{X}}_i^2 = \mathbf{G}_i\dot{\mathbf{X}}_0^2 + \mathbf{H}_i\dot{\mathbf{X}}_0 + \mathbf{K}_i\dot{\mathbf{\Phi}}^2 \tag{A4}$$

where matrices $\mathbf{G}_i$, $\mathbf{H}_i$ and $\mathbf{K}_i$ are defined as follows:

- Central link: $\mathbf{G}_0 = \mathrm{I}_3$, $\mathbf{H}_0 = 0_{3\times3}$, and $\mathbf{K}_0 = 0_{3\times2}$
- Left link:

$$\mathbf{G}_1 = \begin{bmatrix} 1 & 0 & \left(\frac{l_0}{2}\sin\theta_0 - \frac{l_1}{2}\sin(\phi_1-\theta_0)\right)^2 \\ 0 & 1 & \left(-\frac{l_0}{2}\cos\theta_0 - \frac{l_1}{2}\cos(\phi_1-\theta_0)\right)^2 \\ 0 & 0 & 1 \end{bmatrix}; \ \mathbf{H}_1 = \begin{bmatrix} h_{1,11} & 0 & h_{1,13} \\ 0 & h_{1,22} & h_{1,23} \\ 0 & 0 & h_{1,33} \end{bmatrix};$$

$$\mathbf{K}_1 = \begin{bmatrix} \left(\frac{l_1}{2}\sin(\phi_1-\theta_0)\right)^2 & 0 \\ \left(\frac{l_1}{2}\cos(\phi_1-\theta_0)\right)^2 & 0 \\ 1 & 0 \end{bmatrix}$$

being:

$$\begin{aligned} h_{1,11} &= 2\dot{\theta}_0\left(\frac{l_0}{2}\sin\theta_0 - \frac{l_1}{2}\sin(\phi_1-\theta_0)\right) + 2\dot{\phi}_1\left(\frac{l_1}{2}\sin(\phi_1-\theta_0)\right) \\ h_{1,13} &= 2\dot{\phi}_1\left(\frac{l_0}{2}\sin\theta_0 - \frac{l_1}{2}\sin(\phi_1-\theta_0)\right)\left(\frac{l_1}{2}\sin(\phi_1-\theta_0)\right) \\ h_{1,22} &= 2\dot{\theta}_0\left(-\frac{l_0}{2}\cos\theta_0 - \frac{l_1}{2}\cos(\phi_1-\theta_0)\right) + 2\dot{\phi}_1\left(\frac{l_1}{2}\cos(\phi_1-\theta_0)\right) \\ h_{1,23} &= 2\dot{\phi}_1\left(-\frac{l_0}{2}\cos\theta_0 - \frac{l_1}{2}\cos(\phi_1-\theta_0)\right)\left(\frac{l_1}{2}\cos(\phi_1-\theta_0)\right) \\ h_{1,33} &= -2\dot{\phi}_1 \end{aligned}$$

- Right link:

$$\mathbf{G}_2 = \begin{bmatrix} 1 & 0 & \left(-\frac{l_0}{2}\sin\theta_0 - \frac{l_2}{2}\sin(\phi_2+\theta_0)\right)^2 \\ 0 & 1 & \left(\frac{l_0}{2}\cos\theta_0 + \frac{l_2}{2}\cos(\phi_2+\theta_0)\right)^2 \\ 0 & 0 & 1 \end{bmatrix}; \ \mathbf{H}_2 = \begin{bmatrix} h_{2,11} & 0 & h_{2,13} \\ 0 & h_{2,22} & h_{2,23} \\ 0 & 0 & h_{2,33} \end{bmatrix};$$

$$\mathbf{K}_2 = \begin{bmatrix} 0 & \left(-\frac{l_2}{2}\sin(\phi_2+\theta_0)\right)^2 \\ 0 & \left(\frac{l_2}{2}\cos(\phi_2+\theta_0)\right)^2 \\ 0 & 1 \end{bmatrix}$$

being:

$$
\begin{aligned}
h_{2,11} &= 2\dot{\theta}_0\left(-\frac{l_0}{2}\sin\theta_0 - \frac{l_2}{2}\sin(\phi_2+\theta_0)\right) + 2\dot{\phi}_2\left(-\frac{l_2}{2}\sin(\phi_2+\theta_0)\right) \\
h_{2,13} &= 2\dot{\phi}_2\left(-\frac{l_0}{2}\sin\theta_0 - \frac{l_2}{2}\sin(\phi_2+\theta_0)\right)\left(-\frac{l_2}{2}\sin(\phi_2+\theta_0)\right) \\
h_{2,22} &= 2\dot{\theta}_0\left(\frac{l_0}{2}\cos\theta_0 + \frac{l_2}{2}\cos(\phi_2+\theta_0)\right) + 2\dot{\phi}_2\left(\frac{l_2}{2}\cos(\phi_2+\theta_0)\right) \\
h_{2,23} &= 2\dot{\phi}_2\left(\frac{l_0}{2}\cos\theta_0 + \frac{l_2}{2}\cos(\phi_2+\theta_0)\right)\left(\frac{l_2}{2}\cos(\phi_2+\theta_0)\right) \\
h_{2,33} &= 2\dot{\phi}_2
\end{aligned}
$$

Appendix B.2. Acceleration

Regarding the acceleration of i-link, it can be obtained through the derivative of $\dot{\mathbf{X}}_i$ and can be expressed, in matrix form, as follows:

$$\ddot{\mathbf{X}}_i = \mathbf{C}_i\ddot{\mathbf{X}}_0 + \mathbf{D}_i\dot{\mathbf{X}}_0 + \mathbf{E}_i\ddot{\mathbf{\Phi}} \tag{A5}$$

being matrices $\mathbf{C}_i$, $\mathbf{D}_i$ and $\mathbf{E}_i$ defined, for each link, as follows:

- Central link: $\mathbf{C}_0 = \mathrm{I}_3$, $\mathbf{D}_0 = 0_{3\times 3}$, and $\mathbf{E}_0 = 0_{3\times 2}$
- Left link:

$$\mathbf{C}_1 = \begin{bmatrix} 1 & 0 & \frac{l_0}{2}(\sin\theta_0 + \cos\theta_0) + \frac{l_1}{2}(\cos(\phi_1-\theta_0) - \sin(\phi_1-\theta_0)) \\ 0 & 1 & \frac{l_0}{2}(\sin\theta_0 - \cos\theta_0) + \frac{l_1}{2}(-\cos(\phi_1-\theta_0) - \sin(\phi_1-\theta_0)) \\ 0 & 0 & 1 \end{bmatrix};$$

$$\mathbf{D}_1 = \begin{bmatrix} 0 & 0 & -l_1\dot{\phi}_1\cos(\phi_1-\theta_0) \\ 0 & 0 & l_1\dot{\phi}_1\sin(\phi_1-\theta_0) \\ 0 & 0 & 0 \end{bmatrix};\ \mathbf{E}_1 = \begin{bmatrix} \frac{l_1}{2}(\sin(\phi_1-\theta_0) + \cos(\phi_1-\theta_0)) & 0 \\ \frac{l_1}{2}(-\sin(\phi_1-\theta_0) + \cos(\phi_1-\theta_0)) & 0 \\ -1 & 0 \end{bmatrix}$$

- Right link:

$$\mathbf{C}_2 = \begin{bmatrix} 1 & 0 & \frac{l_0}{2}(-\sin\theta_0 - \cos\theta_0) + \frac{l_2}{2}(-\sin(\phi_2+\theta_0) - \cos(\phi_2+\theta_0)) \\ 0 & 1 & \frac{l_0}{2}(-\sin\theta_0 + \cos\theta_0) + \frac{l_2}{2}(-\sin(\phi_2+\theta_0) + \cos(\phi_2+\theta_0)) \\ 0 & 0 & 1 \end{bmatrix};$$

$$\mathbf{D}_2 = \begin{bmatrix} 0 & 0 & -l_2\dot{\phi}_2\cos(\phi_2+\theta_0) \\ 0 & 0 & -l_2\dot{\phi}_2\sin(\phi_2+\theta_0) \\ 0 & 0 & 0 \end{bmatrix};\ \mathbf{E}_2 = \begin{bmatrix} 0 & \frac{l_2}{2}(-\sin(\phi_2+\theta_0) - \cos(\phi_2+\theta_0)) \\ 0 & \frac{l_2}{2}(-\sin(\phi_2+\theta_0) + \cos(\phi_2+\theta_0)) \\ 0 & 1 \end{bmatrix}$$

References

1. Tovi, E.; Zigelman, A.; Or, Y. Dynamics, stability and bifurcations of a planar three-link swimmer with passive visco-elastic joint using "ideal fluid" model. *Int. J. Non-Linear Mech.* **2024**, *167*, 104859. [CrossRef]
2. Song, S.; Kim, J.; Kim, T.; Song, Y.W.; Yu, S.C. Development of a Biomimetic Underwater Robot for Bottom Inspection of Marine Structures. *Int. J. Control Autom. Syst.* **2023**, *21*, 4041–4056 . [CrossRef]
3. Gorma, W.; Post, M.A.; White, J.; Gardner, J.; Luo, Y.; Kim, J.; Mitchell, P.D.; Morozs, N.; Wright, M.; Xiao, Q. Development of Modular Bio-Inspired Autonomous Underwater Vehicle for Close Subsea Asset Inspection. *Appl. Sci.* **2021**, *11*, 5401. [CrossRef]
4. Lyu, F.; Xu, X.; Zha, X.; Li, Z.; Yuan, H. A Snake Eel Inspired Multi-joint Underwater Inspection Robot for Undersea Infrastructure Intelligent Maintenance. In Proceedings of the OCEANS 2022—Chennai, Chennai, India, 21–24 February 2022; pp. 1–6. [CrossRef]
5. Purcell, E.M. Life at low Reynolds number. *Am. J. Phys.* **1977**, *45*, 3–11. [CrossRef]
6. Becker, L.E.; Koehler, S.A.; Stone, H.A. On self-propulsion of micro-machines at low Reynolds number: Purcell's three-link swimmer. *J. Fluid Mech.* **2003**, *490*, 15–35. [CrossRef]
7. Hatton, R.L.; Choset, H. Geometric Swimming at Low and High Reynolds Numbers. *IEEE Trans. Robot.* **2013**, *29*, 615–624. [CrossRef]

8. Wiezel, O.; Or, Y. Optimization and small-amplitude analysis of Purcell's three-link microswimmer model. *Proc. R. Soc. A Math. Phys. Eng. Sci.* **2016**, *472*, 4–25. [CrossRef] [PubMed]
9. Tam, D.; Hosoi, A.E. Optimal stroke patterns for Purcell's three-link swimmer. *Phys. Rev. Lett.* **2007**, *98*, 068105. [CrossRef]
10. Or, Y. Asymmetry and Stability of Shape Kinematics in Microswimmers' Motion. *Phys. Rev. Lett.* **2012**, *108*, 258101. [CrossRef]
11. Kadam, S.; Banavar, R. Geometry of locomotion of the generalized Purcell's swimmer: Modelling, controllability and motion primitives. *IFAC J. Syst. Control* **2018**, *4*, 7–16. [CrossRef]
12. Grover, J.; Zimmer, J.; Dear, T.; Travers, M.; Choset, H.; Kelly, S.D. Geometric Motion Planning for a Three-Link Swimmer in a Three-Dimensional low Reynolds-Number Regime. In Proceedings of the 2018 Annual American Control Conference (ACC), Milwaukee, WI, USA, 27–29 June 2018; pp. 6067–6074.
13. Alouges, F.; DeSimone, A.; Giraldi, L.; Zoppello, M. Self-propulsion of slender micro-swimmers by curvature control: N-link swimmers. *International J. Non-Linear Mech.* **2013**, *56*, 132–141. [CrossRef]
14. Kadam, S.; Joshi, K.; Gupta, N.; Katdare, P.; Banavar, R.N. Trajectory tracking using motion primitives for the Purcell's swimmer. In Proceedings of the 2017 IEEE/RSJ International Conference on Intelligent Robots and Systems (IROS), Vancouver, BC, Canada, 24–28 September 2017; pp. 3246–3251.
15. Giraldi, L.; Martinon, P.; Zoppello, M. Controllability and optimal strokes for N-link microswimmer. In Proceedings of the Proceedings of the 52nd IEEE Conference on Decision and Control, Firenze, Italy, 10–13 December 2013; pp. 3870–3875.
16. Ramasamy, S.; Hatton, R.L. Soap-bubble optimization of gaits. In Proceedings of the IEEE 55th Conference on Decision and Control (CDC),Las Vegas, NV, USA, 12–14 December 2016; pp. 1056–1062. [CrossRef]
17. Wiezel, O.; Or, Y. Using optimal control to obtain maximum displacement gait for Purcell's three-link swimmer. In Proceedings of the 2016 IEEE 55th Conference on Decision and Control (CDC), Las Vegas, NV, USA, 12–14 December 2016; pp. 4463–4468.
18. Alouges, F.; DeSimone, A.; Giraldi, L.; Or, Y.; Wiezel, O. Energy-optimal strokes for multi-link microswimmers: Purcell's loops and Taylor's waves reconciled. *New J. Phys.* **2019**, *21*, 043050. [CrossRef]
19. Ramasamy, S.; Hatton, R.L. The Geometry of Optimal Gaits for Drag-Dominated Kinematic Systems. *IEEE Trans. Robot.* **2019**, *35*, 1014–1033. [CrossRef]
20. Wiezel, O.; Ramasamy, S.; Justus, N.; Or, Y.; Hatton, R.L. Geometric analysis of gaits and optimal control for three-link kinematic swimmers. *Automatica* **2023**, *158*, 111223. [CrossRef]
21. Deng, S.; Cowan, N.; Bittner, B. Adaptive Gait Modeling and Optimization for Principally Kinematic Systems. In Proceedings of the IEEE 2024 International Conference on Robotics and Automation (ICRA), Yokohama, Japan, 13–17 May 2024; pp. 12571–12577. [CrossRef]
22. Gutman, E.; Or, Y. Symmetries and gaits for Purcell's three-link microswimmer model. *IEEE Trans. Robot.* **2016**, *32*, 53–69. [CrossRef]
23. Passov, E.; Or, Y. Dynamics of Purcell's three-link microswimmer with a passive elastic tail. *European Phys. J. E Soft Matter Biol. Phys.* **2012**, *35*, 78. [CrossRef]
24. Alouges, F.; Desimone, A.; Giraldi, L.; Zoppello, M. Can Magnetic Multilayers Propel Artificial Microswimmers Mimicking Sperm Cells? *Soft Robot.* **2015**, *2*, 117–128. [CrossRef]
25. Alouges, F.; DeSimone, A.; Giraldi, L.; Zoppello, M. Purcell magneto-elastic swimmer controlled by an external magnetic field. *IFAC-PapersOnLine* **2017**, *50*, 4120–4125. [CrossRef]
26. Grover, J.; Vedova, D.; Jain, N.; Travers, M.; Choset, H. Motion Planning, Design Optimization and Fabrication of Ferromagnetic Swimmers. In Proceedings of the Robotics: Science and Systems (RSS), Freiburg im Breisgau, Germany, 22–26 June 2019; pp. 79–87.
27. Moreau, C. Local controllability of a magnetized Purcell's swimmer. *IEEE Control Syst. Lett.* **2019**, *3*, 637–642. [CrossRef]
28. Zigelman, A.; Ben Zvi, G.; Or, Y. Dynamics of Purcell-type microswimmers with active-elastic joints. *Phys. Rev. E* **2024**, *110*, 014207. [CrossRef]
29. Serrano, A.J.; Nuevo-Gallardo, C.; Traver, J.E.; Tejado, I.; Vinagre, B.M. Purcell's three-link microswimmer based on IPMC: Simulations in COMSOL Multiphysics. *IEEE Lat. Am. Trans.* **2022**, *20*, 474–480. [CrossRef]
30. Nuevo-Gallardo, C.; Tejado, I.; Hunt, A.; Vinagre, B.M. IPMC-Based Purcell's Three-Link Swimmer: Simulations and Experiments at Low-Reynolds Conditions. *Actuators* **2024**, *13*, 498. [CrossRef]
31. Van Stratum, B.J.; Austin, M.P.; Shoele, K.; Clark, J.E. Comparative Model Evaluation with a Symmetric Three-Link Swimming Robot. In Proceedings of the 2022 IEEE/RSJ International Conference on Intelligent Robots and Systems (IROS), Kyoto, Japan, 23–27 October 2022; pp. 2672–2678. [CrossRef]
32. Grover, J.S. Geometric Approaches to Motion Planning for Two Classes of Low Reynolds Number Swimmers. Master's Thesis, Carnegie Mellon University, Pittsburgh, PA, USA, 2018.
33. Aranda-Escolástico, E.; Guinaldo, M.; Heradio, R.; Chacon, J.; Vargas, H.; Sánchez, J.; Dormido, S. Event-Based Control: A Bibliometric Analysis of Twenty Years of Research. *IEEE Access* **2020**, *8*, 47188–47208. [CrossRef]

34. Hertneck, M.; Meister, D.; Allgöwer, F. Current trends and future directions in event-based control. *arXiv* **2025**, arXiv:2505.22378. [CrossRef]
35. Zhang, X.M.; Han, Q.L.; Ge, X.; Ding, D.; Ning, B.; Zhang, B.L. An overview of recent advances in event-triggered control. *Sci. China Inf. Sci.* **2025**, *68*. [CrossRef]
36. Postoyan, R.; Bragagnolo, M.; Galbrun, E.; Daafouz, J.; Nesic, D.; Castelan, E. Nonlinear event-triggered tracking control of a mobile robot: Design, analysis and experimental results. In Proceedings of the 9th IFAC Symposium on Nonlinear Control Systems, Toulouse, France, 4–6 September 2013; pp. 318–323.
37. Santos, C.; Martínez-Rey, M.; Espinosa, F.; Gardel, A.; Santiso, E. Event-Based Sensing and Control for Remote Robot Guidance: An Experimental Case. *Sensors* **2017**, *17*, 2034. [CrossRef]
38. Wang, Y.; Chen, J.; Mai, X.; Bi, S.; Cheng, Y.; Xi, N. Event-Based Planning and Control for Teleoperation of Hot Line Work Robot. In Proceedings of the IEEE 8th Annual International Conference on CYBER Technology in Automation, Control, and Intelligent Systems, Tianjin, China, 19–23 July 2018; pp. 339–343. [CrossRef]
39. Jie, Z.; Aihua, Z.; Qian, Q. Event Triggered Feedback Linearization Sliding Mode Control for Trajectory Tracking by Multi-joint Robotic Manipulator. In Proceedings of the 2019 International Conference on Robotics, Intelligent Control and Artificial Intelligence, Shanghai China, 20–22 September 2019; pp. 33–40. [CrossRef]
40. Nuevo-Gallardo, C.; Traver, J.E.; Tejado, I.; Vinagre, B.M. Purcell's Three-Link Swimmer: Assessment of Geometry and Gaits for Optimal Displacement and Efficiency. *Mathematics* **2021**, *9*, 1088. [CrossRef]
41. Nuevo-Gallardo, C.; Traver, J.E.; Tejado, I.; Vinagre, B.M. Path Following for Purcell's Swimmers: An Event-Based Control Approach. In Proceedings of the 15th APCA International Conference on Automatic Control and Soft Computing, Caparica, Portugal, 6–8 July 2022; pp. 487–497.
42. Vilanova, R.; Visioli, A. *PID Control in the Third Millennium: Lessons Learned and New Approaches*; Advances in Industrial Control; Springer: London, UK, 2012.
43. Astolfi, A.; Marconi, L. *Analysis and Design of Nonlinear Control Systems: In Honor of Alberto Isidori*, 1st ed.; Decision Engineering; Springer: Berlin/Heidelberg, Germany, 2008.
44. Vasyutynskyy, V.; Kabitzsch, K. Event-based control: Overview and generic model. In Proceedings of the IEEE International Workshop on Factory Communication Systems (WFCS), Nancy, France, 18–21 May 2010; pp. 271–279. [CrossRef]
45. Pettersen, K.Y. Snake robots. *Annual Rev. Control* **2017**, *44*, 19–44. [CrossRef]
46. Traver, J.E. Diseño de un Robot Nadador de Pequeñas Dimensiones Tipo Flagelo Eucariótico Artificial. Aplicaciones Médicas. Ph.D. Thesis, University of Extremadura, Badajoz, Spain, 2023.
47. Newman, J.M. *Marine Hydrodynamics*, 40th Anniversary Edition ed.; The MIT Press: Cambridge, MA, USA, 2017.
48. Long, C.; Qin, X.; Bian, Y.; Hu, M. Trajectory tracking control of ROVs considering external disturbances and measurement noises using ESKF-based MPC. *Ocean. Eng.* **2021**, *241*, 109991. [CrossRef]
49. Yang, H.; Yan, Z.; Zhang, W.; Gong, Q.; Zhang, Y.; Zhao, L. Trajectory tracking with external disturbance of bionic underwater robot based on CPG and robust model predictive control. *Ocean. Eng.* **2022**, *263*, 112215. [CrossRef]
50. Nuevo Gallardo, C. Robots Nadadores Tipo Purcell: Alternativas de Diseño y Estrategias de Locomoción. Ph.D. Thesis, University of Extremadura, Badajoz, Spain, 2024.

Disclaimer/Publisher's Note: The statements, opinions and data contained in all publications are solely those of the individual author(s) and contributor(s) and not of MDPI and/or the editor(s). MDPI and/or the editor(s) disclaim responsibility for any injury to people or property resulting from any ideas, methods, instructions or products referred to in the content.

robotics

MDPI

Article

Design an Adaptive PID Control Based on RLS with a Variable Forgetting Factor for a Reconfigurable Cable-Driven Parallel Mechanism

Elham Khoshbin , Martin J.-D. Otis * and Ramy Meziane

Automatic and Interactive Robotic Laboratory, Department of Applied Science, Université du Québec à Chicoutimi, Chicoutimi, QC G7H 2B1, Canada; elham.khoshbin1@uqac.ca (E.K.); rmeziane@uqac.ca (R.M.)
* Correspondence: martin_otis@uqac.ca

Abstract: This paper proposes a two-layer adaptive proportional–integral–derivative (PID) controller for precise pose control of a six-degree-of-freedom cable-driven parallel robot with eight cables, specifically designed to handle dynamic changes caused by the movement of attachment points. The positions of the attachment points on the base are adjusted to avoid collisions between humans and cables, where humans and robots are working in a shared workspace. The inherent nonlinearity of the robot system was addressed using model identification based on the recursive least squares (RLS) algorithm equipped with an adaptive forgetting factor. This method enables real-time updates to the dynamic model of the robot, thereby ensuring accurate parameter estimation as the attachment points move. The combination of the PID controller and RLS algorithm enhances the system's ability to respond effectively to changing dynamics. Simulation results highlight the superior accuracy, robustness, and adaptability of the proposed approach, making it well suited for applications requiring a reliable performance in dynamic and unpredictable environments. The proposed method can guarantee human safety, while the end effector tracks the desired trajectory.

Keywords: cable-driven parallel mechanism; adaptive controller; recursive least squares; collision avoidance

1. Introduction

Cable-driven parallel mechanisms (CDPMs) have attracted considerable research interest, owing to their advantages, such as lightweight structures, cost-effectiveness, ease of installation, and high precision. These mechanisms are widely used in industrial applications for heavy-load transportation and in haptic systems that require precise motion control. CDPMs encounter a variety of challenges, including workspace analysis [1–3], tension distribution algorithms (TDA) [2,4,5], singularity analysis [6,7], pose control, and collision avoidance [8,9]. Notably, physical design [10,11] remains one of the most critical and complex challenges, as it fundamentally affects the system's performance and feasibility. Cheng et al. 2023 [12] proposed an optimization method for the positions of cable attachment points in a reconfigurable CDPM under various workspace conditions. It formulates wrench-feasibility, wrench-closure, and interference-free constraints as polynomial functions or variables. It minimizes cable forces or maximizes tension factors using advanced optimization techniques that are applicable to different reconfiguration mechanisms, such as rails, unmanned ground vehicles (UGVs), and unmanned aerial vehicles (UAVs). However, designing an RCDPM using movable attachment points to ensure safe human–robot interaction in shared workspaces by preventing cable–human collisions is a major challenge. To address this issue, Khoshbin et al., 2022 [13] proposed adjusting the position of the attachment point along the z-axis on the base. Specifically, when the minimum distance between a human and a cable, estimated using the KKT method, approaches a predefined safety threshold, the attachment points are repositioned to prevent potential contact. As discussed in this paper, such adjustments inherently alter cable lengths and tensions, significantly affecting system dynamics.

Furthermore, Youssef and Otis, 2020 [14] suggested modifying the attachment point positions along the Z-axis to mitigate cable–cable collisions, further enhancing system safety, adaptability, and operational efficiency. Geometric modifications have been implemented for several reasons, such as preventing collisions between cables or between humans and cables and ensuring accurate end effector positioning remains a significant challenge. To address this, various control strategies, including proportional–integral–derivative (PID) controllers, have been investigated to improve performance, stability, and overall system efficiency.

Zake et al., 2020 [15] proposed a visual servo control approach for the ACROBOT CDPM, a 6-DOF system with eight cables, ensuring accurate end effector positioning despite modeling errors and perturbations. This study introduced a new control-stability workspace, although the end effector orientation remained constant. Awais et al. 2018 [16] presented a vision-based control system for a 3-DOF planar CDPM with four cables, using a fixed camera on the end effector. Cable tensions are measured via load cells, whereas a visual marker enables the localization and tracking of the CDPM. This study highlights the impact of camera calibration and marker size on the system accuracy. A robust algorithm integrates camera calibration with real-time visual marker monitoring to improve performance. Bayani et al., 2015 [17] proposed a PID control strategy for a planar CDPM to enhance end effector tracking. The controller parameters were tuned using pole placement, by positioning closed-loop poles at the desired locations. The optimization was performed using differential evolution, particle swarm optimization, and genetic algorithms.

Picard et al., 2018 [18] presented a PID feedforward control strategy for CAROCA, a 6-DOF CDPM with eight cables. Three control schemes are proposed: (a) a PD torque controller with real-time mass input, (b) a PD controller with a mass estimator, and (c) a PD controller with a mass estimator and compensator. Real-time payload estimation is integrated into the feedforward term to compensate for the payload mass and friction, thereby enhancing trajectory tracking. The controller parameters are updated based on the payload mass, thereby achieving greater accuracy than the PD control. The RMS end effector position error was 60 mm for the PD, with a 58% reduction for heavier payloads and a 91% reduction for the feedforward-PD.

Jiesinuer et al., 2021 [19] presented a 3-DOF planar CDPM with four cables and derived its dynamic model using D'Alembert's principle and the principle of virtual work. The proposed approach integrates torque control, cable force optimization, and fuzzy control. A fuzzy algorithm dynamically tunes the PD parameters in real time and achieves higher accuracy than a fixed-gain PD torque controller. Zhou et al., 2023 [20] proposed a fuzzy PID controller for a 3-DOF CDPM with four cables by utilizing an adaptive whale optimization algorithm (FPID-AWOA). This method achieves higher trajectory tracking accuracy than fuzzy PID with particle swarm optimization (FPID-PSOA). FPID-AWOA reduces the tracking errors by 51.2% and 19.5% in the x direction, 64.2% and 49.7% in the y direction, and 29.1% and 12.2% in the z direction, respectively. Khalilpour et al., 2020 [21] proposed a wave-based controller for an ARAS-CAM 3-DOF CDPM, with four cables to manage the cable loss. The design requires no precise calibration or installation, effective control of loosened cables, or reduction in vibrations. The results showed improved performance and smoother tracking compared to conventional cascade controllers. Khalilpour et al., 2019 [22,23] proposed a cascade controller for an ARAS-CAM 3-DOF CDPM with four cables to address the system uncertainties. This approach models the actuator and power transmission dynamics using an inner loop for cable force control and an outer loop with a robust sliding mode. The system stability was analyzed using the Lyapunov method. The results show an improved performance compared to the sliding mode controller. Khalilpour et al., 2018 [24] proposed a robust sliding mode control for a 3-DOF CDPM with four cables to ensure closed-loop stability using the Lyapunov matrix. This method accounts for uncertainties in attachment points and cable models while operating in Cartesian coordinates, without calibration or inverse kinematics. This study analyzes sliding vector surface variations and Cartesian error manifolds. Controller gains were selected to ensure stability under a 10% uncertainty in the end effector's mass and attachment point positions.

Abdolshah, S., and Barjuei, E. S. (2015) [25] present LQ controller for a 3-DOF CDPM with four cables, optimizing a performance index based on Riccati's equation to compute the end effector position, velocity, and motor torque. The proposed controller ensures accurate trajectory tracking while maintaining the motor torque within the design limits. Tho, T.P. and N.T. Thinh, 2021 [26] propose an ANFIS-based control approach for a 6-DOF CDPM with eight cables. This method predicts cable sagging using a first-order Sugeno ANFIS model with 81 rules and three generalized Gaussian membership functions. The inputs include the kinematic structure, cable tension, and tension distribution. Lu et al., 2022 [27] analyzed closed-loop stability using a reinforcement-learning-based control approach for a 6-DOF CDPM with eight cables. This method compensates for the uncertainties caused by friction and cable elasticity. Kumar et al., 2019 [28] proposed an input-output feedback linearization control for a 6-DOF CDPM with four cables. A linear feedback controller was designed, using the pole placement method with and without noise to achieve effective trajectory tracking. However, the workspace considerations have not yet been addressed.

Kiani, A. and S.K.-e. Mashhadi, 2017 [29] proposed a Lyapunov-based adaptive control for the Samen SpaceCam CDPM with four cables, considering a linear model with unknown parameters. The approach employs a model reference adaptive control with an adjustable feedback controller to enhance disturbance rejection and tracking performance. The closed-loop stability was ensured using the Lyapunov function. In 2017, Yoon, J. et al. [30] proposed an adaptive control method for a planar 3-DOF CDPM with four cables to track the desired position. The cables were modeled as axial springs, with an unknown constant stiffness coefficient estimated by the controller. The system generates cable lengths as inputs and maintains trajectory tracking despite a 40% parameter estimation error, thereby reducing tracking error and residual vibrations. Aghaseyedabdollah et al., 2022 [31] proposed an adaptive PID controller in which the PID sliding surface gains were tuned via a fuzzy system. The optimization algorithm optimizes fuzzy membership functions. The closed-loop stability was analyzed using the Lyapunov function. This method reduces chattering and enhances robustness against load disturbances and uncertainties. Santos et al., 2019 [32] proposed a model predictive controller (MPC)-based control framework, consisting of prediction and optimization. This method integrates the actuation redundancy resolution within the MPC, eliminating the need for a tension-distribution algorithm. The results showed improved position tracking performance, outperforming PID and sliding mode controllers. Song, C. and D. Lau, 2022 [33] propose an MPC for a 2-link planar CDPM and a 6-DOF spatial CDPM to track desired trajectories. This paper presents a workspace analysis that reformulates the optimization problem into a convex form under uncertainty. Recursive feasibility and stability are strictly ensured in the nominal case, with inherent robustness under non-nominal conditions.

The control of RCDPMs presents significant challenges, due to their strong nonlinearities and the necessity to maintain performance under continuously changing geometric configurations. Traditional adaptive control strategies, such as the adaptive control presented by Ji, H. et al., (2020) [34], mainly address passive uncertainties, including unknown payload, friction, or cable stiffness, while assuming fixed attachment points. Similarly, advanced methods developed for interaction safety, such as Fuzzy-PID methods presented by Tong, Lina et al., 2024 [35] and Liang, Xu et al., 2021 [36] concentrate on the system's mechanical properties (stiffness/damping) or managing continuous human interaction force. Moreover, a zero-force control framework, based on a fuzzy-PID method presented by Tong, Lina et al., 2024 [35], has been proposed for post-stroke rehabilitation training, where adaptive impedance modulation was used to enhance human–robot interaction comfort. Likewise, works focusing on specialized kinematic designs, such as the method presented by Lei, Yanqiang et al., 2024 [37], remain limited to geometric analysis and do not extend to dynamic control under reconfiguration. However, these studies typically do not address the broader dynamic control challenge in general reconfigurable systems. Recent works on real-time reconfiguration planning and fault-tolerant control have underlined the importance of multi-layer architectures to handle both intentional reconfigurations (for workspace optimization) and unintentional ones (due to cable failure). For example, Raman, Adhiti et al., 2023 [38] effectively employs an interactive multiple model (IMM) adaptive filter for fault diagnosis and operational recovery. Yet, such approaches mainly facilitate decision-making at the planning level and fail to provide immediate real-time compensation for the abrupt changes in dynamic parameters that are directly induced by geometric reconfiguration. These step-like variations generate active uncertainties far beyond the scope of conventional passive uncertainty compensation. Similarly, Raman Thothathri, Adhiti, 2022 [39] integrates screw-theory-based modeling with deep reinforcement learning (DRL) to manage configuration-dependent dynamics. While theoretically rigorous, its heavy computational load and quasi-static assumptions restrict its real-time applicability, and practical constraints, such as tension limits or fast parameter adaptation, are not explicitly addressed.

Most existing controllers are primarily designed for CDPMs with fixed attachment points [18,40–42]. In RCDPMs, modifying attachment points to prevent cable collisions introduces uncertainty, affecting the force transmission, mass matrices, and overall dynamics. These variations, including changes in the cable length, attachment angle, and system dynamics, require adaptive or robust control for effective handling. Frequent modifications may require real-time model updates or dynamic controller adjustment. To enhance reliability, the integration of adaptive control with a primary control strategy is recommended. A promising approach involves real-time system modeling, which allows for continuous updates based on real-time estimation. Recursive least squares (RLS) is a powerful tool for real-time parameter estimation in adaptive control. Initially designed for linear systems with fixed parameters, it can be adapted for time-varying systems using a forgetting factor, prioritizing recent data, while reducing the influence of older data. An RLS with a variable forgetting factor further improves the accuracy by dynamically adjusting the data weighting, thereby enabling the precise tracking of system dynamics. This adaptability allows controllers to respond immediately to changes, thus enhancing the overall performance and stability.

Compared to other methods, such as the adaptive robust control based on singular perturbation theory [43], this paper presents a two-layer scheme that offers a simpler yet dynamically adaptive structure. Instead of estimating uncertainty bounds, it directly identifies and tracks dynamic model parameters, which are crucial for reconfigurable systems with abrupt geometric changes.

As a contribution of this paper, a two-layer control structure is proposed for a reconfigurable cable-driven parallel mechanism, in which, as the first contribution, the first layer adjusts the attachment points on the base in real time to avoid human–cable collisions. As the second contribution, the second layer controls the end effector motion by adaptive PID, based on RLS.

In the second layer, an adaptive PID controller is developed, integrating an online model identification scheme based on RLS, with a variable forgetting factor to continuously update the system model under geometric reconfiguration and model uncertainties. The RLS algorithm dynamically updates the parameters of the nominal linearized model while accounting for changes in the Jacobian matrix and system dynamics caused by large attachment point displacements, thereby incorporating uncertainties directly into the control constraints. The RLS-identified model provides real-time parameter estimates that enable online adaptation of the PID gains to maintain precise trajectory tracking during attachment point movements. This adaptive framework enhances controller robustness and stability, making it particularly effective for RCDPMs, where unpredictable variations in the attachment points significantly influence the system dynamics. Simultaneous management of human safety and trajectory accuracy is achieved by integrating geometric and dynamic control layers, allowing for collision avoidance without compromising tracking performance. This results in a lightweight controller with fast response and strong real-time applicability. So, this two-layer architecture (i) directly identifies and tracks dynamic parameters across reconfigurations, (ii) integrates a constrained tension-distribution layer to enforce safety limits, and (iii) remains computationally lightweight for practical real-time implementation.

This paper is organized into three main sections. Section 2 introduces the mathematical nonlinear model (used as the physical simulation model) and the corresponding nominal linearized models with variable attachment points, along with a two-layer control framework. In the first layer, the positions of the attachment points are estimated to prevent cable–human collisions, whereas the second layer controls the pose of the end effector. Within the second layer, the parameters of the nominal linearized model are continuously updated using the RLS algorithm, which then inform the design of the PID controller. These layers operate concurrently and interact in a dynamic manner. Section 3 presents simulation results that validate the proposed approach. The subsequent section details the controller implemented for the RCDPM model in the MATLAB R2025b simulations.

2. The Schematic of the Proposed Control Architecture with Adaptive PID

This study proposes a control strategy for an RCDPM with eight cables, where eight tensile servomotors control the position of the end effector and eight translation servomotors adjust the attachment points vertically. As illustrated in Figure 1, the proposed RCDPM control structure comprises two layers that operate simultaneously. This design enhances real-time adaptability, enabling efficient collision avoidance and precise trajectory tracking, while ensuring high system performance. System identification estimates a nominal model to adapt to dynamic changes, owing to moving attachment points in the z direction. This model enables real-time controller updates and ensures precise trajectory tracking through continuous tension estimation. Definitions of all parameters are available in Appendix C.

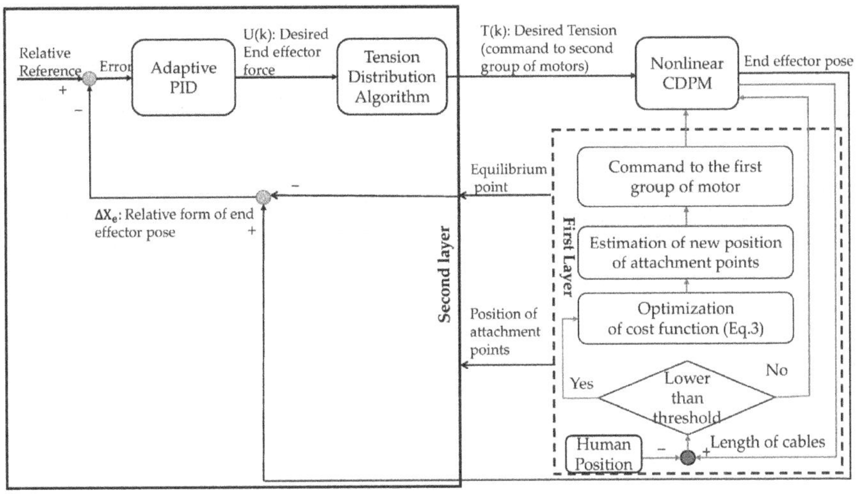

Figure 1. Schematic of proposed two-layer RCDPM control.

The first layer manages the geometric model and collision detection by adjusting the attachment points on the base to prevent collisions and to adapt to dynamic changes. It calculates cable distances, optimizes new positions, and moves attachment points using eight vertical servomotors along the z-axis, while maintaining cable length constraints. These adjustments occur gradually at a lower update rate than in real-time cable tension control.

The second layer controls the pose of the end effector using a dynamic model, ensuring stability and precise trajectory tracking as the attachment points move. Sensors collect input data (e.g., cable tensions) and output data (e.g., end effector positions), and the parameters of the nominal linearized model are updated via RLS. In the RCDPM, both layers interact, requiring careful management to achieve stability and optimal performance. The first layer adjusts the attachment points based on human positions and cable tensions from the second layer to prevent collisions, whereas these adjustments alter the cable lengths and angles, necessitating tension recalibration in the second layer. The second layer controls the cable tension and tracks the end effector, thereby ensuring an accurate force distribution. Although the motors in the first and second layers operate independently, changes in the attachment points (controlled by the first layer) indirectly influence cable tension in the second layer. If tension feedback from the lower layer to the upper layer is unnecessary, the two layers can operate partially independently to improve modularity and efficiency. To manage these interactions, the RLS algorithm continuously updates the system parameters at each time step. This study integrated system identification with PID control [44] to enhance the stability and accuracy of the reconfigurable CDPMs.

The proposed first-layer framework to avoid collisions between humans and cables is detailed in Algorithm 1, whereas Algorithm 2 outlines the controller's implementation steps. In Algorithm 1, function z_new is proposed to estimate the position of attachment points to keep distance between human and cables in safe distance $\min_z \|d_{hi} - d_{hisafe}\|^2$. This algorithm attempts to maintain the maximum distance between cables and humans by displacing the attachment points (Anew) such that the cables move as far away from the obstacles (human or object) as possible. In Algorithm 2, if the RLS update fails due to numerical instability or ill-conditioning, the parameter vector is reinitialized to prevent error accumulation and to restore stability before continuing the estimation. The Matlab code based on the presented pseudocode is available online in [45] and is cited in the paper.

Algorithm 1: First Layer: Attachment Point Position Adjustment

Function Main Kinematic Control Loop (N, A_0, X_{e0}, system_config)
Inputs:

- $N \in \mathbb{N}$: *Total number of time steps (time horizon)*
- $A_0 \in \mathbb{R}^{n_c \times 3}$: *Initial attachment points (for* n_c *cables) in x, y and z directions*
- *System_config: system configuration (e.g., safety threshold* d_{safe}*, acceptable threshold* d_{accept}*, Workspace W, Maximum velocity* v_{max}*, human position* P_h*)*
- d_{safe}: *Safe distance between human and cables*
- $X_{end}\mathbb{R}^6$: *End effector pose over time*
- $X_{e0}\mathbb{R}^6$: *Initial end effector pose*

Outputs:

- $A \in \mathbb{R}^{n_c \times 3 \times N}$: *Updated attachment points over time*
- $X_{eq} \in \mathbb{R}^{3 \times N}$: *Equilibrium points over time*

```
    Initialize:
    Set k ← 1
    Initialize Attachment Points A ← A0
    For k = 1 to N do:
    Compute Shortest Distance (d_min) ← KKTsolver(P_h, A[:, :, k], X_end)
If d_min < d_safe then
    Collision Risk ← True
    Else
    Collision Risk ← False
    End If

    //Check if end effector and cables are within workspace limits
    Compute tensions T ← TensionSolver(A, X_e)
      If any(T < T_min) OR any(T > T_max)
    WorkspaceValid ← False

   L ← CableLengths(A, X_e)
   If any(L < L_min) OR any(L > L_max):
  WorkspaceValid ← False

    # Singularities/poor conditioning
   J ← Jacobian(A, X_e)
      Else If det(J*J') < epsilon
    WorkspaceValid ← False

# Equilibrium proximity constraint
   If norm(X_eq − X_e, 2) > 0.5:
return False

If (Collision Risk = True) OR (Workspace Valid = False)
     Then //Adjustment Needed
       Solving function z_new ← Solve Optimization(Objective Function, Constraints)
      where Constraints include
```

Algorithm 1: *Cont.*

- *Collision Avoidance* $d_{min} \geq d_{safe}$
- *Workspace Limits* $X_e[k] \epsilon W$
- *Maximum velocity of movement* $\|z_{new} - z_{prev}\|_2 \leq v_{max}\Delta t$
- *Maximum distance between the equilibrium point and end effector position* $\|X_{eq} - X_e\|_2 \leq 0.5$

A[:,:,k] ← Update Attachment Points (z_new)
Else
//No Adjustment
A[:,:,k] ← A[:,:,k−1]
End If
Transmit attachment points position to first group of motors in first layer (A[:,:,k])
End For
Return (A, X_{eq}*)*

Algorithm 2: Second layer: RCDPM adaptive PID loop

Inputs:
$N \in \mathbb{N}$: *Total number of time steps (time horizon)*
$X_{e0} \in \mathbb{R}^{n_x}$: *Initial position and rotation of end effector where* n_x *is number of output*
$\theta_0 \in \mathbb{R}^{n_\theta}$: *Initial_model_params* (e.g., *ARX model coefficients) where*
n_θ *is the number of parameters for each output.*
system_config: *System configuration* (e.g., *input/output dimensions, sampling time dt)*
pid_tuning_params: *Parameters for PID tuning*
rls_params: *Parameters for RLS* (e.g., *forgetting factor, initial covariance)*
X_{eq}: *equilibrium point from first layer*
Outputs:
$U \in \mathbb{R}^{n_u \times N}$: *optimal control inputs applied over time*
$X_e \in \mathbb{R}^{n_x \times N}$: *matrix of measured system outputs over time*
$\theta \in \mathbb{R}^{n_\theta \times N}$: *updated model parameters over time*

Begin:
Initialize:
Set k ← 1
Initialize the covariance matrix $P \leftarrow P_0$
Initialize forgetting factor $\lambda \leftarrow \lambda_0$
Initialize input $U \leftarrow zeros(n_u, N)$
Initialize end effector pose $X \leftarrow zeros(n_x, N)$
Initialize model parameters $\theta \leftarrow zeros(n_\theta, N)$
Set dt//Time step
Defined the desired trajectory $X_{desired}$

For k = 1 to N do:
//Update the dynamic model of CDPM (Appendix A to simulate nonlinear dynamics)
$u_{previous} \leftarrow$ *Input from previous step*
X_e*[1:6,k]←* x_m *(Measured current outputs by sensors* (e.g., *pose)*

Algorithm 2: *Cont.*

//Defined ARX model (Equation (A15), Appendix B) in relative form $\Delta X_e = X_e - X_{eq}$
//Update Model Parameters
Defined $\phi \leftarrow$ *ConstructRegressor*(x_m, $u_{previous}$, *gravity, system_configuration*)
$$\phi = [\Delta X_e(t-1)\ldots X_e(t-n_a)\ \Delta U(t-1)\ldots U(t-n_b)]$$
Estimated parameters of ARX
$\theta(k) \leftarrow$ *UpdateRLS*($\theta(k-1)$, ϕ, X, P, λ)
If UpdateRLS failed = true"
Then Log "RLS update failed at time step k = ", k
$\theta(k) \leftarrow \theta_0$ *Reset to initial params*
End If

//Compute Optimal Control Input
Tracking Error(k) $\leftarrow \Delta X_d\,[k] - \Delta X_e$
Pid_gains $\leftarrow$*//Compute* K_p, K_i, K_d *for MIMO*
$\Delta F(k) \leftarrow$ *PID_task(e(k), e_dot, e_int)*
$F(k) \leftarrow F_{eq}(k) + \Delta F(k)$ *//Add equilibrium feedforward (optional but recommended)*
$U(k) \leftarrow F(k)$ *//Input of system in task space*
//Tension distribution with constraints
$J \leftarrow$ *Jacobian*(A, $X_e(k)$)
(T(:,k), status) $\leftarrow$ *DistributeTension*(J, $F(k)$, T_{prev}, *Limits*)
//transmit tension to the second group of motors
End For

Return $(T(:,k), X_e(:,k), \theta(k))$
End

The next section presents more information on system identification using the RLS in the nominal model of the RCDPM. An estimated nominal model was used to design the proportional–integral–derivative (PID) controller. The proposed RCDPM controller consists of two steps. First, an adaptive strategy using real-time RLS updates the linearized linear model to estimate the transfer functions under changing conditions. Second, PID minimizes pose errors, even with model uncertainties, by adjusting cable forces and updating controller parameters for precise tracking. Further details are in Sections 2.1 and 2.2.

2.1. Dynamic and Kinematic Model of 6 DOF CDPM with 8 Cables

This section presents the nonlinear RCDPM model used in the MATLAB simulations to generate end effector poses based on real-time cable tension inputs. In the absence of real-world data, the simulated input-output data validate the RLS algorithm for parameter estimation. The control strategy employed eight tensile servomotors for position control and eight translation servomotors for attachment point adjustments. To simplify the modeling, the pulley dynamics were ignored, and the cables were assumed to be massless and inextensible. The kinematic and linearized dynamic models of the robot [46] are detailed, with attachment points moving per step in the z direction, whereas tensile servomotors regulate cable tensions for precise trajectory tracking. The attachment points are allowed to move in the z direction in this study to simplify the reconfiguration process and focus on vertical adjustments. However, the algorithm is formulated in a three-dimensional form (x, y, z) to maintain generality, so that in future works, the attachment points can also be reconfigured along the x and y directions without modifying the overall structure of the algorithm.

The pose of the end effector is given by $X_e = [x_e\ \varphi_e]^T$ where the $x_e = [x\ y\ z]^T$ and $\varphi_e = \left[\varphi_x\ \varphi_y\ \varphi_z\right]^T$ are the position and orientation of the center of the end effector, respectively. The kinematics and constraints of the CDPM were presented in [13,46]. The dynamic model of the CDPM in the operation space is given by Equation (1) [5].

Eight rectilinear translation servomotors adjusted the attachment points vertically, altering the Jacobian and system dynamics, including the mass, damping, and stiffness matrices. The attachment points were reconfigured in the z direction for each sample. The dynamics presented in Equations (1) and (2) and the kinematic parameters are described in detail in [47]. Equation (1) is the dynamic simulation model of the RCDPM, which is employed in the simulations as a substitute for the physical model. Equation (2) is the linearized dynamic model of the robot, which is derived from the full nonlinear dynamic model (Equation (1)), using the Taylor series expansion around an equilibrium point (X_{eq}). This transformation to relative variables ($\Delta X_e = X_e - X_{eq}$) is essential for implementing our relative controller. It shifts the controller's focus to small deviations from the equilibrium point (X_{eq}), which simplifies the controller's task and makes it more specific to what actually needs to be corrected.

More details of the dynamic model and parameters of CDPM are available in Appendix A. The relative controller, which operates on the deviation from the equilibrium point $X_e - X_{eq}$, performs better than an absolute controller. This is because the relative approach makes the controller's task simpler and more specific. It separates the system's physics from the path-tracking objective, allowing the controller to focus only on what actually needs to be corrected.

$$[M(X_e)]_{6\times6}\ddot{X}_{e_{6\times1}} + \left[C\left(X_e, \dot{X}_e\right)\right]_{6\times1} + [K(X_e)]_{6\times1} + G_{6\times1} = \left[A^T{}_v(\varphi_{e_0})\right]_{6\times6}\Delta F_{ev_{6\times1}} \quad (1)$$

$$M_{0_{6\times6}}\Delta\ddot{X}_e + C_{0_{6\times6}}\Delta\dot{X}_e + K_{0_{6\times6}}\Delta X_e = \left[A^T{}_v(\varphi_{e_0})\right]\Delta F_{ev_{6\times1}} \quad (2)$$

More details on the mass, spring, and damper matrices of the nonlinear and linear models are presented in [47]. The next section discusses the system identification method for estimating the parameter model of the CDPM.

2.2. First Layer: Estimation of the Position of Attachment Points on the Base

The first layer focuses on geometric and kinematic models of CDPM. Modifying the attachment points on the base potentially causes the end effector to fall outside the workspace or deviate significantly from its intended trajectory. To ensure both safety and stability, this paper introduces an optimized cost function for determining new attachment points. This cost function is designed to prevent collisions between humans and cables, and ensure that the end effector remains within the workspace boundaries. The cost objective function is given by Equation (3). $d_{h_{isafe}}$ is the maximum safe distance between human and cable and is chosen to be 0.2 m in this research.

$$J = min_z \left\|d_{hi} - d_{h_{isafe}}\right\|^2 \geq 0 \quad (3)$$

However, there are five constraints:

$$\begin{cases} 0 \leq Z_i \leq 3 \\ d_{hi} \geq 0.2 \\ \left| z_i - z_{i,prev} \right| \leq maximum\ movement \\ x_{end\ effector} \in Workspace \\ Kinematic\ tension : T_{min_i} < T < T_{max_i} \\ \left\| x_{eq} - x_{endeffector} \right\|_2 \leq maximum\ distance\ end\ effector\ and\ equilibrium\ point = 0.5\ \mathrm{m} \end{cases} \quad \forall i = 1, \ldots\ldots, n_{cables}$$

This cost function is used to determine (or minimize) the objective and optimized position of attachment points on the base, while limitations of distance between human and cables and existing end effectors inside workspaces are the main constraints. Also, the maximum acceptable velocity of moving attachment points on the base should be considered. The cost function is solved numerically at each time step, using a constrained optimization approach implemented through MATLAB's fmincon function. This solver determines the decision variables (e.g., attachment point positions) that minimize the cost function while satisfying all physical and safety constraints.

2.3. Second Layer: Pose Control of RCDPM

This section presents the system identification method and PID controller for the second layer to track the desired pose of the end effector.

2.3.1. System Identification

To estimate the mechanism parameters, input–output signals were collected by using a nonlinear dynamic model, owing to the absence of a physical model. The PID controller is designed based on a nominal linearized model, and the parameters of this model are estimated by recursive least squares (RLS), depending on the system characteristics. Linearization with offline parameters, which are fixed over time, is only valid near specific points. For larger movements, the errors increase, requiring multiple controllers and adding complexity and potential instability. In a CDPM with moving attachment points along the z-axis, continuous changes alter the mass, damping, and stiffness matrices, resulting in insufficient fixed-point linearization. Instead, RLS is more suitable because it continuously updates the system model in real time, thereby capturing dynamic variations.

In Section 2.3.2, the parameters of the nominal model are determined by using offline RLS. Offline RLS leverages predefined input and output signals from the initial configuration to estimate the parameters of the nominal model. These estimated parameters remain fixed and non-adaptive, as they are not updated in real time. The use of offline RLS is recommended in scenarios where the exact parameters of the motors and CDPM are inaccessible, providing a practical solution for parameter estimation under such constraints.

2.3.2. Non-Adaptive PID Controller

As shown in Figure 2, the offline RLS identifies the parameters of the nominal model for the PID controller design, providing a simplified representation of the system behavior. The parameters of the model, derived from the pre-collected data, remained fixed, and the PID parameters were tuned accordingly. Offline RLS only estimates the fixed or nominal model, and therefore, the controller remains non-adaptive.

RLS estimates the system parameters using open-loop or closed-loop data [48]. Open-loop offers higher accuracy but risks instability, whereas closed-loop ensures stability but introduces noise, requiring techniques such as instrumental variables (IV) for accuracy. An open loop is preferable for stable systems, whereas a closed loop is safer for unstable systems with appropriate noise filtering. Control Loop 1 outlines a non-adaptive approach with a fixed ARX and controller parameters. In fact, N_1 and N_2 represent the number of time steps for the first and second control loops, respectively.

N_1 corresponds to the kinematic modification layer, which computes the adjustment of the attachment points on the base to avoid collisions.

N_2 corresponds to the dynamic control layer, which performs end effector trajectory tracking through cable tension control.

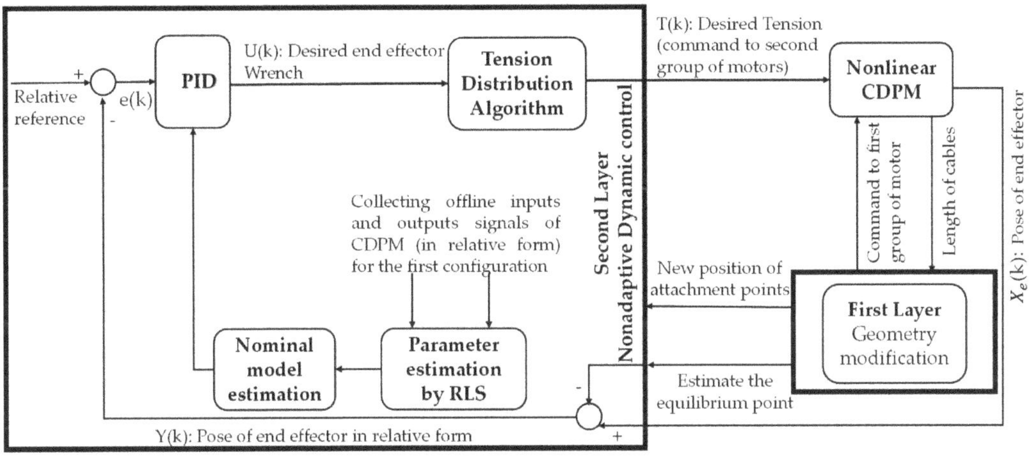

Figure 2. Schematic of non-adaptive PID for RCDPM.

The non-adaptive controller utilizes fixed gains. To determine these fixed parameters, offline RLS (recursive least squares) is employed in this paper. This process involves executing the RLS algorithm only once on pre-collected data (the system's inputs and outputs in the initial fixed configuration of the RCDPM). The goal is to estimate a fixed set of nominal model parameters for the initial equilibrium point. However, the use of these fixed parameters places the final controller in the category of non-adaptive control because, as long as these parameters are not updated continuously during system operation (online), the system lacks an adaptive loop, resulting in low robustness against sudden changes and dynamic uncertainties (such as those caused by moving attachment points), and its tracking performance rapidly deteriorates.

However, in real-world scenarios, varying attachment points alter system dynamics, necessitating controller updates for effective performance. So, this paper proposes that an adaptive PID controller (APID) utilizes an online adaptive loop that includes the RLS algorithm with a variable forgetting factor. This structure enables the APID to continuously and adaptively update the model or controller parameters online to cope with uncertainties and dynamic changes, thereby maintaining high tracking accuracy and stability over time. The next section explores the adaptive PID control for the RCDPM.

Control Loop 1: Non-adaptive relative dynamic control with offline RLS-based parameter estimation

Choosing a safe distance by an expert
Choosing a desired trajectory
First layer: The main control loop steps of the first layer loop
$K_1 \leq 1$ *//Step time index*
Initializing
for *each step index* K_1 ($K_1 = 1$ *to* N_1) **do**:
Step 1.1: *Find the shortest distance between humans and cables by the KKT method presented in [13].*
Step 1.2: *Comparison between the safe distance and the calculated distance*
If the distance is higher than the safe distance, go to step 1.3.
else if the distance is lower than the safe distance, go to the end for.
Step 1.3: *Estimate optimized attachment point positions to a safe position by solving the cost function.*
Step 1.4: *Estimate the equilibrium point based on estimated new attachment points.*
Step 1.5: *Transmit the optimized positions to the first group of servomotors for relocation.*
Step 1.6: *Send the equilibrium point and new attachment points to the second layer.*
end for

Second layer: The main non-adaptive control of the second layer loop (offline RLS + fixed parameters PID controller)
Step 2.1 *Gather outputs x(i,k) and inputs u(j,k) from the nonlinear or physical model with the initial position of attachment points (In the absence of real data, the data obtained from the nonlinear model in Equation (1) is used).*
Step 2.2: *Receive equilibrium points from first layer (step 1.6).*
Step 2.3: *Estimate end effector pose and input in relative form* $\Delta x(j,k)$, $\Delta u(j,k)$.
Step 2.4: *Estimate parameters of the nominal linear model from gathered u and x* via *offline RLS.*
The second layer uses offline RLS to estimate the unknown parameters of the nominal linearized model (θ) *at each time step. These parameters do not directly represent the coefficients* M_0, C_0, K_0, *but rather include the parameters of ARX presented in the form of Equation (4).*
for *each step index* K_2, ($K_2 = 1$ *to* N_2) *perform the following:*
Step 2.5: *Define the desired trajectory for the end effector at the step time* K_2.
Step 2.6: *Design PID for the nominal model based on offline RLS.*
Step 2.7: *Estimate the optimal control force on the end effector.*
Step 2.8: *Using the tension distribution algorithm to generate tension on the cables.*
Step 2.9: *Transmit the tension to the second group of servomotors for tracking trajectory.*
end for

2.3.3. Adaptive PID Controller

When the dynamics of the cable-driven parallel robot change significantly, such as when attachment points vary, the nominal model may become inaccurate, thereby affecting the PID performance. An adaptive proportional–integral–derivative (PID) controller is recommended for systems with substantial dynamic variations. Online RLS can continuously update the system model and adjust the PID parameters to maintain accuracy. If discrepancies arise between nominal and actual systems, controller gains may require re-tuning.

As shown in Figure 3, the proposed RCDPM controller consists of the following:

1. Adaptive Modeling: An RLS-based algorithm updates the nominal linear model in real time, adapting to attachment point changes and noise.
2. Error Compensation: A compensator adjusts the cable tension to minimize pose errors and ensure accurate trajectory tracking.

Controller parameters are continuously updated, based on the identified model for precise control.

An ARX (Auto-Regressive with eXogenous input) model was selected for identifying the cable-driven parallel robot, due to its simplicity, computational efficiency, and suitability for real-time applications. Unlike state–space models that require full knowledge of the system's internal dynamics, the ARX approach relies solely on input–output data, making it ideal for systems with partially known or configuration-dependent dynamics. Moreover, ARX models can be easily updated online using recursive least squares (RLS), allowing the model to adapt to structural changes in the robot. This data-driven modeling framework also integrates seamlessly with control strategies, such as PID or generalized predictive control (GPC), making it a practical and effective choice for real-time implementation. The ARX model in Equation (4) is used for each position and orientation of the end effector as the output, with respect to the z cable tension inputs for each step index k. As can be seen in Equation (1), the output of system is 2 degrees and can be indicated in ARX form as follows: Y is the output of the system in relative form (pose of end effector and input is tension in cables).

$$Y(k)_{6\times1} = -a_{1_{6\times6}}Y(k-1)_{6\times1} + -a_{2_{6\times6}}Y(k-2)_{6\times1} + b_{1_{6\times6}}U(k-1)_{6\times1} \tag{4}$$

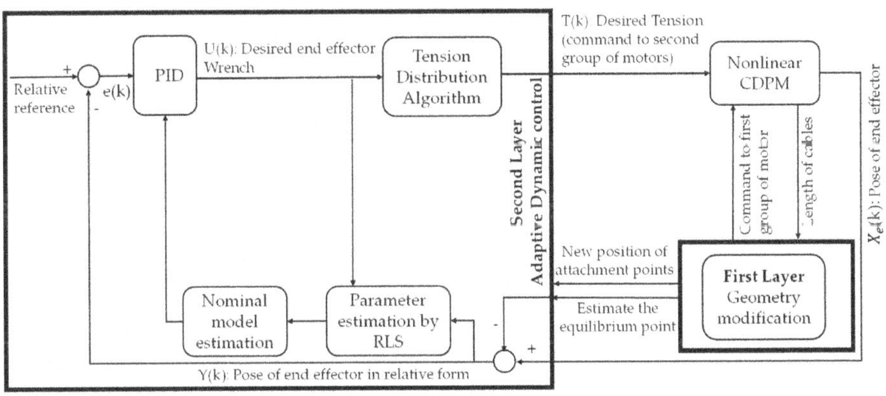

Figure 3. Schematic of adaptive PID for RCDPM.

More details of the ARX model for the CDPM and parameters of θ_i for each output are presented in Appendix B. Equation (4) for a linear parameters variable (LPV) system, in which the parameters of the model are changing over time [49], can be written in a pseudo-linear regressive form, as Equation (5).

$$y_{i,k} = {\Phi_{i,k}}^T\theta_i \tag{5}$$

The parameters for Equation (4) are presented as follows. All parameters of θ_i for each time step compute the matrix in a general format, as follows: (i is number of outputs, n_a is order of output, and n_b is order of input).

$$\theta_i = \begin{bmatrix} a_{1(1)} \cdots\cdots a_{1(i)} & \cdots a_{n_a(1)} & a_{n_a(i)} & b_{1(i)} \cdots & b_{1,n_b(i)} \cdots b_{z(i)} \cdots b_{z,n_b(i)} \end{bmatrix}^T$$

$$\Phi_k = \left[-Y_{k-\tau-1} \quad \ldots \quad -Y_{k-\tau-n_a} \; u_{1,k-\tau-1} \cdots \; u_{1,k-\tau-n_b} \cdots u_{z,k-\tau-1} \cdots \; u_{z,k-\tau-n_b} \right]^T,$$

Control Loop 2 presents the additional details of the adaptive PID controller. a_i are coefficients of outputs and b_i are coefficients of inputs at sample times 1 to N.

The mechanisms for resetting P and adaptively tuning the forgetting factor prevent divergence and instability. Rounding errors and poor conditioning are handled by resetting P for large errors ($|e| > 1$) and at model change points, forgetting factor (λ) tuning is constrained between 0.95 and 1 and adaptively adjusted based on error, preventing divergence of P.

A dynamic adjustment of the forgetting factor is performed according to the magnitude of the error. If the error is large, the forgetting factor is decreased so that the algorithm can respond more quickly to changes. If the error is small, the forgetting factor increases slowly to enhance stability.

These methods are proposed for adjusting the forgetting factor, based on prediction errors. In this study, the forgetting factor is updated dynamically according to the variations in error, in order to maintain a balance between convergence speed and stability.

μ_i in Equation (6) adds a small regularization term to the denominator during the gain calculation, which can enhance numerical stability. In cases where the covariance matrix P is diverging or becoming ill-conditioned, it is reset. This controls the value of P to prevent it from entering an unstable region. The term "becoming ill-conditioned" ($\text{cond}(A) = \| A \| \cdot \| A^{-1} \|$) refers to the numerical instability of the system or Jacobian matrix (A or J) that occurs during attachment point reconfiguration, when the matrix approaches singularity or its determinant tends toward zero. To quantify this effect, we use the condition number, defined as a large condition number (e.g., $\text{cond}(A) > 10^4$), which indicates that the matrix is ill-conditioned and that the system becomes highly sensitive to noise or modeling errors.

Control Loop 2 presents the performance of the second layer, while the first layer avoids a collision between human and cable by changing the position of attachment points, which are the same as the steps of the first layer in Control Loop 1. In Equation (11), the parameter β is a fixed, constant parameter used to tune the sensitivity of the forgetting factor. Its value must be determined through trial and error, based on specific noise characteristics and system dynamics. In the simulations conducted for this study, the value of β was selected to achieve the optimal balance between the convergence speed and the stability of the RLS algorithm. This choice ensures that the variable forgetting factor rapidly adjusts in response to changes in the estimation error. $\varphi_i(k)$ is a column regressor vector in the ARX model, and the inverse term corresponds to the scalar reciprocal of the inner product $\varphi_i^T(k)\varphi_i(k)$. The dimension of $\varphi_i(k)$ is 18 by 1 when $n_a = 2$ and $n_b = 1$.

Control Loop 2: Main adaptive PID control loop based on RLS algorithm with forgetting factor

Choosing a safe distance by an expert

Choosing a desired trajectory

First layer: The main control loop steps of the first layer loop are the same as the first layer in Control Loop 1.

Second layer: The main adaptive control of the second layer loop (online RLS + updated parameters PID controller)

for *each step index* K_2*(*K_2*= 1 to* N_2*), perform the following:*

for i = 1:6 (number of output)

Step 1: *Collect data of inputs u(i,k) and outputs y(j,k) from the nonlinear or physical model.*

Step 2: *Computation of regression vector:*

$$\theta_i = \left[a_{1(1)} \cdots\cdots a_{1(i)} \quad \cdots a_{n_a(1)} \quad a_{n_a(i)} \; b_{1(i)} \cdots \; b_{1,n_b(i)} \cdots b_{z(i)} \cdots b_{z,n_b(i)}\right]^T$$

$$\varphi_i(k) = [y_1(k-1)\ldots\; y_i(k-1) \;\; \ldots\; y_1(k-n_a)\ldots\; y_i(k-n_a) \;\; u_1(k-1)\ldots\; u_1(k-n_{b_1})\ldots u_z(k-1)\ldots u_z(k-n_{b_z})$$

Step 3: *Computation of the RLS gain matrix:*

$$K_i = p_i(k-1)\varphi_i(k)\left[\lambda(k)\varphi_i(k)^{-1}p_i(k-1)\varphi_i(k) + \mu_i\right]^{-1} \tag{6}$$

Step 4: *Computation of estimated output:*

$$\hat{y}_i(k) = \varphi_i{}^T(k)\theta_i(k-1) \tag{7}$$

Step 5: *Error computation (error between estimated output matrix and measurement output matrix):*

$$e_{t_{(6,1)}}(k) - y_i(k) - \hat{y}_i(k) \tag{8}$$

Step 6: *Unknown parameters estimation:*

$$\theta_i(k) = \theta_i(k-1) + K_i(k) * e_i(k) \tag{9}$$

Step 7: *Updating of the covariance matrix:*

$$p_i(k) = \frac{\left[1 - K_i(k)\varphi_i{}^T(k)\right]p_i(k-1)}{\lambda_i} \tag{10}$$

Step 8: *Updating the forgetting factor:*

$$\begin{gathered}\lambda_i(k) = \lambda_{imin}(k) + (1 - \lambda_{imin}(k))^{\propto(k)} \\ \propto(k) = 2^{\beta e^2(k)}\end{gathered} \tag{11}$$

λ_{imin} *and* $\propto(k)$*are the fixed parameters*

end for.

3. Results

To apply the proposed controller, the physical parameters of The INCA robot [47] are modified. To assess the effectiveness of the proposed controller in a reconfigurable CDPM, the attachment points were assumed to move along the z axis on the reel. Figure 4 illustrates the movements at the base. The workspace dimensions are Lx = 3 m, Ly = 3 m, and Lz = 3 m.

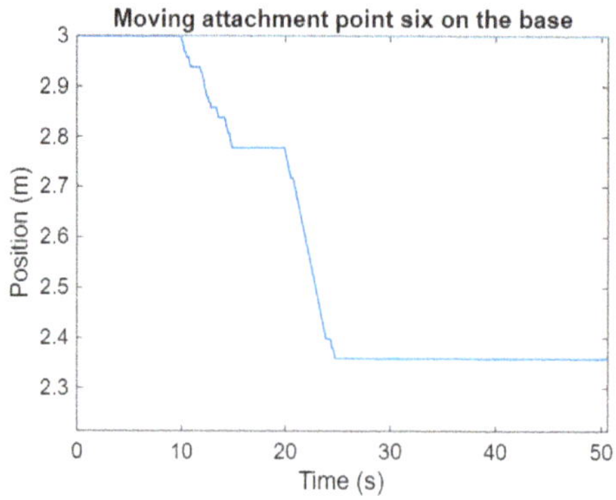

Figure 4. Moving attachment points on the base.

3.1. Collision Avoidance (First Layer)

First-layer optimization estimates the optimal attachment point positions to prevent collisions between humans and cables in a shared workspace, as shown in Figure 5. A human actively moved his arm within the workspace, which required dynamic adjustment.

Figure 4 presents the updated attachment point positions based on this optimization. Meanwhile, the upper attachment points do not change, and the lower attachment points are moved to avoid collisions between the humans and cables. Table 1 lists the initial positions of the attachment points at the bases.

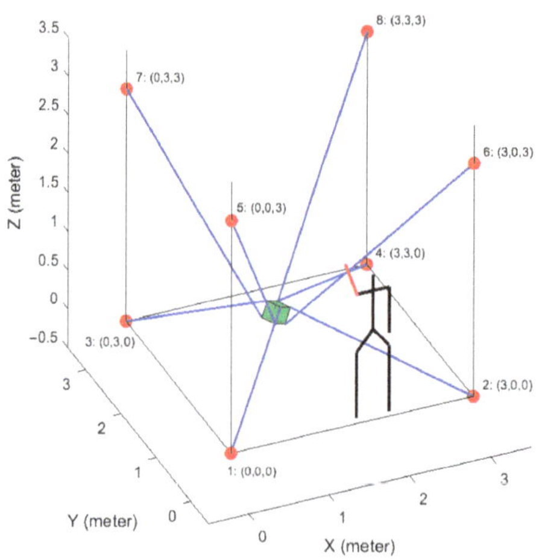

Figure 5. Human and CDPM in the shared workspace.

Table 1. Initial position of attachment points on the base.

O_1	$[0,0,0]$	O_5	$[0,0,3]$
O_2	$[3,0,0]$	O_6	$[3,0,3]$
O_3	$[0,3,0]$	O_7	$[0,3,3]$
O_4	$[3,3,0]$	O_8	$[3,3,3]$

As illustrated in Figure 6, the distance between cables increases when a collision risk is detected, particularly when approaching the predefined safety threshold. The maximum velocity in optimization is 1 m per s. Figure 7 presents a forgetting factor. As can be seen, the forgetting factor decreases at the seconds where attachment point 6 is moving on the base to update the RLS parameters and then increases to one to stabilize the estimated parameters by RLS. Additionally, this change in the forgetting factor is also observed at the moments when the end effector is at the edge of the square signal.

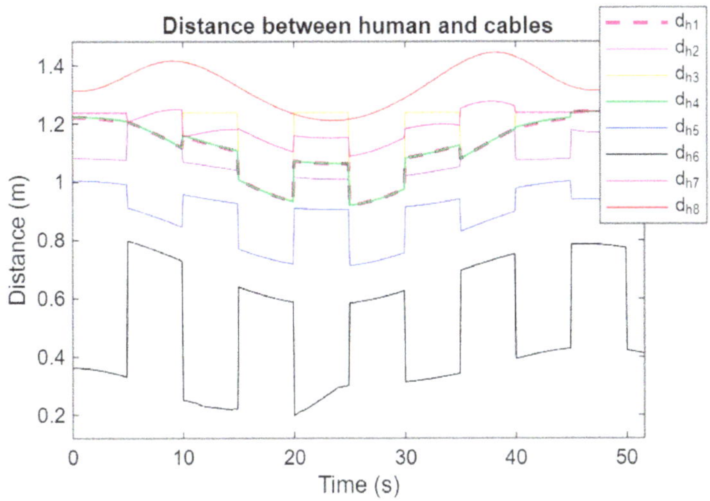

Figure 6. Distance between human and cables.

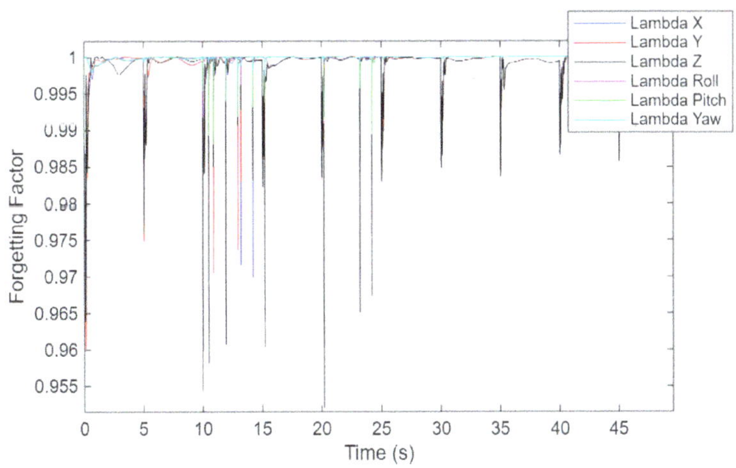

Figure 7. Forgetting factor.

3.2. Tracking Trajectory (Second Layer)

Since the main attachment point relocations occur within the first 50 s, the forgetting factor is plotted only for that period. After this time, the configuration remains stable, and no further adaptation is required.

This method is designed to respond swiftly to sudden changes and prevent abrupt performance degradation. However, in critical situations when the estimation error exceeds one (which may indicate poor estimation or a model jump), the covariance matrix P is reset. Covariance matrix P quantifies the uncertainty in the estimated model parameters and plays a crucial role in calculating the gain vector (K(k)). The size of P is carefully managed by the variable forgetting factor to prevent filter saturation and enable the algorithm to rapidly adapt to sudden dynamic changes (such as the movement of the attachment points).

The second layer optimizes cable tensions using a PID controller, whereas the RLS algorithm is adaptive, continuously estimating the CDPM model at each time step. This ensures precise force generation on the end effector, thereby minimizing the error between the desired and actual poses. A tension distribution algorithm then converts the required end effector force into the corresponding cable tensions, ensuring that all the generated tensions remain positive for feasible actuation. A controller is designed according to the position of attachment points on the base. In the context of CDPMs with dynamic attachment points mounted on a moving base, the implementation of relative control strategies is generally more advantageous than absolute control paradigms. This preference stems from the inherent variability in the system's equilibrium point, which undergoes continuous perturbation due to base motion. Absolute control, reliant on fixed global references, often exhibits instability under such conditions, as it necessitates frequent recalibration of the reference frame, potentially amplifying tracking errors and oscillatory behavior.

Relative control, conversely, operates by minimizing deviations that are relative to the instantaneously computed dynamic equilibrium, thereby enhancing robustness against kinematic uncertainties and external disturbances. This approach leverages feedback on differential states (ΔX), facilitating adaptive compensation for base-induced variations. Tuning PID gains to prioritize relative error reduction yields superior trajectory tracking precision, reduced settling times, and mitigated collision risks in reconfigurable environments. Figures 8 and 9 compare the end effector poses achieved using PID and adaptive PID (APID) controllers with the desired trajectory over the period, in both relative and absolute positions.

As shown, PID struggles with precise trajectory tracking, whereas APID exhibits a greater robustness against model uncertainties. Notably, when the attachment points move on the base, the APID outperforms the PID, maintaining better trajectory tracking. According to Figure 4, significant changes in the attachment points occur at the seconds between 10–15 and 20–25 to avoid collision between human and cables, where the APID effectively compensates for uncertainties, ensuring superior tracking accuracy. In Figure 6, at second 10, when all attachment points are moved, a significant increase in the overshoot is observed in the x and y directions, using the PID controller. Additionally, the highest position error between the PID-controlled system output and the reference trajectory in the z direction occurs at this moment.

Furthermore, attachment points change their position to prevent potential collisions between the human operator and the cables. These dynamic changes in attachment points not only affect the end effector's positional accuracy but also induce rotational deviations, further challenging the PID controller's ability to maintain precise trajectory tracking.

As shown in Figure 4, after 25 s, the attachment points are fixed. Beyond this point, the position and orientation of the end effector stabilize, as all attachment points become fixed. This configuration ensures collision avoidance between the human operator and the cables, guaranteeing a safe and stable operation of the system.

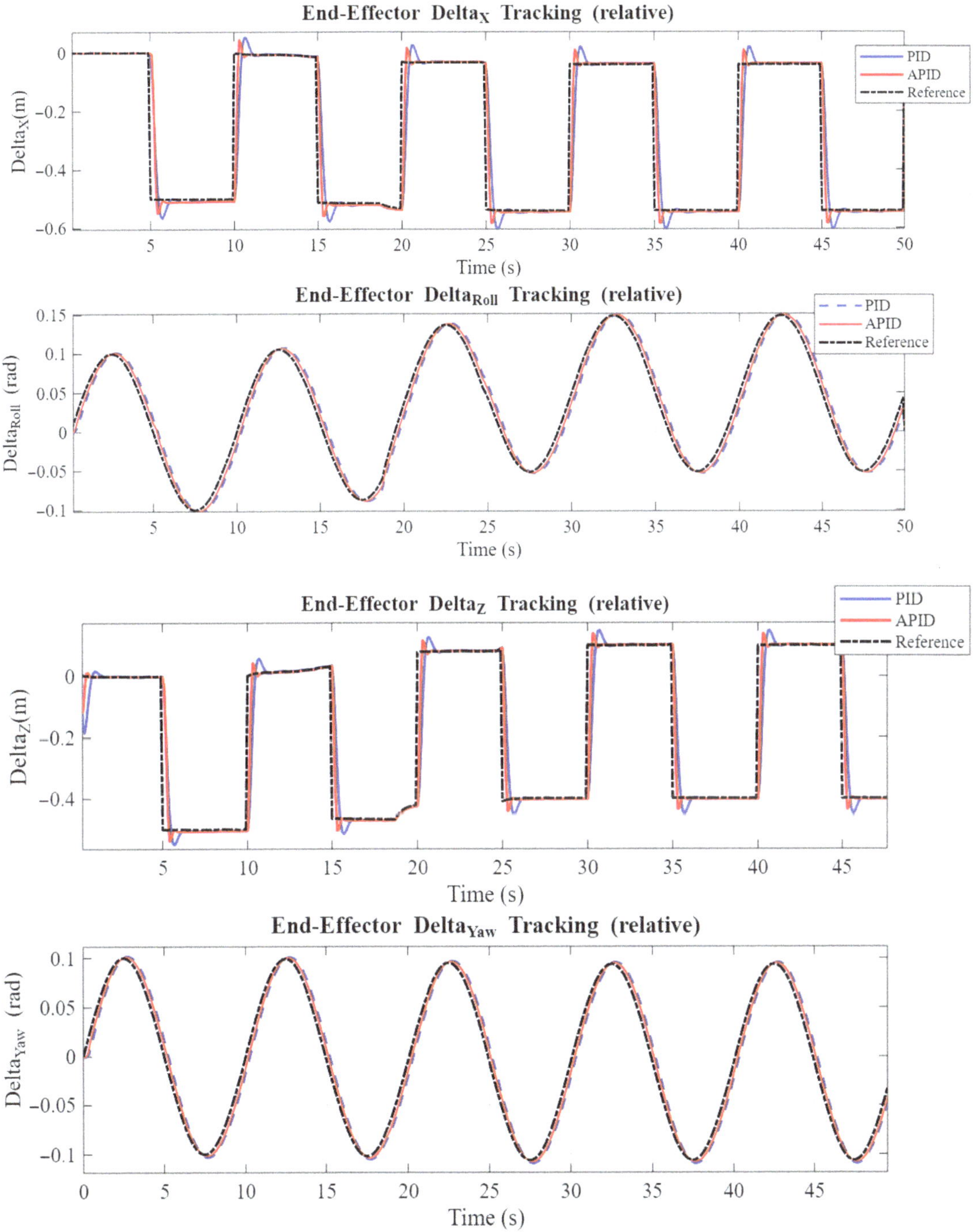

Figure 8. Comparison of ΔX between APID and PID relative pose controllers for RCDPM with online estimated equilibrium point.

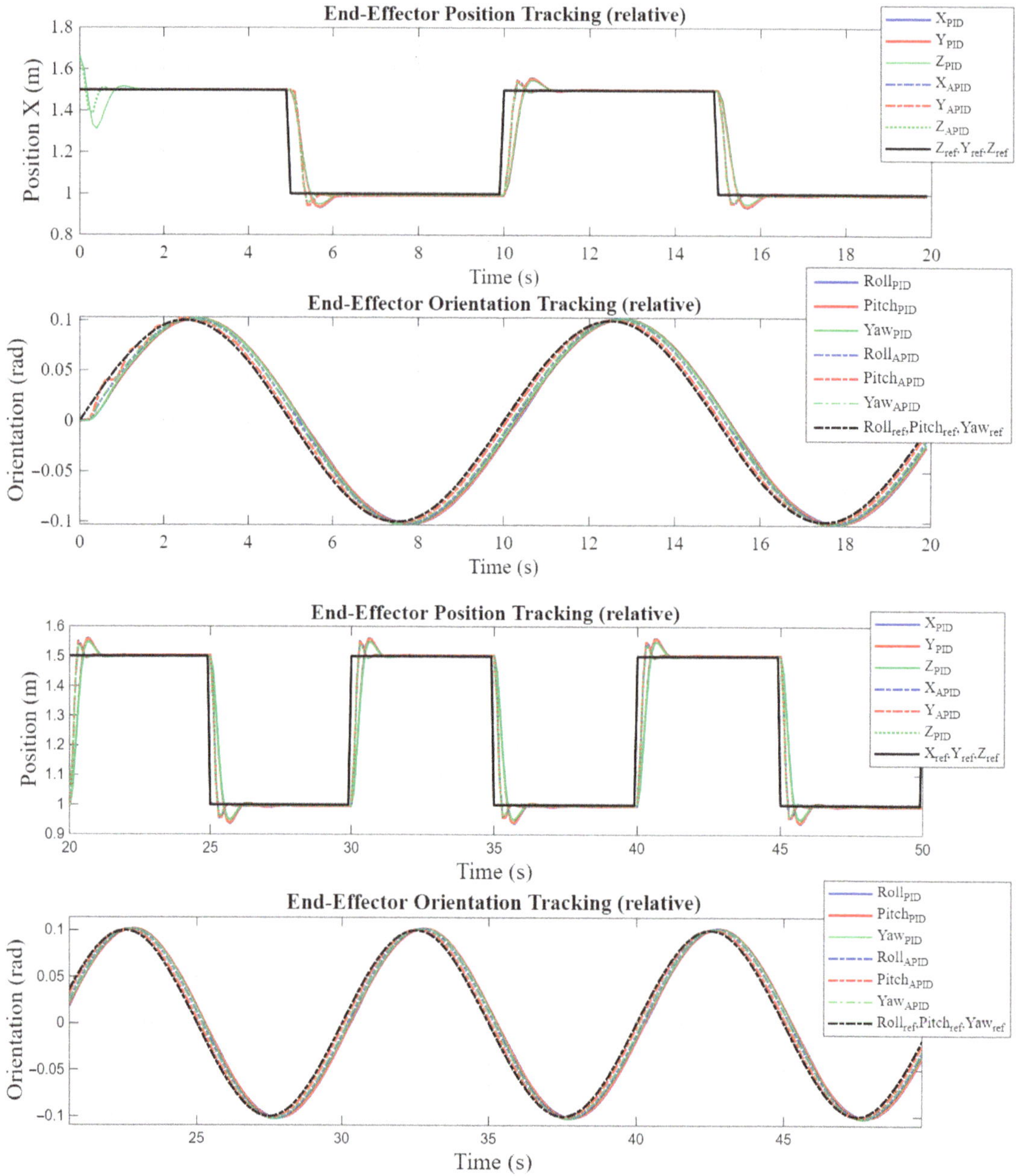

Figure 9. Comparison of *X* between APID and PID relative pose controllers for RCDPM to track the desired trajectory with an online estimated equilibrium point.

Figure 9 illustrates the absolute position and rotation of the end effector. It highlights the lowest tracking accuracy in both the position and orientation of the PID controller, indicating the challenges in maintaining precise trajectory tracking under these conditions

As shown in Figure 10, the mean absolute error (MAE) for PID and APID in trajectory tracking is compared, whereas APID maintains better accuracy, effectively compensating for system variations. In the z direction, PID struggles the most, with error accumulation over time. This improvement is particularly evident in rotational accuracy, where APID outperforms PID in maintaining stable and precise tracking.

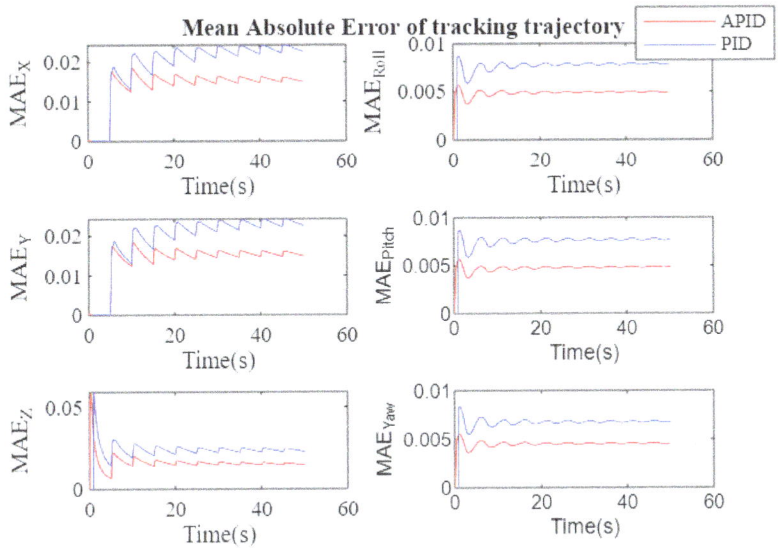

Figure 10. Mean absolute error for PID and APID, with online equilibrium point estimation (relative error).

After designing the PID and APID controllers, the performance of the proposed controller is evaluated under several scenarios as presented in Table 2.

In the first scenario, the attachment points move on the base, and the results of the proposed controller are compared with the LQR controller.

In the second scenario, the performance of the APID controller is compared with PID and LQR when the attachment points are moving on the base and an external disturbance is applied to the system.

Table 2. Three scenarios to test the performance of controllers.

Scenario	Conditions	Primary Goal
1. Dynamic Variation	Attachment points are moving on the base (no external disturbance, no mass change yet).	To prove that adaptivity is necessary. Both fixed-gain controllers do not have perfect performance as the robot's dynamics change.
2. Disturbance Rejection	Attachment points are moving AND an external disturbance is applied.	To prove that APID's adaptive gains plus the integral action make it superior for handling both variations and external forces.
3. Model Uncertainty	Attachment points are moving AND the mass of the end effector is suddenly changed (e.g., ±0% mass).	To test the robustness of the APID's RLS algorithm in estimating and compensating for unknown physical parameters.

Finally, in the third scenario, the mass of the end effector is changing to assess the robustness of the controller in the presence of the changing mass of the end effector.

3.2.1. Scenario 1: Performance of Controllers in the Presence of Moving Attachment Points on the Base

PID struggles to handle sudden changes in attachment points, leading to higher position and rotation errors over time. APID significantly reduces both positional and rotational MSE, especially after 25 s, when all attachment points are fixed. APID is particularly effective for reducing drift in the z direction and rotational errors (Roll, Pitch, Yaw), making it a better choice for trajectory tracking in dynamic environments.

Table 3 presents the mean absolute error (MAE) and root mean squared error(RSME) values for PID, LQR, and APID, highlighting the improved performance of APID. Table 3 further confirms that APID consistently achieves better accuracy across all the position and orientation components, demonstrating its effectiveness in dynamic environments.

Table 3. RSME and MAE for APID, PID, and LQR for first scenario (relative error).

	RSME				MAE		
	PID	**LQR**	**APID**		**PID**	**LQR**	**APID**
X	0.0603	0.061	0.051	X	0.0251	0.026	0.0151
Y	0.0589	0.057	0.048	Y	0.0254	0.024	0.0152
Z	0.0837	0.085	0.047	Z	0.022	0.0025	0.00134
Roll	0.02101	0.023	0.0136	Roll	0.0072	0.0087	0.0048
Pitch	0.0479	0.05	0.013	Pitch	0.0073	0.0084	0.0045
Yaw	0.0604	0.095	0.0134	Yaw	0.0068	0.0075	0.0046

If the PID gains are chosen high enough, they can partially compensate for the necessary input variations resulting from changes in the attachment point geometry (due to changes in the structure matrix). PID tuning is simpler, and it can be empirically adjusted around the worst-case scenario geometry of the robot. Due to the simplicity of its model and less reliance on the accuracy of the $a_{1_{6\times6}}$, $a_{2_{6\times6}}$, and $b_{1_{6\times6}}$ matrices in the ARX model (Equation (4)), PID has a higher chance of maintaining local stability in a portion of the workspace, but its tracking performance will be poor. PID (particularly with its integral term) compensates for the biases caused by changes in T_{cq}, even when the model is not accurate. When large attachment movements occur, PID, with anti-windup and tension-rate limits, remains more stable than LQR.

LQR is inherently designed based on a linearized model. If the gain is optimized for a specific point (e.g., the center of the workspace) and remains fixed during motion, its performance will be poor in other parts of the workspace, because the actual system model constantly deviates from the model assumed by the fixed-gain LQR. APID has better performance due to the model update at each time step to update the gain parameters of controllers.

3.2.2. Scenario 2: Performance of Controllers in the Presence of Moving Attachment Points on the Base and Disturbance

The PID controller includes an integral term that can automatically eliminate steady-state disturbances (such as additional gravitational or frictional forces), whereas a simple LQR without an integral component suffers from steady-state error.

When both attachment points' motion and external disturbance are present, the LQR with fixed gains shows the largest performance degradation, due to high sensitivity to model variations. The simple PID controller is more robust, but its tracking error still increases. The adaptive PID (APID) maintains the best overall performance, since its gains adapt online to geometric and disturbance changes. As shown in Table 4, the APID has better tracking in the presence of moving attachment points and disturbance.

Table 4. RSME and MAE for APID, PID, and LQR for second scenario (relative error).

	RSME				MAE		
	PID	**LQR**	**APID**		**PID**	**LQR**	**APID**
X	0.083	0.092	0.061	X	0.036	0.039	0.019
Y	0.081	0.087	0.057	Y	0.034	0.036	0.017
Z	0.108	0.125	0.069	Z	0.042	0.049	0.023
Roll	0.035	0.041	0.019	Roll	0.012	0.014	0.0065
Pitch	0.054	0.061	0.018	Pitch	0.013	0.015	0.0058
Yaw	0.078	0.098	0.02	Yaw	0.011	0.016	0.0062

3.2.3. Scenario 3: Performance of Controllers in the Presence of Moving Attachment Points on the Base and Variation in Mass

Since this new scenario involves simultaneous attachment point motion and mass variation (+20% and +30%), and only MAE is considered, the trend should follow the same pattern as the previous table. As shown in Table 5, the APID has better tracking in the presence of moving attachment points and mass variation. The updated MAE trends for the two cases are as follows:

Table 5. RSME and MAE for APID, PID and LQR for third scenario (relative error).

Axis	**PID (20%)**	**LQR (20%)**	**APID (20%)**	**PID (30%)**	**PID (30%)**	**APID (30%)**
X	0.0276	0.0293	0.0163	0.0301	0.0325	0.0174
Y	0.279	0.270	0.0164	0.0305	0.03	0.0174
Z	0.0275	0.034	0.0164	0.0319	0.039	0.00176
Roll	0.0081	0.0104	0.0053	0.0088	0.0113	0.0055
Pitch	0.0088	0.0105	0.005	0.0098	0.0112	0.0054
Yaw	0.0085	0.0098	0.0053	0.0099	0.0113	0.0058

3.2.4. Workspace Analysis

The workspace of a cable-driven robot is determined by checking the allowable range of cable tensions inside workspace 3 m $\times$ 3 m $\times$ 3 m. Any point where all cable tensions remain between the minimum and maximum limits is considered part of the workspace. However, the workspace before moving attachment points (blue) and after moving the attachment points (green) on the base, to avoid collision, is presented in Figure 11. As shown, the end effector with square trajectory (red line in center) is kept inside the workspace after moving the attachment point six on the base. The closed-loop stability of the motor system can be analyzed using both analytical and practical considerations. The PID gains are tuned so that the closed-loop matrix $A_c = A - BK$

remains Hurwitz, ensuring asymptotic stability of the system according to the Routh–Hurwitz criterion. The adaptive RLS update with a variable forgetting factor maintains the covariance matrix $P(k)$ as positive definite, contributing to bounded parameter estimates and overall system stability. From a practical standpoint, saturation is possible, but not instability in terms of the Routh–Hurwitz criterion. The classical PID control method is applied to a motor with minimum overshoot. Moreover, the trajectory definition setpoint limits the overshoot, and then vibration is almost nonexistent. Then, it cannot be unstable, considering both the Routh–Hurwitz criterion and mechanical vibrations. The location of the poles of a motor never go outside the negative Laplace plane, whenever the gain. Of course, if the PID/APID gain is set too high, overshoot could occur until it reaches motor amplifier saturation or limit (slew rate, threshold, etc.). Therefore, both mathematically and mechanically, the controlled system remains stable within the defined gain limits.

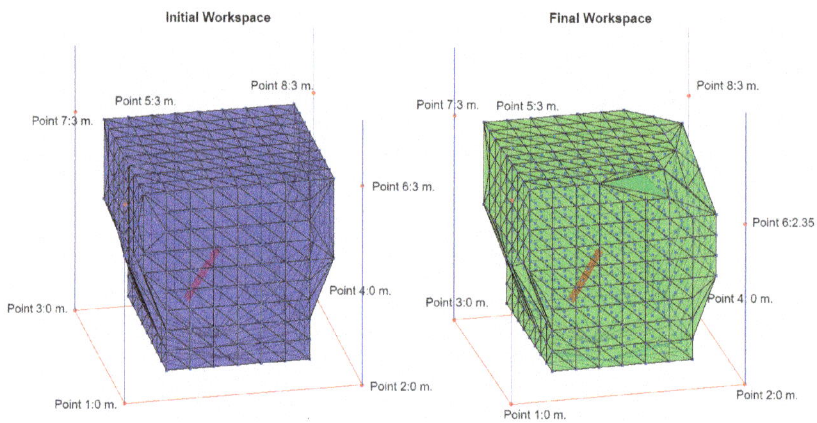

Figure 11. Comparison of initial and final workspaces.

4. Conclusions

This paper presents new two-layer control schematics for the CDPM, where in the first layer, attachment points move on the base to avoid collisions between humans and cables. The second layer generates tension in the cables, using a controller. If the equilibrium point can be estimated online and accurately, the relative controller is better, because it eliminates the error caused by the movement of the attachment points.

If the estimation of the equilibrium point is inaccurate or noisy, the absolute controller is used, but it provides lower tracking accuracy. So, for cable-driven robots with moving attachment points, the relative controller is usually chosen, since the attachment points move frequently and the absolute controller does not perform well.

The added part is an RLS with a variable forgetting factor, used to update the nominal model, which is then used to design the PID. The PID parameters were updated when the attachment points moved on the base. This method yields better results than PID in the presence of uncertainties in the model or moving attachment points at the base.

Although the proposed RLS implementation dynamically adapts the forgetting factor and resets the covariance matrix in critical conditions to enhance stability, it still faces potential numerical challenges when scaled to high-dimensional systems. Real-time deployment may require further optimization, including efficient memory handling and the use of numerically stable RLS variants.

While the proposed methodology has been evaluated in the simulation, the lack of real-world experimental validation is a recognized limitation of this study. Physical testing is essential to assess the model's reliability under realistic conditions, where unmodeled

dynamics, sensor noise, cable elasticity, and actuator imperfections may significantly affect performance. As a part of future work, a robust controller can be added to implement the proposed control framework on a physical cable-driven robot to verify the simulation results. This experimental phase will also help identify potential hardware challenges—such as delays, backlash, and calibration errors—that are difficult to capture in simulation but critical for robust real-time performance.

Supplementary Materials: The following supporting information can be downloaded at: https://osf.io/b4563/overview (accessed on 10 September 2025).

Author Contributions: Conceptualization, E.K.; methodology, E.K.; software, E.K.; validation, E.K., M.J.-D.O. and R.M.; formal analysis, E.K.; investigation, M.J.-D.O.; resources, M.J.-D.O.; data curation, E.K.; writing—original draft preparation, E.K.; writing—review and editing, E.K., M.J.-D.O. and R.M.; visualization, E.K.; supervision, M.J.-D.O. and R.M.; project administration, M.J.-D.O.; funding acquisition, M.J.-D.O. and R.M. All authors have read and agreed to the published version of the manuscript.

Funding: This research was funded by Fonds de recherche du Quebec—Nature et technologies (FRQNT), grant numbers 2020-CO-275043 and 2016-PR-188869. This project uses the infrastructure obtained by the Ministere de l'Economie et de l'Innovation (MEI) du Quebec, John R. Evans Leaders Fund of the Canadian Foundation for Innovation (CFI), and the Infrastructure Operating Fund (FEI) under the project number 35395. Other financial support was also used in this project. The Natural Sciences and Engineering Research Council of Canada (NSERC) Discovery Grant number is RGPIN-2018-06329.

Data Availability Statement: The source code is available for the simulation in the Supplementary Materials section. There is no data associated with the source code.

Conflicts of Interest: The authors declare no conflicts of interest. The funders had no role in the design of the study; in the collection, analyses, or interpretation of data; in the writing of the manuscript; or in the decision to publish the results.

Abbreviations

The following abbreviations are used in this manuscript:

RCDPM	Reconfigurable Cable-Driven Parallel Robot
APID	Adaptive Proportional–Integral–Derivative
RLS	Recursive Least Squares

Appendix A

The motor located on the base is responsible for displacing the cable attachment points on the base, thereby changing the position of the tensioning motors, which are responsible for controlling the robot. Although the structural form of the tensile motor's equations and the robot's equations do not change, the robot must monitor the attachment points online and, if necessary, update the Jacobian matrix and other matrices related to the attachment points. The nonlinear tension motor (actuator) equation is shown below. The difference between this system and other cable-driven robots is that the parameters within the equation that depend on the attachment points are time-varying and must be updated with the change in the attachment points. All equations and parameters in Table A1 are extracted from the model CDPM, presented by Chellal, R., 2017 [47].

Appendix A.1. Nonlinear Dynamic Modeling of CDPM

Appendix A.1.1. End Effector Dynamics

The Newton–Euler equation is used to find the force F_e, including the forces and moments on the end effector. $F_e = [f_e m_e]$

$$F_e = A_e(\varphi_e)\dot{V}_e + B_e(\varphi_e, \varphi_e) \tag{A1}$$

while $A_e(\varphi_e)$ and $B_e(\varphi_e, \dot{\varphi}_e)$ are presented as follows:

$$A_e(\varphi_e) = \begin{bmatrix} M_e I_{3\times3} & 0_{3\times3} \\ 0_{3\times3} & I_{oe}(\varphi_e) \end{bmatrix} \tag{A2}$$

$$B_e(\varphi_e, \dot{\varphi}_e) = \begin{bmatrix} 0_{3\times1} \\ w_e(\varphi_e, \dot{\varphi}_e)(I_{oe}(\varphi_e)w_e(\varphi_e, \dot{\varphi}_e)) \end{bmatrix}$$

The moment of inertia (with respect to the reference) is expressed:

$$I_{oe}(\varphi_e) = R_{oe}(\varphi_e) I_{ee} R_{oe}(\varphi_e)^T \tag{A3}$$

The force on the end effector can be changed to the tension applied on the cables.

$$F_e = W(X_e)T + G = -J^T(X_e)T + G \tag{A4}$$

where F_e is the wrench matrix, $W(X_e)$ is the mapping matrix, and G is gravity.

Appendix A.1.2. Actuator Dynamics

The equation of the actuator dynamics is presented as follows:

$$J_{eq}\ddot{\theta} + f_{eq}\dot{\theta} + K_{eq}\theta = \tau - R_p(T_a - T_{ao}) \tag{A5}$$

$$K_{eq} = K_p {R_{pe}}^2$$

J_{eq} is the diagonal matrix of the inertia moments. $T_{ao} = K_{eq} {R_p}^{-2} L(X_{e_0})$ is the pretension of the driving cables for the initial pose of the end effector. This can be updated at each time step, where attachments are moved on the base. K_{eq} rotational stiffness of the balancing spring.

When the translational motor (the rail) moves in the z direction, the form of the tensile motor's dynamic equation remains unchanged, but these parameters must be updated at every time step: $J(X_e)$, X_{eq} (equilibrium point), length of cables. The structure of Equations (A4) and (A5) remains constant. However, the displacement of the tensile motors (by the translational motors) causes $W(X_e)$ in Equation (A4) and $-T_{ao}$ in Equation (A5) to become time-varying parameters that are functions of the instantaneous position of the translational motors. This is what makes the use of the RLS mandatory for you to adaptively absorb these changes into your ARX parameters (which are complex functions of these matrices).

Appendix A.1.3. CDPM Dynamic (Actuator + End Effector Dynamic)

CDPM model is a combination of end effector dynamic and actuator dynamic in task space. A nonlinear dynamic model of CDPM is presented as Equation (A6), which is presented in [47], which is presented as Equation (1) in the text.

$$\begin{aligned}[M(X_e)]_{6\times6}\ddot{X}_e + \left[C\left(X_e, \dot{X}_e\right)\right]_{6\times1} + [K(X_e)]_{6\times1} + G_{6\times1} \\ = A^T{}_v(\varphi_{e_0})\Delta F_{ev_{6\times1}}\end{aligned} \tag{A6}$$

$$A_v(\varphi_e) = diag(I_{3\times3}, J_{rpy}(\varphi_e)) \tag{A7}$$

J_{rpy} maps the angular velocity, w_e, to the time derivative of the orientation representation $\dot{\varphi}_e$. $\tilde{J}(X_e) = R_p J(X_e) A_v(\varphi_e)$, where $\dot{\theta} = -\tilde{J}(X_e)\dot{X}_e$ to represent the direct relationship between the velocities of the end effector coordinates and the winch speeds.

The tension is limited $[T_{min}, T_{max}]$ within the workspace to ensure safe operation. Coulomb friction is presented in Ref. [47], and is a nonlinear term that complicates the analysis and design of the controller. By removing it, the model takes on a more linear form. Matrices of the mass, spring, and damper of the model are written as follows:

$$[M(X_e)]_{6\times6} = A^T{}_v(\varphi_e)A_e(X_e)A_v(\varphi_e) + \tilde{J}^T(X_e)J_{eq}\tilde{J}(X_e) \tag{A8}$$

$$[K(X_e)]_{6\times1} = \tilde{J}^T(X_e)K_{eq}R_p^{-1}L(X_e) \tag{A9}$$

$$\begin{aligned}\left[C\left(X_e, \dot{X}_e\right)\right]_{6\times1} = [A^T{}_v(\varphi_{eq})A_e(X_e)\dot{A}_v(\varphi_e, \dot{\varphi}_e) + \tilde{J}^T(X_e)F_{eq}\tilde{J}(X_e) + \\ \tilde{J}^T(X_e)J_{eq}\dot{\tilde{J}}\left(X_e, \dot{X}_e\right)]\dot{X}_e + A^T{}_v(\varphi_e)B_e(\varphi_e, \dot{\varphi}_e)\end{aligned} \tag{A10}$$

Appendix B

Linear Dynamic Modeling of CDPM

This section presents the ARX model of CDPM. Equation (A11) is a linear model of the system in relative form. $M_{0_{6\times6}}$, $C_{0_{6\times6}}$ and $K_{0_{6\times6}}$ are presented in [47].

$$M_{0_{6\times6}}\Delta\ddot{X}_e + C_{0_{6\times6}}\Delta\dot{X}_e + K_{0_{6\times6}}\Delta X_e = A^T{}_v(\varphi_{e_0})\Delta F_{ev_{6\times1}} \tag{A11}$$

$$X = \Delta X_e = X_e - X_{eq}$$

To find the MIMO ARX equation, the discrete form of Equation (A11) is written as follows:

$$\dot{X}(t) \approx \frac{X(t) - X(t-1)}{\Delta t}$$

$$\ddot{X}(t) \approx \frac{\dot{X}(t) - \dot{X}(t-1)}{\Delta t} \approx \frac{X(t) - 2X(t-1) + X(t-2)}{\Delta t^2} \tag{A12}$$

Substituting Equation (A12) into Equation (A11)

$$\begin{aligned}M_0\left(\frac{X(t) - 2X(t-1) + X(t-2)}{\Delta t^2}\right) + C_0\left(\frac{X(t) - X(t-1)}{\Delta t}\right) \\ + K_0 X(t) = A^T{}_v(\varphi_{e_0})\Delta F_{ev}(t)\end{aligned} \tag{A13}$$

Simplify the Equation (A13)

$$\begin{aligned}M_0(X(t) - 2X(t-1) + X(t-2)) + \Delta t C_0(X(t) - X(t-1)) \\ + \Delta t^2 K_0 X(t) = \Delta t^2 (A^T{}_v(\varphi_{e_0})\Delta F_{ev}(t))\end{aligned} \tag{A14}$$

This equation can be rewritten as Equation (A15)

$$\begin{aligned}\left(M_0+\Delta tC_0+\Delta t^2K_0\right)X(t)-(2M_0+\Delta tC_0)X(t-1)\\+M_0X(t-2)=\Delta t^2A^T{}_v(\varphi_{e_0})\Delta F_{ev}(t)\end{aligned} \quad \text{(A15)}$$

The output of system $Y(t)_{6\times 1}$ is the pose of the end effector, $X(t)$, which can be presented as a MIMO ARX model with full output coupling.

The MIMO ARX model presented in Equation (A15) can be rewritten as follows:

$$Y(t)_{6\times 1}=-a_1Y(t-1)_{6\times 1}+-a_2Y(t-2)_{6\times 1}+b_1U(t) \quad \text{(A16)}$$

$$Y(t)=\Delta X_e(t)\in R^{6\times 1}$$

$$U(t)=\Delta F_{ev}(t)\in R^{6\times 1}$$

The parameters of a_1, a_2, and b_1 are presented as follows:

$$\begin{aligned}a_1&=\frac{2M_0+\Delta tC_0}{M_0+\Delta tC_0+\Delta t^2K_0}\in R^{6\times 6}\\a_2&=\frac{-M_0}{M_0+\Delta tC_0+\Delta t^2K_0}\in R^{6\times 6}\\b_1&=\frac{\Delta t^2A^T{}_v(\varphi_{e_0})}{M_0+\Delta tC_0+\Delta t^2K_0}\in R^{6\times 6}\end{aligned} \quad \text{(A17)}$$

Appendix C

Table A1. Explanation of parameters.

Component	Dimension	Description
X_e	$\mathbb{R}^{6\times 1}$	End effector pose vector (3 positions + 3 orientations).
$\dot{X}_e$	$\mathbb{R}^{6\times 1}$	Velocity vector.
$\ddot{X}_e$	$\mathbb{R}^{6\times 1}$	Acceleration vector.
Φ_e	$\mathbb{R}^{3\times 1}$	Orientation angles (subset of X_e).
$M(X_e)$	$\mathbb{R}^{6\times 6}$	Inertia matrix.
$C\left(X_e, \dot{X}_e\right)$	$\mathbb{R}^{6\times 1}$	Coriolis, centrifugal, viscous, and Coulomb friction term.
$K(X_e)$	$\mathbb{R}^{6\times 1}$	Stiffness term from balancing springs.
G_x	$\mathbb{R}^{6\times 1}$	Gravity term.
$A_v(\Phi_e)$	$\mathbb{R}^{6\times 6}$	Twist transformation matrix (diagonal blocks: $I_{3\times 3}$ and $J_{rpy}\in\mathbb{R}^{3\times 3}$).

Table A1. *Cont.*

Component	Dimension	Description
$A_e(\Phi_e)$	$\mathbb{R}^{6\times6}$	Mass and inertia of end effector (diagonal blocks: M_e and $I_e \in \mathbb{R}^{3\times3}$).
F_{ev}	$\mathbb{R}^{6\times1}$	Effective input wrench
$J(X_e)$	$\mathbb{R}^{8\times6}$	Jacobian matrix (cable velocities to end effector velocities).
$\tilde{J}(X_e)$	$\mathbb{R}^{8\times6}$	Modified Jacobian matrix (motor velocities to end effector velocities).
$L(X_e)$	$\mathbb{R}^{8\times1}$	Cable lengths vector.
$f_{eq}, K_{eq}, J_{eq}, R_p, K_p,$	$\mathbb{R}^{8\times8}$	Diagonal actuator parameter matrices (friction, stiffness, inertia, radii).
$\theta_{1_i}, \theta_{2_i}$	$\mathbb{R}^{8\times1}$	Position of the first and second groups of motor
$\dot{\theta}_{1_i}, \dot{\theta}_{2_i}$	$\mathbb{R}^{8\times1}$	Velocity of the first and second groups of motor
T	$\mathbb{R}^{8\times1}$	Cable tension vector.
X_{eq}	$\mathbb{R}^{6\times1}$	Equilibrium point vector.
X_{e0}	$\mathbb{R}^{6\times1}$	Initial position and rotation of the end effector vector.
v_e	$\mathbb{R}^{3\times1}$	Linear velocity vector
w_e	$\mathbb{R}^{3\times1}$	Angular velocity vector
M_e	$\mathbb{R}^{3\times3}$	Rigid body of mass matrix
f_e	$\mathbb{R}^{3\times1}$	Translational force vector
A_0	$\mathbb{R}^{8\times1}$	Initial attachment points position
N_1	$\mathbb{R}^{1\times1}$	Time horizon of the first layer
N_2	$\mathbb{R}^{1\times1}$	Time horizon of the second layer
e_i	$\mathbb{R}^{6\times1}$	Error between the estimated output and the measurement output vector
λ	$\mathbb{R}^{6\times1}$	Forgetting factor vector
Φ_i	$\mathbb{R}^{(6\times n_a+6\times n_b)}$	Regressor vector in the ARX model for the ith output

References

1. Rasheed, T.; Long, P.; Caro, S. Wrench-feasible workspace of mobile cable-driven parallel robots. *J. Mech. Robot.* **2020**, *12*, 031009. [CrossRef]
2. Tho, T.P.; Thinh, N.T. An Overview of Cable-Driven Parallel Robots: Workspace, Tension Distribution, and Cable Sagging. *Math. Probl. Eng.* **2022**, *2022*, 2199748. [CrossRef]
3. Pham, C.B.; Yeo, S.H.; Yang, G.; Kurbanhusen, M.S.; Chen, I.-M. Force-closure workspace analysis of cable-driven parallel mechanisms. *Mech. Mach. Theory* **2006**, *41*, 53–69. [CrossRef]
4. Geng, X.; Li, M.; Liu, Y.; Li, Y.; Zheng, W.; Li, Z. Analytical tension-distribution computation for cable-driven parallel robots using hypersphere mapping algorithm. *Mech. Mach. Theory* **2020**, *145*, 103692. [CrossRef]
5. Wang, K.; Hu, Z.H.; Zhang, C.S.; Han, Z.W.; Deng, C.W. Dynamic Modeling and Optimization of Tension Distribution for a Cable-Driven Parallel Robot. *Appl. Sci.* **2024**, *14*, 6478. [CrossRef]
6. Diao, X.; Ma, O.; Lu, Q. Singularity analysis of planar cable-driven parallel robots. In Proceedings of the 2008 IEEE Conference on Robotics, Automation and Mechatronics, Chengdu, China, 21–24 September 2008; pp. 272–277.
7. Diao, X. Singularity analysis of fully-constrained cable-driven parallel robots with seven cables. In Proceedings of the 2015 IEEE International Conference on Mechatronics and Automation (ICMA), Beijing, China, 2–5 August 2015; pp. 1537–1541.
8. Lahouar, S.; Ottaviano, E.; Zeghoul, S.; Romdhane, L.; Ceccarelli, M. Collision free path-planning for cable-driven parallel robots. *Robot. Auton. Syst.* **2009**, *57*, 1083–1093. [CrossRef]
9. Yang, G.; Yeo, S.H.; Pham, C.B. Kinematics and singularity analysis of a planar cable-driven parallel manipulator. In Proceedings of the 2004 IEEE/RSJ International Conference on Intelligent Robots and Systems (IROS) (IEEE Cat. No. 04CH37566), Sendai, Japan, 28 September–2 October 2004; pp. 3835–3840.
10. Almenningen, E.O.; Grøterud, M.; Nørsterud, S. Design, Construction, and Control of a Cable-Driven Parallel Robot. Master's Thesis, NTNU: Norwegian University of Science and Technology, Trondheim, Norway, 2024.

11. Gueners, D.; Chanal, H.; Bouzgarrou, B.-C. Design and implementation of a cable-driven parallel robot for additive manufacturing applications. *Mechatronics* **2022**, *86*, 102874. [CrossRef]
12. Cheng, H.H.; Lau, D. Cable Attachment Optimization for Reconfigurable Cable-Driven Parallel Robots Based on Various Workspace Conditions. *IEEE Trans. Robot.* **2023**, *39*, 3759–3775. [CrossRef]
13. Khoshbin, E.; Youssef, K.; Meziane, R.; Otis, M.J.-D. Reconfigurable fully constrained cable-driven parallel mechanism for avoiding collision between cables with human. *Robotica* **2022**, *40*, 4405–4430. [CrossRef]
14. Youssef, K.; Otis, M.J.-D. Reconfigurable fully constrained cable driven parallel mechanism for avoiding interference between cables. *Mech. Mach. Theory* **2020**, *148*, 103781. [CrossRef]
15. Zake, Z.; Chaumette, F.; Pedemonte, N.; Caro, S. Robust 2½d visual servoing of a cable-driven parallel robot thanks to trajectory tracking. *IEEE Robot. Autom. Lett.* **2020**, *5*, 660–667. [CrossRef]
16. Awais, M.; Park, J.-H.; Jung, J.; Choi, E.-P.; Park, J.-O.; Kim, C.-S. Real-time vision-based localization of planar cable-driven parallel robot. In Proceedings of the 2018 18th International Conference on Control, Automation and Systems (ICCAS), PyeongChang, Republic of Korea, 17–20 October 2018; pp. 462–465.
17. Bayani, H.; Sadeghian, R.; Masouleh, M.T.; Kalhor, A. On the control of planar cable-driven parallel robot via classic controllers and tuning with intelligent algorithms. In Proceedings of the 2015 3rd RSI International Conference on Robotics and Mechatronics (ICROM), Tehran, Iran, 7–9 October 2015; pp. 623–628.
18. Picard, E.; Caro, S.; Plestan, F.; Claveau, F. Control solution for a cable-driven parallel robot with highly variable payload. In Proceedings of the 2018 International Design Engineering Technical Conferences and Computers and Information in Engineering Conference, Quebec City, QC, Canada, 26–29 August 2018; American Society of Mechanical Engineers: New York, NY, USA, 2018.
19. Jiesinuer, A.; Shangfeng, P.; Yang, C. Research on a 3-DOF Planar Cable-Driven Parallel Robot Based on Fuzzy Adaptive PD Computed Torque Control. *J. Phys. Conf. Ser.* **2021**, *1986*, 012124. [CrossRef]
20. Zhou, B.; Wang, Y.; Zi, B.; Zhu, W. Fuzzy Adaptive Whale Optimization Control Algorithm for Trajectory Tracking of a Cable-Driven Parallel Robot. *IEEE Trans. Autom. Sci. Eng.* **2023**, *21*, 5149–5160. [CrossRef]
21. Khalilpour, S.; Khorrambakht, R.; Taghirad, H.; Cardou, P. Dual space control of a deployable cable driven robot: Wave based approach. *Int. J. Robot. Theory Appl.* **2020**, *6*, 11–19.
22. Khalilpour, S.; Khorrambakht, R.; Harandi, M.; Taghirad, H.; Cardou, P. Cascade terminal sliding mode control of a deployable cable driven robot. In Proceedings of the 2019 6th International Conference on Control, Instrumentation and Automation (ICCIA), Sanandaj, Iran, 30–31 October 2019; pp. 1–6.
23. Khalilpour, S.; Khorrambakht, R.; Taghirad, H.; Cardou, P. Robust cascade control of a deployable cable-driven robot. *Mech. Syst. Signal Process.* **2019**, *127*, 513–530. [CrossRef]
24. Khalilpour, S.; Khorrambakht, R.; Harandi, M.; Taghirad, H.; Cardou, P. Robust dynamic sliding mode control of a deployable cable driven robot. In Proceedings of the Electrical Engineering (ICEE), Iranian Conference on, Mashhad, Iran, 8–10 May 2018; pp. 863–868.
25. Abdolshah, S.; Barjuei, E.S. Linear quadratic optimal controller for cable-driven parallel robots. *Front. Mech. Eng.* **2015**, *10*, 344–351. [CrossRef]
26. Tho, T.P.; Thinh, N.T. Analysis and Evaluation of CDPR Cable Sagging Based on ANFIS. *Math. Probl. Eng.* **2021**, *2021*, 4776317. [CrossRef]
27. Lu, Y.; Wu, C.; Yao, W.; Sun, G.; Liu, J.; Wu, L. Deep Reinforcement Learning Control of Fully-Constrained Cable-Driven Parallel Robots. *IEEE Trans. Ind. Electron.* **2022**, *70*, 7194–7204. [CrossRef]
28. Kumar, A.A.; Antoine, J.-F.; Abba, G. Input-Output Feedback Linearization for the Control of a 4 Cable-Driven Parallel Robot. *IFAC-PapersOnLine* **2019**, *52*, 707–712. [CrossRef]
29. Kiani, A.; Mashhadi, S.K.-e.-d.M. Lyapunov-based adaptive control of a cable-driven parallel robot. *Int. J. Adv. Mechatron. Syst.* **2017**, *7*, 193–201. [CrossRef]
30. Yoon, J.; Hwang, S.W.; Bak, J.-H.; Park, J.H. Adaptive control for cable driven parallel robots. In Proceedings of the 2017 17th International Conference on Control, Automation and Systems (ICCAS), Jeju, Republic of Korea, 18–21 October 2017; pp. 416–419.
31. Aghaseyedabdollah, M.; Abedi, M.; Pourgholi, M. Supervisory adaptive fuzzy sliding mode control with optimal Jaya based fuzzy PID sliding surface for a planer cable robot. *Soft Comput.* **2022**, *26*, 8441–8458. [CrossRef]
32. Santos, J.C.; Chemori, A.; Gouttefarde, M. Model predictive control of large-dimension cable-driven parallel robots. In Proceedings of the 4th International Conference on Cable-Driven Parallel Robots, Krakow, Poland, 30 June–4 July 2019; Springer: Berlin/Heidelberg, Germany, 2019; pp. 221–232.
33. Song, C.; Lau, D. Workspace-Based Model Predictive Control for Cable-Driven Robots. *IEEE Trans. Robot.* **2022**, *38*, 2577–2596. [CrossRef]
34. Ji, H.; Shang, W.; Cong, S. Adaptive synchronization control of cable-driven parallel robots with uncertain kinematics and dynamics. *IEEE Trans. Ind. Electron.* **2020**, *68*, 8444–8454. [CrossRef]

35. Tong, L.; Cui, D.; Wang, C.; Peng, L. A novel zero-force control framework for post-stroke rehabilitation training based on fuzzy-PID method. *Intell. Robot.* **2024**, *4*, 125–145. [CrossRef]
36. Liang, X.; He, G.; Su, T.; Wang, W.; Huang, C.; Zhao, Q.; Hou, Z.-G. Finite-time observer-based variable impedance control of cable-driven continuum manipulators. *IEEE Trans. Hum. Mach. Syst.* **2021**, *52*, 26–40. [CrossRef]
37. Lei, Y.; Du, F.; Song, H.; Zhang, L. Design and kinematics analysis of a cable-stayed notch manipulator for transluminal endoscopic surgery. *Biomim. Intell. Robot.* **2024**, *4*, 100191. [CrossRef]
38. Raman, A.; Walker, I.; Krovi, V.; Schmid, M. Cable failure tolerant control and planning in a planar reconfigurable cable driven parallel robot. *Front. Robot. AI* **2023**, *10*, 1070627. [CrossRef]
39. Raman Thothathri, A. Modeling, Control and Estimation of Reconfigurable Cable Driven Parallel Robots. Ph.D. Thesis, Graduate School of Clemson University, Clemson, SC, USA, 2022.
40. Picard, E.; Plestan, F.; Tahoumi, E.; Claveau, F.; Caro, S. Control strategies for a cable-driven parallel robot with varying payload information. *Mechatronics* **2021**, *79*, 102648. [CrossRef]
41. Zhang, B.; Shang, W.; Cong, S.; Li, Z. Dual-loop dynamic control of cable-driven parallel robots without online tension distribution. *IEEE Trans. Syst. Man Cybern. Syst.* **2022**, *52*, 6555–6568. [CrossRef]
42. Sancak, C.; Yamac, F.; Itik, M. Position control of a planar cable-driven parallel robot using reinforcement learning. *Robotica* **2022**, *40*, 3378–3395. [CrossRef]
43. Babaghasabha, R.; Khosravi, M.A.; Taghirad, H.D. Adaptive robust control of fully constrained cable robots: Singular perturbation approach. *Nonlinear Dyn.* **2016**, *85*, 607–620. [CrossRef]
44. Rivera, D.E.; Jun, K.S. An integrated identification and control design methodology for multivariable process system applications. *IEEE Control Syst. Mag.* **2000**, *20*, 25–37.
45. Khoshbin, E.; Martin, J.-D.; Meziane, R. Reconfigurable Cable Driven Parallel Robot—PID Controller. 2025. Available online: https://osf.io/b4563/overview (accessed on 3 November 2025).
46. Bouaouda, A.; Pannequin, R.; Charpillet, F.; Martinez, D.; Boutayeb, M. Dynamic modeling and AI-based control of a cable-driven parallel robot. *IFAC-PapersOnLine* **2023**, *56*, 10021–10026. [CrossRef]
47. Chellal, R.; Cuvillon, L.; Laroche, E. Model identification and vision-based H∞ position control of 6-DoF cable-driven parallel robots. *Int. J. Control* **2017**, *90*, 684–701. [CrossRef]
48. Ghazali, R.; Sam, Y.M.; Rahmat, M.F. Open-loop and closed-loop recursive identification of an electro-hydraulic actuator system. In Proceedings of the 2010 IEEE Conference on Robotics, Automation and Mechatronics, Singapore, 28–30 June 2010; pp. 285–290.
49. Bamieh, B.; Giarré, L. LPV models: Identification for gain scheduling control. In Proceedings of the 2001 European Control Conference (ECC), Porto, Portugal, 4–7 September 2001; pp. 3092–3097.

Disclaimer/Publisher's Note: The statements, opinions and data contained in all publications are solely those of the individual author(s) and contributor(s) and not of MDPI and/or the editor(s). MDPI and/or the editor(s) disclaim responsibility for any injury to people or property resulting from any ideas, methods, instructions or products referred to in the content.

MDPI AG
Grosspeteranlage 5
4052 Basel
Switzerland
Tel.: +41 61 683 77 34

Robotics Editorial Office
E-mail: robotics@mdpi.com
www.mdpi.com/journal/robotics

Disclaimer/Publisher's Note: The title and front matter of this reprint are at the discretion of the Guest Editor. The publisher is not responsible for their content or any associated concerns. The statements, opinions and data contained in all individual articles are solely those of the individual Editor and contributors and not of MDPI. MDPI disclaims responsibility for any injury to people or property resulting from any ideas, methods, instructions or products referred to in the content.

www.ingramcontent.com/pod-product-compliance
Lightning Source LLC
Chambersburg PA
CBHW040748250926
51850CB00007BB/1436
9783725874248